This is a comprehensive, well-presented guide that will be a valuable resource for MBA applicants. It is thorough, relevant and user friendly.

Judith A. Goodman, Assistant Dean, Admissions and Student Services
University of Michigan Business School

While no one book can truly answer the question of "How do I get into the business school of my choice?", Richard Montauk's book comes awfully close!

Henry F. Malin, Director of Admissions
The Amos Tuck School, Dartmouth College

. . . current and comprehensive. . . . Montauk has covered every aspect of the application process. This is a valuable resource for every MBA applicant.

Fran Forbes, Director of Admissions, Graduate School of Business
The University of Texas (Austin)

Drawing on extensive research and experience in counselling MBA candidates, Richard has written a comprehensive, well-balanced book that will be invaluable for anyone considering an MBA.

Connie Tai, Director of Admissions
Rotterdam School of Management

Richard Montauk has produced the most comprehensive and insightful review of how to approach selection of and entry to a good business school. The book is of enormous value to those approaching this critical two-way selection process.

Professor Leo Murray, Dean, Cranfield School of Management (UK)

This book serves as an intelligent guide to help you find your way through the maze of an MBA application.

Kal Denzel, Director of MBA Admissions, IMD (Switzerland)

The subtitle of this book could be "How to Get into Your Favorite Business School in Ten Easy Lessons." Maybe it cannot improve your product, but it can surely help you to improve your marketing, your advertising, and your packaging (of yourself). . . . This book is both amusing and amazing: It is an amusing read that gives you an amazing mass of tips on how to get into your favorite business school.

Gabriella Aliatis, Director of Admissions
SDA Bocconi School of Management (Milan)

How to Get Into the Top MBA Programs provides an excellent description of the intricacies involved in the admissions process of top American and European business schools in a strightforward and easy-to-read format.

Mary Clark, Assistant Director of Admissions, IESE (Barcelona)

Getting into a top MBA program is not as difficult as most people think—all you need is *How to Get Into the Top MBA Programs.* By providing the strategies and advice you need, Montauk's book is an essential roadmap to success. Everything from detailed advice on writing your essays to interviewing strategies is laid out in simple, easy terms. Unless your mother plans to donate a library, or your uncle is on Forbes' list of the world's richest people, I'd recommend that you buy this book.

Tom Fischgrund, editor of The Insider's Guide to the Top 10 Business Schools

Attending a full-time MBA program requires an investment of two years and, typically, more than $100,000 in tuition and foregone earnings. Richard Montauk provides expert advice on how to maximize your return on this investment by giving you an insider's view on how to successfully navigate the tricky process of applying to the best business schools. The secrets of doing well in the applications process—particularly with the written essay questions and the personal interviews with admissions personnel—are exceptionally valuable. If you are serious about applying to one of the top business schools, buy this book first.

Ronald N. Yeaple, Ph.D., author of The MBA Advantage: Why It Pays to Get an MBA

How to
Get Into the
TOP MBA
PROGRAMS

PRENTICE HALL
Paramus, New Jersey 07652

RICHARD MONTAUK

Library of Congress Cataloging-in-Publication Data

Montauk, Richard.
    How to get into top MBA programs / by Richard Montauk.
       p.   cm.
    Includes index.
    ISBN 0-13-246323-7
    1. Master of business administration degree.   2. Master of
business administration degree—Europe—Handbooks, manuals, etc.
3. Master of business administration degree—United States—
Handbooks, manuals, etc.   4. Business schools—Handbooks, manuals,
etc.   I. Title.
HF1111.M66   1996   96-9041
658′.0071′1—dc20   CIP

Printed in the United States of America

10   9   8   7   6

ISBN 0-13-246323-7

ATTENTION: CORPORATIONS AND SCHOOLS

Prentice Hall books are available at quantity discounts with bulk purchase for educational, business, or sales promotional use. For information, please write to: Prentice Hall Special Sales, 240 Frisch Court, Paramus, New Jersey 07652. Please supply: title of book, ISBN number, quantity, how the book will be used, date needed.

PRENTICE HALL
Paramus, NJ 07652

A Simon & Schuster Company

On the World Wide Web at http://www.phdirect.com

Prentice-Hall International (UK) Limited, *London*
Prentice-Hall of Australia Pty. Limited, *Sydney*
Prentice-Hall Canada Inc., *Toronto*
Prentice-Hall Hispanoamericana, S.A., *Mexico*
Prentice-Hall of India Private Limited, *New Delhi*
Prentice-Hall of Japan, Inc., *Tokyo*
Simon & Schuster Asia Pte. Ltd., *Singapore*
Editora Prentice-Hall do Brasil, Ltda., *Rio de Janeiro*

Dedicated to the memory of my father
Howard S. Montauk
1927 – 1988

ACKNOWLEDGMENTS

I wish to thank those people who have been so helpful to the development and writing of *How to Get Into the Top MBA Programs:*

First, the admissions directors and program directors at leading business schools around the world who have been so generous with their time and knowledge in discussing how admissions decisions are made at their schools. In particular, I would like to thank those I interviewed for this book and who have allowed themselves to be quoted at length throughout the text: Fran Hill (Berkeley), Don Martin (Chicago), Linda Meehan (Columbia), Jon Megibow (Darden/Virginia), James Millar (Harvard), Brian Sorge (Kellogg), Judith Goodman (Michigan), Rob Garcia (MIT), Fran Forbes (Texas), Henry Malin (Tuck/Dartmouth), Linda Baldwin (UCLA), Suzanne Cordatos (Wharton); Gabriella Aliatis (Bocconi, Milan), Professor Leo Murray (Cranfield, U.K.), Christy Moody (ENPC, Paris), Mary Clark (IESE, Barcelona), Kal Denzel (IMD, Switzerland), Carol Giraud and Professor Ludo van der Heyden (INSEAD, Paris), Jason Sedine (ISA, Paris), Claire Harniman and Julia Tyler (London, U.K.), Andrew Dyson and Helen Ward (Manchester, U.K.), Alison Mills (Oxford, U.K.), and Gea Tromp and Connie Tai (Rotterdam, Netherlands).

Second, those friends in the admissions field who have in some cases been discussing these and related matters with me for years, and whose comments have influenced the shape of this book in innumerable ways: Mary Boss and Helen Henderson (INSEAD), Monique Mols (Rotterdam), and Josephine Borchert-Ansigner and Christian van Welsenes (NIMBAS, Netherlands).

Third, my great friends who encouraged and supported the creation of Education U.S.A. in the first place: Monte and Sheri Pitt, Pam Levy, Rolf Grun, Dana Clyman, Bart Perkins, and Read Wickham. And, similarly, my friends who so helped the start of our Paris office: Philippe Cothier, Jane Davis, Joerg Otzen, and Eva Wehmeyer.

Fourth, our clients, from whom we have learned a great deal, and particularly those who have allowed their work to be reproduced in the appendix and elsewhere in the book.

Fifth, my colleagues in the United States and Europe, who have been instrumental to the development of my thinking about the applications "game" and to the development of this book as well, particularly Gigi Letts.

Sixth, three editors who have been indispensable to the production of this book: Christa Weil, who has suffered longest and most in helping me and without whom this book might never have been transformed from manuscript form; Sharon Oliver, herself an admissions director, for her insightful comments; and Tom Power, Prentice Hall stalwart. Without their help, it would have been well-nigh impossible to produce this work. Needless to say, any remaining errors are my responsibility alone.

Finally, and most important, my family. I owe a debt too great to be repaid to Karen, Marlin, Ernie, and Clare— and to my mother, Shirley M. Montauk, for her enduring love and support.

Richard Montauk

PREFACE

Approximately one million people seriously consider applying to MBA programs each year. Some hundreds of thousands actually do apply. Not all of them are aiming for the world's best programs, but most of them do want to get into the best program they can manage. They are your competition, the people who can stand in the way of your getting into the school that you want. Maximizing your chances of getting into a top program by outshining this competition is where my company comes in.

Education U.S.A. has been helping people get into top MBA programs for years—better programs than they ever realistically expected to attend. This book can do the same for you. *How to Get Into the Top MBA Programs* was written to give you the kind of information and advice that is simply not available from any other source:

- An *inside view* of *what leading business schools are looking for* in applicants (based upon interviews with over two dozen admissions officers and our own extensive experience)

- Solid, detailed advice to help you *assess and upgrade your own credentials*

- *A step-by-step guide to take you through the whole application process,* showing you:
  - How to *choose the right school*
  - How to determine your *optimal marketing strategy*
  - How to write high quality *essays* for maximum impact
  - How to choose and then manage your *recommenders*
  - What to expect in your *interviews* and how to persuade your interviewers that you have what it takes

- And once you are admitted, you'll learn how best to prepare for business school and to get the most out of your MBA program.

How to Get Into the Top MBA Programs will provide you with all you need to do bang-up applications. If you would still like our help on an individualized basis, however, please contact us. Similarly, if you have any suggestions regarding information you would like included in future editions of this book, please let us know.

Education U.S.A., Inc.
2443 Fillmore St., Suite 330
San Francisco, CA 94115
Telephone (415) 273–1078
Fax (415) 567–1616
E-mail educationu.s.a.@worldnet.att.net

or

126 Aldersgate St.
Barbican, London EC1A 4JQ
Telephone +44 (171) 608–1811
Fax +44 (171) 250–3109

Given that the world's telecommunications system seems to be in a permanent state of flux, by the time you read this book one or other of the above contact numbers may have changed. If so, call the San Francisco telephone number, (415) 273–1078, for up-to-date information.

HOW TO BENEFIT MOST
FROM THIS BOOK

GETTING INTO A TOP SCHOOL IS THE HARDEST PART OF GETTING A TOP MBA

Admissions directors at the world's top business schools admit that the hardest aspect of getting an MBA from their schools is getting in. Getting through a top program may be demanding, but, let's face it, almost 99 percent of the people who enroll get their degrees. At a school like Stanford, however, only 10 to 12 percent of the people who apply are admitted. Harvard sends out 50,000 application packages each year. Only 5,000–6,000 recipients rate their chances high enough to bother applying, and of those who apply only about one in seven gets in. Thus for every hundred people who are interested in applying to Harvard, only one or two are admitted.

　　The reason it is so difficult to get into these schools is clear. The value of an MBA from a top school is immense. As later chapters discuss, graduates of the top schools earn salaries that are, on average, double or more of what graduates from lesser schools make. There is even a pronounced difference in the earnings of graduates from the top-ranked and tenth-ranked schools in the United States (as well as in Europe). Increased salaries are not the end of the story. Greater career choice, increased job security, faster promotions, more interesting work, higher status, and numerous other benefits also result from a top MBA, so it is no wonder that so many people want to get into the best school they can manage.

EDUCATION U.S.A.'s TRACK RECORD

My company, Education U.S.A., Inc., has been helping thousands of business school applicants get into the world's top schools for years. We have been hired by individuals, colleges, and even associations of business executives to help them market themselves or their members. They have often come to us either after failing to get into their desired schools or after recognizing that they did not understand the whole application process well enough to do a good job on their applications. With our help, many of them have gotten into various of the world's finest MBA programs. In fact, it is their view as well as our own that we have generally helped them get into a program about two "tiers" above what they had or could have managed by themselves. In other words, those who were otherwise destined for a top 50 American program have gotten into a top 10 school, and those who were destined for a top 25 program have gotten into a top 5 school.

How to Get Into the Top MBA Programs continues the work we have done with our clients. We believe that this book provides the necessary strategic understanding and detailed guide to the admissions process so necessary for top results. Although it is designed for the individual working on his or her own to get into the best MBA program possible, it also provides a foundation for those of our clients wanting to enhance their experience with Education U.S.A.

GETTING INTO A BETTER SCHOOL

The purpose of this book is to help applicants get into the best business school possible. Schools want candidates who will be successful corporate (and nonprofit) executives, civic leaders, and entrepreneurs. To find them, they assess a great deal of information. Some of this is objective and quantifiable, such as a candidate's Graduate Management Admission Test (GMAT) score, whereas much of it is not, such as what a candidate intends to do in the future. The objective elements of an application, which can be termed a candidate's credentials, are obviously important. The subjective elements, however, are ultimately much more important.

Stanford could fill its class with candidates from the world's top universities—people who graduated in the top 10 percent of their classes, scored in the upper 600s or better on the GMAT, and have worked for the world's preeminent consulting firms and investment banks. Of course it accepts some people who fit this profile, but it actually rejects more of them than it accepts. The point is that schools are looking for more from its candidates than fancy résumés.

Schools admit people rather than résumés. Harvard for example, wants people who have "demonstrated senior management potential," which is not the same thing as getting a high GMAT score. Schools look for leaders—people who work well as part of teams, who are determined to make an impact, and who have thought carefully about how they want their careers to progress. Given a certain baseline of achievement, they will look at far more than someone's grade point average or GMAT score, because those are simply inadequate predictors of leadership, teamwork, and other critical skills.

Schools do consider objective credentials, but only as a part of the total picture of the person. They use all of the information they get, including the essays candidates write, the recommendations submitted on their behalf, and the results of application interviews, to determine whether someone will be a successful business leader, entrepreneur, or whatever.

Darden's admissions director, Jon Megibow, puts it succinctly: "We are convinced that the 'who' is even more important than the 'what.' We look for people who are more than a set of credentials, more than a set of technical or professional skills. The only way to get a handle on the who is by interviewing applicants, by reading their essays to see whether they are multifaceted human beings, and by examining the recommendations. A one-dimensional person, no matter what his numbers—his credentials—will not be successful as a general manager."

In fact, the essays, recommendations, and interviews are doubly useful for schools. They do not only show these leadership and other qualities but also show schools how to interpret the so-called objective data. A grade point average of 3.5 on a 4.0 scale means different things in different contexts. If a student has to work 30 hours per week at a demanding job, that performance looks better. Similarly, if the person is a gifted mathematician but chose to take a lot of writing courses to improve a weakness, that performance again looks better. The only way that schools know how to interpret a grade point average, let alone someone's work experience or aspirations, is by hearing what the applicant (and the applicant's recommenders) say about it. In other words, the essays, recommendations, and interviews not only present new information, they also "frame" the objective data.

How to Get Into the Top MBA Programs shows you how to maximize the value of your credentials by presenting them in the best way. It does this in several ways:

- It shows what leading business schools are looking for in their applicants and exactly how they interpret the different parts of the applicant's folder.

- It explains the nature of the admissions process, including showing who evaluates your application and how the final decisions are reached.

- It explains and illustrates how you can (and should) improve your own marketing efforts—via your application essays, recommendations, and interviews—to increase your chances of admission at the schools you most want to attend.

WARNING: DO NOT JUST COPY EXAMPLES FROM THIS BOOK

It is important to recognize from the outset that by explaining the way the business school admission process works, and by making suggestions as to how you should market yourself, I do *not* want you to look for a magical application that would be perfect both for you and for everyone else reading this book. There is no single perfect application of the one-size-fits-all variety. Instead, this book is designed to provide you with the understanding and, yes, examples, that will allow you to craft an application that shows you in the best possible light. When looking through the various examples of different people's applications, note how they differ dramatically, just as the people themselves do.

The key is to develop your own *personal marketing strategy*. This must be comprehensive, because a disjointed set of essays, or a recommendation that is at odds with what you say about yourself, is the kiss of death for your application. To maximize your chances, you must take advantage of every opportunity to show how professional you are, and why *you* should be admitted.

This book will show you how to prepare applications that distinguish you from the rest of the applicant pool and show you in your best light. It will show you the mistakes applicants typically make, and how (and why) to avoid them.

Admissions directors routinely note that only 10 percent to 20 percent of applicants market themselves really well. This gives you a great opportunity to improve your chances by learning how to do a professional quality application.

WHO SHOULD READ THIS BOOK?

This book is geared toward people who want to get into the best business school they can. It analyzes and discusses each step of the process in a thorough, detailed fashion. Although the text is weighted in terms of getting into the top schools, frankly anyone who wants to improve his or her candidacy to any school, in the top 20 or not, would benefit from an understanding of application strategy.

The book does not assume that you are an American applying to an American business school, although that is the most common situation encountered. The examples used include many Americans but also a number of European and other candidates. Similarly, the business schools considered include the top American and European schools.

WHAT IS INCLUDED IN THIS BOOK?

Part I provides the context for your decisions. It explains why an MBA is such a valuable degree, surveys what are considered the world's leading schools, and shows exactly what those leading schools look for in their candidates. It also shows how best to prepare your candidacy—including preparing for the Graduate Management Admission Test (GMAT), how to choose a school that will be best for you, and how the admissions process works. It concludes with a discussion of how you can finance your MBA studies.

Chapter 1, Why Get an MBA?, explains the advantages of getting an MBA, particularly one from a top program.

Chapter 2, Types of MBA Programs, surveys the different types of programs, including the differences between typical American programs and typical European programs. It also explains what to expect from your business school experience itself.

Chapter 3, How to Use the Rankings, shows what various authorities have considered the top schools in America, Europe, and the rest of the world. It explains the basis for the rankings and urges caution in using them, due to the limitations of their methodologies.

Chapter 4, Make the Most of Your Credentials, explains in detail the qualities schools look for in candidates and how they determine from your application to what extent you possess them. Besides showing what schools look for, it explains how you can augment your credentials to improve your admission chances, even in the months immediately before applying. Included is an extensive discussion of how best to prepare for the GMAT exam.

Chapter 5, How to Choose the Right School for *You*, shows how to find schools that will provide you with the type of program you need, the atmosphere in which you will learn best, and the best reputation among potential employers. It discusses information sources, published and unpublished, that will be most helpful to you in making your decision.

Chapter 6, The Admissions Process, profiles typical admissions officers and shows how the decision-making process works at typical schools.

Chapter 7, Financing Your MBA, explains financing strategies for obtaining your MBA. It lays out the principal means of financing an MBA, discusses your options for financing, and suggests good sources for detailed information on scholarships and loans.

Part II is the core of the book. It takes you through the whole process of developing your marketing strategy and shows you how to use each marketing vehicle—the essays, recommendations, and interviews—to maximum advantage. It takes you step by step through the application process to help you maximize your chances of acceptance.

Chapter 8, Marketing Yourself: General Principles, examines how you can portray your candidacy as bringing the maximum value to a program with a minimum of risk (i.e., risk of losing interest in the program or actually flunking). It includes an extended analysis of how people with different professional backgrounds (and people of different ages, nationalities, and educational backgrounds) are likely to be evaluated by admissions offices— and shows the imperatives that face each type of applicant.

Chapter 9, Understanding the Key Essay Topics, thoroughly analyzes each of the 21 most common essay questions. The most typical mistakes people make are discussed along with suggestions for how you can capitalize on your own strengths and present yourself in the best light.

Chapter 10, How to Write Persuasive Essays, explains what admissions officers look for in your writing. For those who are uncomfortable writing essays, it describes what should be done at each stage of the writing process to produce a high-quality essay package. It also offers a large set of do's and don'ts for writing compact, powerful essays.

Chapter 11, Recommendations, shows how to determine who will be your best recommenders, how to approach them and weed out the lukewarm from the very positive ones, and how to get them to write what you want (without offending them).

Chapter 12, Interviews, shows you how to prepare for the critical interviews. You need to know the strengths and weaknesses of your candidacy, the nature of the school and the program, and the questions most frequently asked in application interviews. This section guides you through each of these interview components and also provides means of dealing with the notorious stress interviews and other difficult interview formats.

Chapter 13, Application Timetable, gives a typical application schedule covering all of the tasks you must perform, from getting information about schools through requesting transcripts and writing your essays to submitting the applications and financial aid forms.

Part III covers the period after you submit your application, including how you can prepare yourself to maximize your business school experience.

Chapter 14, Responding to Wait-Listing, Rejections, and Other Disappointments, explains how to handle wait-listing, being placed on hold, and outright rejections. It also explores how to reapply to a school that once rejected you.

Chapter 15, What to Do Once You Are Accepted, shows you how to leave your job without creating ill will. It then provides detailed suggestions for how best to prepare for business school. Too many people arrive at business school unprepared, with consequent difficulties in surviving the first months of the program. Follow the suggestions in this chapter, however, and you will be ready to get the most out of your MBA program.

Chapter 16, How to Get the Most Out of Business School, suggests how you can maximize the benefits of your business school experience. Drawing on interviews with school program and career service directors, this provides a set of tips for learning efficiently and well, taking advantage of the social and career/job opportunities, and staying healthy and sane.

The *Appendix* provides additional help:

Essay Examples: one hundred fifteen successful essay examples—on over three dozen essay topics—written by applicants to nearly twenty different schools. They are accompanied by commentaries on what each one has done particularly well (and what could have been done to improve already good work). These applicants are from over a dozen different fields; 60 percent are American, most of the rest are European; their educational backgrounds range from less than a bachelor's degree through PhD; and their goals are as diverse as their backgrounds.

The introductory pages to this appendix provide information in summary chart form to allow you to find the right essay fast. If you want examples of people who applied to Chicago, these pages will show you where to look. Similarly, if you want to see examples of essays written by engineers, the introductory pages will show you where to look.

UNIQUE FEATURES

How to Get Into the Top MBA Programs provides a thorough explanation of how you can get into the best schools possible. It guides you through each step of the process, showing you at each point how to develop your own marketing strategy. The unique features include:

- Advice from over two dozen admission directors on every aspect of the applications process
- 120 actual applicant essays, including:
  - Successful applications to eighteen of the world's top schools
  - Submissions by applicants from all walks of life, from accounting to the arts, banking to marketing, consulting to engineering, and so on
- Detailed advice on how to write persuasive essays for maximum impact
- Sample recommendations, from academic and business recommenders
- Solid advice on:
  - How to choose and finance the right program for you
  - How to prepare for business school *and* how to get the most out of the program once you go
- A detailed timetable so you'll know what to do and when
- Complete explanation of what top schools look for in applicants, and how you can meet their needs

HOW TO REALLY PROFIT FROM THIS BOOK

The key to maximizing the value of this book is to start the whole admission process early—earlier than you might believe necessary. As Chapter 13, "Application Timetable," shows, it is ideal to begin the process a year or more before you expect to begin classes. Starting early, and using this book throughout the process, will allow you to complete strong, persuasive applications in the most efficient manner possible.

This book is designed to be used efficiently by people with radically different needs. Some will want to read it cover to cover, but many will want to dip into it for help on specific problems they face. Here are some suggestions for how to get the most out of the book, depending upon your own situation:

YOU ARE IN THE MIDST OF YOUR APPLICATIONS NOW

If you have applications due in just a few weeks, you must read several core chapters of the book immediately to avoid making terrible mistakes. Chapter 4 shows you how business schools will evaluate your applications, Chapter 8 shows you the basics of how to market yourself, and the introduction to Chapter 9 shows you how to think about your essays. You will also want to read the analyses of specific essay questions that you are going to answer. In addition, if you have yet to choose your recommenders, or if they have not yet sent in your recommendations, read Chapter 11 to see how you can improve what they say. Before your interviews, which presumably will not happen until after you have filed your applications, you will certainly want to read Chapter 12 on interviewing. When you have time, read the other chapters, or the executive summaries of them, to understand the application process more fully. Part III, which covers the post-application period, is important reading for you after you have finished your applications.

WHAT IF ONE OF YOUR APPLICATIONS IS DUE IN A WEEK?

Do not panic! This book can get you up to speed fast. Before going any further in your applications, be sure to read the executive summaries of each chapter and read Chapter 8 thoroughly. Then consult the relevant essay topics (the ones you are working on at the moment) in Chapter 9 and look through the discussion in Chapter 10 of how to write a strong and persuasive essay. Also be sure to read Chapter 11 on recommendations before giving the "go-ahead" to your recommenders.

YOU ARE GOING TO APPLY TO SCHOOLS IN THE NEAR FUTURE

If you intend to apply to schools in the next several months, you will probably want to get an overview of the applications process by reading the executive summaries of each chapter now, plus Chapters 4, "Make the Most of Your Credentials," and 8, "Marketing Yourself," which will explain the fundamentals of what you want to demonstrate in your applications. Read Chapter 13, "Application Timetable," to be sure that you do not miss the starting dates for important activities. Then, read each chapter as it becomes relevant to your effort, starting with Chapters 9 and 10, which will show you how to prepare your essays.

YOU WILL NOT APPLY UNTIL SEVERAL YEARS FROM NOW

If you are not going to apply to schools for another two or three years, read Chapters 4, "Make the Most of Your Credentials," and 8, "Marketing Yourself," now. These will show you how best to ready yourself for admission, while you still have the opportunity to improve your credentials dramatically. Then read Chapter 13, "Application Timetable," to determine when to start the process for keeps. Later on you can read the executive summaries of each chapter (about 15–18 months before you intend to go) to prepare for the application process itself.

In general, some chapters will not be relevant to everybody. For example, people who have already done their research and determined which schools to apply to can happily skip Chapter 5, "How to Choose the Right School for You."

A FINAL NOTE: The Application Process May Prove Helpful (As Well as Painful)

Many applicants look upon the task of producing hundreds of details about their pasts, writing dozens of essays about intimate or obscure topics, securing recommendations from old professors and current bosses, and enduring interviews as a modern form of "death by a thousand cuts." They feel that it is trial enough simply to research the schools and figure out which ones would be appropriate for them, let alone to have to manage the data-, paper-, writing-, and time-intensive application process.

If that is your view, keep in mind that the application process, however imperfect it may be, forces applicants to think seriously about where they want to go in their careers and in their lives, and how they are going to get there. Too few people do this at any point, let alone at this most appropriate of times. Applicants to business schools, whether they are in their mid-twenties or mid-thirties, are highly likely to be right at the point where sensible decisions about these matters can yield a lifetime of benefits, and a failure to consider their options carefully can result in opportunities missed, opportunities that will not be offered again. Confronting such important career decisions might open doors you never even realized existed.

CONTENTS

Part I
THE CONTEXT

1
Why Get an MBA?—3

2
Types of MBA Programs—11

3
How to Use the Rankings—30

4
Make the Most of Your Credentials—50

5
How to Choose the Right School for *You*—83

6
The Admissions Process—103

7
Financing Your MBA—110

Part II
MARKETING YOURSELF SUCCESSFULLY

8
Marketing Yourself: General Principles—121

9
Understanding the Key Essay Topics—141

10
How to Write Persuasive Essays—179

11
Recommendations—205

12
Interviews—228

13
Application Timetable—268

Part III
ON THE ROAD TO BUSINESS SCHOOL

14
Responding to Wait-Listing, Rejections, and Other Disappointments—283

15
What to Do Once You Are Accepted—290

16
How to Get the Most Out of Business School—309

Appendix
Application Essay Examples—317

Index—435

Part *I*

THE

CONTEXT

1

WHY GET
AN MBA?

— EXECUTIVE SUMMARY —

■

There are numerous, good reasons to get an MBA.

■

Not all MBAs are of equal value; graduates of the top schools command
a premium in the marketplace.

■

There are many different types of MBA programs:

- European one-year as well as American two-year.
- Part-time (and executive) as well as full-time.
- Programs vary in length, focus, philosophy, and
  structure.

■

To understand what to expect at business school, consult the appendix to
Chapter 2.

Once upon a time, a high school diploma was a sufficient credential to get a good executive job. Then, as more and more people went to college, a high school diploma was no longer enough to land an executive position. A college degree sufficed for a time, but as more and more people got MBAs, even a college degree was no longer enough. That was the case in the 1970s. Since then, the number of people getting an MBA has increased to the point that simply having a degree is insufficient to get plum jobs; the *quality* of the MBA program has become determinative.

This "degree creep" has been matched by the recognition that managers now have far more demands placed upon them than in the past. It is no longer enough just to master a narrow function. In addition to developing strong technical skills, a manager must possess a range of such softer skills as the ability to influence people, manage interfaces with other departments, negotiate with individuals from all walks of life, manage his own career in the newly complicated job environment, and more. A manager must also know how each part of the company fits with the other parts, how the company competes, and how it should compete. The disappearance of much of middle management means that, even at what were once junior positions in a company, this sort of knowledge is becoming more and more critical. It is all the more important in smaller organizations, which are responsible for more and more employment. This increased complexity has made advanced managerial education much more necessary than it was in the past.

Thus the educational key to managerial success is getting an MBA that both trains you well in your chosen field and is of the highest possible reputation. This does not mean that everyone needs an MBA, but there are a host of people who sensibly view it as a major stepping stone to career success.

SOME COMMON REASONS FOR GETTING AN MBA

The MBA is a very flexible degree, which can serve either to broaden your knowledge of business or develop your knowledge of a particular function, such as finance. Therefore, it is often viewed as having something for everyone. Although this is obviously an overstatement, there are certainly many valid reasons to get an MBA. Some of those most commonly expressed by prospective MBA students are that they:

- Want to change careers
- Want to advance in their current fields
- Want to shift from individual contribution to managing others
- Want to learn to manage a technical or artistic field they are currently in
- Are between jobs and want to use the time well
- Seek an intellectually challenging and interesting experience
- Need an advanced degree to obtain a useful job in their country or field
- Want sufficient skills to start and run a business
- Want to grow their small business, but need more skill and credibility (for dealing with lenders or customers) to do so
- Want to improve their pay
- Want to develop their network of contacts

All of these are sensible reasons for getting an MBA. Of course there are others, but it is possible to go into too much detail in enumerating them. London Business School, for example, uses a much simpler classification; it separates people into "vertical" and "transitional." In other words, those wishing to climb the career ladder in their current field are classified as "verticals," whereas those wishing to change fields are classified as "transitionals."

WHAT DOES AN MBA PROGRAM DO?

A good business program will teach things that cannot ordinarily be mastered on the job, such as finance, statistics, and managerial economics. It can also compress the time necessary to learn things that can be learned on the job, but only over a long period and with great effort and luck. In addition, a program shows how different functions work, how they are related, how companies in different industries compete, and how they manage in different environments.

It does all of this by being, in part, a boot camp for managers. Students are drilled in the basics and forced to crunch through a massive amount of material, cooperate and compete with colleagues very different from themselves, and, in general, live life at a speeded-up pace. The net result is a graduate with broadly recognizable skills and attributes.

The positive attributes associated with MBAs from top schools include:

➤ Superior intelligence, as demonstrated by the admissions hurdles they needed to clear

➤ Willingness to invest in themselves, as shown by their pursuit of a graduate degree

➤ Willingness to work long and hard, again as shown by their pursuing an MBA

➤ High motivation: self-starting and self-confident

➤ Desirable blend of theoretical knowledge and practical experience (especially now that the top schools are making sure that their programs are a blend of the two)

➤ Strong analytical skills and a wide perspective, including an understanding of how the whole of the business functions and fits together

➤ Strong communication skills

➤ Willingness and ability to work under great time and performance pressure

The negative attributes are:

➤ Expectations of large salaries and rapid promotions

➤ Lack of loyalty to a company, being devoted instead to their own careers

➤ In sum, being a prima donna.

Of course, a graduate gains more than just a set of skills and attitudes. The reputation and connections of the school, along with a hard-working career services department, will help you to gain an appropriate job. The alumni network of the school, plus the contacts you develop during the course, will be assets forever. Indeed, on your résumé the degree itself will have long-term value.

A WORD OF WARNING FOR CAREER CHANGERS

Many people get an MBA in order to facilitate a career change, but a word of warning is in order. Those who intend to make a dramatic change must plan carefully. It should not be difficult for a medical doctor to become a hospital manager, given her substantial experience in hospital operations. The same is not likely to be true for a commercial photographer who wishes to become an investment banker. This switch will probably only be possible if she has strong quantitative skills and does a great deal during business school to work on projects concerning investment banking, including part-time work of a related nature.

Your prior experience will be important in determining the potential employers that will be interested in you. To overcome a lack of relevant experience in business school:

- Go beyond just taking relevant courses.

- Demonstrate at least a mini "track record" that is relevant to your new field. You can do this by working (1) in this field or a related one during your summer between years and (2) on a part-time basis during your second year. (3) If need be, do something on a volunteer basis to get your foot in the door.

Before blithely assuming that you can make the career change you desire, discuss with the career services officers at the relevant schools whether and how you should go about it.

THE VALUE OF GOING TO A TOP SCHOOL

As the number of MBA holders in the world increases, so does the importance of getting a top-quality MBA rather than just any MBA.

INCREASED PAY

The better the reputation of a school, the more its graduates earn. For example, it is clear that graduates from one of the top five schools in the United States can expect, on average, to earn 50 percent to 100 percent more than graduates from schools ranked nearer to number 50. This pay gap increases dramatically as one goes further down the rankings to those schools near the bottom of the 1200 or so that grant MBAs in the United States.

CAREER CHOICE

Some professions are virtually off-limits to graduates of lesser business schools (let alone those without MBAs). These include investment banking and corporate strategy consulting. The most desirable companies to work for, such as major consulting firms and investment banks, would no more think of recruiting at "Acme" University Business School than they would of giving this year's profits to the Flat Earth Society. These firms look to hire the best and the brightest and they know that the best and the brightest are to be found at the world's leading business schools.

The same is true, albeit to a somewhat lesser extent, in other fields. Making it into consumer marketing positions of responsibility at the world's leading firms also demands that you have an MBA from a top school.

STATUS

This category nearly speaks for itself. Whether for personal or business reasons, being a graduate of Stanford conjures up entirely different impressions and reactions among people you encounter than does being a graduate of Acme U. Status is partially related to the other items listed here, such as salary, but it also reflects the fact that Stanford admits only people who are highly regarded to begin with.

CAREER FLEXIBILITY

The benefits of going to a top school are not limited to your initial job upon graduation. If you decide to change careers in the future (which is becoming more and more common), the quality of your education will be one of the determining factors in your ability to make the switch successfully, and it will also determine how other people rate your chances (and whether they will risk hiring you). The alumni network, and your own personal network from business school, will also be important determinants of your ability to switch. With a strong network willing to help you, your chances are automatically better.

FINANCIAL CONSIDERATIONS

Getting an MBA represents an extremely large investment of money, as well as time and effort. The tuition for a two year program may be $40,000 or more, and the income forgone may be $75,000–$100,000 or more for the two years. Books, computer hardware and software costs, travel to and from the program, and other assorted expenses may add thousands more. The cost of a two year program is thus likely to be upwards of $150,000 or more. A one year program may cost 50 percent to 65 percent as much as this, given the often higher annual tuition at such programs.

Is an MBA worth this large sum? Although not everyone will be financially better off from getting an MBA, those attending the top MBA programs are highly likely to be. In fact, almost no one who attends a top program ends up regretting the experience. An interesting contrast is provided by American law schools, of whose graduates a large majority are sorry they ever went.

The payoff is partly a matter of increased earnings. It is also a matter of increased career options, increased confidence that one can do a given job extremely well, increased security (no matter what happens there are jobs available for people from top schools), and increased status. In addition, most people feel that they lived life more intensely at business school, met the most interesting people they ever have known, and formed their closest friendships there.

It is therefore probably a mistake to view the decision to get an MBA on a purely financial basis, despite the sums involved.

ARE MBAs CURRENTLY IN FAVOR WITH COMPANIES?

The traditional employers of MBAs have been firms in financial services, management consulting, and consumer goods. They remain the biggest employers of MBAs to this date. The trend in recent years, however, has been for smaller firms in a variety of different industries, including high-tech start-ups, to hire them, and for graduates to start their own firms. The mix of employers varies from year to year, depending upon the health of their own industries and, curiously, the attitudes toward MBAs. There seems to be a cycle in the way some companies view candidates with MBAs. At times these companies feel that they need as many MBA holders as possible. At other times they feel that MBAs should be avoided.

This should not be regarded as discouraging news. The fact is that many hundreds of companies are *always* looking for candidates with the attributes associated with MBAs. The demand for candidates from the top schools, therefore, varies from strong to very strong.

CAREER PLANNING

This book is avowedly not a career planning manual. It is important to note, though, that you should view the decision to pursue an MBA as an important career decision, and one that merits considerable thought. The starting point for your decision making should be an evaluation of where you want to go and how best you can get there. If this is a complete mystery to you, by all means consult the career literature, which is abundant.

IS AN MBA RIGHT FOR YOU?

If any of the reasons for getting an MBA that were listed at the start of this chapter struck a responsive chord, an MBA is probably right for you. If you intend to be a better manager, progress rapidly in your current company, start your own business, give yourself better career options, or just earn more money, an MBA is likely to be a sensible investment.

Even after you have decided to get an MBA, however, you have not finished making important decisions. Major issues you will face will include the following: Do you want to pursue the degree now or later? Do you want to go to a full-time or a part-time program? Do you want to go to an American or a European school?

The question of timing is likely to be the first one you face if you have not already made up your mind that now is the time. Chapter 4, "Make the Most of Your Credentials," discusses the amount of experience that is appropriate to maximize your attractiveness to schools.

TYPES OF
MBA PROGRAMS

— EXECUTIVE SUMMARY —

■

Full-time, part-time, and executive MBA programs offer
a wide range of courses:

– The advantages of each type of program are marked.

■

The European MBA model offers a contrast to the American model.

■

Be sure to choose the type of program best suited to your personal needs.

*T*here are now many different types of MBA programs, as well as different means of delivering a given type of program. Thus the business school applicant can choose from full-time, part-time, modular, or distance learning (i.e., by television, video, Internet, and mail) programs. Rather than discuss all of the many different possibilities, however, this section focuses on the major program types: traditional full-time programs (both American and European versions), part-time programs, and executive programs.

THE TRADITIONAL, FULL-TIME AMERICAN MBA

The American MBA has been around for a century now. The initial assumption was that it was to provide training for someone without prior business study, so it was made a two-year degree, with the first year providing an introduction to business fundamentals. Although there have been innumerable changes in the typical program, it retains certain core characteristics. It is still, almost without exception, a two-year program. It has a set of core courses that are required for all or most students. Most students are still relatively young, with the typical age upon entrance currently being 26 or 27. Many schools once accepted a majority of their students straight from undergraduate studies, but now schools require two or more years of experience from most of their students.

American schools have always been the intellectual leaders in business education and they remain, collectively, a bastion of serious research. (The leading European schools have closed this gap, but relatively few of them are truly serious research institutions.) American professors at the leading schools therefore tend to be at the forefront of their fields. This is especially true now that American schools have emphasized developing closer links with industry, so most leading professors spend part of their time consulting to industry in addition to doing research. In fact, the two activities are closely related.

American schools have dramatically changed their programs to integrate the core subjects, incorporate softer skills, and internationalize their focus. These changes are continuing. Different schools have approached the need for change in different ways, as the contrast between the programs at the Amos Tuck School (at Dartmouth College) and the University of Chicago's Graduate School of Business illustrates.

PROGRAM STRUCTURE

The Amos Tuck School of Business Administration ("Tuck") provides an example of a traditional program structure. Tuck is a two-year program devoted to training general managers rather than functional specialists. The academic year is split into three terms. In the fall term, five courses are required:

- Decision Science
- Financial Accounting
- Management Communication
- Managerial Economics
- Marketing

In the winter term, the five required courses are:

- Applied Statistics
- Capital Markets
- Global Economic Environment
- International Leadership
- Organizational Behavior

In the spring term, the required courses are:

- Business Policy
- Corporate Finance
- Managerial Accounting
- Operations Management

In the second year students take twelve (or more) electives. This structure is common to other two-year programs, although many schools have a two- rather than three-term structure. This selection of courses is a good example of a rigorous and modern program, with a good mixture of quantitative courses, such as Capital Markets and Managerial Accounting, and softer courses, such as Managerial Communication and Organizational Behavior. The international dimension is also clear, with core courses devoted to Global Economics and International Leadership. The program's structure is a relatively rigid one: few students are allowed to waive the first-year courses, which represent half of the total number of courses to be taken.

At the other end of the spectrum, the University of Chicago Graduate School of Business ("Chicago") has created a curriculum that offers dramatic freedom of choice to students. Only two courses—Business Policy and an introductory leadership-soft skills course—must be taken by everyone. There are four other core courses, all of which can be waived and replaced by more advanced courses in the same area, or, with faculty approval, an unrelated course may be substituted. Students must take courses in a variety of fields, to meet a distribution requirement, but the specific courses are to be chosen by each student. This structure is highly flexible; only two to six courses out of twenty-one are mandated, and the rest to be chosen to fit a student's own needs.

Most American schools are closer to Tuck than Chicago in their curricula. Although a good deal of freedom of choice of electives is offered, the set of required courses remains at about 40 percent of the total program. Although some schools allow students to waive some required courses, most case-oriented schools (like Harvard, Darden, and North Carolina) do not. They feel that it is essential to have highly knowledgeable students in these courses because these students will effectively end up teaching the novices, through their comments in class and their work in study groups.

Advantages of a Traditional Program (relative to other methods of obtaining an MBA)

- Traditional, well-understood method of getting the degree
- High student satisfaction with most programs
- High interaction with other students
- Ability to take numerous elective courses
- Appropriate for people changing careers who need courses and time to make the change
- Good for those who need to understand the American market or a specific American industry

Disadvantages (relative to other methods of obtaining an MBA)

- Expensive
- Long time away from work
- Student body typically largely American rather than mixed

VARIATIONS ON THE TRADITIONAL MBA

AMERICAN VS. EUROPEAN MODEL

Not long ago there were two relatively distinct models of MBA education. The American model differed from the European on several grounds:

	American	*European*
Length	2 Years	1 Year
Primary Driver	Professorial Research	Industry Connections
Course Focus	American	Global or European
Quantitative or Soft Skills Emphasized	Quantitative	Soft Skills
Student Body	Largely American	Mixed
Selection Criteria Emphasized	Test Scores, Grades	Work Experience and Success
Age of Students	Early Twenties	Late Twenties

There were other differences too, although this type of chart obviously oversimplifies the extent. Moreover, not all programs fit the predominant pattern in either case. In the United States, Thunderbird was (and remains) very similar to the European programs, with its global focus, emphasis upon languages, and the like. In Europe, London Business School, Manchester Business School, and IESE (Barcelona) were (and remain) a mixture of the American and European models—a "mid-Atlantic" model, perhaps.

The differences between the two models have become blurrier in recent years as the American programs in particular have made substantial changes. Most, if not all, of the top American programs have greatly increased the role of such "soft skills" as leadership, negotiation, and teamwork. Related to this, they have tried to improve their connections to industry, to make their courses more relevant and less driven by professorial interest (some would say whim), and also to benefit from being able to place students as interns undertaking projects for companies. They have also worked hard to examine the issues in managing in a global environment, although they generally lag behind the top European programs in this regard. The American programs have sought people with more work experience, rather than those who have only academic credentials. Some things have remained the same, however; most American programs remain resolutely two years long. The European schools have changed less, although the leading programs in particular, such as INSEAD (outside Paris) and Rotterdam, have joined London Business School in having a more quantitative focus to their programs.

The old stereotypes—American schools are intellectually rigorous but their graduates lack managerial and interpersonal skills; European schools produce fine managers who understand the languages and cultural context of different countries but lack substantive skills—clearly no longer apply. But before dismissing the issue, it should be said that some of the old differences between American and European programs remain. American schools still spend a majority of course time on American cases and issues, whereas European schools do not focus so heavily on any one country. American student bodies are still largely American (only 20 percent to 40 percent come from other countries), whereas few leading European schools have more than a large minority from their home countries.

EUROPEAN PROGRAM STRUCTURE

INSEAD offers a typical one-year program structure (although it actually lasts only about ten months). It is divided into five two-month terms:

Term 1:

Introduction to Management
Applied Statistics
Financial Accounting
Management Accounting
Marketing I
Prices and Markets

Term 2:

Finance I (or "Turbo-Finance" for those who are or wish to be finance professionals)
Management Accounting
Marketing II
Managing Organizations
Production and Operations Management

Term 3:

Corporate Strategy
Economic Analysis
Financial Management or Finance II

Choice of two electives

Term 4:

Industrial Policy and International Competitiveness
International Political Analysis
Choice of two electives

Term 5:

Choice of three electives

Twenty-two courses are required to graduate, with approximately fifteen required courses and seven electives. This two-to-one ratio of required to elective courses is about average for the one-year programs, although several leading schools offer almost no choice of electives, with all courses being set, essentially—and no waivers or options available. The shortness of the program and the consequent high percentage of required versus elective courses are different from the longer American programs.

The advantages and disadvantages of attending a European school as described below are based upon one-year programs. Those interested in the two-year programs at such schools as London, Manchester, IESE, and Bocconi are advised to use this list with caution, and to consider the above pros and cons regarding American two-year programs as well.

Advantages:

- For those with substantial business experience, one year may be all that is necessary to broaden horizons and improve skills.
- The time spent away from one's career is limited.
- Good industry connections mean that the best schools do remarkably well in placing their students.
- The internationalism of the top programs, especially regarding the mix of nationalities in the student body, is remarkable.
- Emphasis is placed upon learning languages.
- Teaching of soft skills is often superb.

Disadvantages:

- A one-year program is too short for some to develop enough new skills and contacts to make dramatic career shifts.
- Some programs are too small or too structured to offer much choice of electives.

■ The underlying presumption that students have substantial business experience means that some of the introductory courses move at too fast a pace for novices.

■ Some programs do not force students to acquire substantial quantitative skills, requiring a conscious choice of quantitative elective courses in order to develop these skills.

The European model is attractive to those who intend to work in Europe or for European companies. As with the leading U.S. schools, leading European schools offer worldwide employment opportunities and first-class learning environments. Top American firms that operate worldwide, such as the management consulting and financial service firms, are among the top recruiters of students from them.

It is indeed unfortunate that so few Americans (perhaps a thousand per year) attend these programs, although an American who wishes to work for a Kansas City firm doing business only in the Kansas City region admittedly has no need to cross the Atlantic for an MBA. The fact remains, however, that fewer and fewer younger applicants will be correct in assuming that their careers will be without international dimensions, whether that means working abroad, working for a foreign company in the United States, managing foreign employees, or competing against foreign companies.

PART-TIME MBAS

Part-time MBAs have become more popular both because they offer the opportunity to remain at one's job while also attending school and because more top-quality schools have begun to offer part-time MBA programs. The typical program involves taking one or two classes per term, thereby prolonging the time it takes to get a degree. Those pursuing an American MBA, who would take two years in a full-time program, will take four years or more in a part-time program.

The people who find these programs attractive are likely to be older, with more experience, and many have family responsibilities that prevent them from attending a full-time program. Others are unable or unwilling to leave their current jobs and choose a part-time program as the only realistic means of furthering their business educations.

PROGRAM STRUCTURE

The structure of a part-time MBA does not differ significantly from that of a full-time MBA. The same core courses are generally required, although they may be taken in a slightly different sequence due to the scheduling difficulties that result from students proceeding through the program at varying speeds.

The number of courses that must be completed in order to graduate will almost invariably be the same.

Advantages

- An employer is more likely to pay your tuition for a part-time program than for a full-time program insofar as the former route involves your remaining an employee of that firm, whereas the latter may involve only a promise to return for some unspecified time—typically one year—after you finish your degree.

- By staying on the job you can eliminate the cost and risk of searching for employment at the end of your program.

- You keep getting paid during your studies.

- You do not have to relocate for your studies.

- You can often employ what you learn on the job as you learn it.

- Ongoing relevant work experience may be drawn upon to enhance your performance in the program.

Disadvantages

- You will not be able to commit yourself to your studies and to your classmates the way that you could if you attended school full time. The result is that you will probably feel that you have not gotten as fully to grips with many of your courses as you would have had you been able to be a full-time student.

- The demands made by the combination of a full-time job and part-time study tend to be overwhelming, causing people to feel that they are doing neither of these activities well. The possibility of handling both well, plus a rewarding personal life, is remote.

- Your job performance may suffer so much, due to the effort you must make for your classes, and your unavailability to travel on certain nights, and so on, that you will not increase your responsibilities or salary as you would if you could devote yourself more fully to your job.

- Your company may not be pleased about your planning to subordinate your work effort to three to six years of school.

- When you have completed all or much of your program, your company may not recognize that you have improved your skills and thus may be unwilling to promote you or increase your pay. (On the other hand, the company may fear that you are going to leave it given that you have improved your résumé and your visibility.)

▓ Your classmates are likely to be from the surrounding area, meaning that you may have very few from other countries. This lack of diversity limits your potential learning.

It would be entirely reasonable to choose a part-time program rather than a full-time one, *provided* that you can go to a top 10 or 20 school in doing so. On the other hand, going to a middle-tier school part time at the expense of being able to attend a top 10 or 20 school full time is not a good idea if you have other options.

The bottom line is that a part-time course should be more appealing to the extent that your current job is very attractive to you and is of a type that would permit you to pursue a part-time program, and you are fortunate enough to have a top quality part-time MBA program available in your area.

EXECUTIVE MBAs

Executive MBAs are a relatively recent addition to the offerings of most graduate business schools. For years, the only such program was offered by the University of Chicago. Now there are dozens of executive MBA programs offered by many of the top business schools in the world. (The European version of an executive MBA is often called a modular program, but it is similar enough that the following description fits it also.)

Executive MBAs are to be distinguished both from regular MBAs and from other executive programs. An executive MBA is generally offered on a one-day-per-week basis over two years, or on alternate weekends for two years. Regular MBA programs, of course, meet daily and last up to two years. Other executive education programs, in contrast, may meet for one to ten or twelve weeks, but do not confer an MBA upon completion.

The number of executive MBA programs has grown dramatically in the last two decades because the degree meets the needs of a substantial number of people who are much less well served by traditional MBAs. The typical student at an executive MBA program has more than seven years' experience and is unwilling or unable to leave her job. Or her company is so reluctant to see her go, or so desirous of improving her skills while she continues to work, that it will sponsor her at an executive program. She will thus work on a more or less full-time basis and attend school four days a month.

A typical executive MBA student might be an architect turned consultant, working for a Boston consulting firm that so likes his performance that it will ship him down to New York several times a month to attend Columbia's executive MBA program.

PROGRAM STRUCTURE

Kellogg's two executive master's programs illustrate the structures that are on offer in executive degree programs in the United States and Europe. Its Executive Masters Program (EMP) holds classes on alternate Fridays and Saturdays during the academic year. Students take twelve six-week modules spread over two academic years. Participants can begin in either January or September. The participants have at least eight years of experience and range in age from early thirties to late forties. The North American Program, designed to help facilitate students coming from long distances (indeed the whole of the continent), is quite similar to the EMP except that classes meet every second week on Friday afternoon, all day Saturday, and on Sunday morning. Both programs begin each of the two years with a one week on-campus session. Both programs have ten required modules. Four courses are to be chosen from a set of alternatives to complete the other two modules. This structure, which features a very large percentage of required courses (approximately 83 percent of the program), is in stark contrast to the flexibility of the traditional MBA, which features only nine (waivable) core courses out of twenty-three.

Advantages

- Your employer pays for the course, so you stay out of debt.
- You continue to earn a salary, so your opportunity cost (see Chapter 7) is dramatically reduced.
- You continue to learn on the job.
- You can apply your learning immediately.
- Because executive MBA programs are generally the most lucrative offering for a school, it will usually provide its best faculty and even throw in one or more luxurious trips abroad.
- Your classmates are very experienced, so they will tend to be fonts of information and skill.
- You do not face the risk of having to find a job upon graduation.

Disadvantages

- Many programs offer a very limited choice of courses. People hoping to develop greater functional expertise rather than general management skills may be poorly served as a result.

▣ Students generally do not get to know each other particularly well, and share assignments and knowledge less often than in a traditional MBA program; the meetings are only once a week or once a fortnight and participants do not necessarily live near the school, so there may be no lingering after class to discuss things over a coffee or beer.

▣ As with part-time programs, the need to devote yourself to both a job and classes can interfere with your ability to do either properly. An understanding boss may be a necessity to handle this conflict successfully.

Given that the advantages of these programs so outweigh the disadvantages, why wouldn't everyone want to do an executive MBA? There are two reasons; the first has to do with the individual, and the second has to do with the employer.

Because executive MBAs are designed for people in their thirties and forties, someone in his twenties does not really have the option of attending such a course. In fact, it is probably not a good idea to wait until age 36 to get an executive MBA if you are now 26 and ready, after approximately three years' work experience, to get an MBA. Delaying getting a traditional degree means that you delay its benefits as well—benefits that are not only monetary but also include expanding career choices and options.

It is also difficult to get your employer to pay for your education and forsake some of your current time in hopes of getting sufficient additional contribution from you in the future to make it worth the company's while. You must be in a job that permits you to be absent every Friday (or whatever is necessary), to devote long hours working on class assignments, and to stay in the same office—or at least the same city—for the two years. An employer also has to believe that you will stay with the company for long enough after you earn the degree to offer a good return on their investment in you. The simple fact is that relatively few employees can realistically expect to qualify. Even if they do, others in the company may also be seeking the same deal and the company may choose to sponsor only a small percentage of those who qualify.

OTHER EDUCATIONAL OPTIONS

An MBA is not the only option for those who wish to do graduate business study. If you are interested in developing your skills in essentially one area only, you can do, for example, a master's degree in finance. Specialized master's degrees exist in accounting, business economics, information systems, marketing, operations, and numerous other fields. These are not generally suitable, however, for those who wish to receive training in the usual core courses of an MBA program or pursue courses in several fields.

APPENDIX
What to Expect at Business School

This appendix is designed to give you a feel for what business school will be like in a full-time program. Part-time and executive programs are similar in most regards, with the obvious differences caused by the fact that students are not spending all of their time in the programs. As a result, the first year is not so overwhelming and their social lives tend not to revolve around the schools.

TYPICAL REQUIRED COURSES

Nearly all schools traditionally require the following courses:

- Financial Accounting
- Managerial Accounting
- Economics
- Finance
- Marketing
- Operations
- Organizational Behavior
- Quantitative Methods/Statistics
- Business Policy/Strategy

Some schools have changed their core curriculum, however, so you might find that some things have been added to this list, such as information systems, leadership, or communication skills. The specific courses required at each school will differ, but the listings of those required at Tuck, Chicago, and INSEAD, noted earlier, should give you an idea of the range of courses required at different schools. For further information about the content of the most typical core courses, see Chapter 15, "What to Do Once You Are Accepted," which discusses how to prepare for these courses.

TEACHING METHODS

Four types of teaching are widely used in business schools: lecture, case study, computer simulation, and in-company project. The traditional lecture method, in which students listen and take a great deal of notes but generally participate only infrequently, is still the most common method of teaching. The other traditional method, termed the case method, has been the primary teaching vehicle at Harvard, Darden (University of

Virginia), and several other programs for a long time. Computer simulations and in-company projects are relatively recent additions to most schools' teaching. (The last three teaching methods, which may be unfamiliar to you, are discussed below.)

THE CASE METHOD

The case method is quite unlike the teaching used in most undergraduate courses. In its purest form it involves reading a case—a write-up of a real or hypothetical situation at a company or other organization—and determining what one or another of the participants is best advised to do and why. Complex cases can involve dozens of pages of background reading and dozens of exhibits. The latter lay out, for example, the cost of components used in a dozen products at each of a dozen different production sites, plus the company's financial results over the last ten years. Students are expected to analyze the case from the perspective of what would be best for the company, for one or more departments, and for one or more individuals, and to determine how best the various options could or should be realized. This involves a great deal of analysis, much of it of a "what-if" variety. ("What if we transferred all model X production to our Ireland plant, shut the Greensboro facility, and exited the Canadian market? Would this make sense? What are the likely production, marketing, organizational, and, ultimately, financial results of this policy?") This teaching method is good at teaching students how to structure the analysis of complex problems, set forth several coherent options showing what they plan to do and how they plan to do it, and sell the chosen option to a group of doubting, difficult peers. The drawback to it is that it is not suited to learning basic, technical disciplines such as accounting, which are more easily learned by reading structured textbooks and doing relevant exercises.

The following points are generally made in favor of the case method:

➤ It fosters high involvement on the part of students.

➤ It is realistic in mimicking the real world, rather than just theorizing about it.

➤ It compresses many career experiences into a short period of time.

➤ The overabundance of material forces students to develop efficient time management techniques and to learn to choose what analysis to do and what to skip.

➤ The nature of the case method requires active class participation, and thus develops presentational skills and the ability to "think on one's feet."

➤ It encourages students to think like general managers, examining a problem from an overall, "big picture" perspective.

The following are among the points made against the case method:

➤ It is inefficient for teaching theory that underlies the material.

➤ It encourages ultracompetitive behavior in the fight for class "air-time" (a particularly important problem for the reserved and for those whose English is not truly fluent).

➤ The packaged information in the cases obviates the need for students to go out and find or develop their own data.

➤ With the development of computer simulations and the increased use of in-company consulting projects, schools need no longer depend solely upon cases to mimic the real world.

➤ The general management perspective that students tend to adopt for case analyses results in their not being prepared to work at a lower level when they graduate.

A consensus view appears to be that some use of cases, especially to teach advanced marketing, strategy, and organizational development, is highly desirable. For one thing, the drawbacks of the method are minimized in those settings; for another, at least some use of it helps develop the ability to mine cases for the most relevant information, package it quickly, and respond to wide-ranging questions in a coherent and powerful manner.

COMPUTER SIMULATION

A relatively new method is computer simulation, in which students can run a company or act as head of a department, and get quick feedback about the appropriateness of their decisions from the results of the game. Team competitions, in which students are divided into teams of three to six, are common, especially for the (often required) business strategy course. Teams feed their decisions about a host of variables into the computer at set times. The outcomes of the competition depend not on what has happened in the industry in the past, but on what the respective teams have chosen to do. For example, if nearly every team decides to boost volume, cut price, and push for as much market share as possible, the winner might be the team that has decided to focus on a high price, high quality (and thus low volume) niche that it alone will occupy.

IN-COMPANY PROJECTS

In-company projects, which have long been common in Europe, are gaining currency in the United States as well. Students get a chance to put into practice their newly acquired skills in a real company. Good projects require that students tackle suitably important issues, not just make-work or trivial problems. The usual problem is not student dissatisfaction with projects, but finding enough companies willing to hand large projects over to students. From the company perspective, such projects require getting students up to speed on their company and industry, and then sharing confidential data with them, as well as soothing the employees who would otherwise have had their own chances to make a mark with the same project. Not surprisingly, most schools suffer from a dearth of ideal projects. The exceptions tend to be the most prestigious schools that are also located close to the headquarters of numerous major companies.

WORKLOAD

Top MBA programs demand a remarkable amount of work. During the first year of a program (or the first two-thirds of a one-year program), the demands are particularly great. There are several reasons for this. The first is that the schools are trying to teach all of the major functional areas of business, plus an understanding of micro- and macro-economics, and numerous skills such as communications, leadership, teamwork, and so on. This is a large amount to learn in such a short time, so the workload is inevitably high. (The second year—or last one-third of a one-year program—is less intense, both because students have learned how to play the business school "game" and because they are taking elective courses suited to their interests.)

Another important reason for the time pressure is that the workload of a senior executive or an entrepreneur can be grueling. The MBA program is structured to simulate that load, so that students are prepared for it later on. The excessive amount of work forces students to learn how to manage their time, one of the key skills a senior manager must acquire. Thus a student will almost certainly have to learn to prioritize—to determine which bits of work to do, which to glance at, and which to ignore—as well as how to do all of this efficiently. Furthermore, a student's coverage of material can be greatly enhanced by working with a group of other students, so the excessive demands of the program encourage formation of student study groups. Getting the most out of a study group requires good teamwork skills, something that programs explicitly wish to foster.

So how demanding are these programs? In fact, they are so demanding that it is more appropriate to describe the amount of time a typical student is not working, rather than the other way around. Unmarried students typically take off one evening per week, enough time each day for a physical activity, plus the occasional hour or two to relax. Married students generally spend a bit more time away from their books, but not a lot. Obviously even an understanding spouse and family are likely to be put out by this sort of schedule.

STUDY GROUPS

Study groups, whether formed to prepare for exams or to do a specific project, are among the staples of business school life. The ideal group consists of students with professional competence in a wide range of fields, and with the temperament to work well on teams. Most students find that their own group or groups fall far short of the ideal, so learning how to manage team interaction is of great importance to them.

Groups in some schools are chosen by the students themselves, but it has become more common for the schools to form the groups to assure everyone of a place and to make sure that students have to confront the usual problems that result from highly diverse membership. For example, how should the lazy or quantitatively underprepared student be treated, should one person be allowed to dominate discussions, and so on? From the school's perspective this mirrors the usual problems in working on teams in the real world. Students tend to find group work a valuable experience, but extremely frustrating, which bears out the school's view.

CURRICULAR ORGANIZATION OF THE TRADITIONAL MBA PROGRAM

THE PRETERM

Many programs start with a preprogram, which may last for as little as three days or as long as a month. Some programs are designed only to review subjects such as statistics, economics, algebra, or calculus. These programs are ordinarily optional, with those who have not had prior coursework in these fields being strongly encouraged to take them. Other programs have various team-building, "bonding," and socializing courses and events. The second type are generally mandatory for all incoming students.

THE FIRST YEAR

The first year (or half-year in a one-year program) is likely to be overwhelming unless you have had a very good preparation for it. By very good preparation, I mean that you have already done a bachelor's degree in business, or worked in the type of environment that in many respects mimics business school, such as a management consulting firm. There is so much work to do, so many new concepts to learn, that you are likely to feel that you are drowning. Not only do you have a great deal to learn, you also have to learn how to learn. As time goes on, however, you will figure out how to cut through the massive amounts of reading and detail and focus on the key aspects, whether of textbooks and articles or of cases. Whereas a full case analysis, for example, might take you eight or ten hours initially, in the second term you might manage a similar case in just three hours. Most students feel that the first term is infinitely more difficult than the second, and that the following terms are more or less a breeze.

THE SECOND YEAR

The second year curriculum generally has few if any required courses, allowing students to choose the electives that fit their interests. The second year is inevitably quite relaxed relative to the pressure of the first year, and most of the emotional focus will be on getting the right job rather than surviving your courses.

STUDENT BODY

The student body at most schools looks much as it has for years. The vast majority of students are male—many schools having seen a decline in the enrollment of women since the late 1980s. A large percentage of students come from engineering, financial services and accounting, management consulting, and marketing. These fields, not surprisingly, are also the biggest employers of MBAs. Despite this, the mix of jobs held by the other quarter or so of the class—the group that has not come from the standard pre-MBA positions—is quite stunning. It is not unusual to have such classmates as a former navy commander, a commercial pilot, a fashion photographer, an inventor of a new machine, and someone who sailed the Atlantic in a minuscule sailboat.

Much of the learning experience in a high quality program comes from your fellow students, who can give real-life insights into problems, based upon their recent experiences in similar situations. The range of different jobs, companies, industries, and countries makes for a rich mixture of relevant experience to bring to bear in classroom discussions and study group sessions.

Whatever their work backgrounds, the different students have several things in common. They are invariably highly motivated as well as highly intelligent, and have been highly successful in whatever they have done so far.

These are not just the people you will work with, and compete with, for your time together in business school. You will form lifelong friendships with some of them and may well form a company with some, too. Your business school colleagues represent your future network of contacts, the people who will be your clients and partners and sources of job information when you consider switching companies.

SOCIAL LIFE

Some suspect that the only way that MBA students manage to have any social life at all is by sleeping very little. There is a lot of truth in this. The time pressure inherent in demanding programs ensures that only the truly energetic can manage a social or family life in addition to their studies. The bulk of MBA students, however, are energetic enough to live at least a moderately social existence.

Social life differs greatly from one program to the next. At all schools, however, student clubs will be the focus of substantial time and effort. Many of these are preprofessional clubs designed to help students get jobs in their chosen fields. A management consulting club, for example, would help members get jobs in consulting by inviting speakers and recruiters from large and small consulting firms to visit and discuss the field, and their respective firms, with interested members. Larger schools tend to have a magnificent range of such clubs, covering everything from consumer marketing to non-profit management.

Not all student clubs are an extension of the job search. Many sports and activities clubs can be found on the typical campus. These in particular are likely to be open to spouses and even children. Like their preprofessional analogs, these offer the opportunity to demonstrate leadership and other desirable attributes along with simple energy and love of a given activity.

American two-year programs tend to be better at providing student-run clubs than do the European one-year programs, due partly to the American undergraduate ethos, which holds that extracurricular involvement in student activities is part and parcel of an educational experience, and partly to the greater amount of time available. (Some American schools seem to have nearly as many clubs as students, perhaps to give every student the chance to be president.)

Not all student social life revolves around clubs. Student parties fortunately are a staple of MBA programs, with the excuse for holding one varying from the need to get away from studying when the pressure is greatest to the need to take advantage of the opportunity when the pressure is lowest. In addition, students find innumerable ways to enjoy informal activities with their fellow students and outsiders, although the more isolated campuses make interaction with nonstudents rather problematic.

3

HOW TO USE
THE RANKINGS

— EXECUTIVE SUMMARY —

■

Schools in the United States, Europe, and elsewhere are routinely ranked
by various authorities.

■

These rankings provide handy guides to the reputations of different programs,
but they are subject to many qualifications.

■

Consult them, but do not rely on them.

- Recognize their limitations as well
  as their strengths.

*T*he purpose of this book is not to rank schools, nor to place school X on a list of "top" schools and relegate school Y to the list of also-rans. Other publications devote substantial effort to doing just this—at least for American programs—and the field will be left to them. This chapter will examine some of the more important rankings and discuss the methodologies they employ to reach their conclusions.

Formal rankings have been made for American full-time programs, part-time programs, and executive programs; Canadian full-time programs; British full- and part-time programs; European full-time programs; and, to a very limited extent, programs in the rest of the world. No doubt other rankings exist, but this chapter will focus on those that are the best known and most useful. Each of the following rankings is revised on a regular basis, with the possible exception of *The MBA Advantage,* which is currently in its first edition. (Whether it will be revised regularly is not clear.) These rankings include:

American full-time programs:

- *Business Week*
- *U.S. News & World Report*
- *The Insider's Guide to the Top Ten Business Schools*
- *The MBA Advantage*
- *Which MBA?*

American part-time programs:

- *U.S. News & World Report*
- *Which MBA?*

American executive programs:

- *Business Week*
- *Which MBA?*

British programs (full- and part-time):

- *Association of MBAs*
- *Which MBA?*

Continental European full-time programs:

- *Association of MBAs*
- *Capital*
- *Which MBA?*

Rest of the World:

- *Which MBA?*

Several of these listings do not actually rank schools. The Association of MBAs (AMBA), based in London, accredits schools according to their provision of appropriate facilities, class size, number of courses offered, and so on. Nonetheless, this serves much the same purpose as a ranking in that it attests to the quality of a program. *Which MBA?* chooses which schools to discuss on the basis of their prominence and their international focus. Like the other sources discussed here, it covers only those schools that use English as a language of instruction, including several bilingual programs. The German magazine *Capital* ranks European schools based largely upon interviews with large employers, including the German industrial giants, leading banks, publishers, consulting and accounting firms, executive recruiters, and other service firms. It is included in this discussion because it is now being updated biannually, in contrast to the many journals that prepare rankings on a one-time basis.

The methodologies employed by *Business Week, U.S. News & World Report,* and *The MBA Advantage* (Ronald N. Yeaple) are discussed in some detail later in this chapter.

There is another important, albeit highly unofficial ranking—that provided by word of mouth and received wisdom. In the United States, for example, while some people would refer to the specific rankings of a school in the *Business Week* guide, others would take into account the "traditional" ranking of a school, which often amounts to a combination of the fame of the school's parent university and the ranking of the business school in the past, or to the fame of the school in the local area.

USING THE RANKINGS

The ranking of business schools is a very uncertain science. Organizations that undertake these rankings are confronted by daunting methodological problems. For example, how important is it to have a library of one million volumes rather than 600,000 volumes, and how does that compare with having a student body GMAT average of 625 rather than 645? Is the school with one million volumes and a GMAT average of 625 better than the school with 600,000 and 645, respectively, equal to it, or worse? It is not obvious how the two schools should be compared, even when two relatively simple quantitative measures are employed. The problem is made infinitely more complicated when numerous other factors are considered, especially because many of these are inherently subjective rather than easily and objectively quantifiable.

Several bypasses are available to the ranking organizations. They can examine the opinions of those doing the hiring at major firms, taking the likely employers of MBAs as the ultimate arbiters of worth. To an extent this is correct, of course, insofar as MBAs tend to view the value of their degree in large measure as a matter of what employment doors it opens. Another possible shortcut is to examine the earnings of the graduates of each school, relying again on the market as the arbiter of the value of MBAs from the various schools. Unfortunately, these shortcuts also suffer from limitations. Some are due to the fact that an overall ranking for a school does not distinguish between how its finance graduates do in the market and how its human resources graduates fare. Nor does it take account of the fact that its graduates may do very well locally but not in another region or country. Thus if a school is rated highly because its finance graduates make a lot of money, but you intend to go into human resource management, this school may not boost your salary more than another school would.

SOME WARNINGS

Rankings are useful as a very rough guide to the reputation and quality of different programs. Most people take them far too seriously, however, when considering where to apply. It is inappropriate to take the latest *Business Week* rankings and limit yourself to the top five schools in their list. The schools differ enough in their goals, programs, and atmospheres that a person who will be well served by one may be very poorly served by another. To take an obvious example, a person who is determined to be managing the "factory of the future" and is not particularly interested in general management should be looking at MIT's Sloan School rather than Harvard. Both are superb, but their missions are quite different.

Chapter 5, "How to Choose the Right School for *You*," lists several dozen criteria that are relevant to choosing the right program. Not all are equally significant, and admittedly reputation is critically important. But it would be silly to opt for a school ranked fourth by *U.S. News* or *Business Week,* rather than one ranked seventh, solely because of these rankings if the first had an unsuitable atmosphere, had few electives in the field you want to enter, or suffered from one of a number of other defects that may also be important to you. There is no precision to these rankings; the same publication may reverse the rankings of these same schools next year! The imprecision and variability of the rankings is one reason for being cautious in using them; another reason for caution is that one school will be able to offer you a program geared to your needs whereas another will not.

These concerns give rise to some guidelines for using rankings:

1. Look at as many rankings as possible and consider the consensus rather than any one ranking.

2. Consider even this consensus view as only an approximation of the appropriate tier for a school. Thus a school that is ranked about tenth to fifteenth in various rankings should be regarded as a very fine school, to be taken very seriously, but whether it really should be ranked in the top 5 or merely the top 25 is not determinable.

3. Since you should be looking for the best program to meet your specific subject and other needs, with an atmosphere in which you will thrive, the rankings have only a modest part to play in helping you to find this program. They have little to say about which school will provide the courses that will be most useful, the connections that will matter most for the job and region in which you wish to be employed, the academic and social environment there, and other key factors.

4. More important than the rankings will be the research you do concerning the details of specific programs, which is discussed in detail in Chapter 5, "How to Choose the Right School for *You*."

THE RANKINGS

FULL-TIME PROGRAMS—THE UNITED STATES

The five rankings charted below cover a total of 46 schools out of the approximately 1200 American MBA programs. Although some of these publications list only about twenty schools, I share the opinion of *Which MBA?* that a listing of forty-some schools in fact understates the number of good quality, serious programs available.

	Business Week	U.S. News	Insider's Guide*	MBA Advantage	Which MBA?**
Wharton (U. of Pennsylvania)	1	3	Top ten	8	+
U. of Michigan	2	12	Top ten	12	+
Kellogg (Northwestern U.)	3	4	Top ten	6	+
Harvard U.	4	5	Top ten	1	+
Darden (U. of Virginia)	5	11	Top ten	10	+
Columbia U.	6	8	Top ten		+
Stanford U.	7	1	Top ten	3	+
U. of Chicago	8	6	Top ten	2	+
Sloan (MIT)	9	2	Top ten	4	+
Amos Tuck (Dartmouth U.)	10	7	Top ten	13	+
Fuqua (Duke U.)	11	9	+	19	+
Anderson (U. of California at Los Angeles—UCLA)	12	16	+	9	+
Haas (U. of California at Berkeley)	13	10	+	7	+
Stern (New York U.—NYU)	14	13	+	20	+
Indiana U.	15	20	+	17	+
Olin (Washington U.)	16	33			
Carnegie Mellon U.	17	14	+	14	+
Johnson (Cornell U.)	18	15	+	11	+
Kenan-Flagler (U. of North Carolina at Chapel Hill)	19	17	+	18	+
U. of Texas at Austin	20	18	+	15	+
Simon (U. of Rochester)	21	23		16	+
Yale U.	22	18	+	5	+
Cox (Southern Methodist U.)	23				+
Owen (Vanderbilt U.)	24	27	+		+
Thunderbird (American Grad. School of Int'l. Mgmt.)	25	48			+
Krannert (Purdue University)		21			+
Goizueta (Emory U.)		22			+
U. of Maryland at College Park		24			
Georgetown U.		25			+
U. of Southern California		26			+
Fisher (Ohio State U.)		28			+
Freeman (Tulane U.)		29			
U. of Wisconsin at Madison		30			+
Georgia Institute of Technology		31			

	Business Week	U.S. News	Insider's Guide*	MBA Advantage	Which MBA?**
Carlson (U. of Minnesota)		32			+
Arizona State U.		34			
U. of Iowa		35			+
U. of Georgia		36			+
Smeal (Pennsylvania State U.)		37			+
U. of Illinois at Urbana-Champaign		37	+		+
Weatherhead (Case Western Reserve U.)		39			+
U. of California at Davis		39			
U. of Notre Dame		41			
Wake Forest U.		42			
Broad (Michigan State U.)		43			
U. of Florida		44			+
Brigham Young U.		45			
Eller (U. of Arizona)		45			
U. of Tennessee at Knoxville		47			
College of William and Mary		49			
Texas A & M U. at College Station		49			
Arthur D. Little					+
Jones (Rice U.)					+
Katz (U. of Pittsburgh)					+
U. of South Carolina					+

*The Insider's Guide to the Top Ten Business Schools, ed. by Tom Fischgrund, does not rank the ten schools chosen. Accordingly, this list simply shows whether a given school has been included among his top ten list or not, or is listed as being one of the "other top MBA programs," indicated by a +.

**Which MBA, by George Bickerstaffe, published by The Economist Intelligence Unit, does not rank schools either. This list simply shows whether a given school has been among the 40+ American schools it discusses.

There is clearly no agreement as to which school is *the* best, nor which one is the seventeenth best. There is some reasonable agreement, however, as to those schools considered the real elite of American schools. Considering the *Business Week, U.S. News, Insider's Guide to the Top Ten Business Schools,* and *The MBA Advantage* rankings, the following schools were ranked in the top ten one or more times:

Ranked in top ten by all 4	by 3	by 2	by 1
Wharton (Pennsylvania)	Columbia	Michigan	Anderson (UCLA)
Kellogg (Northwestern)	Amos Tuck	Haas (Berkeley)	Fuqua (Duke)
Chicago	(Dartmouth)		Yale
Stanford	Darden (Virginia)		
Harvard			
Sloan (MIT)			

These additional schools were ranked in the top twenty* by one or more of these guides:

Ranked in top twenty by all 4	by 3	by 2	by 1
Carnegie Mellon	—	—	Simon (Rochester)
Johnson (Cornell)			Illinois
Stern (NYU)			Owen (Vanderbilt)
Texas			
Kenan-Flagler (North Carolina)			
Indiana			

*Or top 22, in the case of *The Insider's Guide to the Top Ten Business Schools* categorization.

PART-TIME AND EXECUTIVE MBA PROGRAMS—NORTH AMERICA

The following is an alphabetical listing of these programs.

	Which MBA?	U.S. News*	Business Week**
Anderson (UCLA)	+	4	5
Carlson (U. of Minnesota)	+	9	
Carnegie Mellon U.	+		
U. of Chicago	+	1	2
Columbia			7
Cox (Southern Methodist U.)	+		19
Fisher (Ohio State U.)	+		
U. of Florida	+		
Freeman (Tulane U.)			20
Fuqua (Duke U.)	+		4
Georgetown U.	+		
Georgia State U.		10	9
Goizueta (Emory U.)			15

	Which MBA?	U.S. News*	Business Week**
Haas (U. of California at Berkeley)	+	7	
U. of Illinois			12
Indiana U.			6
U. of Iowa	+		
Katz (U. of Pittsburgh)	+		14
Kellogg (Northwestern U.)	+	3	1
Kellstadt (DePaul U.)		6	
Krannert (Purdue U.)			13
Kenan-Flagler (U. of North Carolina)	+		
McGill U.	+		
U. of Michigan	+	5	
Owen (Vanderbilt U.)			18
Simon (U. of Rochester)	+		
U. of South Carolina	+		
U. of Southern California	+	8	8
Stern (New York U.)	+	2	11
U. of Texas (Austin)			16
Thunderbird (American Graduate School of International Management)	+		
U. of Toronto	+		
Wake Forest U.			17
Weatherhead (Case Western Reserve U.)	+		10
Western (U. of Western Ontario)	+		
Wharton (U. of Pennsylvania)			3
U. of Wisconsin—Madison	+		

*Part-time programs only; rankings by business school deans and program heads.
**Executive programs only.

FULL- AND PART-TIME PROGRAMS—UNITED KINGDOM AND IRELAND

The *Which MBA?* listing is once again a matter of which schools it chooses to discuss, whereas the AMBA listing represents schools it has accredited, whether for full-time or part-time programs. The *Capital* magazine list is an interesting view of the strength of British programs from the perspective of German, Austrian, and Swiss employers. It should therefore be used with even more caution than might ordinarily be given to a ranking unless you intend to work in Germany, Austria, or Switzerland. (The list is in alphabetical order.)

	Which MBA?	Capital*	AMBA
Ashridge Management Centre	+	20	+
Aston University	+	30	+
University of Bath	+	25	+
University of Birmingham	+		
Bradford University	+	22	+
Bristol Business School			+
Judge Instititute (University of Cambridge)	+	5	
Cardiff Business School	+		
City University	+	31	+
Cranfield School of Management	+	11	+
University College Dublin	+	26	
Trinity College Dublin	+	18	
Durham University	+		+
Edinburgh University	+	24	+
Glasgow University	+		+
Henley, The Management College	+	17	+
Heriot-Watt Business School	+		+
Imperial College	+	27	+
Kingston Business School			+
Lancaster University	+	28	+
Leicester Business School (De Montfort University)			+
London Business School	+	2	+
Loughborough University			+
Manchester Business School	+	14	+
Manchester Metropolitan University			+
Middlesex University			+
Newcastle upon Tyne University			+
Nottingham University	+		+
Open Business School	+		+
Sheffield Business School			+
Sheffield University	+		+
Stirling University	+		+
Strathclyde Graduate Business School	+	35	+
Warwick Business School	+	15	+
Westminster University			+

*These rankings are part of *Capital's* overall European rankings; the missing numbers are largely continental European schools, with the exception of two schools which do not offer English language-based programs: Université de Lausanne (Ecole des HEC) and Europa Institut, Saarland.

FULL-TIME PROGRAMS—CONTINENTAL EUROPE

The question of which European schools should be considered in the top tier is more open to speculation than is true for American schools. Europe does not really have a set of publications equivalent to those which rank American schools every year or second year, with a well-defined set of criteria. The exception is *Capital,* the German magazine, which has apparently settled into a biannual ranking routine. The gaps in its rankings below are largely due to its including British schools, which are included in the list above. (The list is in alphabetical order.)

	Which MBA?	Capital	AMBA*
Bocconi	+	7	+
EAP (Ecole Européenne des Affaires)	+	9	+
ENPC Graduate School of International Business (Ecole Nationale des Ponts et Chaussées)	+	23	
ESADE (Escuela Superior de Administracion y Direccion de Empresas)	+	8	+
European University	+		
Helsinki School of Economics and Business Administration	+		
IE—Instituto de Empresa	+	34	
IESE—International Graduate School of Management (University of Navarra)	+	6	+
IMD—International Institute for Management Development	+	3	+
INSEAD—European Institute of Business Administration	+	1	+
ISA—HEC School of Management	+	10	+
Katholieke Universiteit, Leuven		16	+
Groupe ESC Lyon—CESMA MBA	+	19	+
Monaco Graduate School of Business (University of Southern Europe)	+		
Nijenrode University	+	13	+
NIMBAS (Netherlands Institute for MBA Studies, together with its sister school, U. Bradford)	+	22	+
Norwegian School of Economics and Business Administration	+	29	
Norwegian School of Management	+	33	
Rotterdam School of Management (Erasmus University)	+	4	+
RVB—Maastricht School of Management	+	32	
Theseus Institute	+		

*AMBA accredits these schools, as opposed to ranking them, but this accreditation is indeed a quality certification. Note, however, that not all potentially eligible schools have applied for accreditation, so the lack of it does not necessarily mean that a school has been denied accreditation.

These rankings do tend to miss one type of program, the hybrid American programs with locations in Europe as well as the United States. Two in particular are noteworthy. The University of Chicago offers an executive MBA in Barcelona. The other top American program is the International MBA program in Vienna, run jointly by the University of South Carolina (which has often been ranked America's number one international business program) and the Wirtschaftsuniversität Wien (Vienna Business School).

BUSINESS SCHOOLS IN THE REST OF THE WORLD

Which MBA? provides a useful list of the top schools elsewhere in the world. It notes, however, that the reputation and academic standards of these schools tend not to match those in North America and Europe, but they do offer strong local business connections and networking possibilities.

Which MBA?

Canada:

McGill University (Montreal)
University of Toronto
Western Business School, University of West Ontario

Rest of the World:

University of Cape Town
Chinese University of Hong Kong
Curtin University of Technology (Perth, Australia)
University of Hong Kong Business School
Hong Kong University of Science & Technology
Macquarie University (Australia)
Melbourne Business School
Monash Mt. Eliza Business School (Australia)
National University of Singapore
The University of Sydney
University of Witwatersrand (South Africa)

THE TOP IN EVERYTHING?

DEPARTMENTAL RANKINGS

Are the top schools the best in terms of everything they do? Not necessarily. Although the overall reputation of a school might guarantee that a graduate will be taken seriously, it does not guarantee that every specialization the school offers is of equal quality or renown.

If you want to study a particular subject, especially an unusual one, you will want to consider the quality and reputation of the relevant department and its course offerings at different schools. For example, if you want to study business ethics, a growing field now that many American and some European companies are establishing ethics offices and need to staff them, you might not be well served by an otherwise fine school. In this instance, you might want to attend Bentley College, otherwise known primarily for its technical fields like accounting and information systems, whose business ethics center is the world leader in this discipline and is home to what is arguably the most important journal in the field.

Fortunately a lot of information is offered in the publications listed above. *The MBA Advantage* evaluates the quality of nine departments at each school it rates. Both *Business Week* and *U.S. News* list the top 5 to top 10 schools in a host of different specialties. *U.S. News,* for example, rates the top 5 in:

- Accounting
- Entrepreneurship
- Finance
- General Management
- International Business
- Management Information Systems
- Marketing
- Nonprofit Organizations
- Production/Operations Management
- Quantitative Analysis
- Real Estate

Which MBA? and the *AMBA Guide to Business Schools* also note the strengths of different schools. AMBA in particular shows the specialist MBA programs offered at various United Kingdom schools. If you are looking beyond the specialties covered by these publications, however, you will need to do your homework. For discussions of how to do so, see Chapter 5, "How to Choose the Right School for *You.*"

LIMITATIONS OF THE RANKINGS' METHODOLOGIES

Rankings of schools can be based on different factors. Simple rankings may measure nothing more than one statistical feature of the school, such as the average salary of graduates or the average GMAT score. Others may combine various statistical features. Another approach is to rank schools based upon informed opinion. Business school deans, recruiters of business school graduates, and students at the schools themselves are the most commonly utilized "experts."

The rankings are neither precise nor totally accurate in measuring the quality of programs. They do, however, influence both the number and quality of applicants to specific programs, and, as a result, the number and quality of recruiters hiring graduates of the school.

> You owe it to yourself to find about the different programs. For one thing, the rankings change all the time. There are also a lot of schools not in those rankings—for some reason—that are really good. *Don Martin, University of Chicago*

There are dozens of individuals and organizations that publish rankings of MBA programs. Due to space limitations, it is not possible to analyze the methodologies employed by all of them. Three rankings that use very different methodologies, and so reach different conclusions about the relative value of different schools, are *Business Week, U.S. News & World Report,* and *The MBA Advantage.* These provide an opportunity to examine some of the methodological issues that bedevil the rankings business.

In general it is clear that there are a number of problems any rater of schools must address. What does "best" mean? Is it the school that conveys the most technical knowledge, is most up to date, best prepares someone to be an entrepreneur (or senior manager for a large multinational), nets graduates the highest salaries, increases students' earnings (versus their pre-MBA salaries) the most, best prepares someone in a particular field, or is the least painful to get through? A rater who chooses any one definition to the exclusion of all others is still faced with potentially insurmountable problems. For example, how is the rater to measure which school is the best *today* at preparing entrepreneurs whose success may not be fully visible for another thirty years? (And, of course, even if the rating is generally accurate, it does not mean that the number one school will be the best one for you in particular.)

BUSINESS WEEK

Methodology. Business Week magazine rates MBA programs every even-numbered year in a late October issue of the magazine. It then incorporates these views in its companion book, *Business Week's Guide to the Best Business Schools.* It rates the top 20 schools based upon surveys of two "consumers" of business school services: the students who attend and the employers who hire graduates of these schools. The rating of each school is based upon its combined score, the sum of the students' and employers' opinions.

Advantages of the approach. It is obviously appropriate to know what the two major consumers of business school services—the students who are trained by the schools, and the employers who hire their graduates—think about the programs. Student views of teaching quality, academic atmosphere, career services, and so on are clearly relevant. Similarly, the views of likely employers concerning the quality of a given school, and its graduates, are important when trying to assess how useful a degree from that school will be.

Limitations of the methodology. The employer ratings of schools do not change markedly from one two-year period to the next, but the student ratings vary greatly. The result is that the changes in the overall position of the schools is determined largely by the student satisfaction ratings. These student ratings are highly volatile for a number of reasons. For example, student opinions can be highly affected by a recent matter such as whether or not a popular (or unpopular) assistant professor was granted tenure.

It is important to note at this point that both employer and student surveys are subject to significant sources of potential bias. The student survey, for example, is very open to being "gamed." If you were a student at good old Acme Business School, and you knew that your employment options and starting salaries depended to some substantial degree upon the rating of your school, wouldn't you consider rating the school as better than perfect in every survey category so as to improve your employment prospects? Another potential source of bias concerns the nature of the students who choose to attend different schools. It is quite possible that those attending Harvard are sophisticates who demand the best, who went to Harvard expecting to have the best possible professors for each and every course, and who would be disappointed if they did not have the most famous and pedagogically able professor for each course. Students who go to Indiana University, in the unpretentious town of Bloomington in the middle of America's cornbelt, might have very different, very reasonable expectations. Thus the ratings by these different groups of students might not be readily comparable.

The employer survey suffers from a similar potential problem. Employers hiring from Harvard and Indiana might be hiring for very different positions and expecting very different people from each school. They might pay Harvard graduates $80,000 and expect them soon to be running a region, whereas they might hire an Indiana graduate for $50,000 and expect him to be a solid contributor who will take twice as long to get a promotion as the Harvard graduates. Once again, are employer's ratings of the schools truly comparable?

There are also the usual problems with the selection of the employers for the survey. For example, there is an apparent bias toward larger employers, even though more and more MBA graduates are being employed by smaller, especially high tech, firms. Similarly, there is the problem of potential nonresponse bias.

Capital Magazine, the German publication cited above, also depends upon employers' rankings of schools for its results and thus its methodology suffers from the same inherent problems and limitations.

U.S. NEWS & WORLD REPORT

Methodology. U.S. News & World Report magazine rates business schools each year in a March issue of its magazine. Its methodology is much more complex than that of *Business Week.* *U.S. News* considers four factors: the schools' reputations, placement success, admissions selectivity, and graduation rates. The first three factors are actually composed of multiple subfactors.

Advantages of the approach. The virtues of this approach are clear. First, by explicitly taking many more factors into account than does *Business Week,* it may well do a more thorough job of measuring what makes a business school great. (*Business Week* could retort that its own methodology implicitly takes these other factors into account insofar as its survey respondents—students and employers—evaluate whatever factors they consider relevant.) Second, the ratings that *U.S. News'* methodology produces are quite stable over time, with essentially none of the extreme jumps and falls in individual ratings that have been so marked in the *Business Week* ratings. This is presumably a reflection of reality, insofar as it is highly unlikely that the quality of many business schools would change dramatically in a short period of time.

Limitations of the methodology. A school's reputation counts for 40 percent of its score. This comprises results from two separate surveys. The first is a poll of the directors of all of America's accredited business schools; the second is a poll of the CEOs who run some two thousand American businesses. Both of these polls are subject to potential bias. It is highly unlikely that even a well-informed business school dean will know the operations of other schools so thoroughly that he or she can accurately rate many dozens of them. This is likely to be more true of CEOs, who are not even in the education business. The likely impact of this is that both groups might tend to overrate schools that are already famous, or those that make the biggest splash (perhaps due to their faculty's publications).

Placement success counts for 30 percent of a school's score. This comprises the percentage of students who are employed at the time of graduation and three months later, the average starting salaries, and the ratio of on-campus recruiters to graduates. The possible biases here are several. Average starting salaries are highly industry- and location-dependent. Investment banking pays more than industry, so schools that turn out investment bankers will be favored relative to those that turn out people who go into industry. The same is true of schools that send graduates to New York rather than to Durham, North Carolina. The salaries in the former will tend to dwarf those in the latter, for the same job, given the different costs of living and other factors. Thus Columbia and NYU in New York City will have an advantage over the University of North Carolina. The other possible bias concerns the fact that the data are reported by the schools themselves and it is quite possible that some "cook" the numbers. In reporting starting salaries, for example, will a school include those who take jobs out of the United States? If the dollar is high, and foreign salaries when translated into dollars appear low, the school might choose to forget to include them. When the dollar is low, perhaps the school will remember to include them. The other data can also be manipulated by excluding various categories of students, or by simply lying.

Student selectivity counts for 25 percent of a school's score. This comprises the undergraduate grade point averages, average GMAT scores, and the percentage of applicants the school accepts. Since these are all reported by the schools themselves, they are all open to manipulation. A school can include or exclude various groups of students to manipulate its numbers. For example, should a school include only American students in calculating its undergraduate grade point averages if only the Americans have been graded on the traditional 4 point scale? On the other hand, perhaps it should include the non-American students too, but in that case how should it translate the French 20 point scale or someone else's 100 point scale into an American equivalent?

Graduation rate counts for 5 percent of a school's score. This comprises the percentage of students who graduated on time. This is less open to manipulation than the other factors, although there is still the self-reporting problem.

THE MBA ADVANTAGE

Methodology. Yeaple's book examines the financial aspects of getting an MBA. He looks at the decision of which school to attend as an investment decision. He examines what increase in salary an average graduate of a school can expect to earn upon graduation and five years later, versus the amount of forgone income and direct costs (tuition, etc.) that represent his investment.

Advantages of the approach. The market's verdicts on different programs, expressed in terms of the financial rewards given to their graduates, should be of keen interest to a potential applicant, who is making one of the most important investment decisions of his or her life. The quantitative approach allows for a very objective ranking of schools.

Limitations of the methodology. There are several limitations to this approach. The first is that, whereas money is important (especially for MBA students), it is not everything. Faced with a choice between two schools that offer similar financial benefits for graduates, one would rationally choose to attend the program that offers a pleasant two years rather than two years of living hell.

The second limitation is a technical one: Yeaple has not discounted the costs and earnings to take account of the time value of money. In other words, his method treats a dollar in ten years' time as being worth the same as a dollar today. This flaw, which is perhaps surprising given the author's profession—he is a professor of economics—does not invalidate his conclusions. (He may have failed to discount future dollars because he felt his audience would not understand what he was doing, although this is an amusing assumption about readers who intend to pursue advanced business degrees.)

Another limitation is that a snapshot of how much the graduates of different schools earned in 1992 does not capture all information about the school. The picture might be quite different even two or three years later. The differences in earnings depend upon a number of factors that are not necessarily a function of the school's educational quality or reputation:

■ Graduates of a given school tend to take jobs disproportionately with organizations in the surrounding area. Renumeration at these organizations will be affected by the relative prosperity of the industry they are in, the area, and the country; think of the impact of the fluctuations in the value of the dollar upon the relative value of being paid in dollars, marks, pounds, or lira. Thus Stanford's ranking may vary with the fate of the local high tech industry in which so many of its graduates work, even though the ups and downs of Silicon Valley firms do not mirror ups and downs of Stanford's quality and reputation.

- A graduate's age and prior work experience, specialization within the MBA program, and other characteristics unique to him or her will affect the nature of jobs offered and amount of salary earned.

- Last, the aggregate figures are for a mix of jobs that may change dramatically. Graduates may choose more public-sector jobs, for less money, in the future, thereby damaging the ranking of the school even though the school's quality and reputation remain the same.

An individual who chooses a specialty with a relatively weak department at a given school may make out less well than he would have had he gone to a comparable, or even less well rated, school with a stronger department. In fact, the conclusions Yeaple reaches are based on averages for what incoming students earned prior to business school and what they earned upon graduating, and five years later. If the bulk of students from the University of Chicago, for example, go into finance or consulting positions, but you wish to go into high-tech marketing, the data that Yeaple uses to produce the average benefits for getting a Chicago degree may not be meaningful for you.

The rankings are based upon financial calculations. Thus two schools that produce similar financial benefits for graduates are ranked the same, despite the fact that one school might provide a very enjoyable experience and the other might be ghastly, that one might funnel students into one of a handful of professions and the other might open up far more opportunities. In other words, potentially relevant issues about schools are not included in this methodology.

Yeaple, to his credit, is aware of the types of limitations discussed above and does not simply dismiss them. He is frank in considering the impact that they have upon the value of his conclusions, and for that matter is able to show the relatively minor impact some of them have.

CONCLUSION

The discussion of the limitations of the various ranking methodologies should not be viewed as a criticism of these surveys. In fact, each of the surveys offers very useful information and, taken together, a group of surveys offers a great deal to prospective applicants. In fact, I urge you to purchase the items described above, but I also urge you to be cautious in using them. *Business Week* shows what major employers think of programs, *U.S. News & World Report* gives useful information about admissions selectivity and placement success, *inter alia,* and *The MBA Advantage* shows the financial benefits of attending one school rather than another. These rankings, taken together, promote a good understanding of what the different schools offer in terms of quality and, most especially, reputation. Since the reputation of a school is one of the most important elements in making a choice, it would be foolish to ignore these rankings. The *Business Week* and Yeaple books in particular contain a great deal of useful information beyond their rankings. *The MBA Advantage,* for example, provides very good information regarding the quality of different departments at the schools.

SOURCES

Association of MBAs, *Guide to Business Schools* (FT Pitman, 1995), 11th ed.

George Bickerstaffe, *Which MBA?* (Economist Intelligence Unit, 1995), 7th ed.

John A. Byrne, *Business Week's Guide to The Best Business Schools* (McGraw-Hill, 1995), 4th ed.

John A. Byrne & Cynthia Green, *Business Week's Guide to the Best Executive Education Programs* (McGraw-Hill, 1993)

Tom Fischgrund, ed., *The Insider's Guide to the Top 10 Business Schools* (Little, Brown, 1993), 5th ed.

Ronald N. Yeaple, *The MBA Advantage* (Bob Adams, 1994)

Capital, June 1995

U.S. News & World Report, March 18, 1996

If you are unable to find the books noted here at your local bookstores, I recommend a large multipurpose bookstore in Berkeley, California, through which we order:

■ Cody's
  2454 Telegraph Avenue, Berkeley CA 94704
  Telephone: (510) 845-7852   Fax: (510) 841-6185
  E-mail: Codysbks@well.com

They stock many of these books and will find the others, as necessary. I list this information because we have found their service to be quick and accurate, they are open seven days a week, and they ship worldwide.

4

MAKE THE MOST
OF YOUR
CREDENTIALS

— EXECUTIVE SUMMARY —

■

Schools look for four things: academic ability, managerial and
leadership potential, character, and solid career goals.

■

They examine everything from your undergraduate record to your
work experience to determine whether you have what they seek.

■

You can improve your credentials.

■

You can maximize their value by presenting them in the best light.
- To do so, understand what admissions committees
  value most highly.

OVERVIEW

Stanford has explained what it looks for in candidates: "In reviewing applications, the admissions officers are guided by three key criteria: all admitted applicants must demonstrate solid academic aptitude coupled with strong managerial potential; in addition, diversity among students is sought in assembling each incoming class.

Solid academic aptitude. A candidate's academic ability is evaluated on the basis of proven academic performance as well as skills evidenced by scores on the Graduate Management Admissions Test (GMAT). The Business School seeks applicants with intellectual curiosity who have the desire to stretch themselves intellectually in a rigorous academic program.

Strong managerial potential. Managerial potential is considered in the context of full-time and part-time employment experiences, as well as experiences in nonwork settings and undergraduate extracurricular activities. The School looks for evidence of leadership and interpersonal and communication skills, as well as maturity and the ability to fully utilize opportunities. Letters of reference are relied upon to add insight in the evaluation of these areas.

Diversity among students. Diversity is a critical ingredient in the makeup of each MBA class. Students come from a wide variety of educational, experiential, and cultural backgrounds. The Business School attempts to identify and encourage applications from minorities, women, and residents of countries outside the United States. Having applied, however, members of these groups must meet the competition from the entire applicant pool.

[In addition,] candidates are accepted partially on the basis of their ability to benefit from and contribute to the learning environment."

Other schools look for similar qualities. One easy way to learn what the top business schools want is to look at the recommendation forms they use. These typically ask a recommender to check boxes in a grid, indicating whether the applicant's analytical ability, for example, is in the top 2 percent, 5 percent, 10 percent, 25 percent, 50 percent, or bottom half of those the recommender has seen at similar stages in their careers. Leading schools, whether American or European, ask recommenders to evaluate similar qualities. The schools in the chart below ask their recommenders to rate applicants on the qualities indicated.

SCHOOL

QUALITY	Harvard	Wharton	Tuck	Chicago	UCLA	Michigan	Bocconi Milan	IESE Barcelona	INSEAD Paris
Intellectual Ability/Analytical Ability	X	X	X	X	X	X	X		X
Imagination & Creativity	X	X	X	X	X	X		X	X
Motivation & Initiative	X	X	X	X	X		X	X	X
Maturity	X	X	X	X	X	X	X	X	
Organization/Admin. Skills	X							X	X
Ability to Work with Others	X	X	X	X	X	X	X	X	X
Leadership Potential	X		X		X	X	X	X	
Self-Confidence	X	X			X	X		X	
Ability in Oral Expression	X	X	X	X	X	X	X	X	X
Written Communication			X	X	X	X		X	X
Managerial/Career Potential		X		X	X		X		X
Sense of Humor		X	X		X	X			
Quantitative Ability	X								
General Ability		X							
Self-Discipline		X							
Poise			X						
Enthusiasm				X					
Dependability				X					
Judgment				X					
Respect from Management					X				
Respect from Peers					X				
Flexibility						X			
Personal Integrity									X
Competence in Field								X	X
Professionalism								X	X
Focus on Task at Hand									X

The picture that emerges from looking at this chart suggests that each of these schools is looking for candidates who are quite similar to the Stanford profile. That profile could be summarized as: brains, demonstrated business talent, and outstanding personal characteristics.

Schools obviously want people with the above-mentioned characteristics, but they also want something more. No matter how talented someone is, he or she is unlikely fully to realize his or her potential without a sensible *career plan*. Those who know where they are headed, and how an MBA will help them to get there, will take fullest advantage of the program's opportunities. Their drive and self-knowledge make them more likely to get to the top, making them sought-after MBA candidates.

THE EVIDENCE SCHOOLS EXAMINE

Where do admissions committees look to find out whether you have the brains, managerial potential, personal attributes, and sensible career plan they consider necessary?

	Primary Sources	*Secondary Sources*
BRAINS	Undergraduate record	Work experience
	GMAT scores	Additional coursework, if any
		Essay writing
		Interviewing
MANAGERIAL POTENTIAL	Work experience	Extracurricular and community activities
PERSONAL ATTRIBUTES	Essays	Everything in your file; i.e., wherever *who you are,* not just what you accomplished, is evident
	Recommendations	
	Interviews	
CAREER PLAN	Essays	Work experience
	Recommendations	
	Interview	

COMPONENTS OF SUCCESSFUL APPLICATIONS

UNDERGRADUATE RECORD

WHAT ARE ADMISSIONS COMMITTEES LOOKING FOR?

It does not particularly matter what you majored in at college. More important is that you excel at whatever you do. Quality work, and a serious level of involvement in it, are the most important things to demonstrate in your university studies. This does not mean, however, that your selection of courses is irrelevant. Taking the easiest courses will arouse suspicion about your ability to do top level graduate work. Similarly, MBA programs that are quantitatively oriented will look for success in undergraduate quantitative courses.

HOW IMPORTANT IS IT?

Admissions officers view your undergraduate record as a key indicator of your intellectual ability and your willingness to work hard. The less work experience you have, the more important your college record will be. A strong undergraduate record earned at a leading university will demonstrate that you can make it through business school, especially if you have had a mixture of quantitative courses and courses demanding substantial amounts of writing. Schools want people who can crunch numbers and communicate, as the chart above shows, so doing well in both quantitative and writing courses is a useful means of demonstrating your suitability for an MBA program. The ideal undergraduate record would thus exhibit all of the following:

- Top-quality school
- Demanding course load
- Top grades throughout
- Courses in economics, mathematics (including calculus and statistics), writing, and public speaking

INTERPRETING YOUR RECORD

Not every successful candidate graduates with a 4.0 from Harvard or a First from Oxford in mathematical economics and creative writing, of course, so admissions officers are accustomed to examining undergraduate transcripts with a practiced eye. A given grade point average is more impressive if achieved in demanding courses, with the better grades received in the junior and senior years. A candidate with high grades in introductory courses and low grades in more advanced courses will be considered less favorably.

In addition to getting the best possible grades, you should try to show that you have taken a real interest in your studies and have gotten a lot out of them. You have thus not wasted an opportunity. Taking extra courses in your major, or in complementary fields, can help to show this, as can a successful thesis.

Improving Your Chances After the Fact

If you have already graduated from university and do not possess a sterling record, is it too late for you to do something to help your candidacy? No. You may not be able to do anything about the grades you got as an undergraduate, but you can always take courses at night or on weekends to provide another set of grades—more recent and thus potentially more reflective of your current ability—for business schools to consider. Admissions officers call this "building an alternative transcript." If you have not yet taken any quantitative courses, for example, why not take some statistics or calculus courses at a local community college or continuing education division of a nearby university? To achieve the maximum possible benefit from these courses, you will need to get excellent grades in them. Getting mediocre grades may show that you are interested in improving your background, but will arouse serious questions about your ability to do outstanding work in a graduate business program.

THE ADMISSIONS DIRECTORS' TALK
ABOUT ACADEMIC QUALIFICATIONS

➤ Going to a top university is not necessary. We look at what opportunities existed for that applicant and how well he took advantage of them. If he went to a lesser university, did he capitalize on the opportunities there or not? *Rob Garcia, MIT*

➤ If someone did badly early in college, he can point to his later performance, whether at the end of college or in courses that he takes after college. He can explain his early failures by saying that "back then I was a C student but now I am an A student." This sort of person will probably need to work longer too, though, to confirm that this reformation has truly taken hold. *Judith Goodman, Michigan*

➤ Those people who have not done much with numbers can help themselves by taking a couple of quantitative courses, whether of accounting, finance, or statistics. It gives us a feeling of confidence and comfort when we know people can do the numbers. *James Millar, Harvard*

➤ In some instances you may need to create an "addendum" to your transcript. If you encountered academic difficulties in quantitative courses during your undergraduate years retaking a calculus course or a statistic course may improve your chances.

Achieving "As" in these courses indicates a level of competence as well as a commitment to pursuing an MBA. We are more willing to give the benefit of doubt to someone with a borderline GMAT quantitative score if he or she takes the initiative to address a deficit. It is also beneficial to enroll in business-related courses (i.e., microeconomics, accounting or statistics) should you not have any prior exposure to these core courses. Again, your pre-MBA preparation can say a lot about your determination and commitment. *Linda Baldwin, UCLA*

➤ The less well known your school, the better your other qualifications have to be. *Prof. Leo Murray, Cranfield (England)*

➤ If you are applying two years out of university, the quality of school you went to will count heavily, but if you're applying ten years out, with a successful career under your belt, it really doesn't matter—it fades into the background. *Andrew Dyson, Manchester (England)*

➤ If your academic credentials are not strong, it will be important that you demonstrate that you can handle the program by having a good GMAT and major achievements in professional life. *Carol Giraud, INSEAD (Paris region)*

* The term "admissions director" is used generically, as a catchall title, to denote those in charge of the admissions process at their respective schools, as most people quoted in this book are, whatever the specific title accorded them. I have quoted more than one person from several European schools. In the case of London Business School, Julia Tyler is in charge of admissions; Andrew Dyson is admissions chief at Manchester Business School, as is Connie Tai at Rotterdam School of Management. In the case of INSEAD (Paris), Carol Giraud is the admissions director, whereas Professor Ludo van der Heyden is the faculty member in charge of the admissions committee. The other professor quoted herein, Leo Murray, makes the ultimate admissions decisions at Cranfield (England) as the school's director.

GMAT SCORES

WHAT IS THE GMAT?

The Graduate Management Admission Test (GMAT) is a four-hour-long examination that combines essay and multiple choice formats. This exam, created and administered by an American firm called Educational Testing Service (ETS) on behalf of the Graduate Management Admissions Council (GMAC), is required by virtually every leading business school in the world.

THE PURPOSE OF THE GMAT

There are two closely related main purposes of the exam: to predict which candidates will do well in business school and to assist schools in ranking applicants.

The GMAT is designed to measure your ability to think logically and to employ a wide range of skills acquired during your prior schooling, including the ability to write persuasively and well. The GMAT does not attempt to measure your business competence or knowledge, nor does it require specific academic knowledge beyond that of very basic mathematics and grammar.

The GMAT score provides business school admission officers with a standardized measure to use in assessing all candidates. Admissions officers tend to rely on it most when analyzing students from unusual backgrounds, or when comparing people from substantially different backgrounds. If you went to a university not well known to the admissions officer, for example, you can expect extra emphasis to be placed upon your GMAT score. The GMAT will likewise be used to compare someone at the very top of her class at a weak university with an applicant who did well at a leading university.

THE TEST FORMAT

The test begins with two half-hour essays. A short break is followed by four 25-minute multiple choice sections. After another short break, the last three 25-minute multiple choice sections are given. The exam, including preliminary administrative matters, typically lasts from 8:00 A.M. until 1:00 P.M., making for a very long morning.

The two essays are part of the Analytical Writing Assessment, a relatively new section that requires you to write essays on each of two chosen topics. The two essays are similar in nature; one is termed "analysis of an argument," the other, "analysis of an issue." The former asks you to assess the validity of someone's position, or "argument," in light of how persuasively the writer marshals argument and evidence in support of that position. The latter asks you for a more personal response to an issue that is not resolvable—not a matter of right or wrong—but something you can discuss at length based upon your personal experience.

There are five types of multiple choice sections:

Math

Problem Solving: problems involving arithmetic, basic algebra, and geometry

Data Sufficiency: problems similar in scope to those in the problem solving section, but more abstract in nature

Verbal

Reading Comprehension: questions based upon three reading passages, designed to test your ability to comprehend and analyze the logic, structure, and details of densely written materials

Critical Reasoning: questions based upon short arguments or statements, designed to test your ability to evaluate the strength of the evidence and logic of the reasoning

Sentence Correction: questions requiring you to recognize clear, concise, and grammatically correct sentences

What Your Score Means

You will receive four scores: three regarding your performance on the multiple choice questions and one regarding your essay writing. Your multiple choice "overall" score will be reported on a 200–800 scale. Business schools consider this to be the most important of the four scores. The exam is designed to produce an average score of 500, with one standard deviation equaling 100 points. Thus someone scoring a 700 is meant to be two standard deviations above the mean (average), meaning in statistical terms that approximately 97 percent of the scores were below this. Your "percentile ranking" shows precisely this, the percentage of people scoring below you.

Top schools have average scores in the mid-600s, meaning that their students are typically in the top 10 percent of test takers. The range of scores is substantial, however, so a score of 600 need not be cause for despair.

You will get two other scores, based upon your performance on the multiple choice sections. Your verbal score will give you a percentile ranking for the verbal portion of the exam, whereas your quantitative score will give you a percentile ranking for the math portion. Schools are generally more interested in your overall score than how you achieved it, albeit with some notable exceptions. Quantitatively oriented schools will want to be sure that students can handle numbers, so applicants without prior coursework in quantitative fields or other evidence that they can handle numbers will find their quantitative performance on the GMAT closely scrutinized. Similarly, those candidates who are not native speakers of English will find their verbal scores closely scrutinized (along with their TOEFL scores).

The fourth score is based solely upon the Analytical Writing (or essay) portion of the exam. One grade is given, on a zero to six scale. The average grade is about 3.5 (scores are reported in half point increments). Schools typically consider a 4 to be acceptable and anything higher a good performance. Copies of the essays are sent to the schools for them to read if they care to, but there is as yet no consistent use of the actual essays. Some schools examine both, some read only the Analysis of an Argument (in preference to the Analysis of an Issue) essay, some read the Issue rather than the Argument, and some read neither, taking into account only the quantitative grade. As you would expect, the weight given to the writing score will depend heavily upon the nature of the candidate involved. Someone who graduated *summa cum laude* from the journalism program at Columbia and then worked as a *New York Times* reporter is unlikely to be rejected as a poor communicator due to a 3.5 score, because he has already demonstrated many times over that he can think and write well under time pressure. On the other hand, an Italian engineer who has never worked in English before may be viewed with doubt if she does not score at least a 4.

How to Prepare

You have two options if you wish to prepare seriously for the GMAT: You can prepare on your own using specially designed preparatory books, or you can take preparatory classes. Self-preparation has several substantial advantages. It is (relatively) low cost, offers complete flexibility of schedule, and allows you to tailor your preparation to suit your own needs. On the other hand, preparatory classes also offer several advantages. They force you to start preparing in earnest well in advance of the exam, they guide you through the mass of potential preparatory material, they offer you an expert on call when you have questions, and they give you the opportunity to study with other people (and compare yourself with them). Finally, their price and inconvenience will be outweighed for some people by the higher scores they are likely to produce.

The appropriate choice for you will depend upon the kind of person you are, your financial resources, your goals, and other variables. Those who almost certainly should take a prep course are those who:

- Have not taken similar tests before
- Tend to test below their overall ability level
- Lack the self-discipline necessary to prepare on an individual basis
- Need substantial help on one or more parts of the exam, such as those who have let their math muscles atrophy

Getting the Most Out of Your Preparation

If you decide to follow the self-study route, make sure that you do two things. First, buy and use several of the popular prep books, because no one book on its own contains sufficient discussion of the strategies, techniques, and fundamentals required. (If forced to choose just one guide, I would opt for the *Cliff's GMAT Preparation Guide,* by Jerry Bobrow (Cliff's Notes, Inc.). Second, be sure that you practice on past GMAT exams rather than on the very different exams created by the various prep book authors. Old exams are available from only one source, *The Official Guide for GMAT Review* (Graduate Management Admissions Council), making it required reading. (If unable to find these books at your local bookstore, consider ordering them from Cody's, which stocks them year-round. For information about contacting Cody's, see the end of Chapter 3.)

You will need to keep to a regular review schedule, such as spending two hours a night twice a week, and six to eight hours on weekends, for six to eight weeks before the exam. Having a study partner can ease the strain and provide you with someone who can explain something that mystifies you (and vice versa). The best partner is likely to be someone with the opposite strengths to yours. Thus if you are strong at math, find someone strong at verbal questions.

If you decide to take a preparatory class, shop around. Numerous quality courses exist, so be sure that the one you choose meets your needs in terms of time, duration, location, reputation, instructor, price, and any special requirements that you might have. For example, if you are not a native speaker of English, you might be best off with a course specifically designed for non-native speakers.

How to Register for the GMAT

The GMAT Bulletin of Information provides a registration form as well as information about the dates, locations, and price of the exam. You can obtain a bulletin by contacting:

Graduate Management Admission Test
Educational Testing Service
P.O. Box 6103
Princeton, New Jersey 08541-6103
U.S.A.
Telephone: (609) 771-7330   Fax: (609) 883-4349   E-mail: gmat@ets.org

The exam is given in March, June, October, and December of each year. To be sure that you will be able to take the exam at the site you prefer, plan to register several months before the actual exam date. (The GMAT will soon be available on a "computer adaptive" basis in many locations, which will permit taking the exam on any one of hundreds of days. Contact ETS for more information.)

It is not easy to prepare for the GMAT at the same time that you are investigating schools and preparing your applications. To avoid this problem, and give yourself the time to prepare properly, try to take the exam before you intend to apply. Besides avoiding the time conflict problem, you will have the chance to prepare better and retake it if necessary.

Receiving Your Score

Your scores are now available, by telephone, approximately three weeks after you take the exam. Otherwise, you will get them by mail approximately four to five weeks after the exam. ETS has been slowly reducing the time it takes to grade the exam, so expect these figures to decrease in the next few years.

THE ADMISSIONS DIRECTORS GIVE A COMMON-SENSE VIEW OF THE GMAT

ITS USES (Yes it matters, but more for some people than for others.)

➤ Studies have shown that the GMAT verbal score is the single best predictor of class performance, so we look for a certain baseline performance. The average for our international group is close to the American average. *Henry Malin, Tuck*

➤ The GMAT score is as important as any other single element in the admissions process. Its importance, however, will vary from applicant to applicant. Someone who has a 3.8 GPA from the five-year engineering program at Dartmouth and gets only a 39th percentile quantitative score on the GMAT will not particularly concern us. The same score for an English literature major would be more of a problem because it may be the only predictor of his or her quantitative abilities. Of course, there is a numbers game at work. Programs tend to be rated according to their average GMAT scores, so other things being equal we will take people with higher rather than lower scores. *Jon Megibow, Darden*

➤ The analytical or quantitative component of an MBA program can be a rude shock to a liberal arts major. The GMAT quantitative percentile can provide assurance that this person has the quantitative ability to function in the classroom. *Fran Hill, Haas (Berkeley)*

➤ We look at the precise score only if we have a problem elsewhere in the application, but otherwise it only matters that the applicant has reached our required minimum score. *Professor Leo Murray, Cranfield (England)*

➤ Someone with a GMAT score that is below the average of the people we admit, with other credentials also below their average, will be turned down. Someone with same GMAT score, but with other credentials above the average of those we admit, is quite likely to be admitted. We examine the GMAT score in the context of the whole application. Of course, someone with a score below 550 (or 600 for a native English speaker) will have to make up for that in a big way. *Carol Giraud, INSEAD (Paris region)*

➤ Having a very high GMAT score does not guarantee admission because having a high cognitive ability is not enough. But, conversely, someone with a 560 GMAT can be admitted if the other parts of the application (work experience, interview, etc.) are really positive. Of course, it's better to have both. *Gabriella Aliatis, Bocconi (Milan)*

SCORES

➤ The mean score of our 4,000 applicants was 620. The mean score for admitted students was 660. *Linda Baldwin, UCLA*

➤ When someone has taken the exam more than once, we take the highest of their scores. We might not really look at the total score: we might concentrate on either the verbal or quantitative score, depending upon the person's background. For an engineer, we might look at the verbal score to make sure that he has the necessary skills.

For a foreigner, we might want to see a 35 or 40 verbal score. The total score can be a matter of someone excelling on just one-half, so we want to make sure that that's not the case. *Rob Garcia, MIT*

ANALYTICAL WRITING

➤ We still don't know what to do with the analytical essays. We do look at it for foreign applicants if their multiple choice verbal score is weak, to see if they can communicate. For now, we look at the analytical score, not the essay itself. *Rob Garcia, MIT*

➤ We do read the Analytical Writing essays, although it is difficult given that they are hand-written. *Fran Hill, Haas (Berkeley)*

➤ We seldom read the essays, because it is time consuming and difficult. We do look at the Analytical Writing score: a 4 is O.K., a 4.5 is definitely O.K. We use the TOEFL too to understand their English abilities. *Gabriella Aliatis, Bocconi (Milan)*

➤ We read many of the essays, mainly to help determine whether the person can string together a logical argument. *Julia Tyler, London*

ADVICE FOR PREPARING

➤ Many applicants do not adequately prepare for the GMAT. Excusing poor performance by saying that you just don't test well or that your job is too demanding to permit time for study won't work. We allow you to take the GMAT twice and we will consider the highest score. If you have trouble on the first take of the GMAT, it is not advisable to simply retake it without analyzing your weaknesses and/or taking action—whether it means enrolling in a college algebra/geometry class, signing up for one of the test preparation services, or embarking on an intense self-paced test prep. *Linda Baldwin, UCLA*

INTERNATIONAL STUDENTS

➤ For Americans we look more closely at the quantitative score; for international students we look more closely at the verbal score. International students (non-native English speakers) average perhaps 40 or 50 points less than Americans, but the overall average is 657. *Suzanne Cordatos, Wharton (Lauder Institute)*

➤ We look for similar GMAT scores from foreigners as from natives. They'll be in the same classroom with Americans, working in English, so the standards should be the same. We do, however, look at the TOEFL score, which might help offset a marginal GMAT verbal score. *Judith Goodman, Michigan*

➤ We expect non-native speakers of English to get lower scores. For the Scandinavians and Dutch, maybe 20–30 points lower; for others maybe 50 points lower, but we wouldn't "credit" someone with more than 50 points.
Andrew Dyson, Manchester (England)

➤ It is very hard to compare people from different backgrounds. We use the GMAT score to help do this, although there is no set means to use it. The very rough equivalent of an American scoring a 650 would be:

British:	630–640 (the test is an American exam, so anyone other than an American faces a cultural handicap that goes beyond language)
Indian:	630-640
Scandinavian and Dutch:	620–630
German:	610–620
French:	600
Latin American:	580–600
Spanish and Italian	580
Indonesian:	550

Remember, this is a very rough equivalence table. *Connie Tai, Rotterdam*

➤ English mother-tongue applicants that we admit tend to have scores in the 650 and above range. Non-mother-tongue applicants tend to be in the 600 and above range. *Carol Giraud, INSEAD (Paris region)*

VERIFYING THE GMAT SCORE

➤ We require one handwritten essay from applicants. We check it against the handwriting on the GMAT analytical writing essays to make sure that the same person took the GMAT. *Alison Mills, Oxford*

SHOULD YOU RETAKE THE EXAM?

If your score will not get you into the quality of program you want, then you may need to retake the exam. Before deciding that this is necessary, however, you should analyze your application to see whether your GMAT score will actually handicap you significantly. Remember that many people with scores in the upper (and even lower) 500s get into top programs because they marketed themselves well (and had something worth marketing). You may be better off applying the time you would otherwise spend studying for the GMAT working on your essays or improving your other credentials.

If you have scored substantially below the normal range of those accepted at schools you want to attend, you may need to retake the exam. Your starting point should be a section by section analysis of how well you did. The only way to do this is to see a copy of your actual exam. This is available if you choose the "hand-scored" option, which ETS makes available for a small charge. You will get the actual exam returned to you, showing your correct and incorrect answers.

This will allow you to see in detail what you did well and poorly. Without this, you will only know the total number of questions you got right and wrong, split between the math and the verbal sections.

EXTRACURRICULAR ACTIVITIES

WHAT ARE ADMISSIONS COMMITTEES LOOKING FOR?

Admissions officers hope to see a pattern of substantial involvement and increasing responsibility in one or more extracurricular activities. Top business schools want to admit people who are (and will be) successful leaders of groups. Extracurricular activities offer an ideal opportunity to demonstrate leadership inclinations and skills.

The specific activity is not particularly important. What matters is that you cared enough about it to pursue it throughout college and to contribute significantly to it. The depth and impact of your involvement will also be more important than the number of activities in which you participated. If you were a member of the college film society, for example, writing the monthly newsletter and serving on the board of directors will demonstrate that you were actively engaged in it. It would be even better if you were the president, of course, especially if you managed to increase the number of films shown from three to twelve per week.

Extracurricular achievement is particularly important for those with limited work experience. As Yale notes, "full-time post-college work experience is highly desirable, although students whose extracurricular accomplishments demonstrate exceptional organizational and leadership abilities may sometimes be admitted directly from college."

WORK EXPERIENCE

WHAT ARE ADMISSIONS COMMITTEES LOOKING FOR?

Work experience is probably the single most important substantive element of your application. Schools are trying to assess your management potential and the best way to do so, in their opinion, is to determine your managerial success to date. In other words, the best predictor of your future success in management is your past success in management.

You are expected to have worked for at least a couple of years prior to applying, but not necessarily much more than that. The appropriate amount of work experience will differ according to the school you are applying to, of course, with some European schools expecting double or triple the experience required by most of the American programs.

The amount of work experience, beyond the required minimums, tends to be much less important than the nature and quality of the experience. Those applicants whose undergraduate performance was comparatively weak, however, should consider working a little longer in order to lessen the currency of grades and course selection and to increase the amount of good information to show to the admissions committee.

NATURE OF EXPERIENCE

It almost does not matter what type of managerial or professional experience you get! Many successful candidates take the tried-and-true path to business school by working in a traditional feeder industry. They work for accounting firms, consultancies, investment banks, or advertising firms, or work in marketing for consumer goods firms. They get good training in these companies and, because these firms recruit MBAs heavily, they are very welcome at business schools, which always want to produce graduates who will be in demand.

These candidates tend to compete among themselves for places at the top schools. They are reckoned to be smart, hard working, and well trained, which should get them a place at a top school, but the fact that there are so many of them with similar credentials means that schools limit how many will be taken. Schools look for diversity in their applicants, including people with different work experience. This opens the door for people who have been journalists, government administrators, managers of art galleries, research scientists, and everything else under the sun. These unusual backgrounds bring an unusual perspective into the business school, something that is highly valued. Thus it is not clear which type of background, the usual or the unusual, is the more likely to help you gain acceptance.

LENGTH

The optimal amount of experience depends upon the school and the nature of your job. American schools generally take younger applicants than do European schools. Whereas students in American schools are typically 27 when they begin, students in some European programs might average 30 or older. Thus while the candidate for an American program might "peak" at three to six years of work experience, that same candidate might be better off applying to some of the European programs after five to ten years of experience.

Schools see a certain amount of high quality experience as necessary to:

- understand how complex organizations work (and how you might fit in them);

■ have had the opportunity to take initiative to solve technical and organizational problems;

■ know where you are headed;

■ know which classes to take in business school; and,

■ have relevant comments to make in class and in study groups.

Too much experience, according to this analysis, would be impossible. On the other hand, an MBA is meant to provide help to people early in their careers, and recruiters come to schools looking for students at a relatively early stage in their careers. Therefore schools want to have candidates who have some, but not too much, experience.

The optimal amount of experience also depends upon your specific job. If it takes four years to get a valued professional credential, such as becoming a Chartered Accountant, applying to business school before reaching this point would seem silly. On the other hand, it is nearly always considered acceptable to apply once you have reached the natural break point in a career, such as after a four-year military enlistment has expired.

The weaker your other credentials, the longer you should work before applying, because you will need more impressive work experience to show that your real talent was not properly reflected, for example, in your undergraduate grades.

IMPROVING YOUR CHANCES

The key to impressing admissions officers with your work experience is not a matter of your specific job or industry, or even of how long you have worked. What you accomplish is the key. Admissions officers want to see people successfully take on responsibility, manage people, projects, and assets, perform complicated analysis, and wrestle with difficult decisions. They want people to progress in their jobs and develop relevant skills, with consequent improvements in responsibilities, salary, and title. People who meet these criteria will be highly valued no matter what industry they come from.

To impress admissions people with your work experience, demonstrate as many of the following as possible:

■ First and foremost, you have been successful at whatever your job involves. (The easiest way to demonstrate this is to be given significant salary increases and promotions.)

■ You have worked well with other people.

■ You have managed other people. Managerial experience is important insofar as it allows you to show that you are able to do what is, after all, the one thing required of people who wish to get to the top of companies, whether large or small.

- No matter what your job has required of you, you have done more (and exceeded your boss's expectations).

- You have had a wide range of experiences, each one requiring different skills (analytical, interpersonal, etc.).

- You have acquired substantial skill in your job, both technical and inter-personal.

- You have done a better job than anyone in a similar position.

The sum total of this is that you present a picture of someone with senior management potential, a person who has not only already accomplished things but also built a strong foundation for greater future success.

As you will see in later chapters, these components of work experience are exactly what the business schools will ask you to write essays about, your recommenders to comment on about you, and even what you are likely to be asked in interviews. The application examples throughout this book, in Chapters 8 and 11 and the Appendix, show people who have looked for and taken advantage of opportunities to do more than what was simply inherent in their positions.

If your work experience gives you little to write about, you face an uphill battle in your applications. Consider waiting a year and devoting that year to making an impact in your job. Focus on developing your skills, assuming new and different responsibilities, and impressing one or more potential recommenders to maximize your chances of success when you do apply.

WHAT THE ADMISSIONS DIRECTORS SAY ABOUT WORK EXPERIENCE

WHY IT'S IMPORTANT

➤ We want people to work for several years. They need not only the work experience itself, but the growth and maturity that the time brings. They will have the opportunity to work with people, to look over the shoulders of several people they might want to emulate, and to learn whether the MBA is the right next step for them. *Judith Goodman, Michigan*

➤ There's no substitute for time spent in the trenches. In fact, recruiters often tell us that three years of work experience is the minimum they want to see. *Fran Hill, Haas (Berkeley)*

➤ We generally prefer more experience rather than less, but someone who wants to totally change careers will be worse off the more experience she has. She's better off making the career switch as soon as possible. *Gea Tromp, Rotterdam*

CONCERNING INEXPERIENCED AND YOUNGER CANDIDATES

➤ We take about 10% of our class each year with little or no experience and they need to be really exceptional—first class degrees and extracurriculars and perhaps some informal business experience. *Andrew Dyson, Manchester*

➤ A very young candidate has to have a very good undergraduate record, a very good GMAT score, and has to be very active regarding extra activities. Someone who has been working part-time or has his own business during university would be an appropriate candidate. The very young person would have to be a very exceptional candidate because the person with work experience will always be at an advantage. For one thing, we always prefer the experienced person because of the contribution he can make in class. *Connie Tai, Rotterdam*

WHAT TYPE OF WORK EXPERIENCE IS MOST DESIRABLE

➤ Our MBA Program, like most, is oriented to large corporations, banks, and consulting firms. Increasingly we find MBAs opting to work within small-to-mid-size companies, high tech/multimedia companies, entertainment companies, not-for-profits and entrepreneurial ventures. Our interdisciplinary study areas provide courses, internships, mentorship and career opportunities that meet these unique interests.
Linda Baldwin, Anderson (UCLA)

➤ We're looking for progressively responsible experience.
Suzanne Cordatos, Wharton (Lauder Institute)

➤ Not everyone has management experience before applying. It's simply not feasible in many corporate structures or in government. Nonetheless, many have a pretty good grasp of it even without having done it. Even if they haven't been able to manage, they may have a lot to offer this place. For example, they may have a technical skill or something else which might be of great value here. We're looking for project leadership, for initiative, for someone who knows what's going on in the organization as a whole, not somebody who stays in his cubicle. Maybe he was supposed to stay in his cubicle, but he didn't—he got out. He had a real itch to see the broad picture. He got onto some project teams, some advisory boards. And that's what we need here— that spirit. *Brian Sorge, Kellogg*

➤ We value bringing in the person from education or the Peace Corps as well as from Wall Street. They'll work together in groups and learn from each other.
Judith Goodman, Michigan

➤ How highly are blue chip feeder companies valued? That is probably more important for my associates in placement, since these people are generally easy to place well. What is of greatest interest to me is how well people have performed on whatever path they have chosen. *Jon Megibow, Darden*

➤ It always makes a good impression if you've worked for a well-known company, but that's not the only thing that matters. If you've worked for a smallish firm, for example, perhaps you've had a lot of responsibility and accomplished a lot, more than you could have in a larger, more famous firm. *Connie Tai, Rotterdam*

➤ It doesn't particularly matter which company someone's worked for; what matters is to what extent he or she has made the most of the opportunities there.
Julia Tyler, London

WHAT IS TOO MUCH EXPERIENCE?

(The American and European programs differ dramatically. The American programs generally take younger candidates, but they are also more willing to accommodate much older students.)

> ➤ We are seeing more and more applicants in their 40s and 50s, in the health care industry particularly, who see the need for management skills and want to be prepared. This has been a surprise, but we will take them if their credentials are strong and they have convincing reasons for doing the program. *Judith Goodman, Michigan*

> ➤ We start looking carefully when someone is 32 or 33. We do admit people at that age or a bit older, but we want to be sure that it makes sense for them and that they will not be frustrated in the classroom. They are likely to contribute a lot, but we want to be sure that they will also learn a lot. Beyond 35 the chances are very slim. Our program is designed very specifically for people in the early stages of their careers. We believe that people, if they are going to be senior managers, will be senior managers by their late 30s or 40. If they haven't made it by then, the MBA won't transform them into somebody they are not. *Carol Giraud, INSEAD (Paris region)*

> ➤ It's a harsh labor market out there. The older someone is, beyond his early thirties, the fewer the job offers he'll get. We don't want to take someone who'll do the program and then find that he can't get a job. *Julia Tyler, London*

> ➤ Once someone gets past about 35 years of age, we start to look closely to make sure that he or she will be able to work along with much younger students. *Connie Tai, Rotterdam*

COMMUNITY AND OTHER OUTSIDE ACTIVITIES

WHAT ARE ADMISSIONS COMMITTEES LOOKING FOR?

The term "community activities" is intended to cover all organized pursuits outside of your employment. It might include working for a political party or helping a youth group. Schools are pleased to see involvement in community activities, both because it suggests that your heart is in working order and because it shows you to be a "doer." Doing voluntary work for your community can have as many different benefits as the different forms it can take.

Schools expect people without particularly heavy job responsibilities to be involved in more than just watching television every evening. Schools prefer "joiners" to loners. The MBA is not a degree for people who dislike being involved in group activities. Schools do not particularly care which activities you pursue, as long as you are active in something. If you take on responsibilities and leadership roles, of course, you will be viewed favorably.

If you intend to be involved in non-profit management, or to attend a school like Yale, which bills itself as a public management program, you will be viewed with suspicion if you have not been involved in substantial community activities.

This discussion of community activities is not meant to exclude other outside activities. Playing sports, making movies, or acting in local theatrical productions would be looked upon just as favorably if you have taken on responsibilities and leadership roles.

RECRUITING RECOMMENDERS

Doing voluntary work is an excellent way to develop good references. You will be working in a hand-picked activity in which you will be able to control your environment. You can choose a position that is just right for you, or you can create a position that offers some benefit to an established organization. Charitable organizations are not like regular corporations; they know that they are highly dependent upon volunteer workers and consequently are willing to go out of their way for anyone who makes a difference in helping their constituency.

If you have not had substantial leadership experience in your job, community activity presents an important possibility for developing the necessary experience and skills to convince an admissions officer that you have leadership and managerial potential.

WHAT ADMISSIONS DIRECTORS LOOK FOR IN EXTRACURRICULARS AND COMMUNITY SERVICE

➤ In terms of their extracurricular and community activities, we look for leadership in any capacity. We want to know what they did with their time. We want people with a passion about something; we don't care what that is.
Suzanne Cordatos, Wharton (Lauder Institute)

➤ We look for applicants with a variety of experience as well as their work. They are the more interesting people; they also make better students. These students give a lot more to the community and to each other, so they work well in teams. Community service is prevalent at Columbia: at the undergraduate and graduate levels. The students tend to be involved, whether it's in sports, music, or whatever. Of course, there are obviously some people who are so outstanding in one specific area that we accept them. *Linda Meehan, Columbia*

➤ In general we expect people to have been involved with something in college, to have achieved a leadership position. (We look at individual cases, though, so we would view a foreigner differently.) We would expect a person working a forty hour per week job, who doesn't have to travel much, to do something else too, whether it's family, activities, or whatever. We do check what they say to see whether something is just résumé patter or something they are seriously involved in. *Henry Malin, Tuck*

YOUR PRESENTATION

The first part of this chapter examined the credentials business schools are looking for—in other words, the substance of your application. Now it is time to consider the way in which you present yourself. How much difference does it make if you write marvelously and make the strongest possible case for yourself? How much does it matter if you get impressive people to write persuasively on your behalf? And how important is it that you come across well in person?

THE ESSAYS, RECOMMENDATIONS, AND INTERVIEWS

The credentials you bring to the application are one thing; your presentation of them is another. Your presentation matters greatly for several reasons. You have the opportunity to color the interpretation of all of the objective data by explaining its context and how all of the different pieces fit together. In addition, sharp admissions officers will cross-check your essay assertions, for example, with what you say (and how you say it) in your interviews, to get as honest a picture of you as possible. Your performance also provides important additional data for the admissions decision. The essays, for example, reveal your writing ability and your ability to sustain a closely reasoned argument. The recommendations reveal the extent to which you have impressed some of the most important people you have worked and studied with. The interviews reveal not only your oral communication skills but also your presence and other important leadership attributes. (In fact, these communication vehicles demonstrate much more than this; for an in-depth view, refer to the individual chapters in Part II.)

Although it is always easier to make an impressive presentation when your substantive credentials are strong, the extent to which you take full advantage of the opportunity to present your case as effectively as possible will tell the admissions committee an immense amount about your abilities and your willingness to work hard to attend their program.

MAKING THE ULTIMATE DECISIONS

THE CRITERIA TRADE-OFF

The question inevitably arises, how do admissions directors determine whom to accept, given that some applicants will have outstanding job records but unimpressive grades and GMAT scores, whereas other applicants will have the reverse set of strengths and weaknesses? In other words, how do admissions directors trade off the different admission criteria? There is no set answer to this. There are, however, three considerations to keep in mind:

First of all, it is important to understand that the top schools do not need to make many such trade-offs. The Stanfords, Whartons, and London Business Schools are in the enviable position of having many applicants with sterling undergraduate records and impressive work experience, which negates the need to trade off criteria.

Second, schools will weight criteria differently depending upon the applicant. For example, someone who has worked for only two years can expect to have his undergraduate record, extracurricular activities, and GMAT scores count very heavily because his work experience is too slight to provide a great deal of information about him. Someone with seven years of work experience can expect that somewhat less weight will be placed on the academic measures; her extensive experience provides a great deal of information about her, making her experience a much more important indicator of her potential than it was for the two year man.

Third, different schools will have different priorities, causing them to apply a somewhat different set of criteria, and criteria weighting, to the process. A school like IMD (in Lausanne) considers work experience to be far and away the most important criterion. INSEAD (outside Paris), which takes a younger group of students, places relatively less weight on work experience and more on the undergraduate record and GMAT scores (although work experience is still its most important criterion).

FILLING THE CLASS

Business schools have come to believe in the virtues of diversity. They feel that a mixture of nationalities, industry, and job backgrounds in their student bodies enhances the learning process and also makes for a more attractive group of graduates, given that employers need a wide range of potential recruits. Schools have responded to their relatively new-found desire for diversity mainly by marketing intensively to hard-to-attract groups, rather than by dramatically reducing their admissions standards for them.

THE TARGETED GROUPS

The groups targeted vary somewhat by area. American schools are always concerned to get sufficient minority students, European schools tend to monitor their geographic balances closely, and programs throughout the world would like more female students. INSEAD adjusts its geographic balance through its marketing policy rather than its admissions policy. When it is getting a great number of French or British and relatively few German applicants, for example, it eliminates advertising targeted toward France or Britain and increases that for Germany.

Targeted groups may have a slight edge in the admissions process, but it is not pronounced. Most admissions officers would concur with Harvard's James Millar, who notes, "We don't have a certain number of places reserved for engineers or whatever. Every applicant competes with every other applicant."

ADMISSIONS DIRECTORS DISCUSS WHICH GROUPS ARE UNDERREPRESENTED AT THEIR SCHOOLS

➤ We would like to see more people from advertising, nonprofits (that perspective is really valuable), manufacturing, more women and American minorities. In any given year, the economy dictates who you have most of among your applicants. *Henry Malin, Tuck*

➤ If we want to see more of anything, we want to see more women apply. We don't get a lot of foreign women in particular. *Rob Garcia, Sloan*

➤ We value diversity, but we would never sacrifice quality to achieve representation. If that means that one year we had overrepresentation in one industry and underrepresentation in another, we would be comfortable with that. *Fran Hill, Haas (Berkeley)*

➤ We have fewer foreigners than we'd like, which is probably due to our location. We would particularly like to have more Europeans. *Jon Megibow, Darden*

➤ We would like to get more American and German applicants. We don't have quotas: we just take the best people who apply. *Andrew Dyson, Manchester (England)*

➤ Like most business schools, we have a large number of people from engineering, consulting, accounting, or banking backgrounds, but the people from less typical backgrounds do enrich the class. They come in with the ability to actually question those consultants and say, "It doesn't work like that if you're managing a hospital," or whatever. That adds a bit of grit which makes the pearl in the oyster better. *Julia Tyler, London*

- ➤ We would like to see more Latin Americans and Asians—groups that tend to look more to the United States for training, more Central and Eastern Europeans, and more Germans. We would also like to see more people coming from the public sector and less traditional backgrounds. *Carol Giraud, INSEAD (Paris region)*

- ➤ Companies across the board, from industrial firms to consulting firms, are concerned that business schools are in danger of getting only stereotypical candidates. In other words, the person who understands how to manage his career very well—how to trade off length in job vs. salary and so on—but who as a result is never going to take real risks. We now have a scholarship from L'Oreal to attract people from off the beaten path. That diversity is something that companies want and appreciate *Professor Ludo van der Heyden, INSEAD (Paris region)*.

- ➤ There are always too many engineers applying. They aren't appreciated here in the UK, so they look to escape their positions. A growing number of people are trying to escape IT jobs—not from IT consultancies, just from companies. They never get to run companies; they're kept in boxes as boffins (nerdish experts). I'd like to see more people from the public sector. I also have a strong predilection for people who look like they're actually going to go manage something, not just take traditional MBA jobs in consulting or on Wall Street or in the City. *Professor Leo Murray, Cranfield (England)*

FOR INTERNATIONAL STUDENTS

This section is designed to provide students from outside the United States with information about the special difficulties they face when applying to American programs. For example, top American schools will generally accept only certain degrees earned at certain types of foreign institutions.

Although this section is designed explicitly for non-American applicants applying to American schools, the concerns it addresses are common for anyone applying outside his or her own region. Thus an American student applying to a European school may face similar concerns about the validity of his or her degree or college. So if you are applying outside your region, this section may alert you to the key issues you will face in addition to the normal ones faced by all applicants.

ADMISSIONS POLICIES

Most of the top MBA programs require that students have a minimum educational background roughly equivalent to an American bachelor's degree. A number of European schools, however, will accept applicants who have not completed the equivalent of a bachelor's degree but who have made up for this by acquiring substantial work experience or professional credentials such as membership in the Institute of Chartered Accountants. These schools generally require at least five years of work experience before they will consider such an applicant.

For those American schools that want educational credentials similar to an American bachelor's degree, however, the following list gives a rough indication of what level of education is likely to be deemed acceptable. Be sure to double check with each institution you are interested in, because substantial differences in criteria do exist.

Australia and New Zealand: see United Kingdom and British-styled systems.

Canada: four year bachelor's degree from English-speaking provinces; three year bachelor's degree from Quebec.

Central America: see Spain and Latin America.

China (People's Republic): bachelor's degrees requiring four years of study at a university are generally acceptable.

Denmark: Academingenior or Candidatus are generally acceptable, even in the case of Candidatus degrees requiring only three years of study.

French and French-styled systems: degrees (diplomes or maitrises) which require a baccalaureate plus four years of further study from a university or Grand Ecole.

Germany: Magister Artium, Staatsexamen, or University Diplom are generally acceptable. Fachhochschulen graduates may or may not be eligible.

India, Pakistan, Burma, Bangladesh, Nepal: bachelor's or master's degrees requiring at least four years of study are generally acceptable, but BA, B.Com, and BSc degrees alone are often unacceptable.

Indonesia: Sarjana or Sarjana Lengka awarded after five years of study is acceptable, but the Sarjana Muda (requiring only three years of study) is not.

Hungary: Oklevel requiring at least four years of study is generally acceptable.

Mexico: see Spain and Latin America.

Netherlands: The following are generally acceptable: Doctorandus, Ingenieur, or Meester. Kandidaats, Propaedeuse, and H.B.O. diplomas are often considered unacceptable.

Philippines: bachelor's degrees requiring either five years of work or four years of work and one year of graduate study are generally acceptable.

Poland: Magister, Dyplom, and Inzynier are generally acceptable.

Russia and former states of the U.S.S.R.: diploma requiring five years at a university or institute.

Spain and Latin America: Licenciado, Licenciatura, or Bacharel is generally acceptable.

Switzerland: Diplom, Diplome, and Licence, requiring at least four years of university study, are generally acceptable. The following are often considered unacceptable: Betriebsokonom, HWV, Econ. ESCEA, Ingenieur ETS, Ingenieur HTL, and Ingenieur STS.

United Kingdom and British-styled systems: there is no general rule in effect as to British-style education. Some MBA programs require that a candidate possess an Honours Bachelor's Degree whereas others accept a standard Bachelor's degree as well. Some programs require a First Class or Upper Second result, whereas other schools are open to candidates with a Lower Second or even a Third. Many programs distinguish between university and polytechnic degrees, although this distinction no longer applies to the United Kingdom itself (given that the United Kingdom has converted its polytechnics to universities). Most programs in the United States, unlike those in the United Kingdom, for example, do not accept professional qualifications, such as Chartered Accountancy associateships, without the aforementioned educational credentials.

ACADEMIC RECORDS

American schools almost invariably require that records be translated into English and the translation be officially notarized.

GRADES

The grading systems in use in your country may or may not be familiar to the admissions staff at business schools to which you are applying. If you have any doubt about this, be sure to have your school send an explanation of the grading system (in English), showing especially the percentage of students who typically get each mark. For example, if your school uses a 20-point system, the top 5 percent of students might have averages of 13-15 points. It is important to point this out, because a poorly informed admissions officer might try to translate your grade of 14 into a 2.8 average in the American style 4.0 system (by simply dividing by 5). This 2.8 is a very mediocre grade, likely to place a student in the bottom half of his or her class. Your 14, on the other hand, might put you in the top 5 percent of your class, something you should want a school to know.

Showing your class rank can thus be very helpful. Another matter of concern to admissions officers is the overall quality of your school. Having your recommenders place it in appropriate context, or having your school note its usual place in the pecking order of local schools, can be helpful, at least if your school is generally well regarded.

STANDARDIZED EXAMS: GMAT AND TOEFL

The GMAT exam is difficult enough for Americans, so it is likely to be doubly difficult if English is not your first language. Americans have the advantage of taking the exam in their native language. The exam is also familiar to them because they take similar exams to get into their undergraduate programs. As if this were not enough of an advantage, they also have ready access to preparatory materials and classes, and those who intend to get into the leading business schools generally take extensive prep courses. If you are a non-native speaker of English, on the other hand, you owe it to yourself to prepare thoroughly for this exam. Although schools will take into account the fact that English is not your first language, they will not accept a dramatically lower score.

The Test of English as a Foreign Language (TOEFL) exam is required by all the leading American schools, and many of the European schools, for all those who are not native speakers of English. The only general exception is granted to those who did their bachelor's degree in an English-speaking country. Unlike the GMAT, it is not a complicated test. If you are comfortable speaking and reading English, it should pose little problem for you. Scores in excess of 600 are generally required at the top schools. Try a sample exam to make sure that you can manage this. If this is difficult, consider taking some English courses or spending time in an English-speaking environment. Frankly, if you are unable to score approximately 600 or better on this exam you will not be able to succeed on the GMAT—the English requirements of which are much greater—nor will you be able to survive a rigorous MBA program. To register for the TOEFL, get a free copy of the TOEFL Bulletin of Information (which contains the registration form) by the creators of the exam, the Educational Testing Service, at:

TOEFL Office
P.O. Box 6151
Princeton, New Jersey 08541-6151
U.S.A.
Telephone: +1 (609) 951-1100   Fax: +1 (609) 771-7500
E-mail: toefl@ets.org

ENGLISH LANGUAGE ABILITY REQUIRED

Stanford explains the level of English required in good graduate business schools: "All students must be able to understand rapid, idiomatic English, spoken in lectures and group discussions by persons of widely varying accents. Students from non-English-speaking countries must be able to express their thoughts quickly and clearly in spoken and written English, and be able to read it with ease. The quantity and quality of academic work required at the Business School cannot be accomplished without such mastery of the English language before arrival on the campus. This point must be emphasized, as the Business School expects its students to submit numerous reports, take written examinations regularly, and participate in classroom discussions."

EXTRACURRICULAR AND COMMUNITY ACTIVITIES

Extracurricular and community activities are not always a priority for applicants outside the United States. As a result, schools may not expect to see as much in this category as they do for Americans. By the same token, to the extent that you can do something significant, it will help to distinguish you from other foreign applicants and make you look like a better "fit" for an American program.

TERMINOLOGY

American usage tends to differ from that used elsewhere. In the United States, a *college* is similar to a *university* (rather than to a high school), the difference being that a college typically focuses on only one area of study and/or grants no degrees higher than a master's degree, whereas a university typically is a collection of colleges and grants degrees up to and including doctoral degrees. A *faculty* refers to the professors teaching at the school rather than to a specific department. Last, a *school,* in American parlance, refers to an educational institution of any level, from grade school (ages 5–12) to graduate school (ages 22 and up).

ADDITIONAL INFORMATION SOURCES

To learn more about being a student in the United States, consider contacting the United States Information Service (USIS), a government agency housed in most American consulates around the world. Many of these have college advisory services and all of them have libraries that contain many books about life in the United States, and about student life.

Many capital cities also have an educational advising center. These centers have a variety of names: the Institute for International Education, the Fulbright Commission, or the Home Country–American Educational Foundation. These offer numerous services, including lectures about the application process, in addition to well-stocked libraries with many school brochures and guides to schools.

A useful guide to many of the issues discussed above is *MBA: A Guide for International Students* (Educational Testing Service).

WHAT ARE WE REALLY LOOKING FOR? THE ADMISSIONS DIRECTORS SPEAK

IN GENERAL

HARVARD: One thing is most important: a sense that this person has long term general management potential. We certainly look for people who are successful in functional roles, but their abilities should transcend functional "pipes." We look for people who can take a CEO's perspective. This is related to the philosophy behind the case method we use so extensively. This interest of ours manifests itself in a lot of ways. Our application is more detailed than those of many schools. We also look closely at the types of experience they have had and the people they have worked with. For example, we want to see anything related to leadership, whether of clubs, teams, or professional organizations. We also look for people who are as multidimensional as possible. *James Millar*

CHICAGO: We are looking for a good combination of intellectual and interpersonal skills. *Don Martin*

TEXAS: We often say that we want "real people who want to solve real problems in real time," real roll-up-the-sleeves people. We do our best to evaluate a person's commitment, drive to lead, and ability to add something unique to the Texas MBA program. Our admissions process doesn't try to fill a "typical MBA candidate" mold. We'd much rather have our students break it.

We accept people with drive, with a history of contribution and a record that shows it. Of course, satisfactory grade point averages and GMAT scores are considered important, insofar as they are further evidence of an individual's personal commitment and effort. And for all intents and purposes, two or more years of work experience are necessary; our average student is 27 years old and has had significant job experience with rising levels of responsibility. But we also strive to build each admitted class with people of different educational backgrounds. We accept MBA candidates with Fine Arts degrees as easily as those with Finance backgrounds, provided such individuals have displayed the professionalism and maturity needed to contribute. *Fran Forbes*

TUCK: As the smallest of the national business schools, we often say that "each seat counts." We look for the usual qualities such as academic excellence and bringing valuable work experiences to the classroom, but we also look for something different. We want students who have personal qualities which will fit well in our very collegial atmosphere. We also look for the type of person who contributes to the community and who will be a loyal alum of the school. *Henry Malin*

COLUMBIA: We are looking for people with professional promise. We assess this by looking at the applicant's résumé as well as their recommendations. Since this is an academic program, we do need to assess the applicant's academic ability. This is accomplished by carefully evaluating both their transcripts and their GMAT scores. Columbia requires international, non-English-speaking applicants to take the TOEFL exam. Some of our competitors are more focused on GPAs and GMAT scores. *Linda Meehan*

DARDEN: All of the top schools articulate the same desires; they all look for the same qualities. There are two things which other schools also value, but on which we place special emphasis because of the unique situation here. Oral communication skills and interpersonal abilities are critically important. In a case method environment, where 50 percent of someone's grade is based on contributions in class, strong communication skills are a pedagogical necessity. Strong interpersonal skills are valued because students are assigned to study groups for the whole first year, so being able to work in a group is critical. These skills are also sought due to the general management nature of the program. These are two things a general manager requires. In addition, diversity is a necessity for a case method environment. Filling a class with Bainies or McKinseyites would kill the discussion because they would tend to have nearly identical views. It is my job to balance the class. *Jon Megibow*

HAAS (Berkeley): We're looking for bright people; we're looking for energetic people; we're looking for creative people. We're also looking for people who have really given a lot of thought to how they want to see their careers progress, who have examined carefully what they've done this far, and basically what their goals are—not a particular salary dimension, but the kind of opportunities they are interested in professionally. *Fran Hill*

UCLA: We look for responsible people who take risks and enjoy taking the lead. Intelligence, a strong commitment to achievement, and positive interpersonal skills are highly valued. We have an interest in individuals who have a comfort level interacting and communicating with a wide range of people. Breadth in academic background and life experiences often facilitates discourse among diverse groups. *Linda Baldwin*

MIT: There are a lot of things that are important to us that grades and test scores don't indicate. Is this person a leader? You can see that in the essays and the recommendations. There are things that are more important to us than the GMAT score, such as the essays and recommendations, career success, and to a lesser extent the extracurriculars. We want to understand what opportunities were available to this person and whether he or she took advantage of them. *Rob Garcia*

CRANFIELD (England): It's also a question of what we don't want. It's important to have people who will gain from the program *and* contribute to it. We don't want people who'll just go through the motions in order to tack three little letters after their names. We don't want people who'll be complete pains in their study groups. When we accept an accountant we want someone who can get his study group through accounting. It is an important learning issue. The personalities of people are quite important to us.
Professor Leo Murray, Cranfield

IMD (Switzerland): We appeal to a niche market. Our students are older, more mature, and with more experience. Our typical student is 30 years old, with six-and-a-half years of work experience. We have a small, collegial program. We look for people who can teach as well as learn. Our first concern is work experience. We look at the quality of experience. We want to see increasing responsibility and career progression. We are different from other schools insofar as we look for real international scope in an applicant's experience. Over 75 percent of our students have lived and worked outside their country of origin. The second thing we look for is the international threshold, including languages. We also look at intellectual ability, which we assess through the person's academics, interpersonal skills, leadership ability, and so on. We are looking for people who have the potential to be strong, international general managers. Third, people need to convince us that IMD is the right place for them. They need to know the program; it is a very different kind of program from any other. *Kalpana Denzel*

INSEAD (Paris region): (1) The key thing we're looking for is *achievement;* it can come in any form. Primarily we're looking for professional achievement, but if somebody is younger and hasn't as much experience they may be able to demonstrate that through what they have done elsewhere in their lives, whether it be voluntary work or extracurricular activity. We use that as an indicator that the person has the potential to succeed in the future. We're looking for people who have had an impact, who have made a contribution in their environment that most other people would not have been able to make in the same situation. (2) We're looking for people who are *internationally minded* and therefore open to other cultures. Language skills, or at least an inclination to learn other languages, are also very important. (3) Personally, I like to look for people who are *adaptable.* Life changes ever more quickly, so people need to be adaptable and able to stand on their own feet and contribute in almost any circumstance they find themselves in. (4) Of course, we're looking for a basic level of intelligence and maturity and the other usual things as well. *Carol Giraud*

MANCHESTER (England): We won't rule out anybody because of one factor. We look first to make sure that the person can do our program, then we look at motivation and character and whether our quite different program is right for them. So we start with the undergraduate record and GMAT, then we go on to the essays and recommendations and such. You do not need to be Einstein to complete an MBA—the threshold is quite low. So we look at other things: progress on the job, motivation for doing an MBA, career plans. *Andrew Dyson*

LONDON: We want people who are extremely intelligent, who are very motivated, and who can see that it's to their benefit to work in groups, however difficult that may be. We put a lot of emphasis on group work. So we aren't necessarily looking for somebody who'll come in with highly polished group skills, because that's something we help people with, but we want people to whom this challenge is not just absolutely frightful. *Julia Tyler*

OTHER FACTORS

VALUE OF LEGACY STATUS

➤ Being a legacy (son or daughter of someone who went to Harvard) has absolutely no impact on your chances of being admitted. It is absolutely not a factor. *James Millar, Harvard*

➤ If it is truly a borderline case—two people who are equally qualified—we would consider the one who had family members attend MIT, but only if it is a borderline case. *Rob Garcia, MIT*

FUTURE GOALS/CAREER FOCUS

➤ There is no substitute for direction and purpose. You get that only as a result of intro-spection and planning and effort. It's that kind of self-direction, self-motivation, and focus that make for progressive and dynamic careers. People who know where they're headed are always an asset to the program. *Fran Hill, Haas (Berkeley)*

➤ It doesn't particularly matter what career a person wants, just as long as he can artic-ulate how Sloan will help him get there. *Rob Garcia, MIT*

VALUE IN THE PROGRAM

➤ What makes somebody good whilst they're here? They're involved not just in their learn-ing but also join the sports tournament and go off to Paris for the tug-of-war contest or whatever. It's somebody who recognizes that there's a community here. They're people who are active in getting clubs going. They're people who'll get someone good to come in and speak at their affairs. It's somebody who, on their week-long shadowing project (on which they follow a senior executive for a week to understand what he actually does and how he does it) says that it shouldn't stop at a week and convince the sponsoring com-pany that they should actually be paid to go with the executive to China because it's so interesting. So the way to put it is that they're engaged. *Julia Tyler, London*

5

How to Choose
the Right School
for *You*

— EXECUTIVE SUMMARY —

■

The first step in choosing a school is to know well what you want
from an MBA.
– Consult the appendix to this chapter (The Ideal Business School)
to understand the key variables relevant to your choice.

■

Researching the schools is a time-consuming, involved process.
– Start with the recommended guidebooks, then investigate specific
schools in depth.
– Consult the relevant rankings, but do not regard them as gospel.

■

Your search will not be complete until you have:
– Visited the most likely choices.
– Checked out these schools with leading firms in
your chosen field.

■

Apply to an appropriate number and range of schools.

*Y*our selection of a school should be driven by two actions: (1) analyzing yourself and your needs well enough to determine what programs will be most appropriate for you, and then (2) getting into the highest quality, best reputed of these programs.

It is essential that you really get to grips with both sides of this equation. Your reasons for getting an MBA will help pinpoint which schools are right for you. If you carefully analyze your own needs you are likely to opt for the right program. By the same token, if you do only a cursory analysis of the different programs, looking just at their slick brochures, you are likely to choose the wrong program.

KNOW YOURSELF—
AND WHAT YOU WANT FROM AN MBA

Your decision to go to business school represents a milestone, and few decisions will equal this one in significance. You want to get it right. The starting point is knowing what you want to accomplish by getting an MBA. Chapter 1, "Why Get an MBA?," discussed some of the more common reasons for getting an MBA. What are yours? Do you want to change from sales to marketing, from nursing to hospital management, from being a research associate at a consulting firm to being a managing partner at the same firm, or from one industry to another?

Your reason for getting an MBA will color your choice of schools. In some cases, your reason will narrow your range of choices to a mere handful. For example, if you intend to move to Utrecht to be near your wife's family, you may want to attend a Dutch business school to learn about the local market and make good contacts there. If so, you may want to look at the Rotterdam School of Management, NIMBAS, Nijenrode, or the HES (Higher Economics School, in a rough English translation) Rotterdam. Tuck or Darden, a large ocean away from Holland, might seem irrelevant.

Your relative ability—your strengths and weaknesses where business schools are concerned—will also help you narrow your choices. If you are among the world's top few thousand candidates, you will probably focus your attentions on the top 10 or 20 schools.

The process of choosing schools to apply to is likely to be an iterative one. As you understand better what you are looking for in an MBA program, you will be able to choose programs that better meet your needs. And as you research schools and learn what they have to offer, you may change what you are looking for from an MBA and thus what you will demand in a program.

RESEARCH THE SCHOOLS

STEP 1: Develop general knowledge about MBA programs.

Before narrowing your search to a handful of schools, you should become acquainted with what the various MBA programs have to offer.

1. Take a look at the appendix to this chapter, where several dozen possible criteria for choosing a school are discussed. This will introduce you to the wide range of factors that might be relevant to your choice of schools.

2. Read several of the publications devoted solely to the question of which school to choose. The best of the guides are listed at the end of this chapter, along with a brief description of their contents. Publications such as *The MBA Casebook, The MBA Career Guide,* and *Which MBA?* provide good overviews of numerous programs, covering the quantitative (such as the number of students and the most popular concentrations) and the subjective (such as what the programs are most famous for).

3. You should also read the rankings produced by *Business Week* and *U.S. News & World Report,* to get a rough approximation of the reputation of the different schools. See Chapter 3, "How to Use the Rankings," for more information on the different rankings.

STEP 2: Start getting information about specific schools.

Your initial efforts should have generated a preliminary list of schools that might be appropriate for you. Now you should start to investigate these schools more seriously.

1. Look more carefully at the information contained in the various guidebooks to business schools. Consider which criteria are most important to

you. Two criteria should weigh heavily in your thinking at this point. (a) What do you intend your concentration to be? If you intend to study marketing, you may be safe going to any leading school, since they all offer numerous courses in marketing (although some of the leading schools are more famous for it than are others). If you intend to study health systems management, however, some schools will offer many relevant courses whereas others will offer none. (b) What type of learning environment is best for you? Some people need to get their adrenaline flowing through competition and fear. If so, there are several schools that should be ideal for them. For other people, these schools would be disasters because these people learn best in collegial, supportive environments. If one of these environments would be much better than the other for you, be sure that you know which schools fall in which category. (c) Consider what additional criteria are particularly important for you. The most likely criteria include location, size, teaching quality, starting dates, and cost.

2. Get information from the schools themselves. Have each send you its brochure and course catalog, being sure that you get the schedule of courses that were actually offered the previous year (rather than just mentioned in the catalog). The brochure will explain the school's philosophy, what it seeks in applicants, and what makes it noteworthy. (Do not, however, believe all that you read.) In addition, ask for any recent newspaper and journal articles about the school that it has on file.

3. Learn when you can meet the schools' representatives. They will travel to MBA forums, which are gatherings held at cities around the United States and the world, at which schools set up booths and give out information about their programs. The MBA forums are convenient affairs for meeting representatives from a large number of schools, but they can be too crowded and hectic to provide good opportunities for lengthy questioning of any one representative. Schools also send their representatives around the world to do "dog-and-pony shows" to sell the programs to potential applicants. These information sessions are often less hurried than the MBA forums, thereby providing the opportunity to question representatives at greater length.

STEP 3: Focus on the most interesting schools.

By the time you have finished the first two steps, you should have a good understanding of which schools are most likely to meet your needs. It is now time to investigate these schools carefully.

1. Talk with each school's alumni to learn more about the schools. Schools are generally glad to give you the names of alumni living near you who have volunteered to discuss the respective programs. Recent alumni, in particular, can be good sources of information about the atmosphere of the school, its academic strengths and weaknesses, the ease with which they did (or did not) get a job in their chosen field, and the types of students who seemed most pleased by their selection of this school.

2. Talk with a school's competitors to learn what the weak aspects of a school might be. (Take these comments with at least one grain of salt.)

3. Examine the résumé books of schools that interest you. Each school prints a book of résumés of its current students that it sends to potential employers. (Although not all schools give them out freely, some, such as the Swiss school IMD, have even begun posting them on the Internet. If a school does not post them, or give them out for the asking, you may need to resort to a ruse such as having a friend in the human resources department of a company request one on your behalf.) The résumés of the students will provide you with a very detailed picture of the student body, thus giving you an understanding of the quality and nature of student that is attracted to the program.

4. Visiting the school is an important part of your research. There are a host of things that you are unlikely to find out in any other way. Schedule your visit with the admissions office. They will make it possible for you to attend any information sessions they are doing, sit in on one or more classes, and meet students. You should by all means do all of this. Sitting in on a class, for example, is critically important. You should be certain that the classroom atmosphere is one in which you will thrive and there is no way to be sure of that short of seeing one, or preferably several, in action. The classes of different schools tend to differ substantially, so do not assume that what you see at one school will be duplicated at another.

   You should also talk with a representative group of students. If you attend this school, you will soon be spending all of your waking hours with people just like them, so be sure that they are people you would be comfortable with. I suggest that you not limit yourself to those students the admissions office arranges for you to meet, because those who volunteer to do this may not be entirely representative of the student body. You can meet plenty of students by just going to the school's cafeteria and joining a group of students who will certainly remember when they were going through the same process, making it quite likely that they will spend whatever time they can with you.

5. Most important, if you know what field you intend to enter, contact the leading firms in it. Be sure to include the firms you would most like to work for. Ask their human resource people most responsible for hiring which are the schools where they actively recruit. Have them explain why they choose these schools, their impressions of strengths and weaknesses of the respective programs, what types of people they choose from each (to the extent that this differs by school), and how many individuals they generally hire from each school. Ask them which other schools they would be particularly happy to receive résumés from. (They might not recruit at some schools for logistical reasons and would be glad to hear from students at those schools. Similarly, they might be glad to hear from the best students at certain schools that they feel produce strong graduates, but in too small a number to warrant proactive recruiting efforts.)

This is a critical step to finding the right school for yourself, but the one most frequently skipped because it involves a bit of honest effort. By the way, the connection you make with these firms' human resource people should be viewed as an advance networking effort, so treat these folks well and keep in touch with them.

I recommend that you not start your efforts with the human resource professionals, because you will be imposing upon their time as it is, and to do so without knowing anything about schools will prove embarrassing. Approach them for such a favor when you have some reasonable idea of what's what in MBA programs and can thus use their time efficiently.

DETERMINE HOW MANY SCHOOLS TO APPLY TO

Some people want to go to a specific school and would not even think about going to one of its rivals. This may or may not be short-sighted, but those who feel this way do not face any problem in determining how many schools they should consider. If you would be content to attend one of a number of schools, you must consider how many applications you should file. This will depend upon several factors:

■ Are you determined to go this year? If so, you must apply to enough schools to be sure of getting into at least one of them.

■ What are your chances at the schools you favor? If your credentials are better across the board than those of the average student accepted at these schools, you need not do a great number of applications. If your credentials are not superior, however, be prepared to do more applications.

■ How many applications can you do without sacrificing the quality of essays, and so on? Conscientious applicants who prepare for the first application by gathering the necessary information about themselves and establishing how to market themselves effectively generally find that the first application takes about the same amount of time and effort as the next five applications altogether. (There is a large "fixed cost" to starting the process, but after that, by the time you are doing a fourth or fifth application you have already, for example, responded to many of the same essay questions.)

■ How many applications can you afford, given the fees schools charge for applying?

Many serious applicants apply to about six to eight schools. For all but the very strongest candidates (who will apply only to the most demanding programs), it is appropriate to spread your applications across a range of schools. Thus you can apply to one or two "likely" schools, two or three "possible" schools, and two or three "stretches." "Likelys" are schools to which you are likely to be admitted. These are schools at which admittees have substantially lesser credentials than you possess. For example, your GMAT score is 40-50 points higher than the school's average, your undergraduate grade point average is 0.5 points higher, and your current salary is 25 percent higher. "Possibles" are schools where your credentials are about equal to the average for those admitted. "Stretches" are the flip side of "likelies": your credentials are substantially lower than those of the average person admitted. Your GMAT score might be 40–50 points lower, your grade point average 0.5 points lower, and your current salary 25 percent lower.

Why separate schools into these three categories and apply to some in each category? If you apply only to schools in one category, you are likely to miss out on an opportunity. If you do not apply to some "stretches," you may not get into the highest quality school possible. If, on the other hand, you do not apply to a "likely" or two, you risk not getting into any school at all.

Given that schools do not just look at quantitative data in determining which applicants to accept, you should try to understand your chances at different schools beyond the raw numbers mentioned above. The easiest way to do this is to examine the résumé books mentioned earlier in this chapter. Looking at the résumés of individual students at a given school, when combined with the quantitative data such as GMAT scores, should make it clear where you stand relative to the typical admittees.

A strategy to minimize your effort is to apply first to your top choice schools and await their decisions. If one of them accepts you, you need not apply to your second choice schools. On the other hand, if they reject you or wait-list you, you can go ahead with further applications. This strategy will work, however, only if you apply relatively early to your top choice schools, to give them time to make their decisions and still give you time to apply to other schools.

CHOOSING A PART-TIME OR EXECUTIVE MBA PROGRAM

Choosing a part-time or executive MBA program is necessarily somewhat different from choosing a full-time program. Your choice of program will probably be limited to those within your immediate area, or within an easy airplane commute—for those with the means or the understanding employer. Therefore some of the criteria used for determining the most appropriate full-time program, such as available housing, will no longer be relevant because you will probably not be moving. Some of the other criteria may be less important than would be the case if you were to attend a full-time program. The career services office may be unimportant for you if you intend to remain with the same employer after you complete your degree.

Other criteria are likely to become more important. A program's schedule may not fit within your own, thereby eliminating it as a possibility. For example, an executive program that requires that you attend it for several weeks in the summer right when you will need to attend your industry's most important trade fair in a distant city may make it impossible to attend that particular program.

In spite of these differences, choosing a part-time or executive program still resembles the selection process for a full-time program. The courses must be of value to you, with an academic atmosphere suited to your desires. When you are choosing between several schools that offer what you want, reputation is still likely to be the most important criterion.

Be careful in evaluating an executive MBA program, however, because it is not the same as a school's traditional MBA program despite being related to it. The executive program may use somewhat different faculty, have a very different student body, and/or have largely different teaching methods—more or less use of the case method or consulting projects. The atmosphere may be very different as well. A school might have a full-time program that you rated highly because of its large number of electives, but the executive program may rate less well if it offers no electives. Thus you need to rate the executive program independent of the traditional MBA program regarding such matters.

Although the executive program may be quite different from the traditional program at a school, the two do share more than just a common facility. The fact is that the brand name of the school, which has probably been developed largely through its traditional program rather than its executive program, will affect the perception of the executive program. Therefore the quality of the school's traditional MBA program, and its rankings in the various media that perform such services, might well be a factor in your decision.

HOW THE ADMISSIONS DIRECTORS THINK YOU SHOULD CHOOSE
THE RIGHT SCHOOL FOR YOU

➤ Take your time and don't rush things. There are at least several schools that people could fit in well with, so they should do it realistically and apply to a range and focus on learning as much as possible about the several that interest them the most. They should do it realistically and get advice from a lot of people. Then pay attention to what they say. Too many people get into a mind-set that says "I'm going to this school and no other," and then they don't pay attention to what other people say. That leans toward a lack of openness, and in a situation that's about learning, if people aren't open to learning from the outset, they face a big problem. *Brian Sorge, Kellogg*

➤ Treat this as a research process. Use books, brochures, and guides, and talk with alums and students. Then make up your own mind. Don't just look at one ranking and treat it as the bible. *Henry Malin, Tuck*

➤ We strongly recommend that people come and visit the campus and sit in on classes. There are a ton of misperceptions about it in the press, but if you visit it you can find out for yourself what it's really like. This is an investment like buying a house. I wouldn't buy a house without seeing it. People go to extraordinary lengths when buying a house, but only to superficial lengths when choosing a program. *James Millar, Harvard*

➤ If I were giving my daughter advice on how to choose a school, I would suggest that she start by considering what industry she wanted to be in. Then she should talk with as many people in that industry as possible and see which schools they recommend and which they attended. It is also important to look carefully at placement statistics: who recruits these students, which companies hire them, and how many are placed and at what salaries. Visiting the campus and talking with the professors and students should be an integral part of her decision-making process. Other questions that are important for her to have answered are: is the student body diverse; will I be comfortable there; does it represent the real world; and, does it have a strong international program. In today's business world, this is imperative. *Linda Meehan, Columbia*

➤ If this is one of a couple of schools someone wants, she should visit and get a sense of it. She should look at a campus visit as a two way exchange. She should request an interview. She should definitely get into a class and she should try to meet with students, even casually. She should see what she thinks of these students to see if this is the right program for her. *Don Martin, Chicago*

➤ If you are not going to test drive a car before you buy it, you will not make a wise decision. If you want to attend Darden but do not visit it, absent important circumstances preventing you from doing so, it looks like you are not interested enough or savvy enough to do so. We look for savvy decision makers who will make good general managers, so we will ordinarily reject someone for either of those reasons. *Jon Megibow, Darden*

➤ One of the most important learning tools is the person sitting next to you. If the caliber of the person next to you isn't as good as you, an MBA is a wasted investment because you'll be doing more teaching than learning. *Kal Denzel, IMD (Switzerland)*

➤ They should think about why they want to do an MBA. They should talk to a lot of people who have done programs that interest them to help figure out which would be best for them. They should also talk with employers they might want to work for, to see which schools these companies recommend. Then they should visit the schools on their lists and talk to a lot of students about the programs. *Mary Clark, IESE (Barcelona)*

AVOID THE LIKELY PITFALLS IN CHOOSING A SCHOOL

Some warnings to keep in mind as you go through the search process:

▨ Start the process early, because you need to gather a lot of information and you should give yourself time to reflect on what you learn at each step.

■ Do not take the rankings too seriously. They are no better than rough proxies for a school's quality and reputation (see Chapter 3 for more on the limitations of business school rankings). They obviously do not take account of your specific set of key criteria. Look for high quality programs that will satisfy your needs.

■ Be wary of schools with learning environments that are not hospitable to *you.* Do not put yourself through months of hell and the disappointment of performing poorly due to a bad match between you and the learning environment of a school. For example, if you are a reserved person, the free-for-all quality of a case method program may not be appropriate.

■ Be aware that your interests may change as you go through the search process, because you can alter what you want to do and better understand what would help you. As a result, your criteria for schools should change to reflect your changed interests.

■ Do not be swayed by spiffy school brochures. The quality of a school is not directly related to the quality of the pictures in its brochure.

■ Do not be swayed by warm (or cold, or inefficient) admissions people. They are not the ones who will be teaching you or helping you to get a job upon graduation. (A blessing, perhaps, considering how many schools manage to lose people's requests for brochures and application forms.)

■ Do pay attention to the quality of the careers service, because your job fate can be dramatically improved by a top-notch department.

■ Remember: Eliminate schools that do not offer the program you need.
  – Eliminate those with inappropriate learning atmospheres.
  – Eliminate those with other important negatives for you, such as location and size.
  – Include the highest quality schools you believe you can get into (and yes, pay attention to consensus views of the rankings).
  – Be swayed from the highest quality school(s), for example, only by big money scholarship offers to go elsewhere.

■ Ultimately, any of dozens of schools can give you a great learning experience and help your career prospects dramatically, but it is up to you to take advantage of the opportunities afforded you (for more, see Chapter 16).

FINAL DECISION CRITERIA

The most important criteria for each applicant will of course differ substantially. Some applicants will be greatly cost-constrained, leading them to choose schools that have lower tuition or offer financial aid. Others will choose schools only in a given area. Others will look for the best quantitative finance school they can get into.

No matter which criteria are relevant to you, it would be highly appropriate to determine which schools will give you the courses you most want, in an atmosphere in which you think you could thrive (collegial vs. competitive, lecture vs. case method, faculty open door vs. isolated, etc.), and in a location that is appropriate to your current circumstances and future goals. Having taken account of these and the other criteria you regard as most important for you, the final choice among those schools that meet these criteria probably should come down to the school's reputation. If you were a financial economist considering Chicago and Simon, for example, it would be peculiar to chose Simon if you were admitted to both. Although Simon is very well regarded, it is not a contender for the mantle of best business school in the world, as is Chicago. Reputation is not everything, but among schools that do not differ dramatically in their ability to deliver what you are looking for, reputation should ordinarily be the critical factor.

RECOMMENDED READINGS

MBA Casebook (Hobson's, 1997), 320 pages. Provides an extensive listing on 160+ schools, with especially good coverage of Europe and, newly, of the United States, Asia Pacific region, and Eastern Europe. In addition to the usual description of the program (comprising the length of the course, starting date, entry requirements, tuition and fees, national origins of students, course structure and offerings, description of the facilities and the career service office), it provides an in-depth profile of a typical recent graduate of the school. This profile describes his reasons for attending the program, what was particularly valuable for him in it, how (and why) he directed his future career, and how this program has improved his ability to perform his current job. This set of profiles is extremely useful for potential applicants to see both what is unique about different schools and what career moves are possible with an MBA in hand, both of which are very useful for career planning. (Available from Hobson's Publishing, 159–173 St. John Street, London EC1V 4DR, UK, telephone +44 (171) 336 6633, fax +44 (171) 608 1034.)

MBA Career Guide (published by Professional Career Guides), approximately 220 pages. Published twice annually, this is a highly informative guide both to leading business schools and to the job market MBAs face upon graduation. Regarding business schools, it includes: a "Dean's Diary" featuring interviews with leading business school deans; profiles of leading schools in the United States, Europe, and Asia, plus a statistical overview of the top schools; and, a discussion of issues of particular concern to MBA applicants. A recent issue, for example, highlighted entrepreneurial programs and also examined new developments in business school career services departments. Regarding the MBA job market, it includes profiles of firms that hire large numbers of MBAs, often with accompanying interviews of their CEOs or other senior executives and profiles of recent MBA graduates that have joined these firms. In addition to writing about career matters, the MBA Career Guide's sister firm has developed a careers service itself, both for current MBAs and also for more seasoned executives. As such, it hosts MBA recruitment fairs and lists current job openings likely to appeal to its readership. (Available from The MBA Career Guide, 3601 Locust Walk, Philadelphia, PA 19104, telephone (215) 243–0582, fax (215) 243–0590 *or* 46 Delancey Street, Regent's Park, London NW1 7RY, United Kingdom, telephone +44 (171) 284–4697, fax +44 (171) 267–1941.)

George Bickerstaffe, *Which MBA?*, 7th ed. (The Economist Intelligence Unit, Addison-Wesley, 1995), 504 pages, $17.25. A particularly sensible view of over 100 full-time programs, with approximately 45 North American programs, 45 European programs, and 15 programs in the rest of the world, plus over 60 part-time and executive programs (on the same geographic basis). Admittedly under-inclusive, but especially good coverage of part-time and executive programs.

Ronald N. Yeaple, *The MBA Advantage* (Bob Adams, 1995), 301 pages, $12.95. An interesting discussion of the financial benefits of attending one of forty leading American schools. Even more useful, perhaps, for its insights into the different programs' strengths and weaknesses, including a rating of up to eight departments at each.

Tom Fischgrund, ed., *The Insider's Guide to the Top Ten Business Schools*, 5th ed. (Little, Brown, 1993) 328 pages, $11.95. The best book on the market for understanding ten leading American schools, including the academic environment, student social life, recruitment, and job search process at each.

John A. Byrne, *Business Week's Guide to the Best Business Schools*, 4th ed. (McGraw-Hill, 1995), 351 pages, $14.95. Essential reading for its well-known rankings of America's top schools, but equally valuable for its discussion of the schools themselves.

John A. Byrne, Cynthia Green, *Business Week's Guide to the Best Executive Education Programs*, (McGraw-Hill, 1993), 248 pages, $14.95. Describes the top executive MBA programs in the United States, plus the top shorter programs (which do not grant degrees).

Two publications *in German* cover the U.S. and European schools, respectively:

- *MBA-Studium und Business Schools in den USA*, by Birgit Giesen, Nicola de Menezes, and Hans Dieter Trommer (Joerg E. Staufenbiel, 1995), 25DM.

- *Europaische Studiengage und MBA-Programme in Europa*, by Birgit Giesen, Nicola de Menezes, and Hans Dieter Trommer (Joerg E. Staufenbiel, 1995), 25DM. In addition to extensive coverage of German business programs, it describes over two dozen leading business schools elsewhere in Europe.

As I have already noted at the end of Chapter 3, if you are unable to find the books noted here at your local bookstores, you can order from Cody's.

APPENDIX
THE IDEAL BUSINESS SCHOOL

Few people will consider all of the following criteria to be important, but they are listed here to spur your thinking about what you would most like in a program. The most important criteria will depend upon your specific needs, but on average they include course offerings, school reputation, location, academic atmosphere, school size, facilities, and teaching quality. In my experience, the one item that applicants tend not to weight heavily enough is the quality of the career services function. Schools of equal quality and reputation tend to have very different rates of success in placing their graduates in desirable companies and positions.

GENERAL

REPUTATION. Is the school considered one of the best schools in the world, especially in your particular specialization? Is it particularly well known and respected where you would most like to work? As Chapter 3 discussed in detail, the various school rankings should not be considered definitive. Pay more attention to the opinions of those in charge of hiring at companies of the type you wish to work for.

SIZE. Smaller schools often engender a friendly, family atmosphere. Large schools, on the other hand, are able to provide large numbers of both elective course options and skilled professors. (Smaller schools tend to be better rated by students, larger schools by employers.)

LOCATION. What part of the world would you prefer to be in? Ann Arbor, a delightful and beautiful town, is home to a world-class university (the University of Michigan) but not to world-class corporate strategy consulting firms, so do not expect to work part-time for Bain & Co. or the LEK Partnership during your second year. By the same token, your spouse's employment options may also be limited, although Detroit is near enough to offer some scope. On the other hand, one can live very well very cheaply in Ann Arbor. New York provides a stark contrast to each of these points. Living there may be wildly exciting, but very expensive. Employment options during your second year, and for your spouse, are likely to be extensive.

The question of whether to go abroad is often a matter of whether you intend to work in the country where the school is located. Other compelling reasons to attend business school abroad include: wanting to work for a target company from the other country; wanting to improve a foreign language; wanting to experience another culture in order to be ready to work in international businesses; or wanting to attend a better quality school than is possible at home.

The location of a school also helps determine its social environment. Schools in large cities tend not to foster the degree of social bonding among classmates that schools located in small towns do, largely due to the lack of other entertainment options.

One additional locational factor to consider: How important is it to be close enough to your home to allow easy visits?

FACILITIES. The ideal school should of course have top quality research facilities, including a traditional library and extensive on-line services.

RELATIONSHIP TO UNIVERSITY. For some, a stand-alone business school is preferable because it means that there will never be a question as to which institution the professors and administration owe their loyalty. For others, a business school that is part of a major university will be better because the university will offer courses on related (or unrelated) subjects and social stimulation as well.

TUITION. American state universities tend to be cheaper than private schools, but the budget crunches of state and federal governments mean that there is upward pressure on their tuitions and downward pressure on the quality of their offerings, making them something of a long-term risk.

MISSION. Some schools view their jobs as training general managers. Other schools look to train functional specialists. All want to train people who intend to get to the top of their chosen fields. Related to this, some schools require that students specialize in a field of their choice, meaning that they must take at least a set number of courses in that field. Others permit a free choice of electives.

PROGRAM

STARTING DATES. The ideal school would offer the chance to start at any time of year or, failing that, at the best time for the individual involved, but most schools offer only one, two, or three starting dates.

TERM LENGTH. Long semesters lift the pressure of constant examinations and papers, but miniterms of six to eight weeks make it possible to sample a variety of areas (some of which do not merit a fifteen-week term, but which would be valuable and well covered in half that time). A good compromise would be a first half of the program structured in longer courses and the second half structured in shorter ones.

PROGRAM LENGTH. The program would be very short for those already well advanced in their careers. Those who are switching fields would have a longer program available to help them reorient themselves. The longest programs would be offered to those without significant business backgrounds.

JOINT DEGREES. The ideal school would offer you a chance to do a master's or doctoral degree in a related subject of interest, such as economics, law, medicine, international studies, or whatever. (This is likely to be possible only if the school is part of a university.) The leading American business schools have long offered this possibility, but it is rare in Europe apart from the British universities. Rotterdam School of Management is a notable exception, offering a joint MBA-MBI (Master's of Business Informatics) program, which does not lengthen the program's requirements.

EXCHANGE PROGRAMS. Ideally you could take a term at another top school, one that offered you the opportunity to study in another language or pursue a specialized topic in greater depth, or just be close to that character you met last year who resembles the young Cary Grant or Rita Hayworth.

INTERNATIONALIZATION. It is not clear what is necessary for a program to be considered truly international. Perhaps many of the cases and courses should focus on international management issues, or at least not be strictly American. Another possibility is that the students and professors should come from many different countries. Yet another approach is to offer projects abroad and exchanges with schools in different countries. An emphasis upon language learning is essential to an international program. In assessing the internationalization of schools, you could look at these factors that actually measure the programs' inputs, or you could look at the outputs—the percentage of graduates who take jobs abroad or jobs that include a large international component.

CURRICULUM

PREPROGRAM. For students who need help in algebra, calculus, statistics, computer usage, or languages, the ideal school would offer preparatory courses in the relevant subjects before school begins.

CORE COURSES. The ideal program would "square the circle" and allow you to opt out of or substitute advanced courses for any core courses about which you are already knowledgeable without losing the benefits to less well prepared students of your contributions in these courses, and vice versa when you are the neophyte and others are the experts. Some schools do not permit waivers of introductory courses in order to keep a cohort or group together. Case method schools in particular feel that much of the teaching comes from students who are knowledgeable about the specific subject matter, so the school must keep those who are already expert in a subject in these classes to teach the novices. Whether this is a key issue for you will depend upon your background. Undergraduate business majors, with work experience in a management consulting firm, for example, may prefer programs that allow them to substitute advanced courses for the basic courses in the core program.

"TOUCHY-FEELY" COURSES. The school should offer courses that capture the nonmathematical elements of management in as rigorous and productive a fashion as possible. They should include training in negotiation, communication, teamwork, leadership, interpersonal skills, and other soft skill areas that graduates ten years out of business school almost invariably describe as being of great importance to them.

INTEGRATION. In the past, most schools taught courses that were neatly divided into functional areas. Thus a marketing course resolutely stuck to marketing topics, without, for example, considering the impact of marketing decisions upon manufacturing operations. It is now generally recognized that such compartmentalization is not only artificial but also harmful to students who fail to integrate their knowledge of different functions. Although schools recognize the nature of the problem, only some of them have succeeded in developing truly integrated programs.

ELECTIVES. The number of electives should be immense. You would thus have the chance to become a specialist in an area of interest. The areas of specialization have increased dramatically in recent years, with some schools offering specializations in arts management, hospital management, international finance, luxury goods marketing, or purchasing. Be sure that the school runs each of the courses it lists in its catalogue each year. Award bonus points to the school that adds sections to courses that are oversubscribed.

NONBUSINESS COURSES. Similarly, courses offered in other departments of the university should be available for credit. These would ideally include everything from languages to econometrics.

PROJECTS. Numerous courses will offer the chance to perform consulting projects for credit with local companies. The teams will include executives of the company as well as other students, thereby giving you a chance to put your learning into practice while making valuable contacts. These also serve as helpful integrating devices, both for showing how different functions relate and for demonstrating the value of the soft skills. These projects tend to be more readily available in schools situated in a region that is home to many companies; schools in splendid rural isolation tend to find it difficult to place students in good consulting projects due to the lack of local firms.

PEDAGOGICAL ISSUES

TEACHING METHODS. Teachers can use lectures, the case method, computer games/ simulations, or company projects in a course. Some courses lend themselves to one method rather than another. An ideal school might utilize lectures for introductory economics, statistics, and accounting classes, but offer case courses, or mixed lecture-and-case courses, in fields like marketing, organizational development, and corporate strategy.

A consensus view appears to be that some use of cases, especially in advanced marketing, strategy, and organizational development, is highly desirable. The drawbacks of the method are minimized in those settings, whereas at least some use of it helps develop the ability to mine cases for the most relevant information, package it quickly, and respond to wide-ranging questions in a coherent and powerful manner. (For a further discussion of the case method, see the appendix to Chapter 2, "Types of MBA Programs.")

Schools noted for their extensive (or exclusive) use of the case method include Harvard, Darden, and North Carolina. Most schools use a combination of teaching methods, although some schools eschew the case method altogether.

WORKLOAD. All of the good schools require substantial work, but there is still a large disparity between the load at the least and most demanding schools. This is likely to be especially important for those students who have families with whom they wish to spend time. Just how hard do you want to work? (Be careful in asking about this, by the way, because even asking may mark you as someone insufficiently determined. Rely in part on the various guidebooks for this information, and pay close attention at school information sessions when someone else is silly enough to inquire about it. When visiting a school, ask students how hard most people work, but do not take their replies at face value since students love to complain about how hard they have to work.)

MATHEMATICAL SOPHISTICATION. The ideal school for the mathematically sophisticated would use advanced math in any course that could be taught better and faster with it. For the mathematically desperate, however—the so-called poets—the ideal school would use little math beyond simple algebra, or it would upgrade their skills in a well-thought-out manner.

CLASS SIZE. Smaller classes offer students the benefit of substantial interaction with, and attention from, the professors as well as a chance to participate relatively frequently. On the other hand, with more students you find a greater likelihood of students with relevant current experience commenting on matters. Small classes offer no chance to be anonymous and to hide, whereas larger classes—especially in courses using the case method—force students to compete for air-time. On balance, however, most students prefer small to medium-sized classes.

PROFESSORS. The ideal professor probably combines three related activities. He is dedicated to teaching and is always available in his office for conversation and assistance. The same professor is also a world famous consultant who spends a great deal of time with companies spread across the world, thereby increasing his knowledge and making contacts that might be useful when it comes time to help you find a job. The ideal professor is, moreover, someone who devotes substantial energy to research and publishing, to increase his fame and that of the school.

Although it is impossible to square the circle and have professors both be readily available and be international consultants and prolific authors, a school can foster an open door policy that encourages professors to be on campus and readily available to students for at least some portion of each week. Students routinely prefer teachers who teach well over those who do high quality research at the expense of quality teaching. At a minimum it is possible to say that teachers who teach only in the executive program, whose courses are so oversubscribed that you will be unable to enroll in their classes, or who are on sabbatical while you are attending the school, are likely to have little impact upon your learning. The greatest danger exists for someone who chooses a school because one or two famous professors are there. He may be unable to get a class with either of them, or changes his intended field of concentration and thus chooses other professors for study after all.

Teaching quality does tend to be highest at those schools that promote largely on the basis of teaching rather than research. Many schools have student evaluations of professors printed for student use in choosing courses.

You are unlikely to be sent a copy if you request this by mail, but on a school visit you should be able to get a copy from the bookstore, the registrar's office, or an individual student. Look at this to see how students really feel about teaching quality at the school.

STUDENTS

STUDENT BODY. The composition of the student body will have a major impact upon your learning experience, your enjoyment of the program, and even your ability to get desirable jobs in the future. The large amount of teamwork embodied in most programs guarantees that much of your time will be spent discussing classroom issues with other students. The other students should be experienced enough that you can learn a great deal from them. On the other hand, they should not be so skilled, relative to your own level, that you will be unable to compete with them. One thing that they definitely should be is friendly and willing to share—both their time and their knowledge. The ideal school would have an atmosphere that emphasizes cooperation more than competition (unless you are the type of person who relishes a great deal of competitive interplay). This is not to say that competitiveness is necessarily bad: it inspires some to work harder and perform better. The question is whether *you* want a more competitive atmosphere or a more cooperative one. (See the discussion regarding atmosphere that follows.)

You can determine a lot about the nature of a school by looking at the makeup of its student body. The University of Texas, for example, has a strong technology management program and thus has many engineers and others with technology backgrounds in its student body. However, one-third of its student body has liberal arts degrees. This is in contrast to Purdue's Krannert School, at which only approximately one-seventh of the student body comes from a liberal arts background. If you have a liberal arts background, Texas might be a better bet if you are worried about being able to handle the curriculum successfully. Schools want students who will fit in, and you should choose schools on that basis as well.

Other aspects of the student body that might be of keen interest are the types of jobs people have held before business school, the age range, the percentage of women students, the percentage of minority students, and the percentage of international students. In general, the more diverse the student body, the more you will be able to learn.

ATMOSPHERE. The relationship between students varies dramatically from school to school. Four factors tend to determine the degree of competitiveness among students. The more work that is done in teams and graded on a team basis, the less competitive the atmosphere is likely to be. If students' grades and class rank are displayed to the class and to potential employers, the atmosphere is likely to be more competitive. The use of a mandated grading curve inspires competition, since an improvement in one student's grade means another's must suffer. Last, the number of students who are flunked out of the school has a large impact. Many schools try to retain every student they enroll, thereby easing student fears, whereas one or two schools deliberately maintain a reign of terror by flunking out a substantial percentage of students at the halfway point.

The relationship between students and faculty is partially dependent upon the factors listed above, but it is likely to be determined more by other factors. Schools that are geographically isolated are likely to cause students and faculty to be closer because the opportunities for socializing are relatively limited for each group. Professors in such programs are also likely to do less consulting work, thereby minimizing the competition for their time. Schools in more isolated environments are also likely to try to capitalize on this situation by being more teaching- than research-intensive. The smaller a school, the more likely professors are to be on a first-name basis with students and to welcome social interactions with them. The same is true of schools with smaller class sizes.

QUALITY OF STUDENT LIFE. The ideal school would have students active in a wide range of activities, from national clubs to sports to such preprofessional organizations as the "management consulting club." Be sure that your favorite activities are available, whether at the school itself or nearby.

Student lifestyles may vary a great deal, depending upon both the program and the student. A program in New York City may influence a student's life less than one in the country. Thus at a school like Tuck in the middle of New Hampshire, most student socializing is done with other students, both because the students tend to be gregarious and well suited to one another and because there are not a lot of opportunities for meeting other people in the surrounding area.

(A sore spot at some schools is that spouses are not really included in the school's social life, not introduced to one another, and not helped to get jobs.)

ADMINISTRATIVE SERVICES

ADMINISTRATION. The ideal administration does not pander to transient student concerns such as the promotion of a popular, if unpublished, assistant professor, but does its effective best to be helpful.

CAREER SERVICES. The ideal career services office gets a number of companies to recruit on campus. It helps to market students to employers by distributing résumé books (filled with the résumés of current students) and other information. It gets companies to keep their offers open until a set date so that you can consider all offers without pressure to take an "exploding offer" (one that provides a bonus if you accept right away but that will lapse entirely if you do not take it immediately). Placement services will also include extensive help in résumé (c.v.) preparation, cover letter writing, and interviewing skills, including videotaping of mock and real interviews. In addition, the ideal career services office should provide extensive career management assistance, intervening early to help those who intend to make dramatic career changes. Its assistance is not limited just to the traditional employers of MBAs such as the consulting firms and investment banks, nor is assistance limited only to the most popular or closest cities, but includes distant countries as well.

JOBS

JOBS. The ideal school is overwhelmed by on-campus interviewers, with several recruiting companies per graduating student (and the same for summer jobs). The school is large enough, with such a substantial reputation, and close enough to a major metropolitan area, that recruiters flock to it. The school successfully places large numbers of students in the most prestigious fields, such as management consulting, as well as in the specific field you intend to work in. The kinds of companies recruiting on-campus include those you would most like to work for. Check what percentage of graduates have not landed a job within three months after graduating, and then find out to what extent they are people like you.

ALUMNI. The older and larger the school is, the more alumni it will have. Because alumni can be useful in providing useful pointers to jobs, or indeed jobs themselves, their number and influence is important. Alumni affect the ranking of the school by virtue of their degree of career success and also by the amount of money they raise for the school. A large, dedicated alumni group is thus a very useful asset.

LOCAL CONNECTIONS. Regional schools often have better local connections than any national or international school can match. For example, NIMBAS, a fine Dutch school with campuses in Utrecht (The Netherlands) and Bonn, is not ordinarily considered a rival of INSEAD or London Business School, long top-ranked among Europe's business schools. For those considering jobs in Holland or the German Rhineland, however, NIMBAS might well be a savvy choice given the school's locations and connections.

6

THE ADMISSIONS PROCESS

— EXECUTIVE SUMMARY —

■

Most schools have more than one person read your file,
guaranteeing that you will not be rejected by someone
who is having a bad day.

■

Admissions professionals, mindful of the need to fill classes with human
beings rather than data points, seek to understand who you are as well as
what you have accomplished.

■

In addition to admissions professionals, some American schools involve
students in admissions decisions, whereas most European schools also
use faculty members.

*C*hapter 4, "Make the Most of Your Credentials," described what the schools are looking for in their applicants, but it did not describe the mechanics of *how* this decision is made and *who* makes it. If you are like most applicants, this process is utterly opaque. This chapter is devoted to explaining the admissions process.

A school's admissions professionals will determine whether to admit you or not based upon the whole of your applications folder—your job histories, educational achievements, extracurricular and community involvements, honors and awards, essays, recommendations, and interview evaluations. Not every admissions officer will weight the different elements in the same way, or for that matter grade them in the same way, but the way the process is followed will hold true for each and every applicant to a school. And while the admissions process at different schools varies somewhat, it varies much less than might be expected—partly because admissions officers at the various schools talk with one another about what procedure each follows—but probably owing more to the desire schools have to be thorough in their evaluation of candidates. Schools go to great lengths to be sure that they have given every applicant a fair chance.

"ROLLING" VS. "ROUNDS" ADMISSIONS

Applications can be processed in either of two ways. Schools using *rolling* admissions evaluate applications as they are submitted. Applicants generally learn of the school's decision within about a month of the completion of their files, although there is considerable difference in the speed at which various schools respond.

Schools using *rounds* split the application period into three or four separate miniperiods. For example, the first round, or miniperiod, may cover Oct. 1–Nov. 30. All applications received in that period are lumped together and evaluated at one go. This means that someone applying early in October will not learn of the school's decision until approximately mid-December. Although this system can mean delays for the applicants, it does make life easier for admissions officers.

Whether they use a rolling or rounds approach, admissions officers gear their schedules to having sufficient time to evaluate each applicant with care. This involves being prepared for long days and nights during crunch periods, especially as the final deadline approaches. The admissions offices always urge you to get your applications in early, claiming that this improves your chances of admission. The reality, however, as Chapter 13, "Application Timetable," discusses in detail, is that the timing of your application is quite insignificant except for those few applicants who have a very complicated message and background, which a tired admissions officer facing deadline pressure might not have the energy to comprehend appropriately. The vast majority of applicants will still get a proper reading and analysis of their applications. The reason that admission offices press for early submission of your application is actually to spread their workloads over the whole admission cycle.

Please note that your application will receive no attention from admissions officers until it has been completed, meaning that *everything* that is required has been received by the school. Thus if your second recommendation has not yet been submitted, the admissions secretarial staff will keep your file open until they receive the recommendation, at which time they will indicate to the admissions officers that your file is now ready.

THE STANDARD AMERICAN MODEL

WHO ARE THE ADMISSIONS OFFICERS?

The director of admissions is typically someone who has worked in business school admissions for some years. *At the top schools,* this generally means someone who has had at least five years' experience as a more junior admissions officer at the same school, or an equivalent amount of time in charge of admissions at a less prestigious school. He or she may not have an MBA, but in this case will probably have a human resources background.

Directors *at other schools* are likely to include those with similar backgrounds in human resources, and recruitment in particular, and those who have recently graduated from the school's MBA program. All schools like to have some of the latter involved to provide a realistic flavor of the program to applicants who attend school information sessions, and also because these recent graduates have a potentially different appreciation of which applicants will fit well and contribute significantly to the program. What all the admissions officers share is dedication to their schools and a concomitant drive to admit only the most qualified group of applicants they can find.

HOW ARE DECISIONS MADE?

Most American schools follow a similar procedure, known as a "blind read." Two admissions officers are given copies of an applicant's file and asked to categorize it. Although there are up to six or eight possible categories, insofar as "wait list" or "hold over" can be considered separate categories, for simplicity's sake I will refer to just three categories: "accept," "reject," and "don't know." If both admissions officers rate the applicant as an "accept," then no more work needs to be done: she is accepted. Similarly, if both admissions officers rate her as a "reject," she is rejected.

On the other hand, if they disagree about her, or both rate her as a "don't know," then her file will be considered further. At this point some schools have the admissions director make the final decision whereas others have admissions officers decide as a group. In some schools, the process works in the same manner except that the admissions director may quickly scan each file, including those that were rated a clear "accept" or "reject" by the two initial readers, to make sure that nothing is amiss in the process.

The mix of different backgrounds and talents on the part of the admissions officers leads to occasionally spirited discussions about how to rate a given applicant, but this is generally viewed as a positive because the school is looking for a diverse group of students and wants an admissions team that is appreciative of a range of different backgrounds and talents.

Recently, the career service departments at certain schools have become involved in the admissions process. Although it is easy to find jobs for the typical applicant, such as an engineer who wishes to enter management in the same industry he has worked in for the last four years, it may be difficult to help an atypical applicant find a job. In such cases the admissions director is likely to chat with the career services director to get his or her opinion regarding the employability of such applicants. (The candidate who intends to change careers is thus well advised to make it clear that the proposed change is a realistic one that suits her talents, and is one that she will pursue vigorously and intelligently.)

THE CRITERIA

Admissions officers have a lot of information about you when it comes time to make their decisions. As the last chapter showed, most applicants assume that the admissions process is devoted to weighing applicants' grade point averages, GMAT test scores, and number of years of work experience, and they therefore make a fundamental mistake. Admissions committees are made up of human beings, generally those who have chosen to work in a human resources capacity, and consequently they are particularly interested in admitting real human beings rather than a set of statistics. You will find it hard to gain admission if you are just so many data points on a page. (Applicants who can make themselves real, that is, human, are more likely to gain supporters among the admissions officers. You should therefore take every opportunity to distinguish yourself from the mass of the applicant pool and make your human qualities apparent.) It takes so much time and effort to accept or reject a given applicant because admissions officers try very hard to understand her, not just to glance at her test scores.

Are the criteria the same for everyone? Yes and no! At the margin, the admissions office must take account of the makeup of the overall class. The school will wish to have an appropriate mix of students in terms of industry experience, job function, nationality, and the like. The admissions director will be responsible for making the necessary trade-offs to "balance" the class. This generally involves no more than the pushing up, or down, of a few applicants on the admissions acceptance ladder. Few schools try to reach a quota for given categories, with the exception of American schools that are desperately afraid of having too few minorities, but all of them want to avoid an overrepresentation of a specific industry, nationality, or other factor. Many schools, however, have specific types of candidates that they might wish to see more of. Almost all of them would like to see more women. Many would like to see more nontraditional applicants, such as public sector managers and people in the arts, especially those with quantitative skills.

THE STUDENT-INVOLVEMENT VARIATION

The student-involvement model of the admissions process is essentially identical to the standard American model, but with one important exception: the involvement of students in the process. Kellogg is most famous for this practice. The usual way in which schools make use of students is in interviewing applicants rather than in evaluating their files and making final decisions about them.

STUDENTS IN THE APPLICATION EVALUATION PROCESS

Judith Goodman, admissions director at The University of Michigan's business school, which has recently introduced students into the admissions process, explains their involvement: "We have both students and admissions professionals involved. We use approximately thirty second-year students who volunteer to help. They are put through a rigorous training process before they take part. They do much of the evaluative interviewing for us because we like to have their different perspective on things. They are fresh from the different industries and jobs, and they are active in the school right now, so they can evaluate how well these applicants have done in their jobs and how well they are likely to be received by prospective employers once they graduate. The students can also tell how well the applicants will do academically and how much they will be able to contribute to classes and study groups. Although admissions professionals aim to determine the same things, they are not quite as close to the action as the second-year students are, so we welcome their involvement. Final decisions, however, are still made by admissions professionals who of course take into account the students' input."

THE EUROPEAN VARIATION

Most European schools eschew the American practice of having admissions professionals make admissions decisions. These schools have their admissions professionals prepare the files on each candidate and then present them to the admissions committee, which is made up of professors from a variety of disciplines. The admissions officers therefore act more as advisors than decision makers.

The procedures of these schools tend otherwise to resemble those at American schools. Many, for example, use the "double blind" reader approach in which two professors on the admissions committee read an applicant's file and categorize it as "accept," "reject," or "don't know." Those rated by both professors as "accept" are indeed accepted, those rated as "reject" are rejected, and in cases where the two professors disagreed or marked "don't know" the file is handed on to a third professor or, more often, the whole committee for a final decision.

(Using professors to make the admissions decisions might be expected to elevate the importance of academic credentials, but this appears to be true to only the slightest extent. Whether this is due to the influence of the admissions professionals in the process is unclear.)

The use of professors to make admissions decisions is quite rare at the leading American schools, leading to my designation of the practice as the "European variation."

ADMISSIONS DIRECTORS EXPLAIN HOW THEIR SCHOOLS PROCESS THE APPLICATIONS

➤ We don't screen out anybody based on their numbers. We read everybody's application. We read the essays first, the recommendations second, and the transcript and GMAT score third. We start with what they say about themselves, then what others say about them, and finally we look at the objective data. We look at the objective data pretty closely, but that is not all that we consider. Just because your numbers are above average doesn't mean that you'll get in and just because your numbers are below average doesn't mean that you won't get in. *Henry Malin, Tuck*

➤ We admit a couple hundred very strong applicants outright. We then interview 1,000–1,400 people for the remaining positions. We generally conduct the interviews in person, but for those in inaccessible places we'll conduct one by telephone. These are people who have made the first cut. We admit over half of them. *James Millar, Harvard*

➤ All of our applications are read by three people. The first reader is a second-year student who has been trained to analyze applications. He or she does a rating together with written comments and a recommendation to admit, deny, or analyze further. The second reader is an assistant or associate admissions director. He or she reads the file "blind," meaning that he or she doesn't know what the first reader has said. The second reader also makes comments and a recommendation. The third reader is me. I don't read things word for word. Instead I focus on whatever the first two readers regard as weaker or less competitive. *Don Martin, Chicago*

➤ The first reader of an application recommends an action. I then give it a second reading. If I agree with the first reader, then the decision is made. If we do not agree, then a third admissions officer will read it. If we are still uncomfortable, we hand it to the faculty oversight committee for a final decision. About 70 percent of applications are decided by two readers, another 25 percent with a third reading, and the last 5 percent will go to the faculty committee for a decision. *Jon Megibow, Darden*

➤ There's a kind of two-step process as we winnow out applications. One is an academic threshold—where your undergraduate record, or graduate record, and your coursework, plus your GMAT are taken into consideration. If we're confident that you could do well in the program, meaning that you would contribute in the classroom, keep the faculty happy, and challenge the other students, then you're advanced to the second stage in the review process where some of the more qualitative factors are taken into account. *Fran Hill, Haas (Berkeley)*

➤ The admissions officers actually have no vote on who is admitted. The admissions committee, which consists of professors of finance, organizational behavior, strategy, technology management, and decisions sciences, votes on each candidate. If you believe in modern management theories, commitment is important, so we increase the faculty's commitment to a promotion (class) by making the faculty responsible for who is admitted. INSEAD works on this high-commitment model. We also include a few alumni on the admissions committee, because that real-world input is useful for calibrating the value of outside references and judging managerial potential. *Professor Ludo van der Heyden, INSEAD (Paris region)*

➤ If there is a spark in the file, we give them the benefit of the doubt and bring them in for an interview. They then have the chance to market themselves. *Kal Denzel, IMD (Switzerland)*

➤ Two of us read a person's application. We look at undergraduate grades and the GMAT first, then we look at the quality of their work experience. We look at their salary advancements, accomplishments, and responsibilities. Then we look at the essays and examine their career objectives and how RSM could help them to meet their objectives. Next we look at the recommendations. If we both agree that the person is a strong applicant, we invite him or her to an interview. If we aren't so happy with the application, we refer it to the whole admissions committee for a second look. So no one can be rejected without being viewed by at least three people. (Our admissions committee is chaired by the dean. Other members include the director of the MBA program, our director of career planning, our marketing director, and our admissions director.) *Connie Tai, Rotterdam*

ADVICE ON HOW TO COMMUNICATE WITH THE ADMISSIONS OFFICE

➤ One group of candidates risks not getting in despite having good credentials and good applications: the ones who call us constantly. The most appropriate way to contact us is to send a short E-mail message. *Rob Garcia, MIT*

➤ Make it easy on the admissions crew by sending in the whole application at one time rather than piece by piece. *Mary Clark, IESE (Barcelona)*

7

FINANCING YOUR MBA

— EXECUTIVE SUMMARY —

■

Calculate the full cost of an MBA.

■

Consider your options in terms of programs and financing alternatives.
- There are many financing strategies available, but few are realistic unless you start working on them early in the process.

INTRODUCTION

Going to business school is a very expensive proposition. If you attend a full-time program, you have to give up your salary, pay tuition and other fees, and pay your room and board for the duration of your studies. Despite this, the financial consequences of attending a top school suggest that it is a very good investment. Indeed very few people who have pursued an MBA at a top drawer school regret having done so, and those who are convinced that they want the degree are unlikely to be deterred by the cost.

The question of how you will finance your MBA studies is nonetheless of critical importance. Whereas the full detail on the subject of financial aid are beyond the scope of this book, this chapter will help you understand what options you have and what strategies you can employ.

CALCULATING YOUR EXPENSES

The *direct cost* of attending a given school will depend upon its tuition rate, living expenses in the area, and the duration of the program. Schools are quite good about providing applicants with information about these costs (based upon the experiences of their current students), in the application materials they send. A typical listing of expenses would include the following, often broken down into much greater detail:

- Tuition
- Room and board
- Books, computer, software, and other supplies
- Health insurance
- Personal expenses (laundry, clothing, recreation, etc.)
- Enrollment, activity, and other school fees
- Local transportation
- Flights home
- Loan payments
- Child care
- Miscellaneous

To this should be added the expense of moving to the school if it is far from your current residence.

The total may be as little as $20,000 per year or as much as $60,000. This may seem like a fortune, but the increased earnings enjoyed by graduates of top programs tend to dwarf that amount, as we have seen in earlier chapters.

The figures above represent the direct costs of the program, but the *indirect costs* are also important. The opportunity cost—or money forgone—is the amount of money you could have earned had you continued working rather than going to business school. Similarly, if your spouse has to take a lower paid job or change careers, this also represents a potentially substantial opportunity cost. These costs will vary according to the length of the program, and, in the case of your spouse's job prospects, the location of the program you choose. (New York City offers job prospects that Ann Arbor may not.)

THE TIMING OF THE OUTLAYS

Some of these expenses must be paid before beginning the program, whereas others will be due on a semiannual basis, and still others will be payable on a monthly basis or more frequently. Tuition is likely to be due before the school year begins, whereas room and board, books and computer-related expenses, health insurance, and school fees are likely to be due prior to the beginning of each year, or on a semiannual basis. Most of the other expenses will be payable on an as-used basis.

HOW MUCH DEBT IS TOO MUCH?

The general rule is that the better the school you attend, the more you are likely to earn, both in your first job out of business school and throughout your career. Attending a better school thus makes a high level of debt more affordable than would be the case if you attended a lesser school.

Nevertheless, the question of how much debt is appropriate for you depends upon your individual circumstances. If you intend to take a relatively low-paying public sector job upon graduation, you may view a $75,000 debt as inconceivable. If you took a job at a leading investment bank, on the other hand, that same $75,000 would probably look highly manageable. This fact could well alter your choice of jobs, which might or might not be a problem. If you have to focus on the salary and bonus of your first year, in order to facilitate debt repayment, to the exclusion of all else, you may take a job that is not appealing in terms of the actual work, the industry involved, or your growth prospects. This would be an unfortunate consequence of your debt situation.

Let's put the question of borrowing into perspective. In terms of the amounts you will have to repay, someone who borrows $50,000 for ten years at 8 percent to 10 percent interest will face a monthly payment of approximately $600–$660. This would ordinarily require an annual income of at least $48,000–$54,000—well below the starting salaries of most people graduating from top programs. Of course, someone borrowing say, $25,000 for ten years at the same 8 percent to 10 percent interest will pay only half as much per month and needs a salary of only $25,000–$28,000. These figures suggest that the size of a loan necessary to fund an average student will not be large relative to his or her post-MBA earning capacity.

SOURCES OF FINANCING

Frankly, the largest source of funds is likely to be your own savings—another reason to work for several years before applying. The second largest is loans, with scholarships and other sources making up the remainder.

How Do People Typically Pay for Their MBAs?

Program Type:	Full-Time	Part-Time	Executive
Funding Source	Savings	Salaries	Companies
	Debt	Savings	
	Part-time jobs	Companies	
	Other		

The first place to look for financial aid is the school itself. Schools have a variety of means of helping students. They often have scholarship, assistantship, and loan funds available. These funds may be limited according to the student's nationality, residence, ethnic background or gender, financial need (possibly calculated with the parents' income included), or relative quality (i.e., an applicant in the top 10 percent of an entering class in terms of prior scholastic achievement, GMAT scores, and estimated managerial potential may be offered scholarship money or an assistantship when an applicant at the "bottom" of the entering class might not be). Thus schools can allocate funds on the basis of need, merit, or as a means of attracting certain types of students. (Check with each school you are considering to ascertain what types of institutional aid are available and what application forms are required.) Note that the bulk of their aid is likely to be in the form of loans and may be limited to citizens and residents of the country the school is in. This is particularly true of American schools.

The next place to look is at government aid programs. In the United States, the federal government has subsidized loan programs that the source books listed at the end of this chapter describe in detail. These are available primarily to American citizens and permanent residents. American state governments tend to provide help via the reduced tuition charged at state schools. Many state schools charge somewhat less for nonresidents than private schools do, and much less for state residents. Many states also provide scholarship aid for residents attending school in that state, and a few even provide it for attendance at out-of-state schools. Residence is an important concept where state schools are concerned. Most states require you to have lived in the state for at least one year to be considered a resident. Documentary evidence that they may take into account includes local bank accounts, drivers' licenses, voter registration, rent receipts, and telephone bills. For more information regarding these programs, and for general residence requirements, see the books listed at the end of this chapter or contact the relevant state scholarship office.

European students, especially Scandinavians, may qualify for aid from their respective governments for attending a top quality school no matter where it is located. Similarly, there are numerous grants available for nationals of a European Union nation who will attend a school in another EU member country.

The next place to look is at the organizations that have funded general purpose or specialized grants that may be applied to business studies. The Fulbright Foundation, for example, has paid for many Americans to go abroad and many foreigners to attend American institutions. Between 4,500 and 5,000 Fulbright grants are given each year. There are innumerable organizations—foundations, clubs, fraternal organizations, labor unions, churches—that have funded grants for the best and brightest or neediest, so see whether you qualify for one or more. (For descriptions of these organizations and their programs, see the list of publications at the end of this chapter.)

Banks are often willing to lend against the prospects of your glowing future. This is particularly true for students with solid roots in the community. Home equity loans are an option for those who already own their residences. In the United States, the Graduate Management Admissions Council (GMAC) has developed programs called MBA LOANS and Executive MBA LOANS for American citizens and permanent residents, as the Association of MBAs (AMBA) has done in Great Britain.

Your *employer* is a potential source of aid, of course, so check to see what arrangements your firm has previously made for other employees who have gone to business school. Discuss your situation with the personnel in charge. If your firm has not sponsored someone before, you may need to work hard to convince it of the value of doing so. (The bigger the firm is, the more likely it is to have a program in place to offer assistance.) Among the points you might make: agreeing to remain with the firm for a specified number of years after completing the degree (with your improved skills), and trying to do any large projects that the school requires (and that are an increasingly prominent part of many MBA programs) in conjunction with the firm, so that the firm gets the "free" advice of a group of talented business students and perhaps that of a professor as well. Be sure to ask your chosen school about how best to present "sponsorship" to your employer. Schools tend to be well informed about how other, similar employers have felt that they benefited from sponsoring someone, and will know how other students have successfully pitched the idea to their own firms. Weigh the value of getting assistance from your employer versus the commitments you may need to make to remain with the firm after you graduate.

If you are a U.S. *veteran* you may qualify for special assistance programs.

Beg your *spouse* to support you through the program.

Lastly, consider re-acquainting yourself with your *parents*. Their financial aid may involve fewer restrictions and qualifications than other likely sources of financing, not to mention the fact that it may be your only realistic choice for assistance.

FINANCIAL STRATEGIES

1. To avoid paying large tuition bills, consider an American state university such as Michigan, Berkeley, UCLA, North Carolina, or Texas. The tuition for nonresidents is generally only two-thirds that of the same-quality private schools, and it is often possible to qualify as a resident for the second year of the program. (Residents pay only about one-fifth to one-third of the tuition charged at private schools.)

2. Maximize your earnings during the summer between the two years of the program. To do so, start your quest for the high-paying jobs at consulting firms, investment banks, and so on, before you start the program. Contact the placement office in advance to see what jobs are generally available and what it takes for students to get them. Be realistic in considering whether you fit the profile of those likely to be offered such employment.

3. Work during the second year of the program for the same consulting firm or investment bank that employed you during the summer. Note that the better the school, the more you can make in part-time jobs. This is, however, very location dependent. Harvard students can work in downtown Boston consulting firms, which are a fifteen-minute drive away, but the same is not true for Tuck students, who are hours away.

4. Reduce your opportunity cost of attending school by opting for a shorter program. In the United States, for example, Kellogg offers a twelve-month program for students with an undergraduate business degree. In Europe, the standard MBA program is approximately one year rather than two.

5. Persuade your firm to pay your way. This is most readily done by attending a school part time or by attending an executive MBA program. The former will require limiting your choice to local schools and the latter may require your waiting until you have the requisite seven- or ten-plus years experience. These options will also allow you to stay on salary.

6. Borrow money from an appropriate school or government, or, better yet, find a grant for which you qualify. The key to getting grants, by the way, is to investigate them well in advance of when you are going to use them. A grant could require that the application be submitted eighteen months before the relevant school term is to start. This is an extreme example, but it is never too early to start searching for applicable grants.

7. Save money before going to school. (Nearly half of all students use their savings to fund their MBA studies.)

8. Upon completion of your degree, ask your new employer to reimburse your tuition or to pay off your loans. The willingness of employers to do this depends upon the strength of your negotiating position and the current practices of such firms. For example, management consulting firms have done this in the past when they have collectively had trouble getting enough recruits, and have refused to do so in other years.

IS THE FINANCIAL AID DECISION INDEPENDENT OF THE ADMISSION DECISION?

Does it hurt you to admit to a school that you do not have the necessary funds to finance all of your MBA program? For virtually all schools, the answer is no. Schools generally determine which students to admit, then consider how to dispense their financial assistance. Those schools without money available for financial aid will nonetheless suggest other likely sources of aid, such as government loan programs.

A few schools, however, expect that the students in private industry, at least, will have been able to save a substantial amount toward their graduate education. Failure to have saved a reasonable amount reflects a possible lack of seriousness and planning. This is particularly likely to be the view of those schools—principally those in Europe—that have very little money available to fund needy students.

SPECIAL NOTES FOR INTERNATIONAL STUDENTS

Students attending schools outside their own countries often are not eligible for financial aid from the schools they attend. International students attending an American school typically must be able to demonstrate their ability to pay for at least the first year of study and sometimes the whole program before a school will issue a Certificate of Eligibility for the appropriate visa.

CONCLUSION

Expect to pay for most or all of your MBA yourself. The more difficult it will be for you to finance an MBA, the sooner you should begin to line up the necessary financing. Choose a slightly lesser school only if you can save a large amount, but note that the difference in salaries upon graduation from even slightly different quality schools can be immense.

INFORMATION SOURCES

Bart Astor, in *The Official Guide to Financing Your MBA*, (GMAC), $12.95, provides an excellent starting point for the aid available from American schools and the federal government. With entries for nearly 400 schools, it shows whether they offer graduate assistantships (and whether these are available for first year students), scholarships based solely upon merit, scholarships based solely upon financial need, scholarships that give preference to women or minorities, or a delayed payment plan. It also lists organizations that provide scholarships for graduate study, but is somewhat incomplete on this score.

Other guides to the American financial aid scene are:

- *Financing Graduate School*, Patricia McWade (Peterson's, 1993), $14.95
- *The Graduate Scholarship Book: The Complete Guide to Scholarships, Fellowships, Grants, and Loans for Graduate and Professional Study*, 2d ed. (Prentice Hall, 1993), $19.95
- *Graduate Guide to Grants* (Harvard University, 1993), $25.00
- *Grants for Graduate Study*, 3d ed. (Peterson's, 1991), $59.95

For non-Americans considering study in the United States:

- *Funding for U.S. Study—A Guide for Foreign Nationals* (Institute of International Education), $39.95

For Americans considering studying abroad:

- *Financial Aid for Study and Training Abroad* (Reference Service Press), $40.00

For Britons:

- *Guide To Business Schools* (Pitman). Lists sources of scholarships and other publications devoted to the subject. In particular, it describes the Association of MBAs loan scheme.

■ *The Grants Register* (Macmillan)

For international students generally:

■ Contact the embassy or consulate of the country where you intend to study to see what scholarships they know of, and what information sources they can recommend, that are appropriate for foreign nationals.

■ Check financing sources in your own country to see which, if any, will allow you to use financial awards outside the country.

As already noted in Chapter 3, if you are unable to find the books listed here at your local bookstores, try Cody's.

Part *II*

MARKETING
YOURSELF
SUCCESSFULLY

8

MARKETING YOURSELF: GENERAL PRINCIPLES

— EXECUTIVE SUMMARY —

■

Understand how you compare with the competition.

■

Learn how admissions officers will view your candidacy based upon their expectations of people from your field and educational background.

■

Capitalize on your strengths, while minimizing your weaknesses, in light of their expectations.

■

Show how you bring unique value to the school, without being so unusual as to be perceived as a risk.

■

Use themes to focus your marketing effort.

The first part of this chapter shows you how to determine what you should emphasize in your application. Your areas of emphasis depend upon several factors: what the top business schools want, what your competition offers, and your relevant strengths and weaknesses compared with these applicants. The second part of the chapter begins the discussion of how to capitalize on your strengths and to make the strongest possible argument for your acceptance. This discussion continues throughout the following chapters, which explore the marketing vehicles you need to master: the essays, recommendations, and interviews.

DETERMINING THE SUBSTANCE OF YOUR MESSAGE

YOUR STRENGTHS AND WEAKNESSES VERSUS THOSE OF THE COMPETITION

Chapter 4, "Make the Most of Your Credentials," explained what schools seek in their applicants. You should therefore have a reasonable idea of what your own strengths and weaknesses are. This, however, is not really enough; at this point you should go one step further in determining how you stack up versus the competition.

Start your analysis of the competition you face by getting the summary data about entering students provided by every program. Four programs are highlighted below:

	Darden	Kellogg	UCLA	Wharton
Applications Received	2,297	5,807	3,348	6,354
Enrolled	260	617	315	767
Female	29%	30%	30%	28%
Male	71%	70%	70%	72%
Minority Students	17%	17%	19%	19%
American Indian	<1%			
Asian or Pacific Islander	3%			
Black/African American	8%			
Hispanic	8%			

	Darden	Kellogg	UCLA	Wharton
Average Age at Entry	27	27	27.6	27.3
Full-Time Work Experience	99%	99%	99%	99.6%
Countries Represented	24	35	26	53
International Students	13%	23%	18%	31%

GMAT Distribution

	Darden	Kellogg	UCLA	Wharton
Below 400	<1%	0%		
400–490	2%	3%		
500–590	16%	19%		
600–690	63%	61%		
700 and above	19%	17%		
GMAT range of middle 80%			570–710	590–730
Mean	643	—	650	657

GPA (Grade Point Average) Distribution

	Darden	Kellogg	UCLA	Wharton
Not Calculated	14%			
Less than 2.5	3%			
2.5–2.99	22%			
3.0–3.49	42%			
3.5–4.0	19%			
GPA range of middle 80%		3.0–3.6	3.1–3.85	
Mean	3.20	(middle 50%)	3.5	3.51

TOEFL

	Darden	Kellogg	UCLA	Wharton
Mean	630	632		

Undergraduate Major

	Darden	Kellogg	UCLA	Wharton
Business Administration	29%	19%	22%	21%
Economics	18%	20%	22%	23%
Engineering/Science	25%	21%	25%	—
Humanities/Social Science	27%	40%	27%	
Liberal Arts & Sciences	—	—	—	31%
Other	1%	—	4%	8%

Each school also gives a geographic distribution of students, showing what percent come from abroad, and, within the United States, what percent come from each region of the country.

Other schools provide this much, or more, data on their entering classes. Some schools give more detail about the age distribution of students, their experience distribution, the fields they were working in at the time of applying, and their salaries. These "class profiles" are generally included in the information packages schools send potential applicants. Some of the guides to schools, as Chapter 5 discussed, also provide such information.

With these data in hand, it is a simple matter to determine how you stack up relative to the average candidates in terms of your academic credentials, GMAT score, amount and nature of experience, salary, international background, and the like. Although this, combined with the information in this book, may well be enough for you to make this determination, it is possible to go still another step further.

As mentioned earlier, schools have long put together books with the résumés of their students. They distribute these books to potential employers to help them determine which students might be of interest for upcoming job openings. These books have traditionally not been given to applicants, but there are ways around this problem. You can ask a human resources person at your company to request one. The second way is to look up the school's Web page on the Internet. IMD, the Swiss school, has led the way in posting the résumés of all of its students for anyone with Internet access to examine.

The advantage of examining the student résumés of a given school is that you can see just where you resemble many of the current students and where you differ. You can also get a real sense of what a school is looking for when you read the precise details these résumés give on each student. This will allow you to tailor your message to the school's specific interests. In fact, even if you only reconnoiter the students at one or two schools at a given level, you will soon know what qualities you offer that are likely to strike an admissions officer as unusual and valuable.

A SHORTCUT TO THE STRENGTHS AND WEAKNESSES ANALYSIS

Each person will be more than just a member of a category; a person who happens to be an accountant will not be the same as all other accountants. By the same token, knowing what category you fall into, especially the job category, can help you determine how you are likely to be viewed by admissions officers. Although admissions officers will not assume that every accountant has the strengths and weaknesses listed here, these are likely to be their starting presumptions.

The following chart is intended to make this process of identifying where to focus your efforts a bit easier by showing the presumed strengths and weaknesses of different categories of applicants. In terms of strengths, or reasons to admit you to a program, these may give you some ideas for things you can emphasize about yourself as good reasons to value you. If you are a member of one of the most traditional categories of applicants to MBA programs, however, recognize that just having the strengths noted here will be insufficient reason to admit you. You may need to be demonstrably stronger than others in the same category (and perhaps even freed of the category's typical weaknesses). The job/industry categories that generate large numbers of applicants include: accounting, consulting, engineering, finance, and marketing. The chart shows what are presumed to be weaknesses unless evidence is presented to the contrary.

CATEGORY	LIKELY STRENGTHS/REASONS TO HAVE THEM IN THE PROGRAM	LIKELY WEAKNESSES
Job/Industry		
Accountant	Understanding of accounting (good for study groups) Seriousness of purpose Exposed to numerous businesses and industries (if CPAs) Quantitative skills	Undynamic Not a leader Dull, no sense of humor Quiet, unlikely to engage in risky class discussions Huge numbers with interchangeable skills and experience available!
Computer Programmer	Bright Technologically up-to-date Quantitative skills	Poor interpersonal skills Not a leader Unwilling to develop "soft" skills
Consultant	Bright Smooth, good communicator Strong research and analysis skills Integrator Leadership	Just getting "ticket punched," without truly wanting to be in program Arrogant, even by MBA standards Limited management experience Huge numbers with interchangeable skills and experience available!

Category	Likely Strengths/Reasons to Have Them in the Program	Likely Weaknesses
Job/Industry (cont'd)		
Engineer	Quantitative skills Technologically up-to-date Team oriented Used to rigorous academic setting	Lacking outside interests Lacking communications and interpersonal skills Huge numbers with interchangeable skills and experience available!
Entrepreneur	Determined Small business focus Real understanding of business nuts and bolts, not just theory Integrator	No patience for "book learning"
Finance/Banking	Quantitative skills Understanding of accounting (good for study groups) Strong research and analysis skills	Huge numbers with interchangeable skills and experience available! Lacking people management skills Arrogance
Human Resources	Social and interpersonal skills Knowledge of compensation, selection, training, and related issues Team player	Lack quantitative abilities! Interested in business problems or just people's feelings? Not enough guts to make managerial decisions?
Lawyer	Communication skills Accustomed to hard work Smart	Lack quantitative abilities! No ability to adopt business perspective Lack ability to work with others
Marketing	Communication skills Integrator Understands customers	Limited management experience Plenty of brand management types available
Military	Good leadership training Management experience Determined	Cultural misfit (business chaos instead of military hicrarchy) No business experience

CATEGORY	LIKELY STRENGTHS/REASONS TO HAVE THEM IN THE PROGRAM	LIKELY WEAKNESSES
Job/Industry (cont'd)		
Nonprofit	Few available in application pool Unusual perspective	Cultural misfit in ultra-capitalist MBA world Not enough guts to make managerial decisions
Sales	Communications skills Interpersonal skills Understands customers Self-confident	Lack analytical skills Short-term focus
Scientist	Bright Quantitative skills Team player	Interest in business? No sympathy for economic motivations Unwillingness to develop "soft" skills
Writer, Photographer, Artist	Unusual perspective Creative problem solving Communication skills Strong individual performer	Lack quantitative skills! Cultural misfit in ultra-capitalist MBA world Little ability to lead others Little dedication to business Not marketable at end of program
Nationality*		
German	Hard working and determined Likely to focus in heavy industry Good team player (at least when other members are strong) Strong secondary and university education Represent a major market	No sense of humor No interest in the underdog Technical arrogance Limited English ability
Irish	Amiable Team player Good communicator	Lack of drive Romantic dreamer rather than pragmatist

*By nationality, I do not mean German American, but one who is native-born German. (One reason for choosing these nationalities, and being very blunt about their supposed shortcomings, is that I number Germans and Irish among my own ancestors.)

Category	Likely Strengths/Reasons to Have Them in the Program	Likely Weaknesses
Age		
Older (late 30s or older)	Experience and industry knowledge Willingness to share experiences in class	Lack of energy (if over 40–45) Unwillingness to sit through the basics Inability to work with youngsters as equals Impatience with theory

Job, nationality, and age are by no means the only determinants of an admissions officer's expectations. For example, your *college major* is another. If you majored in Egyptology, an admissions officer will probably picture you differently than would be the case if you had majored in American Studies. Similarly, your *family background* can influence expectations. If you are from a wealthy background, for example, you risk being perceived as spoiled. (To combat that, you would be wise to show how you took advantage of all the opportunities such an upbringing offered and have done things a spoiled, sheltered person would never contemplate.)

CAPITALIZING ON YOUR STRENGTHS; MINIMIZING YOUR WEAKNESSES

Once you have analyzed your situation and recognize where you stand, you should be aware of what an admissions officer is likely to see as strengths and weaknesses. Your job now is to capitalize on this understanding.

First, you will want to support any of the strengths you do indeed have. You can relate stories in your essays that show you, for example, as an effective leader. Just as important, you can (and should) have your recommenders provide supporting examples. The interviews give you a further opportunity to amplify your strengths. The following chapters show you how to use these three communication vehicles most effectively.

Second, do whatever you can to minimize your weaknesses, or, better yet, show that you do not suffer from them. Once again, it is a matter of addressing them through each of the vehicles at your disposal: the essays, recommendations, and interviews. In other words you should maximize your *reward/risk ratio*. Schools want students who will make major contributions to their programs (i.e., provide a reward for accepting them) without involving substantial risks of academic and other types of failure. The higher the reward/risk ratio, the better your chance of appealing to a school.

EXAMPLES

The tasks facing people with different profiles will of course be different. A research associate (or, so to speak, a junior consultant) at a major management consulting firm faces a very different task from that of a commercial photographer in trying to maximize the reward/risk ratio. The junior consultant is likely to be regarded as very bright, with strong research and analysis skills, and a good overview of business, without being much of a risk to a program. She has already gone through the difficult screening process of the consulting firm, which was much like the screening process of a business school. After three years in consulting, she knows enough about business and about how to do business analysis that there is essentially no danger that she will fail out of a program, or lose interest in business, or be unplaceable in a good job upon graduation. She therefore looks like an absolute cinch to be admitted because she brings good experience and qualities to the program without any risk, meaning that her reward/risk ratio looks very high indeed. The problem for her, however, is that she is but one among thousands of junior consultants, all of whom bring similar qualities. To improve her chances of admission, she must show that she is quite different from these other consultants in terms of the range of her work, the depth of her understanding of a given industry (or two or three), the extent of her direct work with clients, her success to date, and how she intends to employ her MBA in the future (based, of course, upon a realistic scenario of how she will do so).

The commercial photographer is in a nearly opposite situation. In his case, the problem is not what he brings to the program. He is likely to be the only photographer applying, so he has considerable uniqueness value to start with. His problem involves the risk side of the ratio. An admissions director is likely to worry that he will be unable to handle the program's quantitative demands and that he will fail out of the program early on. Similarly, she may worry that he will lose interest in business and simply go back to photography midway through the program. She will probably also worry that his lack of work in a traditional field may make the normal employers who recruit at the school reluctant to hire him. To improve his chances of admission he needs to address each of these concerns. He may, for example, want to take several quantitative courses prior to applying to show that he has the ability to do quantitative work. By doing this he also shows that he is sincerely interested in business, is not applying on a whim, and is likely to complete the program. Last, he will want to show where he is headed with his MBA and how he intends to get there. This will involve explaining what skills and experiences he already has, plus showing how he will acquire other relevant skills and experiences during the business school program (through part-time work, club activities, course projects, etc.), to be able to land a job with the type of employer that interests him.

The junior consultant would make a terrible mistake if she were to concentrate on the risk side of the ratio; she must show her unique value. The commercial photographer would make a terrible mistake if he were to concentrate on the reward side of the ratio; he must reduce the risk he poses.

— ESSAY EXAMPLE —

The essays written by Joerg, immediately below, provide a good example of how to capitalize on a category's strengths and minimize the expected weaknesses. He was finishing a doctorate in mechanical engineering at a leading German university when applying. If you look at the chart earlier in the chapter, you can see that a German engineer carries a lot of baggage, a lot of expectations. Joerg wanted to reap the benefits of being a German engineer, so he made it very clear that he was determined, conceptually able, well grounded in fundamentals, and a solid team player in working with other strong engineers. In fact, he was able to show that he was quite exceptional on these counts, thereby increasing the "reward" side of the reward-risk ratio. He also neutralized the potential weaknesses for someone of his profile. He showed that he was a deeply caring, humanitarian fellow in helping someone involved in political difficulties escape from China. He showed that he was not an arrogant, insular German by demonstrating his international involvement. His essays have other virtues as well, but these are the most important ones for us for the moment.

1. **Briefly describe your career progression to date. Elaborate on your future career plans and your motivation for pursuing a graduate degree at Kellogg. (400 word limit)**

    I have followed a traditional German route to a serious business career by pursuing my education in Mechanical Engineering to the doctoral level. In spring 1993 I will complete my ME education in approximately 2.5 years less than the average student requires, without sacrificing the breadth or depth of my studies and apprenticeships, even while doing this at Germany's finest engineering school.

    My engineering efforts have been meant to prepare me for a business career combining engineering and marketing skills. The marketing side of the effort started with my work for two business consulting firms in the late 1980s. I had to support myself throughout my studies since my parents are disabled. I consequently sought the highest paying outside jobs I could get which also fit my school schedule. The first of these jobs was with a computer consulting firm, Consultax. One of my projects for Consultax involved helping a marketing consultancy, Wehmeyer Marketing, develop and implement a new marketing information system.

    My work for Wehmeyer Marketing Consultancy, whose principal activity was textile consulting, convinced them to hire me away from Consultax. Wehmeyer wanted me to apply my computer and textile engineering skills, as well as the ability I had demonstrated to understand quickly the marketing dimension of a business. I ended up managing numerous projects which combined technical and marketing elements, including, for example, the analysis of potential textile suppliers in Mauritius.

Since early 1991 I have been managing a research project* at Hans Schwarzkopf GmbH to develop a new machine to measure the shape stability of chemically treated fiber and hair. This work, which will also satisfy my ME doctoral thesis requirements, should result in one or more patents once it is completed this spring.

My career, while focused upon engineering, has started to straddle the marketing area as well. I very much wish to combine my engineering knowledge with marketing and general management skills. I would prefer to do so by getting an MM at Kellogg, given its international reputation in these areas (and emphasis on teamwork). For the future, I hope to do marketing work for a technically based company, perhaps in the reinforced composite material field. And, not surprisingly, I would like eventually to run such a firm.

described in detail in my employment history

2. **Your background, experiences, and values will enhance the diversity of Kellogg's student body. How? (400 word limit)**

My very strong technical background, project management expertise, and international exposure will, I hope, enhance Kellogg's student body.

The strength of my technical background—which will shortly include a Ph.D. in Mechanical Engineering and already includes substantial engineering work experience in a variety of engineering disciplines—should be clear. While there will be other engineers in the Kellogg Program, I suspect that few will possess the same depth and breadth of knowledge and experience which I have acquired.

My project management experience, described briefly in my employment history, has involved the development of a device to measure the shape stability of hair and fiber. This project has required me to motivate, integrate, and control people in various parts of Schwarzkopf Co., ranging from technicians in workshops of different companies to scientists in chemistry laboratories (and even to company owners).

My international background consists of several components. I am of course German and have worked and gone to school in Germany for most of the last 20-plus years. On the other hand, I have also sought out opportunities to live and work abroad. These experiences have included working in a Japanese factory and doing marketing/engineering work in Mauritius, as well as being a research intern at the University of Wisconsin, Madison. In addition I have worked in various parts of Europe.

I recognize, however, that my experience will not benefit others at Kellogg except to the extent that I am what Americans call a "team player." I certainly regard myself as precisely that, one who enjoys people of different skills and interests, and, for that matter, different nationalities. My experiences in different disciplines (from chemistry to mechanical engineering to marketing) and different countries (from Japan to Europe to Mauritius) have caused me to enjoy greatly being part of multifaceted teams. I have sometimes led such teams, as I am now doing at Schwarzkopf, but I have also enjoyed participating in research groups as a very junior member. I derive great satisfaction from being able to contribute and thus hold up my own end, while simultaneously learning from others with very different skills. My enjoyment of multidisciplinary groups is actually one of the reasons that I look forward to combining my engineering skills with what I hope will be my strong marketing and general management skills in the future.

3.a. It's the year 2030 and your autobiography has just been published. What do the book reviews say? (150 word limit)

(As translated from the Japanese)

Mr. Otzen's view of the first twenty years of his career—perhaps uniquely for a German industrialist—provides a lighthearted view of his climb to the top of Du Pont's Asian operations. There is little surprise that his polymer processing background, combined with his marketing skills, led him to Du Pont. Similarly, his long-time interest in Asia explains his early posting to China. The surprises, of which there are many, come instead from his uninhibited joy in virtually all that he did. He loved the early engineering challenges which yielded his treasured patents. But he also loved the managerial side of his career, particularly working with people from every conceivable country and background. This combination appears to explain at least part of his success.

Volume 2, much anticipated by this reviewer, will cover his controversial years as CEO of Du Pont and then as Germany's Commerce Secretary.

3.b. What are your most valued accomplishments outside of work? Why? (150 word limit)

Through my long involvement in Jülich's International Club, which is dedicated to helping the foreign scientists working at the Research Center Jülich, I met Fanxhia Ling,* a Chinese woman anxious to get her son out of the PRC. This couldn't be arranged until she returned to China, so she needed someone to help from within Germany.

I eventually arranged for Li Ling* to come to Germany, but only after countless interventions on his behalf. I arranged his admission, without interviewing, to Karlsruhe University. The PRC refused him a passport several times due largely to his Tiananmen Square activities, but each time I was able to convince both Chinese and German officials to intercede for him. Then I convinced the German Embassy to give him a second chance to prove his German was acceptable and to grant him a student visa.

He is now a student here, and we are friends.

These are pseudonyms; their real names, due to his/her involvement in the Tiananmen Square activities, should remain undisclosed.

3.c. For fun I . . . (150 word limit)

For fun I travel as much as I can. Of course there are other things I greatly enjoy doing, ranging from skiing to scuba diving, but the most satisfying of my pursuits is traveling.

My sort of traveling may not suit every
I have met through the International Club of
and their families. I prepare for each visit by lear
raphy, and culture of the region. By staying with
other countries through the eyes of the local residents

Because this discovery process exhilarates me so much
United States, nearly a dozen European countries, and parts
interesting thing still awaits me: to see Li Ling's family in China

FIT IN—STAND OUT

Another way to think about the reward/risk ratio is, as many admissions
put it, a "fit in–stand out" problem. *Fitting in* means that you are accepted b
classmates as belonging in the program rather than being regarded as an od
If you can do the course work, subscribe to the program's goals, and get on we
with the other students, you will fit in. *Standing out* means that you bring something unique to the program, something that distinguishes you from the other
students. At some level, all of the programs are quite similar in terms of what
would make someone fit in or stand out, but at another level this may vary. Having
basic accounting skills would help you to fit in at any program. Being a fluent
speaker of four languages might make you stand out at Darden (which has a high
percentage of American students) but would help you fit in at INSEAD, where
students must speak at least three languages by the time they graduate.

The trick, obviously, is to fit in and stand out at one and the same time. It is
not sufficient to do just one of these things. Saying that you really fit in, that you
look like a composite of all the other students, gives the school no reason to want
you there because you bring nothing different and therefore nothing special.
Saying that you really stand out, that you do not resemble any of the other students
in any relevant way, is similarly useless because you will be seen as too risky to have
in the program. If you really have nothing in common with people, the likelihood
of your not getting along with others in the program is high, as are your chances
of failing. The way to straddle this apparent divide is to fit in on certain key dimensions and be different on other specifics. Most people will tend to fall more on one
side of the divide than the other. The consultant need not worry that she will fail
to fit in; her problem is showing how she stands out. The photographer need not
worry about standing out; his problem is showing that he fits in.

MAXIMIZING THE IMPACT OF YOUR APPLICATION

The admissions director for a top business school is confronted with thousands
of applications for each class. He or she is meant to read the lengthy folders on

me jobs with descriptions
:s, and so forth, and uni-
ommendations, interview
it were not enough, every
n, there are applicants try-
e sights at an MBA fair, for
a top school's admissions
:ouple of minutes with the

eaning that they could suc-
get something useful from
is undifferentiated mass of
'd is to "position" yourself

[rotated text in torn region:] one. I enjoy going to stay with the people Jülich, which assists visiting scientists ing all I can about the history, geog- iends, however, I am able to see rather than as a tourist. have explored much of the of Japan. But the most (See essay 3b.)

directors your ity.

133

eal with this problem of too
many applicants trying to capture the a... dmissions directors who are
overwhelmed by the onslaught. To cut through all of this communications haze,
you must have a very sharp and clear image that is readily noticed and understood and valued.

Let's look at an example that is dear to my heart. There are many types of
whiskey, even of scotch whiskey. Nonetheless, there are a number of products
that are distinctively positioned in the market for scotch. For example,
Laphroaig is a single malt scotch with a peatier, more iodine taste (and "nose")
than its competitors. Its unique attributes allow it to market itself to consumers
who consider themselves beyond the "beginners'" scotches and who want the
strongest possible taste they can find. Macallan, on the other hand, is exceptionally smooth and even bears a certain resemblance to cognac. It tells consumers that its product is aged in old sherry casks, which impart a distinctive hint
of sherry in the nose.

These two products compete in the very high end of the scotch market, yet
each is positioned to be completely unique. Their marketing efforts aim to make
it very clear what key attributes they possess, and they are very successful. Both
are held in extremely high regard by serious malt scotch whiskey drinkers,
although they are considered virtually unrelated to one another. The result is
that each can claim a price premium for its distinctiveness that would be impossible were they positioned to compete head-to-head.

APPLYING THE CONCEPT TO YOURSELF

How does this apply to you? You must distinguish yourself from others in the applicant pool who may apply to the same schools you do. Business school applicants are not all the same; your job is to show your uniqueness. By appearing unique, you increase your value. After all, if you are the same as 2,500 other applicants, what school will really care if they get you rather than one of the other 2,500? By making yourself unique you also make yourself more memorable. Remaining anonymous will not help you. Far better if an admissions committee remembers you, perhaps even having a shorthand expression for use in discussing you. Being the "woman who runs the binational airport," as one of the people whose essays we include later in the book might have been characterized, means that you are remembered and can be discussed as a unique person. Contrast this with the sort of person who is discussed as "Which one is she? Really? Could I see that file again? I don't remember reading that one before."

JUXTAPOSITION

The easiest positioning effort, frankly, is simply to show that you have the traditional strengths of your category to an unusual degree, with none of the weaknesses. For example, if you are an accountant you can try to show that you are truly an exceptionally good accountant (the best in your cohort of thirty-seven at Deloitte's Chicago office), plus you are blessed with a sly sense of humor.

It is wonderful if you can take this one step further. If you happen to be a stand-up comedian who has played some of Chicago's professional clubs, you can show that you actually have two generally incompatible competencies. This juxtaposition of the unlikely (how many stand-up comics work as CPAs in their day jobs?) will certainly leap out at an admissions officer and make sure that you are remembered and viewed very favorably.

GENERAL POSITIONING VERSUS SPECIFIC POSITIONING

To what extent should your positioning be different for each target school? Since no two schools are exactly the same, you might want to position yourself differently for each school. On the other hand, doing markedly different applications for each school is a lot of extra work. Not only do you need to write your essays differently, but you also need to have your recommenders write each recommendation differently. For example, if you intend to apply to MIT to study manufacturing (to take advantage of its "Global Strategic Management in

Consulting") and to Kellogg, to study marketing (to take advantage of its well-known marketing curriculum), you will face the difficulty of being a persuasive applicant for both.

Take a modified approach; have a general positioning strategy that you can fine-tune to fit the needs of specific schools without making major changes in your application. Emphasize different aspects of your experience for a given school; don't try to recreate yourself for it. This assumes that you will not be applying to one school in order to do marketing and another in order to do manufacturing. (Obviously, if you have not yet resolved what you intend to do at business school and afterwards, you may need to do very different applications to each program.)

Any positioning approach that you take must be something that you can reinforce via specific, powerful examples.

THE MECHANICS OF POSITIONING: USING THEMES

Positioning is meant to provide a method for presenting a very clear picture of you. A simple way to achieve this is to use several *themes* to organize your material. When writing your essays, for example, relate all or at least most of your material to your chosen themes. If your material is organized around three or four themes, your positioning will be very clear and easy to grasp.

The themes you use will be different from those others will (or should) use. Because business schools are looking for some very definite features in all of their candidates, however, you should have one or two themes that other strong candidates will also use. Chapter 4, "Making the Most of Your Credentials," showed that schools are always concerned to find people who (1) are determined to succeed and (2) will profit from an MBA, now.

Business schools want people who will accomplish things, despite the inevitable obstacles they will encounter. Success in spite of difficulties is what determination is all about. At age 25 you might have had moderate success without having tried very hard or without having confronted substantial obstacles but this good fortune is unlikely to continue for your whole career. Thus you should show that you have accomplished things only after overcoming significant difficulties placed in your way.

Top schools believe that the education they offer is valuable, and they want to admit students who will get the full measure of this value. Such students are those who want an MBA for the right reasons and who are at the proper point in their lives and careers to get the most out of it. This is one reason schools want students with at least several years of work experience. Those with experience are likely to know where they would like to head in their careers and what they currently lack in order to achieve their goals. This means that they are able to appreciate what an MBA offers them. It also means that they will figure out how to maximize the benefit of a program by choosing the appropriate courses, making the right contacts, and marketing themselves effectively to potential future employers. Those who have not thought through their own futures, or who do not appreciate where their talents and interests lie, are not likely to maximize the benefits of an MBA and are thus likely to be rejected by the best schools. This means that you are obligated to show *your need for an MBA*—and that it is best done *now*.

The other organizing themes you choose will be those that are appropriate to you. The essays in the Appendix show some examples of what others have chosen; look at several of them from this perspective. In general, here are a few of the many possible themes around which you can organize parts of your application, and some idea of who might make use of them:

- Number-crunching analyst: World Bank economist
- Warm, loving "Saint Bernard": human resources consultant specializing in outplacement
- All-round synthesizer: as an architect you have had to bring together the work of various types of engineers, interior decorators, lawyers, accountants, city planners, and clients
- Functional specialist: you have become an expert in tax planning for international companies, utilizing triple-tiered corporate structures based in Liechtenstein, the Channel Islands, and the Caymans
- Polyglot: you speak five languages fluently, with substantial knowledge of multiple cultures
- From an unusual background: you lived five years in a nunnery
- Risk taker: your idea of fun is scuba diving in the North Sea—or your idea of how to earn a living is going short in developing markets

HOW MANY THEMES SHOULD YOU USE?

There are practical limitations to the number of themes that will help you. If you use too few, you have very little maneuvering room in writing your essays because everything has to fit with just one or two organizing themes. If you use too many, you end up doing no organizing whatsoever and your positioning will no longer be clear. The trick is to balance these two factors. Using *about four themes* is generally appropriate because with that number you do not constrain your efforts so much that you appear boring, but you are focused enough that admissions committees reading your applications will know what you are about. The key is that they should be able to summarize your positioning in three or four short phrases: you are determined; you need an MBA, now; you are a marvelous synthesizer; and, you are a real Saint Bernard. If this is what a committee comes away with, they have you pegged in just the way that will serve you best: you are an individual to them, yet one whom they can get a handle on.

THE ADMISSIONS DIRECTORS DISCUSS HOW YOU SHOULD MARKET YOURSELF

WHY MARKETING YOURSELF MATTERS

➤ If someone doesn't do a good job of presenting himself, he won't get in, despite having very good quantitative credentials. Just having good grades, GMAT and work experience won't get someone in. *Rob Garcia, MIT*

➤ It's rare that someone does a great job marketing himself. I assume that the majority of people applying are not one-dimensional drones, but too many come across that way. We have more than enough applicants with fine credentials to fill our classes several times over, but that is not enough. We want people who have personal strengths as well as paper strengths. What a delight to find someone who is lively, personable, engaging, and multidimensional. *Jon Megibow, Darden*

➤ Maybe 10 percent of people do a great job of marketing themselves; far more do a truly rotten job. *Henry Malin, Tuck*

➤ It's important that someone market himself well to us because ultimately he'll have to be able to do the same thing in marketing himself to employers. So we consider his marketing efforts carefully. We don't want graduates who will be unable to market themselves. *Connie Tai, Rotterdam*

MARKETING ADVICE

➤ People often do not look at the total picture they're presenting. Oftentimes the different pieces simply don't fit. The essays should fit together. If there are themes which someone wants to emphasize he should make sure that they stand out. *James Millar, Harvard*

➤ Prepare ahead of time. Most applicants fail to think through the process as they should. For example, it is important to be sure that this school is right for you, because that fact tends to come through in your application and substantially influences the decision. *Don Martin, Chicago*

➤ A lot of people are afraid to reveal themselves but I think they'd be surprised by the number of things that might help them: what they've gone through, their struggles, how they've gotten to where they are, are all important. People hide those, but I think that how anybody got to where they are is important. *Brian Sorge, Kellogg*

➤ The people who do the most impressive job of marketing themselves are the people who know what LBS is all about. These are the people who've been through the school literature, but also talked to alumni, current students, and faculty. They've visited the school or, if unable to do that, have made themselves fully aware of what the program is about. They've read the general literature to educate themselves about what to look for. The worst applications are from people who feel they're rushed and can't take the time to do the research and don't really even know what the MBA is about. *Claire Harniman, London*

➤ The ones who impress are the ones who have thought about who they are, what they want, what an MBA can give them, and above all about the links between these things. Therefore they can be precise and to the point, even in interviews. So it's not just somebody who has a stunning undergraduate or employment history up to now, which sits there isolated. It's the person who convinces us that they are thoughtful and reflective about what they want out of an MBA and have thought about what aspects of themselves fit, and what aspects don't, and are able to explain both. *Julia Tyler, London*

LYING/INCONSISTENCY

➤ We have such a thorough application process that when we have a complete file we have: the individual telling us about himself—how he sees himself; through the recommendations we've got input from people who know him well; then we've got the interview with someone who may not know him well, but does know INSEAD well and they tell us about him. We can quickly see whether there's any inconsistency in the file. We no longer see much lying—much less than we used to. *Carol Giraud, INSEAD (Paris region)*

A SIMPLE POSITIONING EFFORT

"I always loved science, beginning in childhood. The only courses I loved in high school were hard sciences and math, so I ended up becoming a research scientist. I worked as a research chemist. My dedication—a willingness to work extremely hard to finish work on time—came to the attention of my boss who started to use me as a project manager. He valued my combination of technical ability and sociability; I got on well with the other researchers in the lab. I have enjoyed this project management work, but I would like it more if I felt that I had the managerial tools to do the job as well as possible. I therefore would like to get an MBA sooner rather than later."

The paragraph above is a no-frills positioning effort. It is not meant to be a realistic essay someone would write in describing her career to date, future goals, and reasons for wanting an MBA. Instead, it is meant to illustrate that it is possible in a very short space to develop some important organizing themes. We know, in just a few short lines, that this woman is a good scientist who intends to remain involved with scientific efforts. She is a determined worker also. We know that an MBA would be appropriate for her, and that she could make good use of

MBA skills immediately. This miniportrait thus shows several clear themes: technical specialization, determination, and a pressing need for an MBA. It also show a logical progression to her career. In other words, she has the fundamentals of her positioning effort already in place.

THE MARKETING VEHICLES

You have three primary vehicles for getting your message across to business schools: the essays, recommendations, and interviews. You will need to be consistent within and across these three vehicles to gain the maximum positive impact. The following chapters will show you how to make the most of them.

CONCLUSION

The penalty for failing to capitalize on your strengths and to prepare a powerful application is, all too often, rejection. Schools have plenty of qualified applicants who took the time to figure out the process and to do a good application. Failure to do these things suggests that you are not able to do so, or at least do not care to. In either case, you are unlikely to be viewed as showing top management potential, at least at the moment.

Your application to a top business school will be read differently from the application of an eighteen-year-old for a part-time job. You are competing with the best and the brightest of several continents to get into programs that offer great benefits to those who succeed. The competition for these positions is intense, and the business schools feel justified in expecting high quality applications. Given that the applicants are expected to have some prior work experience, and that they are applying to graduate programs in business, business schools expect that applicants will have at least a reasonable idea of how to market themselves. They also expect applicants to treat the process seriously insofar as the program will take up to two years of the person's life and affect his or her earning potential and career choices forever.

9

UNDERSTANDING THE KEY ESSAY TOPICS

— EXECUTIVE SUMMARY —

■

Familiarize yourself with the topics you need to address.

■

Learn how to use the essays to market yourself effectively

■

Avoid the numerous traps that are built into the essays.

*O*ne leading business school states, "While we believe that previous academic records and standardized test results are useful tools for (our) evaluation, we find several less quantifiable indicators to be of equal or greater importance. Please keep this in mind as you complete the questions. . . . Use these short essays to show us your personality, motivation, goals, leadership abilities, and communication skills." (IESE, Barcelona)

Essays offer you the chance to show schools who you really are. Take advantage of this opportunity. Recommenders can show only a part of who you are, since most of them are instructors or employers and have thus seen you in only one context. Similarly, interviews are not under your control to the same extent as the essays, which can be rewritten and reexamined to make sure that the "real you" is presented.

Rather than imagining that an ultraserious admissions committee is going to read your application, imagine that a pleasant chap with a glass of port in one hand is examining your essays, hoping to find something that distinguishes you and makes it possible for him to know you even without having met you.

Your essays can and should present a clear picture of you, but they do not need to tell all. Sketching in the main points with appropriate stories will show who you are. In fact, whenever possible, try to tell a story rather than write an essay. The task will seem lighter.

This is your chance to choose which parts of your past and yourself to highlight, and to determine how people should view them. This is a precious opportunity; take full advantage of the chance to color your readers' interpretations.

This chapter analyzes the essay questions; the following chapter shows you how to write your responses. 115 examples of actual essays written by applicants are available in the Appendix. The chart at the beginning of the Appendix shows where to find specific examples, classified by the background of the applicant, the school applied to, and, of course, the specific question asked.

QUESTION:
WHAT ARE YOUR CAREER OBJECTIVES
AND REASONS FOR WANTING AN MBA?

WHY THE QUESTION IS ASKED

Schools ask this question for a number of reasons. They want to make sure that you have given substantial thought to your future career. They want to see that an MBA fits with the future that you envision for yourself. They want to understand why now is the time. Although schools will not, for reasons of political correctness, confess to this on the record, I believe that they are especially desirous of finding women who will not retire from the workforce for long periods to raise a family. Top schools want people who will get to the top of the business world, so anyone who looks likely to drop out of business *for whatever reason* will be viewed as suspect.

THE TYPICAL APPLICANT

Many people apply to business schools because they are unhappy with their current situations and are hoping to do virtually anything as long as it is different from what they currently do. Too many of them have no idea of where they are heading, just what they are running from. Their response to this question tends to show that they do not have a realistic career plan. They either describe their hoped-for jobs in vague, rosy terms, saying that they hope to find something liberating, empowering, with substantial responsibilities and high pay, or they mention a popular career like investment banking, for which nothing in their past even remotely qualifies them.

Other applicants discuss the virtues of an MBA, including the fact that it can increase graduates' skills, salaries, and career options, which the reader in the admissions office knows quite well in any case.

A BETTER APPROACH

This is a truly critical essay. You will be manifestly unsuccessful in writing the other essays if you have not thought carefully about your future career. It will be extremely helpful to know where you are heading when you try to answer many of the other essay questions. Start with this essay. Do not go on to the other questions until you have completed—at a minimum—a good draft of this essay.

The place to start is obvious: what do you want to be, now that you are all grown up? If you do not currently know with any degree of assurance, explore the possibilities by consulting the relevant career literature and discussing the possibilities with family and friends. Only after you have settled on an approximate goal will you be truly ready to apply for an MBA. This does not mean that you must be certain of where you are headed, but you should, at a minimum, be able to articulate several possibilities that you intend to explore and that are clearly related to your experiences, strengths and weaknesses, and likes and dislikes. Show that you are being realistic in your planning.

Once you know in general terms where you are headed, how does an MBA fit into your plans? In other words, what is it that you need from an MBA program in order to get where you want to go? There are innumerable reasons that would be quite sensible for wanting an MBA. For example, perhaps you want additional:

- General management perspective
- Understanding of various functional areas
- Knowledge of one specific area (although this might be better served by doing a specialized master's degree rather than the inherently more generalist MBA)
- Exposure to people from different backgrounds (cultural, functional, etc.)
- Understanding of for-profit (rather than nonprofit) firms
- Knowledge of business approaches beyond your own industry
- Understanding of analytical techniques not readily learned on the job

Perhaps you seek to advance in an industry that requires people to eventually jump from a nonbusiness area to the management side of the business. You might be knowledgeable about directing plays, for instance, but want to be able to run a theater; or you wish to gracefully jump from one segment of the business world to another—for instance, from marketing to finance, or from the creative side of a corporation to business management.

The next point is to show that an MBA is right for you *now*, not in several years. The younger you are, the more likely this is to be a critical issue. Standard reasons for wanting an MBA now are:

- You have reached a natural break in your career. For example, you are about to finish a four year tour of duty in the Navy.

- You cannot progress further in your career without one. In some fields, for instance management consulting, this might be more an issue of needing to have your "ticket punched" than needing the actual knowledge, but it is a well understood reason nonetheless.

- You could progress without one, but you would do so much more slowly than you would with an MBA.

- You are involved in a family business, and need to take over the reins sooner rather than later.

Take the approach that you have already had substantial accomplishments but that you could nonetheless go much further, faster, if you had an MBA (and the sooner the better). Above all, do not make it sound as though you know little and have done less.

Be sure that you tie this specific school's offerings to your needs, to show that you know and value the fine points of this program.

ADVANTAGES OF THIS APPROACH

Our approach will allow you to show that you know where you are going and that you therefore have a good chance of actually getting there. It will also show you to be sensible concerning what should be a matter of great concern to you—your career. Failure to demonstrate clear thinking about this will mark you as someone not ready for an MBA. You are likely to miss out on a great deal of the value of an MBA if you do not know what you want out of it, which depends upon where you are headed. Similarly, showing the admissions committee that you have not been serious in thinking about where you are headed suggests that you may not even be serious about business, which is likely to be particularly damaging if you are, say, an arts graduate working in the nonprofit sector at the moment.

QUESTION:
WHAT WOULD YOU CONTRIBUTE
WHILE AT OUR SCHOOL?

WHY THE QUESTION IS ASKED

Schools want to know what you consider a "contribution." They also want to have certain skills and experiences represented in the student body. This essay gives you a chance to show what you bring to the mix.

THE TYPICAL APPLICANT

The typical applicant mentions a set of boilerplate. First, he claims that he is a very hard worker. Next, he says that he will try to contribute to class discussions, and the fact that he is an accountant will be very valuable in this regard. Last, if he is really thinking hard, he may note that he is a good guy whose company will be enjoyed by one and all.

A BETTER APPROACH

The first step is to show that you will fit into the school's student body. In other words, you are not hopelessly strange. You have the attributes normally expected of top managers, such as intelligence and determination. In addition, you are accustomed to dealing with others like you and you have typically compared favorably with them. In other words, you will not be intimidated by your classmates.

   The second step is to show that you would add something valuable to the workings of the school. These workings are not just in class, but equally important outside of class. Thus, your being able to work well on a team, and in a study group or project team, will be useful here. The usual things that applicants mention are worth noting in passing but should not be the focus of your effort if you can find something more interesting to discuss. The "usual" includes:

- Knowledge of industry A, technology B, function C
- Computing skills
- A second language
- Personal characteristics: sense of humor, likeability, determination

Each of these can be worthwhile, but they are best not dwelt upon unless you possess them to an unusual degree. For instance, one of the candidates ("Joerg") whose essays we reprint in the prior chapter and in the Appendix notes that his engineering skills are of a very high order indeed. He can say this because the breadth and depth of his knowledge were extraordinary. (He was finishing a PhD in mechanical engineering from Germany's finest program, had done top-flight work in testing the shape stability of fibers, and had significant assignments in North America, Japan, and Africa as well as in various parts of Europe. Comparatively speaking, someone with a bachelor's degree and three years of experience in reverse-engineering widgets might be better served looking for something else to emphasize.)

Unusual items that you could emphasize might include:

- A different perspective. Are you from an unusual part of the world (at least insofar as where most of this particular school's students come from)? Have you worked with unusual people, for instance workers with disabilities?

- Knowledge of an unusual industry, technology, or function. Consultants, engineers, and accountants are, if anything, overrepresented in MBA programs, but professional tennis players and jazz musicians are not.

- Unusual work conditions. Perhaps you are a corporate strategy firm research associate, which is a common position for an applicant, but you have done your cost analysis work for a client brewery in Lagos rather than Milwaukee.

- Personal qualities that are all too rare, such as a sterling sense of humor. But you will need to back this up with solid evidence.

- Unusual outside interests. A person who has published a successful book, been ranked in squash, started a successful part-time business, or whatever, has something unusual to talk about. *You* might not think any of these things are significant, but you are probably better off at least mentioning them than dwelling upon the fact that you are yet another junior accountant. For example, you might think that being a top squash player is irrelevant, but remember that one U.S. Supreme Court Associate Justice allegedly chose his clerks largely in the light of skill on the basketball court. While idiosyncratic, this is by no means atypical.

Remember, too, that a skill that might be considered typical at MIT might be quite rare elsewhere.

The last component of this essay is to show that you are the sort of person who will share knowledge with others in the program. In other words, you are the sort of person who will work well with other people and value their contributions, too.

ADVANTAGES OF THIS APPROACH

A knowledge of what distinguishes you from other applicants is particularly important in answering this question. What you would contribute to a program is best answered by thinking not of the skills many of your peers share but those that seem uniquely yours. Doing so will allow you to appeal to schools hoping to diversify their student bodies on as many dimensions as is possible.

QUESTION:
WHAT DO YOU HOPE TO GAIN
FROM OUR PROGRAM?

WHY THE QUESTION IS ASKED

This question is meant to reveal how you view an MBA program and degree. Are you thinking of it narrowly or broadly? Do you have a clear reason for wanting an MBA yourself?

THE TYPICAL APPLICANT

Too many people mention the amount of money they will make after they have their MBA. Others describe the technical skill or skills they will acquire. And many just mouth the platitudes of how marvelous MBA degrees are, as if trying to convince the admissions staff of this fact.

A BETTER APPROACH

Treat this essay just like the "why do you want an MBA, and why from our school" questions. Start by explaining what you hope to accomplish in your career and what you lack in order to do so. Show how an MBA will help you acquire some or many of the skills and other assets you lack, thus helping you to reach your goals. Then note how this program in particular will be most appropriate for you in addressing these needs. Make it clear that you will gain more from this program than others because it best fits your needs.

Do not stop there, however, because if you do you will make it seem that you are so unworldly as to think that a top-quality MBA program is nothing more than a skill transfer mechanism. In fact, as this book has emphasized, you will gain from the credential itself and the network you can tap into. You can expect to have career opportunities open up to you that someone without a top MBA will never have. And, yes, you can expect to make more money. The problem, however, is to show that you are savvy enough to appreciate the many career benefits offered by a top MBA without looking like a greedy creature intent upon nothing more than maximizing his or her salary. The best way to do this may be to note the ancillary benefits of the school's network without talking about the money or credentials.

ADVANTAGES OF THIS APPROACH

Following this approach will make it clear that you have a well-considered reason for getting an MBA. It fits into your own career scheme and is not something you are pursuing just because it is trendy to do so, or because you need your "ticket punched." It will also be clear that you have thought through your choice of school.

QUESTION:
WHY HAVE YOU APPLIED TO THE
OTHER SCHOOLS YOU HAVE?

WHY THE QUESTION IS ASKED

Schools typically ask this question to learn two things. First, they want to learn how much you value their school relative to others you might be considering. And second, they want to understand how much you value an MBA.

THE TYPICAL APPLICANT

Most applicants make one of several mistakes. Some applicants tell Bentley College that they are applying to Harvard and MIT. Bentley College is a good school, but it does not realistically expect applicants to choose it over Harvard or MIT. Listing these other Boston area schools tells Bentley that he or she does not really want to attend it, that it is just a backup in case Harvard and MIT both say no. Bentley is unlikely to get excited about such applicants. If an applicant tells Harvard that she is applying to Bentley College, Harvard is likely to conclude that she does not really see herself as being of Harvard quality and that she does not have the self confidence necessary for a top program.

Other applicants reveal that they are not certain of what they want from their MBA education by listing very different types of schools. Applying to both Harvard and Darden, two case method schools that educate general managers, makes sense, but applying to Harvard and Theseus, the French school devoted to training telecommunications managers, suggests that the applicant has not yet decided what he is seeking.

A different type of mistake is made when someone states that he is applying to school X and no other, for fear of offending school X. If an applicant has good reasons for wanting an MBA, it is highly likely that more than one school will serve his needs quite well. If this is the case, he will be determined enough to want to go to any of a number of schools. Failing to list other schools, therefore, suggests that he is not really serious about getting an MBA.

Another mistake is made when applicants simply state that school X is the best, famous for its (fill in the blank), and is what they have always hoped to attend. This is a mistake insofar as it represents a missed opportunity to market oneself.

A BETTER APPROACH

Start by showing what you need in order to meet your goals. For example, perhaps you are an experienced sales representative who wishes to move into general management. Despite your knowledge of sales, you do not know much about accounting, finance, strategy, organizational development, or the international aspects of business; you may be looking to acquire substantial skills in these areas. Depending upon the kind of company, and industry, you are aiming for, some of these areas are likely to be much more important than others. Thus your pitch might be:

My goal: work for my current firm, but in general management

What I am lacking: general management skills, especially in finance, marketing, and strategy

Then show how school X will be right for you. You do this by showing how it meets your requirements. If you want to become a consumer marketer, note that school X has a host of relevant courses. What besides course offerings might be important to you? You might choose on the basis of the languages used at the school, the nature of the student body (age, functional backgrounds, etc.), the reputation of a specific department—and thus the quality and number of companies looking to recruit, say, consumer marketers from the school. Refer to our earlier discussion about how to choose a school.

Apply these factors to the other schools you are considering. Note that each school will be acceptable in terms of meeting the bulk of what you are looking for, but note also that school X is more desirable insofar as it offers more consumer marketing courses or whatever. It is unlikely that any one school will be the most desirable on all counts, which gives you the opportunity to say good things about each school in terms of how it meets your needs. Your conclusion, however, should emphasize the factors that favor school X, thereby putting it at the top of your list.

ADVANTAGES OF THIS APPROACH

This approach will help make it clear that you are serious about getting an MBA. In addition, it shows that you have researched this and other schools; it reinforces your seriousness about getting an MBA at the same time that it shows you to be a sensible decision-maker gathering data for this important decision. This approach also shows that you value school X, and for substantial reasons—because it better meets your needs than do other schools.

QUESTION: IN WHAT OTHER WAY WILL YOU PURSUE YOUR DEVELOPMENT IF OUR SCHOOL REJECTS YOU?

WHY THE QUESTION IS ASKED

This question helps schools determine two things about you first, how carefully you have planned for your future, and second, how determined you are to succeed.

THE TYPICAL APPLICANT

The typical applicant notes that he will reapply next year if school X turns him down this year.

A BETTER APPROACH

The starting point is to state what your goals are, and what you lack in order to meet them. (For a full discussion of this, refer to the "Why Have You Applied to the Other Schools You Have" analysis.) This will help to demonstrate that you have given serious thought to your future career.

Your needs can probably be met, at least to a reasonable degree, by another MBA program. You will thus almost certainly note that you are applying to other schools.

You should also consider whether some part-time educational programs would meet at least some of your needs. A local school's offering of introductory marketing courses may not suffice to make you into a crack consumer marketer, but they will almost certainly be better than nothing.

Another possibility may be training programs that your company offers. Or, you could shift jobs (either within your company or by switching companies), in order to learn about a different function or even a different industry. As you will recall from our discussion of why to get an MBA, further job experience is not likely to provide you with the conceptual understanding that is part and parcel of an MBA. Companies seldom feature lectures on quantitative methods for managers or applications of the capital asset pricing model. MBA programs are set up to increase dramatically your intellectual capital, whereas companies are set up to make money, preferably sooner rather than later. A new position or company is not likely to provide you with all that you hope to get from an MBA program, but something is better than nothing.

The last option is self-study. You can always read the interesting popular books in a given field or, better yet, the textbooks used at business schools. This is a difficult way to learn, however, and it is unlikely that you will be able to learn advanced quantitative methods in this fashion.

The conclusion is always that you would prefer to get an MBA, but you will do whatever you can to gain as much knowledge as possible.

ADVANTAGES OF THIS APPROACH

This approach shows that you have considered your future with care. It also shows that you are hungry for improvement in your knowledge and skills, and that you are determined to succeed and action-oriented. If going to school X will not work you will go to school Y. If you cannot go to a top school you will look to learn on this or another job. The picture that you convey is therefore one of a person striving to reach his or her potential. Remember that you are applying to an educational institution, so showing that you are hungry for knowledge and determined to improve yourself by acquiring it is a "can't miss" proposition.

QUESTION:
DESCRIBE YOUR CURRENT JOB

WHY THE QUESTION IS ASKED

This question may not help schools assess the candidacies of, for example, research associates from McKinsey because the admissions committee already knows what the typical McKinsey R.A. does. For people in less familiar positions, however, this question enables a much clearer understanding of an applicant's background.

THE TYPICAL APPLICANT

Most applicants simply list a few of the elements of their formal job descriptions or just list their job titles. If you were to say simply that you were a marketing associate for a computer firm, an admissions committee would know almost nothing about your responsibilities. Do you provide field support? Do you do on-line research only? Do you do competitor analysis? Do you liaise with the research and development staffs in the development of more user-friendly products? Do you analyze the productivity of different advertising media or promotional campaigns? What do you *do?*

A BETTER APPROACH

There are usually numerous elements to a given job. You must figure out and list the many things you do. Next, you must determine which are the most significant parts of your job and which are most consistent with the position you are attempting to communicate, and then characterize them as favorably as possible. The following should help you with this process.

Is your job important? Most people would say so only if they are egotists or are making a lot of money and enjoying a very impressive title (Senior Executive Vice President for Marketing and Strategy, perhaps).

Assuming that you are not in this situation, does this mean that your job is unimportant and that you will have to be apologizing for it? No, of course not. A job is of real importance under a number of different circumstances. In particular, work gains significance whenever two things are true about it. First, the degree of uncertainty is high, and second, the potential impact upon the firm's success is great. In other words, is there a fair likelihood that an average-quality performer in your job would make a hash of things? And, if so, would that really affect your firm's performance, or that of one of its components? If the answer to both of these questions is yes, then your job is of real importance.

What must you do to perform successfully? In other words, what challenges do you face? For example, if you are in sales support, one of your biggest headaches might be to get the junior people in marketing, who report directly to the regional marketing manager, and report on only a dotted-line basis to the regional sales manager, to provide the current competitor analysis material to the sales department. This can be characterized as a liaison role. Or, if the relationship is particularly poor, you might describe your role as conflict resolution—particularly in light of the fact that sales and marketing often have an antagonistic relationship.

Perhaps your greatest challenges are satisfying two different bosses with two completely different agendas. If you are in a matrix structure, reporting to the regional manager and an engineering director, you can expect to be unable to please either one. The regional manager is probably concerned with making money, today, and wants everyone to work as a team without regard to functional specialties. The engineering boss, on the other hand, wants her people to maintain their specialized skills and the prestige of the engineering department. Working on cross-functional teams without taking time out for updating technical skills may strike the former as standard practice and the latter as anathema. To perform your job well may require balancing these conflicting desires.

If the last two occupants of your job were fired, say so. This will make your performance look all the more impressive.

A number of other circumstances can lend importance to a job. The more senior the person you report to, the more important a job will look. Similarly, the fate of prior occupants of your job may be relevant. If the last occupants were promoted high in the organization, the job will appear to be one given to high-fliers, thereby increasing its significance.

Have your recommenders discuss these points, too.

What is the nature of your work? There are many different types of work. A market researcher is generally doing analytical work. A brand manager is likely to be doing a combination of analytical work and influence work insofar as she must analyze the factors for the brand's relative success or failure in different market and competitive conditions in her country, and then try to influence the manufacturing, packaging, or whatever department, to take the action she wants in order to address these factors. She typically will have no power over these departments and will have to rely on her influence skills (personality, reasoning, expertise, etc.) instead. A restaurant manager will probably be most concerned with managing people, whereas a technical manager may be most concerned with the management of physical processes.

Many other aspects of your work can also be characterized. Is your job like being in the army: crushing boredom interspersed with brief moments of sheer terror? Are you expected to perform at a steady pace to a predictable schedule or do you work like a tax accountant, 50 percent of whose work may take place in three months of the year? Are you supposed to be the steadying hand for a bunch of youngsters? Are you supposed to be a creative type who will respond flexibly to each new situation rather than simply referring to the corporate manual?

Do you supervise anyone? How many people, of what type, are under your supervision? What does this supervision consist of? For example, are you in charge of direct marketing activities, necessitating that you monitor the phone calls of your direct reports and also analyze their performance versus budget and various economic and industry factors?

Do you have control of a budget? If so, what is the amount you control, and what amount do you influence?

What results have you achieved? Results can be looked at from many different perspectives. From a strategic perspective, what have you achieved regarding the market, customers, and competitors? From a financial perspective, what have you done regarding costs, revenues, and profits (not to mention assets employed, etc.)? From an operational perspective, what have you done regarding productivity of your unit, or of your direct reports, or of yourself; what have you done regarding the percentage of items rejected, or bids that fail, and so on? Similarly, from an organizational perspective, have you taken steps such as altering the formal organization or introducing new integration or coordination mechanisms? Provide numbers whenever possible to buttress your claims.

How has your career evolved? Did you have a career plan in place before graduating from college or university or soon thereafter? If so, did you pursue it wholeheartedly? Did it include a focus on developing your skills and responsibilities? What, if anything, has altered your original plan? What was your reaction to events that altered or affirmed this plan? When dealing with the development of your job with a given employer, be sure to note the employer's *reasons* for promoting, transferring, rewarding, or praising you as well as the *fact* of these things.

ADVANTAGES OF THIS APPROACH

It is important to take this question very seriously. The answers will provide you with much of the ammunition you will use in responding to other questions. Your current job is of inherent interest to business schools. They will always want to know what you are doing, and with what success, because that suggests a great deal about your talents and interests, the way your employer views your talents and attitude, and why you might want an MBA.

Taking a broad view of the job description enables you to put the best light on your responsibilities and performance. It also allows you to build the basis for later essays where you will be able to save space by referring to this write-up rather than listing the same things when space is at a premium.

QUESTION:
DESCRIBE YOUR WORK EXPERIENCE

WHY THE QUESTION IS ASKED

This question is, of course, intended to elicit what you have done over the course of your career, what impact you have had. It is also designed to give you an opportunity to show what you have learned about yourself and your abilities.

THE TYPICAL APPLICANT

Most applicants simply list what they have done in the past without showing what has driven their career choices and changes. The result is a list in which the elements appear nearly unrelated to one another.

A BETTER APPROACH

Look at our discussion of the "Job Description" essay. Then think in terms of telling stories rather than simply listing events dryly. A good story has conflict; that is, it has obstacles placed in the way of the hero. The hero may be unable to overcome each of the obstacles, but he tries hard and is unwilling to give up.

One possible approach is as follows. Find a theme that unites the elements of your job history. For instance, you show how you responded to challenges that were initially daunting. You tried hard and learned how to do what was required. As you learned better how to do the job, you started to take more initiative. In fact, once you mastered your initial responsibilities, you understood them in a broader context. Having done so, you moved up to the next level of responsibility—or you are now at the point of needing further scope for your talents but cannot move up without an MBA or years of experience on the job.

The telling of your career story should focus upon where you have come from and where you are now headed. If you have changed your direction, explain what happened to change your direction. If you have had your decisions reaffirmed by experience, describe them and how they convinced you that you were on the right track.

This essay is closely related to the "Your Career and the Reasons for Getting an MBA" essay.

ADVANTAGES OF THIS APPROACH

Telling stories that focus on obstacles and the attempt to overcome them makes this essay interesting to read. Focusing on your personal development in response to challenges is well aimed for an audience of educators. They are preconditioned to appreciate your developmental capabilities.

This approach also sets up your need for an MBA. You have been overcoming obstacles by learning how to perform new jobs, and you have acquired new skills and knowledge; now you need to take another step up.

WHAT ONE CHANGE WOULD YOU MAKE IN YOUR CURRENT JOB (AND HOW WOULD YOU IMPLEMENT THIS CHANGE)?

WHY THE QUESTION IS ASKED

This question is designed to reveal how savvy you are about organizational matters and how analytical you are about your company's operating and strategic needs.

You may be too junior to have run a department or a company, but that should not stop you from thinking about its operations and environment. How much perspective do you have on these things? Can you write a persuasive analytical piece showing that you have been able to step back from your own tasks to take a more senior manager's view? If not—if you can see only your own job's details—you are missing a chance to show that you are in fact senior management material.

THE TYPICAL APPLICANT

Most applicants fail to define what this question is really asking. The question itself is open to several interpretations. For example, does it ask you to improve things for you or for your company? How realistic must you be in your suggestion? Must this be an aspect you can indeed change, rather than something that only a very senior manager could affect? All too many applicants end up interpreting the question to mean, "How can *you* make your own job easier to do?" Consequently, they make themselves look self-centered and concerned only about the minutiae of their jobs, since any meaningful change would require someone else's intervention.

Virtually all applicants run into the implied follow-up question: If this proposed change is such a good idea, why haven't you done all you could to implement it? Failing to answer this can make an applicant look hypocritical or ineffectual. If he claims that a change in the pattern of his sales calls will dramatically improve his results, why has he never tried to convince his boss of this? Is it that he does not really care about the company's success or that he cannot imagine persuading his boss to make any change? In either case, the force of the applicant's suggestion is diminished by failing to address this issue.

A BETTER APPROACH

Focus on the benefits for the company rather than personal benefits. In other words, show that the reason the change makes sense is that the company's balance sheet will improve, or some other equally important advantage will accrue, not that your job will become easier.

You may have spotted only one change the company should make. If so, you should certainly discuss it. On the other hand, if you have several possibilities, choose the one that will best do the following:

■ support your positioning effort, including your current need for an MBA (which can be shown by suggesting that you have outgrown your current responsibilities)

■ show that you are thinking about how your job relates to others

If you do not have any obvious changes in mind, how can you develop some? For one thing, you can look at the examples of this essay included in the Appendix. Beyond this, consider the following possibilities:

■ Should the nature of your *reporting relationship* be changed? For example, perhaps you report to a regional manager but would be better off reporting to a functional one. Or perhaps you are matrixed—reporting to two different bosses in different departments—and the matrix structure is preventing decisions being reached in a timely fashion. If so, simplifying the reporting relationship might be appropriate.

- Should the nature of your *responsibility* be changed? For example, are you currently responsible for revenues but not costs, or assets employed? Should you have complete profit and loss (or return on assets employed) responsibility?

- Should the various *control systems* be harmonized? For example, perhaps the accounting systems are designed to control one thing whereas your bonus is tied to something contradictory.

If you are describing proposed changes in, say, the design of your job or the way in which you are evaluated or controlled, you will want to show that the current standards cause suboptimal performance in a way that your proposed change will not. You may also need to show that the proposed change will not lead to new problems or that any such problems will not be as large as the ones currently faced.

Deal with the implementation issue head-on. In other words, answer the implicit follow-up question as to why, if this change is such a good idea, you have not yet made it happen. Maybe you have just learned of the need for this change, in which case you have not had the time to do anything about it. For example, maybe you just started this job, or you have just gotten new responsibilities; or perhaps a recent problem first exposed the need for change. Another possibility is that you have been aware of the problem for some time but have been engaged in gathering the necessary data to analyze the situation fully.

The question's phrasing is hypothetical: "What change would you make?" This seems to eliminate the possibility of discussing a change that you have recently made. In fact, business schools would love to have you discuss a change you have actually enacted; the only reason that they phrase the question thus is because so few applicants have a real example to talk about. If you have actually implemented a substantial, praiseworthy change, by all means discuss it.

ADVANTAGES OF THIS APPROACH

This approach shows that your primary concern is the company's welfare. It also shows that you have analyzed your environment and are aware of the areas of weakness and strength. Using a real example is better than using a hypothetical one insofar as it shows that you actually take action and have an impact.

QUESTION:
WHAT ARE YOUR STRENGTHS AND WEAKNESSES?

WHY THE QUESTION IS ASKED

This question is clearly designed to elicit your opinion of yourself. Modest people, and people from cultures less egocentric than that of the United States, have a hard time responding, because it obviously asks you to brag a little. Less self-assured applicants find it hard to be honest and to mention their shortcomings. This question provides a good gauge of how self confident (or arrogant), accomplished (or boastful), decent (or manipulative), mature, self-aware, and honest you are.

THE TYPICAL APPLICANT

Most applicants list a large number of strengths and one or two weaknesses. Their weakness is generally a strength dressed up as a weakness ("I am too much of a perfectionist." "I work too hard.").

A BETTER APPROACH

Start by choosing two or three primary strengths. Use these to organize your essay by grouping other strengths around them. For example, if you claim that you are very *determined,* you might discuss your *patience* in working hard for a long time in order to achieve something important as related to this determination. The problem is not generally finding something good to say about yourself. Usually the problem is limiting yourself to a manageable number of strengths. You want to have few enough that you can discuss them in a persuasive fashion rather than just listing them. Using two or three as central organizing devices (i.e., themes) helps to achieve this.

Remember that simply listing strengths is a very weak way of writing. To make your strengths credible and memorable, use illustrations of them. Instead of bragging about being determined, note your five-year battle to overcome childhood leukemia.

The bigger problem, however, is finding a weakness to discuss. Simply calling a strength a weakness ("I work too hard") is not sufficient. This tactic is used by countless applicants, and its insincerity is nearly guaranteed to repel those reading your essays. For one thing, *you have failed to follow instructions;* you were asked to list a weakness and failed to do so. In addition, a failure to recognize your own weaknesses means that you are blind to something very important. It is far better to recognize your weaknesses and thus be in a position to try to overcome them than to pretend that they do not exist. If you recognize that a weakness exists, you are in a position to make a constructive change. Being willing to discuss a weakness is thus a sign of maturity, and, consequently, a strength in itself.

Do not carry a good thing too far, though, and discuss huge flaws such as your drug addictions. Your choice of a flaw may depend upon exactly how the question is phrased. If you are asked for a weakness, you can certainly discuss the lack of skills or knowledge that currently limit your managerial success and that have occasioned your desire for an MBA. This is an easy version of the question. The hard version asks you about your *personality* strengths and weaknesses. The focus on your personality means that you cannot simply respond by discussing what skills you want to acquire. To respond to this you must discuss a true personality flaw. One approach is to look at the dark side of one of your strengths. If you are a very determined person, does that mean that your drive is accompanied by a terrible temper? Or perhaps it means that you are too willing to trample upon peers' feelings? If you are a strong leader, does that mean that you do not always value the inputs of your subordinates? If you have been very successful doing detail-laden work, have you overlooked the big picture? Are you so concerned about quality that you find it overly difficult to delegate or share responsibility?

Be sure to avoid discussing a weakness that will be a major handicap at a given school. For example, if you are applying to a quantitatively oriented program, be leery of talking about your difficulties with numbers.

Be careful to discuss your weakness differently from your strengths. The correct space allocation is probably about three- or four-to-one, strengths to weakness. You will note that I say "weakness," because you should discuss only one or two weaknesses. When doing so, do not dwell on your description of it, or of the problems that it has caused you. Do so briefly, thereby limiting the impact that the specifics will have upon admissions officers. Then note what steps you take, or have taken, to try to overcome it.

You want to describe yourself as having numerous strengths that relate well to your positioning effort, without sounding arrogant.

ADVANTAGES OF THIS APPROACH

Grouping your strengths in an organized fashion will give you the chance to cover a lot of ground without taking a scattershot approach. Emphasizing strengths is obviously appropriate. Writing about them in some detail, with appropriate illustrations, will make them memorable. The use of illustrations also makes your claims realistic rather than boastful.

Describing your weakness in a cursory way, and being detailed about the steps you take to overcome the weakness, will gain you points. It shows you to be willing to face up to your flaw without the flaw itself being emphasized. This offers you the best of both worlds.

QUESTION:
WHAT ARE YOUR MOST SUBSTANTIAL
ACCOMPLISHMENTS?

WHY THE QUESTION IS ASKED

This question obviously gives you a chance to "blow your own horn." You can brag a bit about what you have accomplished in life. Moreover, you have the chance to put your own spin on what you have done. A particular accomplishment is all the more impressive when you explain the obstacles you had to overcome in order to succeed.

The question also allows schools to learn more about you insofar as you must explain why you consider something to have been a substantial accomplishment. Some accomplishments are of obvious significance. Winning the Nobel Prize for Physics is obviously significant; you probably do not need to elaborate on the fact of having won it. Other accomplishments are much more personal. For example, if you had stuttered as a youth and finally ended your stuttering in your twenties, this might be an extremely significant accomplishment for you personally. You have probably done things that have had more impact upon the rest of the world, but for you this accomplishment looms larger. You will probably want to talk about it as an example of your determination and desire to improve yourself. This essay gives you the chance to do so.

This question gives you an opportunity to discuss matters that are unlikely to be listed on your data sheets or mentioned by your recommenders. Even if you just discuss accomplishments of a more public nature, including something listed in your data sheet (or discussed by your recommenders), you can personalize it in a way in which just listing it (or having someone else talk about it) does not do.

THE TYPICAL APPLICANT

Most applicants use the whole of their essay to try to demonstrate that their *accomplishments* are impressive; they focus on their accomplishments and not on themselves. These accomplishments, by the way, tend to be things like making the high school basketball team or graduating from college or university. Another mistaken tendency is to list a string of things rather than to explain one or two in detail.

A BETTER APPROACH

The first step is to determine which accomplishments you will discuss. Your criteria for choosing appropriate accomplishments will be familiar. Which ones will help your positioning effort? Which will be unusual and interesting for admissions committees to read about? Was this accomplishment truly important to you?

The following criteria are also helpful guides:

- You had to overcome major obstacles, showing real determination in doing so.
- You learned more about yourself.
- You came to understand the need for further skill development and thus, perhaps, an MBA.
- You used real initiative, perhaps by pushing a bureaucracy to respond or bypassing one altogether.
- Your success was unexpected.
- You worked extremely hard toward a clear goal.
- Your impact can be clearly seen (i.e., you were not simply tagging along with someone else who did the real work).

If you are trying to show that you have had a lot of relevant business experience despite being only 23, you will probably want one (or preferably more) of these accomplishments to be in the business realm. Not every accomplishment will fulfill all of our criteria, but you should be able to include most of them in the course of the full essay.

In writing the essay, go into sufficient detail to bring the events to life, but do not stop there. Discuss why you consider this a substantial achievement, why you take pride in it, and what you learned from it. Did you change and grow as a result of this? Did you find that you approached other matters differently after accomplishing this?

The admissions committee will read this for more than a brief description of the items you list on your data sheet. It will want to learn more about these accomplishments and more about the private you, if you discuss significant accomplishments of a personal nature here. It will want to know what motivates you and what you value. It will also want to see how you have developed as a person and as a manager.

ADVANTAGES OF THIS APPROACH

This question gives you a lot of latitude, as our criteria suggest. Using it to show more of the real you will help you to avoid the usual problems people create for themselves on this essay. You do not want to restate the facts you have already listed on your data sheet; you want to show that you have been ready to face challenges, determined to overcome obstacles, and able to accomplish things that have mattered to you. The essays in the Appendix show a limitless number of potential topics; the excerpted essays were successful because they revealed their authors' characters while explaining the personal importance of their achievements.

QUESTION:
WHAT HAVE YOU DONE THAT DEMONSTRATES YOUR LEADERSHIP POTENTIAL?

WHY THE QUESTION IS ASKED

Top schools expect to produce top managers, that is, leaders. They are looking for applicants who have already distinguished themselves as leaders, since past performance is the best indicator of what people will be like in the future.

THE TYPICAL APPLICANT

All too often, applicants discuss being part of a group that achieved something noteworthy without making it clear that they themselves were leaders in this effort.

A BETTER APPROACH

This question is deceptively similar to the "Substantial Accomplishment" essay. The "Substantial Accomplishment" essay, as I explained, asks you to describe a real achievement (and what it means to you). The "Leadership" essay, on the other hand, is not looking so much for an "achievement" as it is for an understanding of how you *led an effort* to achieve something. In other words, your emphasis should be upon your *leadership* rather than the achievement.

To write this essay, you must understand what leadership is. One obvious example is *managing* people who report directly to you. Less obvious examples involve pushing or inspiring non-subordinates to do what you want done. How? Leading by example, using your influence as a perceived expert in a relevant field, influencing through moral suasion, or influencing by personal friendship? You might have led people through direct management or through influence. Describe your methodology—what strategy did you employ? And why? You may not have been deliberate or extremely self-aware in your actions, of course, in which case you might wish to discuss what you did and why it was or was not a good choice. What problems did you confront? What did you learn about managing or influencing people? Would another strategy, or different actions, have been better choices? Why? (Do you have a philosophy of leadership?)

You should emphasize that your leadership qualities are the sort that describe a future CEO rather than a high school football hero. In other words, such qualities as maturity, thoughtfulness, empathy, determination, valuing other people's input, the ability to influence or manage very different types of people, the ability to integrate disparate inputs into a unified perspective, and integrity are highly desirable.

You are free to choose something from your business career, but you might wish to choose something from your extracurricular or private life, too.

ADVANTAGES OF THIS APPROACH

Viewing this question as concerning your understanding of leadership, and the ways in which you yourself lead, will result in an essay with the appropriate focus. It is not your achievement that is paramount here; it is your method of approaching and resolving leadership issues that concerns the admissions committee. If you show yourself to be aware of the leadership issues inherent in your situation, and extract some suitable comments regarding what worked or did not work, and why, you will have the core of a good essay.

QUESTION:
DESCRIBE AN EXPERIENCE IN WHICH YOU DID NOT REACH YOUR OBJECTIVES
(AND WHAT YOU LEARNED FROM THIS)

WHY THE QUESTION IS ASKED

This question is essentially asking: Are you mature enough to admit that you have made a mistake? Did you learn from it? Can you change and grow?

THE TYPICAL APPLICANT

Most applicants focus more on the mistake they made, or failure they suffered, rather than what they learned from it.

A BETTER APPROACH

You have a great deal of latitude in choosing your failure or mistake. Several factors should govern your response. (1) Try to further your positioning effort. If you are trying to present yourself as a worldly international negotiator, you might wish to show how you flubbed your first negotiations with people from another culture due to your lack of understanding of how they valued different components of a deal. (You can then go on to explain that this started you on the path of investigating the values and beliefs of your negotiating partners and opponents in all future deals, something you believe has underpinned much of your success.) (2) Show that you have truly learned from your mistake. One implication of this may be that you will want to choose a failure from your more distant past, not last week. You will not have had much of an opportunity to learn from a recent failure, whereas a failure from two or three years ago may have afforded plenty of opportunity to learn. The reason is that you generally need some time to reflect upon matters in order to benefit fully from them. (3) If you choose a distant failure, you are not saying that you are currently making these mistakes. It may be better to admit to having been prone to mistakes long ago, not currently.

Having chosen your failure, do not belabor your description of it. Remember that it is what you learned from this failure that is critical here, not the failure itself. Consider what you learned from the experience concerning yourself, your job, your company, your industry, how to manage people and so on. One key piece of learning may have been that you came to see your need for much more conceptual knowledge, such as that which you hope to acquire by doing an MBA.

> When describing failure, a sense of humor may help. If I were writing this essay I might describe my work on a retail strategy case for a UK brewer. I spent several months on this case without understanding that the "fruit machines" that were frequently mentioned as a new cash generator for pubs were gambling machines suitable for Las Vegas rather than dispensers of actual bananas or oranges. As a result, I could hardly contribute to the discussions concerning their future potential. I should have paid more attention in pubs to see what was involved rather than just keeping quiet when these machines came up in discussion. In writing this essay, I could then go on to note how I resolved to learn the details of clients' operations rather than treating them at just an abstract, strategic level.

ADVANTAGES OF THIS APPROACH

The emphasis here should be upon your development. We learn more from our mistakes than from our successes. A willingness to admit mistakes and then try to learn from them is one hallmark of a mature adult. It is also the trait of someone who will benefit from more formal education.

QUESTION:
DISCUSS AN ETHICAL DILEMMA YOU HAVE FACED

WHY THE QUESTION IS ASKED

The ongoing debate over the proper role of business in society has made ethics an important issue in a manager's training—or so the admissions officers will tell you. The reality may be somewhat different. Business schools have felt the need to talk about ethics as a result of the various scandals of the 1980s and 1990s, although it is clearly a subject of limited interest for most of the professors. The need to appear interested in the subject, at least to critical outsiders, has probably been as important as anything else in generating the use of this question.

For some schools and some admissions officers, this question is a sincere attempt to understand your ethics. For others, the question is not so much about ethics as it is just another chance to see your writing and read another story about you.

THE TYPICAL APPLICANT

Most people have trouble finding something to discuss, so they end up choosing something trivial. In discussing it, they think that a question about ethics must call for a holier-than-thou stance, so they sound like refugees from a sensitivity training session.

A BETTER APPROACH

The toughest part of this essay is to find a suitable subject. Here are some possible topics:

- People versus profit. For example, should you fire the Italian researchers you have working for you now that your firm no longer markets in Italy? They are too old to be hired by someone else. On the one hand, you may feel that you owe it to the shareholders to maximize their returns. On the other hand, you feel concern for the researchers. Is it a clear-cut decision? Maybe, but that will depend upon the circumstances. If the company promised the researchers that they would be employed until they reached retirement age, and this was one of the things that helped lure them from another firm, you will probably feel one way. If the researchers have been working second and third jobs at the same time that they have been officially employed by your firm, you may feel differently.

- Your career versus someone else's. When you are in a meeting and your boss takes credit for your idea, what should you do?

- Taking advantage of someone's lack of knowledge or opportunities. Should you sell a product to someone who does not know that it will be inappropriate for his needs? By the time he figures this out you may have moved on to a new division in the company so you will not face his fury or the long-term consequences of having an angry customer.

The essays in the Appendix contain interesting examples of other ethical dilemmas. Note that you can also consider writing about something that happened in your private rather than your business life. In fact, such dilemmas are a part of everyday life, so failing to find one runs the risk of appearing unaware of the moral dimension of life.

This question is asked in one of two different ways. In one version, you are asked simply to describe an ethical dilemma and what you thought of it. In the other version you must describe an ethical dilemma and what you did in response to it. The second type obviously is more demanding than the first because you must have a situation that you ultimately managed well. Some situations may lend themselves to excellent management, but the nature of a "dilemma" suggests that there may not be a perfect way to handle it.

In writing this essay you will want to show that there was truly a dilemma, at least on the surface. You will probably want to show that you explored and investigated the nature of the problem, since you were no doubt reluctant to make a snap decision when it appeared that any decision would have substantial adverse consequences. If you are called upon to describe what you did, rather than just what you thought, you will want to show that you explored every option and did your best to minimize the adverse consequences.

The tone of your essay is another minefield. If you sound like an innocent seven-year-old who believes that it is always wrong to lie, you will not fit in a world of tough senior managers who constantly need to make hard decisions with rotten consequences for somebody. On the other hand, if you sound like a Machiavelli, for whom the only calculus depends upon personal advantage, and for whom the potential suffering of other people is irrelevant, you will be rejected as a moral monster. You need to be somewhere in the middle, someone who recognizes that the world and the decisions it requires are seldom perfect, but that it is appropriate to try to minimize adverse consequences as best one can. Only in extreme circumstances would it be appropriate to walk away from the decision (and the job).

ADVANTAGES OF THIS APPROACH

It is critical to find a subject you can get your teeth into. Our examples may help you find such a subject, one with layers of detail and dilemma. If you go into depth in exploring it, without sounding like a naive child or a totally cynical manipulator, turn it about and examine it from different angles, and weigh the various options thoughtfully, you will show yourself to be senior management material.

THE MOST IMPORTANT TREND
FACING BUSINESS

WHY THE QUESTION IS ASKED

This question is designed to find out whether you have thought about the "big picture," are aware of the issues currently facing industry, and have the ability to discuss a big topic in a sophisticated fashion.

THE TYPICAL APPLICANT

Most people discuss the most headline-grabbing item they can think of. In past years this would have been global warming or the moral imperatives of business—with special reference to apartheid in South Africa. Their discussion, moreover, tends to resemble the headlines of tabloid newspapers: Global Disaster Forecast! Major Changes Needed Now! No research informs the essay. The other approach—too often seen—is that of cribbing all too obviously from a recent lead story in *Business Week* or a similar magazine.

A BETTER APPROACH

Do you have any real views on this subject? If you firmly believe, for example, that the Internet will change how your particular business operates more than the telephone and computer have, then you will probably want to choose this as your topic.

Most applicants do not have such a clear-cut opinion. Instead, they have some not overly well-informed opinions about a handful of topics, any one of which could fit well here. If this is your case, choose the topic that shows you off to best advantage. It should enable you to (1) express sensible but not blindingly obvious views, (2) enhance your positioning, (3) show why you want an MBA, and perhaps, (4) show why this school is right for you. This is a rather daunting set of criteria. You may not satisfy each one, but at least it gives you a target. A quick look at one of the many possible topics reveals how to get started.

Globalization. This is an old favorite response to this essay question. It is a truism that the increasing globalization of business is continuing to have substantial impact upon how business is conducted. Is this topic right for you? It would be highly appropriate for someone applying to a school outside her country, or one that uses a language other than her own for many of its courses. It would also be highly appropriate for someone applying to an internationally focused program such as the Lauder program at Wharton, the University of South Carolina's highly rated international business program (either in the United States or at its companion program in Vienna at the Wirtschaftsuniversität Wien), or one of the European schools whose whole *raison d'etre* is training international managers.

How will you discuss globalization? You might begin with an explanation of how you became aware of this issue in the first place. Have your own company's operations been dramatically affected by foreign competition? Then discuss in what other ways business is being affected by increased international competition. Next, move on to the underlying trends that will cause greater globalization and, finally, examine the impact this is likely to have upon your industry overall. Your degree of specificity will depend in large part upon the allotted space. This discussion will help you demonstrate why you want to attend a school that has a serious international focus.

What are some of the other possible topics?

- Deregulation and Privatization
- Service Management (i.e., the change from industrial to service management concerns)
- Changing Demographics of the Workforce (or Managing Diversity)
- Flattening of Organizational Structures (or the Change from Hierarchy to Network)
- The Information Revolution
- The Internet
- Environmental Limitations
- Quality Management (although this is already a time-worn subject)
- Political Turmoil

Is this list exhaustive? By no means; a sensible list might be two or three times this long. Don't assume that your chosen topic is inappropriate simply because it is not listed here.

Does it matter which topic you choose? The answer to this is, yes and no. It matters that you choose something that strikes admissions committees as being quite important—at least after you have explained why it is important. But what is likely to matter more is how you discuss the topic you have chosen.

When discussing any of these topics, remember to follow good essay writing practice. Be specific when possible, referring to events in your own (business) life when you can. Be upbeat rather than defeatist. For example, if you are discussing globalization, do not wallow in the possible future demise of the "American-ness" of baseball (or whatever). Instead of looking just at the negative side of change, look, too, at the opportunities and challenges that will come in its wake. You should be able to give a sophisticated treatment to your subject, but this is likely to be the case only after you have done some reading. Has *The Economist* written extensively about this subject? If so, you should know its position, as well as that of other sophisticated journals, and provide relevant quotations to demonstrate your awareness. Look at the examples in the Appendix to get a feel for ways to be a sophisticated commentator without sounding vague or jaundiced.

ADVANTAGES OF THIS APPROACH

This topic should be a godsend, in that it allows you to do so much to further so many of your positioning efforts while ostensibly discussing an abstract concept. You can show, for example, that you have a real need to learn much more about organization design and development, thereby necessitating an MBA. At the same time you will show that you have given real thought to a complex issue.

QUESTION:
WHAT DO YOU DO IN YOUR SPARE TIME?

WHY THE QUESTION IS ASKED

Good managers tend to be able to make friends and to socialize easily. This is all the more important in a non-hierarchical, manage-by-influence rather than power world. This question is designed to reveal more about you and to see whether you would fit into the school's social life (and perhaps add to it). This is likely to be much more important for small schools than for large ones, for isolated schools than for urban ones, and perhaps for stand-alone business schools than for those that are part of a university. The reason is that a smaller, more isolated school will tend to have a very close-knit student body, so someone who does not fit well may have a miserable time.

A person with balanced interests, who is not consumed by business to the exclusion of other things, will be able to survive the ups and downs both of business school and of a managerial career.

THE TYPICAL APPLICANT

Many applicants treat this question too lightly and end up simply listing five or ten things they enjoy doing. This does nothing to help their cases.

A BETTER APPROACH

Start by thinking of the things you really enjoy. You probably have a pretty good-sized list. Choose one or two to talk about. Your selection criteria should include the following:

The activity matters to you.

- You know a lot about it.

- You can make it interesting to read about.

- It aids your positioning effort.

- The activity's *distinctiveness* (will 90% of the applicants write about this?) is apparent.

The appropriate activities to discuss are those that will help your positioning. For example, if you have been a corporate librarian, you may want to reassure schools that you are a very tough and determined person. If you enjoy technical mountain climbing, by all means discuss this rather than your chess-by-mail games. The former shows you to be a highly unusual librarian whereas the latter suggests an all too stereotypical one who prefers solitary, contemplative pursuits. Topics to avoid no matter what include watching soap operas or situation comedies on television, sleeping, drinking with the lads, hanging out in pool rooms, etc.

The next step is to write the essay in an appealing fashion. Since your spare time is indeed your own, any activities you pursue should inspire you with real *enthusiasm,* at least if you are a basically enthusiastic sort of person. Given that business schools want enthusiastic students, you are obligated to sound enthusiastic even if you are not.

The other key to your essay will be to show that you are *highly knowledgeable and sincere* about the activity. These characteristics are desirable on their own and, equally important, they show that you really do participate in this hobby, sport, or activity. This essay lends itself to "hypercreativity"; make it clear that you are not simply claiming to climb mountains or whatever you discuss.

One way to sound enthusiastic, knowledgeable, and sincere is to go into detail in describing what you do. If you are a mountain climber you may want to discuss one of your best climbs. Why did you choose to tackle this particular mountain; why this particular route? How did you choose your team? What criteria did you employ, and why? What were the major challenges that you faced? How did you handle them? What was the aftermath of this climb? Describing these and other matters will also *individualize* you, because even someone choosing the same topic will have had entirely different experiences.

The other quality you should strive to communicate is that you are a very *likeable* person. You want to be regarded as interesting and pleasant company. This is especially true for people whose positioning is that they are number-crunching accountants, or otherwise relatively isolated.

Should you discuss one or two activities? This depends upon the number of activities you pursue that meet our criteria and how much space it will take you to describe each one appropriately.

ADVANTAGES OF THIS APPROACH

Choosing only one or two activities to discuss shows that you know how to prioritize and makes your discussion seem focused while giving you the opportunity to interest the admissions committee in what you describe. Discussing unusual activities will also help the committee to remember who you are.

Choosing activities that further your positioning effort has an obvious payoff. Discussing them enthusiastically permits you to build enthusiasm *for you* on the part of the committee.

QUESTION:
TELL US ANYTHING ELSE YOU CARE TO

WHY THE QUESTION IS ASKED

This question is asked for three reasons. First, it gives you a chance to add important information that other essays may not capture. Second, it gives you a chance to explain a weakness or gap in your record, or why your boss did not write a recommendation for you. Third, it will ascertain whether you are able to weigh the value of the additional information you are giving the admissions committee versus the effort required for them to read another essay.

THE TYPICAL APPLICANT

Many people write something, but few benefit thereby. Too many complain about what happened long ago or make excuses for their own failings (or substitute an essay from another school).

A BETTER APPROACH

First, ask yourself whether anything important to your positioning has been left out. If there is an important credential or overcoming of a major obstacle that you have not been able to discuss, and it will substantially help your positioning effort, then use this essay to bring it to the admissions committee's attention. Resist the natural inclination, however, to gild the lily. Do not tell a third story showing how politically astute you were on the job. If you have explained how well you analyzed a production problem, and a recommender is describing another such effort, do not even think of describing a third one here.

What sorts of things are most likely to qualify for inclusion here? With some schools you will not otherwise have the opportunity to discuss your community activities or other things you have pursued outside your proper job. For example, you might wish to describe your managing of the political campaign of a friend who ran for office in your city. Or you might wish to describe what you did in setting up a successful business that you ran on weekends. You may have a specific skill you wish to demonstrate that will not otherwise come across, or you may have rectified a weakness in your record. Perhaps you did poorly at math during your university studies but have since been sufficiently motivated to learn enough math to understand Einstein's general theory of relativity.

If you have found something that will be important enough in saying good things about you and furthering your positioning, by all means use it, but what if you think you have six or eight such items? In this case, follow the usual approach and select one, or at most two, of these. This essay is meant to augment the basic application, not substitute for it. You do not want to risk overwhelming admissions officers with too much material, nor do you want to fall into the trap of just listing items.

Do not worry about adding to an application that is already complete. If you do need to write more, be sure that it is only one or two items of clear importance. Do them justice by discussing them sufficiently to make their nature and value clear.

ADVANTAGES OF THIS APPROACH

Lists are seldom of value. It is far better to choose one or two things and then describe and discuss them in sufficient detail as to make them believable and memorable.

BRIEF NOTES ON ADDITIONAL ESSAYS

QUESTION: WHAT HAVE YOU CONTRIBUTED TO A RECENT GROUP EFFORT?

1. Focus on your contribution, rather than the group's accomplishments, although it is useful to show that you helped the group succeed.

2. One of the requirements is that you made a major contribution to the effort.

3. Consider also:
   - what difficulties were presented
   - what skills you employed
   - the group dynamics
   - how you influenced people or managed them
   - how you got others to contribute
   - how you reduced conflict
   - how your efforts complemented those of others.

4. What was the result?

5. Would the skills you expect to add from an MBA program have helped in this project?

QUESTION: WHAT DOES DIVERSITY MEAN TO YOU? HOW WILL YOU CONTRIBUTE TO THE DIVERSITY OF OUR PROGRAM?

1. You can define diversity in terms of nationality, language or culture, job history, age, educational background, political opinions, sex, aptitudes, or any of dozens of other matters. Your choice is likely to reflect your own experiences and, of course, ways in which you are different from the norm at the program to which you are applying.

- You should certainly have already asked yourself what this school is looking for and how you can appear valuable to it, so to be asked what diversity you can add should really just be making explicit something you have already had occasion to consider.

2. The second part of this question is largely a repeat of the "how will you contribute to the school" question, so refer to the discussion of that question.

QUESTION: DISCUSS A PROFESSIONAL PROJECT THAT CHALLENGED YOUR SKILLS

1. Start by determining what your professional skills are.

2. Look at the most challenging professional project you have faced, preferably one that was successful for you, or one that taught you valuable lessons.

3. After trying to remember it in real detail, abstract exactly which skills you used (or should have used, but have only come to appreciate since then).

4. Remember the attributes your readers are looking for: analytical ability, interpersonal skills, leadership ability, dedication, integrity, and so on.

5. Which of these attributes can you illustrate via one of your projects? Which are most important to your positioning effort? Which will be the most interesting to read about? Which can you get someone else to back up in a recommendation?

QUESTION: DESCRIBE A REPRESENTATIVE WORK DAY

1. This is most important for people in jobs that are not run of the mill where business schools are concerned.

   - For auditors at a major accounting firm, for example, this is not as critical as for someone who is a political liaison person.

2. Do not load into one day every important thing you have done in the last two years.

   - Be sure to show a reasonable range of your typical activities, however. If possible, these would include research and analysis, leading meetings, supervising the work of subordinates, influencing colleagues, negotiating, and so on.

3. Show teamwork, leadership, analysis, communication skills, etc.

QUESTION: COMMENT ON THE ADVANTAGES AND DISADVANTAGES OF ATTENDING OUR PROGRAM

1. This is clearly related to the other questions about why you want an MBA, and what other steps you will take if rejected.

2. Discuss the school's strengths and weaknesses in general.

3. By showing what you are looking for in an MBA, show which of these strengths and weaknesses are most relevant for you.

4. Be kind to the school, but not unrealistic in your evaluation of it.

   ■ Schools want to believe that they do a generally good job, but they are not foolish about this.

   ■ Do not, for example, pretend that a school that offers only a few manufacturing courses is blessed with a strength in this area.

5. Compare this school with the appropriate competitors, showing that you know what real advantages it offers.

RULES FOR APPROACHING OTHER ESSAY QUESTIONS

It should be apparent after reading the above analyses of essay questions that a *thoughtful* approach is required when confronting any essay. Remember that a question does not exist in a vacuum. Instead, it is part of the whole application and should be answered in the context of how you wish the whole application package to read.

You will have started by determining what themes you wish to emphasize and how you will maximize your reward-risk ratio. As part of this, you will have chosen the "stories" you want to tell about yourself. This initial effort provides you with the context for an essay. When it is not clear which story to tell, remember these general rules for selection:

■ The story is interesting.

■ It is unusual.

■ It shows you to have senior management qualities.

■ It reveals something not fully revealed elsewhere in your application.

■ It is a story you should tell, rather than one a recommender should tell.

■ It will aid your positioning effort.

■ It can be backed up by a recommender.

HOW TO WRITE
PERSUASIVE ESSAYS

— EXECUTIVE SUMMARY —

■

Examine your past and present (and goals for the future), and develop
the information that you will need to write persuasive essays.

– See the Appendix for a step-by-step guide.

■

Sift through the material to establish your most effective themes.

■

Outline, then draft, a complete set of essays before finalizing any one of them.

■

Follow this chapter's advice to maximize the impact of your essays.

■

Allot substantial time to reorganizing and redrafting: remember,
"There is no such thing as good writing, just good rewriting."

*A*s a leading Dutch business school's brochure says: "Prepare your essays carefully, for they are your opportunity to provide unique information about yourself, your ambitions and your interests. Essays are evaluated for substance, writing ability, and skill in organizing and presenting thoughts." (Nijenrode Business School.) If you intend to rely on your "numbers" to get you admitted, you will be missing the opportunity to dramatically improve your chances. In fact, the better the school, the more likely it is that the objective data in your application will not determine your fate and that the essays in particular will weigh heavily in the decision.

Admissions officers will judge you on the basis of what your essays reveal about your writing ability (including your ability to persuade, structure and maintain a well-reasoned argument, and communicate in an interesting and professional manner), honesty and maturity, understanding of what the program offers and requires and how well you would contribute to it, and clear understanding of where you are headed. They will want to learn *what* you have accomplished, *who* you are as a person, and *how well you can communicate*. Admissions officers never take the approach of teachers who said, "I'll grade this on the basis of the content, not your writing style."

This chapter is designed to help you actually write your essays. You have learned from prior chapters the type of thing you are likely to want to say, but not *how* to say it; this chapter addresses that need. In addition to reading this chapter, however, learn about successful essay writing by examining some of the many examples contained in this book.

THE WRITING PROCESS: GETTING STARTED

SAVING TIME: APPLICATIONS ON DISKETTE

One of the pains of applying to schools is filling in the finicky little boxes on the application forms. (Who still has an old typewriter around for completing them?) A good alternative now exists for the leading American and European schools. A firm called Membership Collaborative Services has produced software that allows you to replicate admissions forms on your computer. The information that is common to all of the applications, such as your name and address, undergraduate university, etc., needs to be inputted only once. The software then places this in the right blanks on each application form. For information, contact:

> Membership Collaborative Services, Inc.
> 740 South Chester Rd., Suite F
> Swarthmore, PA 19081
> 1-(800) 516-2227 or (610) 544-9358
> fax: (610) 544-9877
> E-mail: mcs@multi-app.com

The price for their whole library of application forms on diskette is approximately $50, plus shipping and handling. Or you can download this free from their web page: http://www.multi-app.com/multi-app

Admissions directors seem quite happy to get the information in this format, so do not be concerned that your application will be at a disadvantage if you use this procedure.

BEFORE STARTING TO WRITE

Before starting to write, let us review what we know about your audience and its decision criteria.

Your audience is the set of admissions officers who will read your application. Chapter 6 described them as conscientious but nearly overwhelmed by the volume of material they read. They are highly familiar with the determinants of business school and career success. Thus they will examine your application for convincing evidence of your intellectual ability, managerial and leadership potential, personal characteristics, and career plan. Being in the education business, they value applicants who clearly value learning and education. They will also like evidence that a person makes the most of opportunities, whether they be great or small.

By communicating effectively—showing that you understand what they are looking for, presenting your material in an organized and concise fashion, and not exaggerating or lying—you will gain credibility as a reliable source of information about yourself and as an appropriate candidate.

What top business schools are looking for. The four principal criteria mentioned above—your intellectual ability, managerial and leadership potential, personal characteristics, and career plan—are common to all of the top schools. (For more detailed information, reread Chapters 4 and 8.)

What does a particular school look for? All schools look for certain traits, such as leadership ability. Yet not every school is looking for exactly the same sort of candidate. Some will concentrate on finding very internationally focused applicants, for example, whereas others want those who are technologically oriented. If you are aware of what a given school is looking for, you can emphasize those aspects of your candidacy that are most suited to their needs. The starting point for learning about a school's specific interests, as discussed in Chapter 5, is to read the material it publishes about itself and speak with its current students and recent graduates.

This chapter focuses on writing individual essays successfully, but bear in mind that each essay is part of a whole application package, consisting of multiple essays, résumé data, recommendations, and interview evaluation. To make sure that you keep your eye on the need to provide a well-integrated, consistent application, do not try to finish any one essay until you have done at least a rough draft of all of the essays for a given school.

PLANNING

It is important to plan your writing. Planning forces you to think about what you will write before you get tied up in the actual writing. Too many people take the opposite approach, writing random paragraphs, hoping to be able to glue them together later, or trying to write the whole of an essay before thinking about it. The results of these approaches are all too predictable. The material included is a haphazard selection of what might be presented and the writing is not necessarily organized and coherent. No amount of editing will cure this problem, which is not merely a problem of word choice or transitions. The greatest problem with the write-before-thinking approach is that, after expending great efforts, writers are disappointed with the results and must go back to what should have been the starting point—*thinking about what they should say.*

1. DEVELOPING YOUR MATERIAL

All too many essays sound the same. The poor admissions officer who has to read five thousand essays, or many more, gains no understanding of an applicant who writes half a dozen essays that could have been written by any of another five hundred applicants to the same school. Few applicants take the time to ask what makes them unusual or unique (or valuable). *Your goal is to develop materials that will help you to write stories unique to you, which no one but you could tell.*

Pulling together the relevant material for your application essays will take substantial effort, especially if you have been working for a number of years at different jobs. The material that might be relevant to the essays could come from virtually any time in your life, and be from any episode or experience.

The best way to start the process of generating material is to fill out the "Personal Organizer" in the appendix to this chapter. As you can see at a glance, there are numerous things to note. Try to fill this out over a period of time, because you will be unlikely to remember everything this calls for in one sitting. Referring to your résumé should be helpful. In fact, you might find it helpful to refer back to earlier versions of your résumé, if you still have them. You may also want to look at your school and university transcripts to refresh your memory.

Consider keeping a notebook (or notebook computer) handy for jotting down ideas, stories, or details about your past or your goals for the future. Reading this book and the many examples in it may also spur your memory. I encourage you to take personal notes in the margins regarding your own experiences.

When you have completed the Personal Organizer, you should have far too much material to use in your essays. This is as it should be. You should feel that you have a wealth of material from which you can pick the most appropriate items.

2. ORGANIZING YOUR MATERIAL

Once you have generated your raw material, what will you actually say? If you have already read Chapter 8, you may have determined what your main themes will be. Now is a good time to recheck that they still make sense in light of the information you have available. Do you have good stories to tell that illustrate your being a brilliant analyst? Have you the right grades in the most closely related courses to claim this? If not, now is the right time to reconsider your positioning. Think in terms of what would be appropriate organizing themes given the information you do have.

After you have generated your information, you must organize it. There are many methods for doing so. One good one is to try to see what the core of your message is. In other words, what key points are you trying to make? If you can state these, the next step is to group your supporting material according to the appropriate points.

OUTLINING

To organize your thinking effectively, it is generally a good idea to outline your essay. This will save you time because the outline will make it clear whether you have too much or too little material, and provides a logical means of organizing your material. It will also allow you to make changes early in the process rather than work on something that does not belong and end up eliminating it only after you have squandered time on it. In other words, it is a check on your thinking.

There are several outlining methods commonly used. Two common ones are:

Informal Outline, using bullets and dashes:

➤ xxxxxxxxxxxxxx
  – xxxxxxxxx

➤ xxxxxxxxxxxxxx
  – xxxxxxxxx

➤ xxxxxxxxxxxxxx
  – xxxxxxxxx
  – xxxxxxxxx

Formal Outline, using Roman numerals, letters, and numbers:

I. xxxxxxxxxxx
    A. xxxxxxxxxxxxx
    B. xxxxxxxxxxxxx
        1. xxxxxxxxx
            a. xxxxxxxx
            b. xxxxxxxx
        2. xxxxxxxxx
II. xxxxxxxxxx
    A. xxxxxxxxxxxxx
        1. xxxxxxxxx
    B. xxxxxxxxxxxxx

It does not particularly matter which outlining method you use. It only matters that it can perform the important functions needed: pulling together related material, showing how idea groups relate to one another, and showing which ideas are primary and in what ways supporting ideas are to be subordinated. You may even find that you start with an informal outline and progress to a more formal one as your ideas become clearer.

3. THE ROUGH DRAFT

The third step in the writing process is a rough draft. Be sure that you are not too demanding of yourself at this point. Even though you want to do a good job, here "the perfect is the enemy of the good." If you are unwilling to write down anything that is less than final draft quality, you are highly likely to be unable to write anything at all. Rather than take this perfectionist approach, be sure to limit your goal to that of producing a rough draft that incorporates most of the basic points you want to make. Do not be concerned if the order you had planned to follow no longer seems to work well, or if you cannot quite express the exact thought you have, or if your word choice is inexact. Get something reasonable down on paper as a starting point.

Writers use any number of different strategies when they start writing. No one method is to be recommended above others. This is very much a matter of personal preference. You can use any of these methods; choose the one (or invent one of your own) that gets you started on the road to producing a reasonably complete draft.

Start with the conclusion. Writers who use this method feel that they cannot write the body of the essay until they know what they are leading up to.

Start with the introduction. When an introduction lays out clearly what will follow, it in effect controls the body of the paper. Some writers like to start with the introduction in order to make sure that they have a grip on the body of the paper before trying to write it.

Start with any of the paragraphs of the body. Some writers like to pick any self-contained part of the body of the paper and write it up, then move on to another part, and then another. These writers like to build the substantive parts of the paper first, and then provide an introduction and conclusion based upon this substance.

Write several different drafts, starting in different places. This approach involves taking one perspective or starting point for writing a draft, then plowing through the entirety. Then the writer does the same thing from another perspective or starting point. Later, the writer can choose one draft or another, or cut and paste using pieces of each.

A majority of people use the third method—writing paragraphs of the body of the paper. They typically write them individually, then place them together in their predetermined order, and only then develop an introduction and conclusion. They take this approach because they know certain aspects of the subject well and can write about them easily, but require more thought to fill in the remaining pieces, such as the introduction and conclusion.

TWO WAYS TO AVOID WRITER'S BLOCK

Many people find themselves "blocked" when they try to write. They sit and stare at the paper or computer, and it stares back at them. To avoid this, be sure to avoid putting pressure on yourself to do too much at once. When you are in the early part of the writing process, try simply to get the basic elements of your thinking about each subtopic down on paper. Do not worry about the quality of what you are writing until you are editing.

Technique one. After you have thought about an essay, try to write down on index cards phrases that convey your various ideas. (Or, of course, use a computer to do the same thing.) Don't plan for too long; just write down the phrases as they occur to you. Then organize the cards into related groups of ideas. Write paragraphs expressing these ideas, perhaps trying to link the related ones together. Then, see if you can place these paragraphs into a reasonably logical order. Next, put this structure into a proper outline, to see if it makes sense. If it does, link the paragraphs with appropriate transitions. If it doesn't, try reordering the paragraphs.

Technique two. If it is still too difficult to get rolling with this method, involve a friend in the process. Explain to your pal what you are trying to convey. Have her take notes on what you are saying. Organize those notes into a logical order, with her help, and then explain yourself to her again, being sure to follow your notes to keep things in order. If you record this, and transcribe your recording, you will have a solid rough draft, which you can start to edit.

---

4. EDITING YOUR ROUGH DRAFT

Remember that "the only good writing is rewriting." When you start to edit your rough draft you are doing your first part of this rewriting.

One of the most important aspects of the editing stage is its *timing.* Editing without a break between the drafting and the editing stages will limit your insight into the flaws of your draft. You will not see where you skipped a needed transition or explanation because you are too close to the original writing. If you can take a break, preferably at least a night, or better yet, a week, you will be better able to read your draft from the perspective of an outsider.

Make sure that you have edited your draft for substance—for what points will remain and what points will be eliminated—before you start editing the language. Otherwise you will devote time and effort to improving the wording of material that should be discarded. (And, even worse, you are likely to keep it in your draft if you have gone to the trouble of making it sound good.) This section assumes that you will revise your essay three times. In fact, if you are a good writer and have taken the time to think through an essay before doing your first draft, you might well need to edit it only once or, more likely, twice. By the same token, if you are struggling with an essay it might require more than three revisions to sort out the problems.

One warning: do not view editing as taking the life out of your essay. In fact, editing's role is to clear out the dead wood, making your points stand out as clearly as possible.

REVISING YOUR FIRST DRAFT

The initial revision should focus on the essay as a whole.

Do you accomplish your objective? Does your essay directly answer the question? Is your main idea clear?

Revise for content. The typical rough draft may have too little and too much material, all at the same time. It will have just touched the surface of some portions of the essay, without providing explanation or convincing detail. At the same time, it may have discussed things that do not contribute significantly to your major points.

A good essay eliminates extraneous material while including all the information necessary to make your point. Your reader needs sufficient *evidence* to accept what you are saying, so be sure that you have adequately developed and supported your main idea. Material that does this belongs, but material that is unrelated to the main idea should be eliminated.

Finally, avoid belaboring the obvious (admissions directors know what an audit is), but do not assume an inappropriate amount of technical knowledge (admissions directors may not know the difficulties in writing a certain type of code).

Revise for organization. A well-organized essay will group similar ideas together and put them in the proper order. To be sure that your draft is in an appropriate order, try to outline it. If it is easy to produce an outline from the draft, and there is a clear logic to the flow of the material, you can be reasonably certain that you have a well-ordered essay. Otherwise, reorder your material.

Revise for length. Is your essay approximately the right length? If it is substantially longer than the stated word limit, consider how to reduce the supporting material. If it is shorter than allowed, consider whether to leave it at that length (which is a good thing if the essay successfully communicates what should be your main points) or to expand it by making additional points or providing additional supporting material.

REVISING YOUR SECOND DRAFT

Assuming that you have successfully revised the first draft of the essay and the content is as you wish it to be, turn your attention to the components of the essay: the paragraphs, sentences, and individual words.

Revise paragraphs. A proper paragraph should make only one major point. The easiest way to organize a paragraph is to start with a topic sentence—one that makes the major point of the paragraph—and then to explain or illustrate that point in following sentences. For business writing, starting most or all paragraphs with a topic sentence is often appropriate, particularly for inexperienced writers.

Look next at the length of your paragraphs. Most writers tend to one extreme or the other: either all their paragraphs are very short or all are very long. A mixture of lengths is a good idea. Having most of your paragraphs between 30 and 150 words is a good idea. The occasional paragraph that is substantially shorter or longer is fine, but they should be the exception rather than the rule. The reasons for this are simple: Too many short paragraphs make you look simple-minded, unable to put together a complex idea or group related ideas together, whereas long paragraphs will discourage reading by any but the most conscientious reader. Use short paragraphs for emphasis; use long paragraphs for discussion of complicated points or examples.

The three methods you can use to develop your main idea are to provide *examples, explanation, or details.* Writing without these three components tends to be unsatisfying and unconvincing. Generalities ("I am a very determined fellow") are unconvincing unless supported with specific examples and explanations.

Revise for flow. Even when you have well-written paragraphs placed in the right order, your writing may still be difficult to read because it lacks suitable transitions between ideas or other means of showing how the ideas relate. For our purposes, the most important method of relating ideas will be using transition words and phrases. Some typical transitions include:

Purpose	Typical Transitions
Amplification	besides, furthermore, moreover
Cause and effect	therefore, consequently, as a result, accordingly
Conclusion	as a result, therefore, thus, in conclusion
Contrast	although, but, despite, however, on the one hand/on the other hand
Example	for example, for instance, specifically
Sequence	first, second; former, latter; first of all

One other easy way to connect paragraphs is to have the beginning of one paragraph follow directly from the end of the prior paragraph. For example, if you have just said "I needed the chance to show what I could do without overbearing supervision" at the end of one paragraph, the next one could start out

"My opportunity to prove myself came with the founding of a new office in Toronto." In this example the relationship between the two paragraphs is ensured by having the second grow organically from the end of the first.

Be sure that each sentence follows logically from the prior sentence.

Check your introduction. Make sure that it not only introduces your subject but also grabs the audience whenever possible. (If you are writing seven essays for a given school, for example, at least two or three of them should have attention-getting introductions.) A good introduction is interesting as well as good at introducing your main points. It should appeal to the reader and set the tone for the whole essay. There are many effective openings. You can state an important and interesting fact, refer to something currently in the news, refer to a personal experience, ask a question that you will answer in your essay, or simply state your general point of view. Do not restate the question; it wastes valuable space and is a weak, plodding way to begin.

Check your conclusion. A good conclusion does one or more of the following:

- pulls together different parts of the essay

- rephrases your main ideas (without repeating anything word for word)

- shows the importance of the material

- makes a recommendation

- makes a forecast

- points toward the future—showing, for example, how you will make use of something you have learned

- gives a sense of completion

It should not make a new point that belongs in the body rather than the conclusion, nor should it sound tacked on. The concluding paragraph should develop "organically," if you wish, from the material that preceded it.

Revise sentences and words. Most essay writers pile on long sentence after long sentence. Avoid this by breaking up some of the longer sentences to provide variety. Use short sentences to make important points, long sentences to explain complex ideas or develop examples. Also, use a variety of sentence structures to maintain reader interest. Eliminate sentences that sound awkward or choppy when read aloud.

Edit your sentences to eliminate imprecise or wordy language. For example, use "although" instead of "despite the fact that." Add vigor to your writing by eliminating clichés, using fresh and interesting descriptions, and trying to write as much as possible with nouns and verbs, rather than primarily with adjectives (which slow the pace and reduce impact). Similarly, write in the active voice.

Revise for tone. Your tone can be assertive without being arrogant. Your essays should sound confident, enthusiastic, and friendly. Be sure to avoid pleading ("I'd give anything if you would just let me in") and whining ("I never do well on those awful standardized tests; it's so unfair that schools even look at the results").

One way to check the tone of your paper is to read it aloud. Read it first to yourself and then, once it sounds appropriate to you, try reading it to a friend. Get his suggestions regarding how easy it is to understand what the strong and weak points are, whether there are any mistakes in it, and whether it sounds like you. Does it reflect your personal style? The ideal essay should sound just like your voice, but with repetitious and awkward phrasings and use of such filler as "you know" and "like" eliminated. It should sound relaxed rather than formal, but still flow smoothly.

Some applicants, remembering a high school text, try to avoid writing in the first person. In fact, it is not only appropriate to use "I" when writing your essays, it is essential that you do so. You are being asked to give personal statements, so do not write in the distant and aloof third person.

REVISING YOUR THIRD DRAFT

Revise again for style. See the comments above.

Revise for grammar, punctuation, and spelling. The way to spot grammatical mistakes and faulty punctuation is to read your essays over slowly, preferably after having put them aside for some time. Reading them aloud can also help this process. Even if your sense of grammar is keen, however, consider having a friend whose grasp of grammar is extremely good read over each essay. Spell-check the final product.

Check the length (again). One of the key factors affecting most of the essays you will write is that the business schools generally prescribe their maximum length. Failing to observe this constraint raises questions about your willingness to pay attention to the rules that will apply in other situations, so avoid going over the limits. Most schools do not mind your slightly exceeding the limits on one or two essays, but a pattern of exceeding the limits strikes even these schools as unfair. They have established these limits to provide a level playing field for the applicants; someone who exceeds the limits is trying to assert an unfair advantage.

Three revisions is not a magic number, but will be a minimum for most people. There is nothing wrong with putting your work through more revisions.

5. GIVING YOUR ESSAYS TO SOMEONE ELSE TO CRITIQUE

After you have edited the essays to your own satisfaction, or gotten stuck, hand them to several people whose views on writing you respect. They can provide you with an objective view that you may not be able to bring to the essays yourself. They can be particularly useful in determining whether your attempts at humor are working, whether the essays convey a true sense of who you are, and whether you have left out important connections or explanations. Pay attention to their opinions, but do not give up control of what are, after all, your essays, not theirs. Do not let them remove the life from your essays.

6. PROOFREADING

Why proofread your paper if you have been careful in composing the final draft? No matter how careful you have been, errors are still likely to crop up. Taking a last look at the essay is a sensible precaution.

What are you looking for? Basically, the task at this point is no longer to make sure that the structure is correct; it is to spot any errors or omissions in your sentences and individual words. Errors tend to show up most often where prior changes were made. Combining two paragraphs into one, for example, may have resulted in the loss of a necessary transition phrase. Grammatical mistakes can also live on.

As with any task that is essentially a matter of editing, your *timing* is of the essence. Wait until you have already finished what you consider to be your final draft. If you can then put this draft down for a few days, you will be able to give it an effective last look. If not, you risk being unable to see mistakes because you are still too close to the writing. Another useful precaution is to have a friend proofread your essays.

SOME TIPS FOR GOOD WRITING

Do:

Give yourself the time to do the essays right. Start early; it will take time to do the essays. The results will also be better if you take time between steps rather than trying to finish an application in a hurry. Expect to spend ten to twenty hours getting organized for the effort, and then averaging perhaps five to ten hours per essay, with the most difficult (and first) efforts taking longer.

Answer the question. Do not ever substitute an essay on another topic, even if it was your best essay for another school. The likely result of doing so is an automatic rejection for inability to do as directed. It is occasionally appropriate to combine your answers to two questions into one if the answers you will give are inevitably linked, but be sure to explain what you are doing and your rationale for doing so.

Use humor, but only if it works. Few people can write humorous prose, or recount humorous stories effectively, but if you can manage it you will definitely distinguish yourself. To check whether you are succeeding, have several people read to make sure that it works on paper as well as it would if you were to tell it. Be sure that it is not vicious humor, as this has no place in a business essay.

Keep the focus on you. For example, do not get carried away in describing the outcome of a project without showing how this relates to you and your efforts.

Explain events whenever appropriate. Many of the things you have done are mainly of interest because of what you learned from them, what you thought about them, and why you did them.

Favor a full description of one event rather than a listing of several. It is generally better to describe one event or accomplishment at some length rather than to mention a number of them without explaining why you undertook something, what it meant to you, and what you learned from it.

Be specific. The more specific you make your writing, the more you personalize it and the better the chance that it will be interesting. Generalizations, without specific information and examples, are vague and weak, and not necessarily believable. Examples add interest to generalities as well as making generalities clear.

Be reluctant to cast everything in black-and-white terms. Readers will tend not to trust or believe essays that give only one side of an argument. For example, if you are suggesting making a change in your company's organizational structure, you may be right, but it would be peculiar if absolutely no argument could be advanced to provide some support to the opposing viewpoint.

Use bold and italics to increase readability, but resist overusing them. Bold print and italics are helpful in making your meaning clear, so use them with moderate frequency. The essays you are asked to write are much too short, however, to use titles, subheadings, and the like.

Use an appropriate amount of space. It is generally acceptable to exceed word or line limits slightly, but doing so consistently or without a good reason suggests that you are unable to get to the point or establish appropriate priorities.

Find someone to edit your work. Explain what you are trying to accomplish and who will be reading your essays, so that your "editor" can both determine whether you are meeting your objectives and correct your grammar. The test of your writing is what the reader understands, not what your intent may have been.

DO NOT:

Start to write until you have restated what your most important contributions to this program will be. Reread this school's brochure and the other materials you have gathered on it and remind yourself of why you are applying to it (beyond its high ranking or reputation). Read the recommendation forms that the school uses to see specifically what this school wants in its applicants.

Use your limited space to recite information that is available elsewhere in the application, such as listing your part-time jobs, or mentioning your GMAT results.

Give superficial answers. Take the application seriously and work accordingly.

Pretend to be someone other than yourself. It will not be supportable with your own history and will sound phony.

Lie or exaggerate. Doing so causes all of your assertions to be doubted.

Think that an essay limit also defines the required amount to write. No one has failed to get into a business school for failure to write the maximum number of words on an essay. When you have said all that you intend to say, stop.

Feel compelled to write the optional essay. When schools ask if you have anything else to add to an application, far too many people use the opportunity to write another essay or give details about their candidacy. Resist the urge unless you will add something that will give an important perspective to your candidacy.

Use a minuscule type size to shrink an essay to a given number of lines, or reduce its borders to nothing. Remember that your readers have to read literally thousands of essays and will not appreciate being forced to squint or use a magnifying glass.

Start by saying, "In this essay I will write about . . ."

Use cute or meaningful quotations unless they fit perfectly and do not make people wince when they read them. Too many people seem to have been taught to start everything they write with a cute epigram, regardless of the fact that it may not fit the subject well and all too often does not match the desired tone of the essay. Shakespeare, Napoleon, Churchill, and Mark Twain all said a lot of marvelous things, but that does not necessarily mean that you should quote them.

Use a definition to begin your essay, absent a very strong justification. This is too often a sophomoric way to begin, so avoid using this crutch.

Use only bullet points. Writing an essay requires that you use full sentences.

Complain about the essay topic. The person reading your essay may be the one who thought up the topic. Besides, you should avoid complaining in general.

Discuss your low grades, poor GMAT score, or other weak aspects of your record, unless you have a very good reason for doing so. If, for example, you worked full time and attended school full time, saying so provides the context within which to judge your grades. A simple explanation is appropriate.

Bore the reader. A fresh and well-written essay will aid your application effort.

Use a fancy vocabulary for its own sake. Use the simplest possible language to explain your meaning precisely.

Preach. In writing your essay, provide support for your viewpoint but do not keep repeating your belief. You have plenty of opportunity in the introduction or conclusion to state your opinion; resist stating your opinion throughout the body of the essay, too.

THE ADMISSIONS DIRECTORS DISCUSS HOW TO WRITE THE ESSAYS

WHY THE ESSAYS MATTER SO MUCH

➤ The essays provide a test of succinctness: how well you can write them in a short space and still stand out. Business writing of course is typically short. On the practical side, the essays are meant to be kept short because there is a limit to how much we as an admissions office can get through. *Judith Goodman, Michigan*

➤ The skill in writing, the skill in organizing, and the content all show people's intelligence and the extent to which they have considered where they are headed and why. Their personality, motivation, skill, and intelligence come across in each essay they write, no matter what the topic. *Fran Hill, Haas (Berkeley)*

SHOULD YOU EVER EXCEED THE WORD LIMITS? (That all depends)

➤ Word limits should be kept in mind when writing essays but talented writers occasionally can make good use of a few extra words, and it's O.K. if they have something to say and say it well. *Fran Hill, Haas (Berkeley)*

➤ We will read beyond our word limit, but after a person writes twice as much it's basically over. Part of our goal in establishing word limits is to create a level playing field by having a highly structured process. We are interested in applicants' ability to play by the rules. *James Millar, Harvard*

➤ One should never exceed essay word limits, nor should one ever submit extra essays. Students who refuse to acknowledge word counts, and who assume that if they give you a long-winded essay, particularly when describing their career, figure this is going to be impressive, but actually it's the biggest turn-off ever. It means they've not read the application form or they're not able to express themselves concisely; if they can't do that they'll have problems on the program. *Julia Tyler, London*

ADVICE

➤ Put simply, the person who does thoroughly research his/her MBA options, will in most cases write more effective essays. *Linda Baldwin, UCLA*

➤ They have to be readable. People should use a decent size font and language people can understand. *James Millar, Harvard*

➤ Some are very personal; these are often the ones that hit me. When I read one that whines about undergraduate grades, I can't help but think, "Let's get on with it." *Linda Meehan, Columbia*

➤ Be sure to check for accuracy, grammar, and spelling, because it is a real turn-off if those things are not right. Be sure that you answer the questions we ask, not the ones another school asks. If you send us an essay that was originally done for Wharton, we will assume that you should go there. When people do not follow the instructions, we wonder what they will do when they are here. Be sure to give the essays real thought. *Don Martin, Chicago*

➤ Too many people write the optional essay. In most cases it doesn't add much value. Applicants often use other schools' essays, and that is pretty apparent, and typically worthless (or worse). My advice for most people is simply to skip the optional essay. *Henry Malin, Tuck*

➤ My advice on writing the essays is:
  – Plan ahead. The essays take time to write well.
  – Make a list of points to include.
  – Prepare your narrative.
  – Be succinct but say enough that it shows depth and thought.
  – Put it in good form. No matter what you are saying, typos and poor grammar destroy it. *Judith Goodman, Michigan*

MOST COMMON MISTAKES

➤ We see three main problems: (1) They didn't answer the question. (2) Their answer was so brief that we don't know if they have nothing to say or lack the writing skills to express themselves. (3) Last, poor form: grammar, style, etc. We don't know if they lack the skill to write properly or failed to check their work.
Judith Goodman, Michigan

➤ The biggest mistakes are: poor proofreading—not running a spell-check, for example; sounding arrogant; and, trying to use an essay from another school's application that doesn't fit our question, like taking an "ethical dilemma" and slamming it into a question about the characteristics of a superb manager. This really leaves a bad taste.
Henry Malin, Tuck

➤ The worst essays may be those that fail to answer the question, or those that make statements that can't be supported by the person's history. *Julia Tyler, London*

➤ The biggest mistake in writing essays is making broad, sweeping, general statements without supporting them with facts and examples of what they've done.
Mary Clark, IESE (Barcelona)

REUSING YOUR ESSAYS

Business schools want to learn similar things about their applicants so they tend to ask many of the same (or similar) questions. This is good for you to the extent that you can reuse your essays and cut down on the amount of work you have to devote to additional applications.

On the other hand, few things annoy admissions officers more than to receive essays that were obviously first written for another school, particularly if the other school's name was left in them. It is possible to recycle your essays as long as you do so intelligently. The reason for doing so—to save time and effort—is compelling enough that almost everyone will try to use the best essays in more than one application.

There are several situations that require you to make more of a change to a previously used essay than just to switch school names:

- Your positioning for this school may be different, requiring that you alter your essays sufficiently to reflect your changed positioning.

- If you applied to one school that required just a few essays, you may have packed brief descriptions of several events into one essay. When writing for a school that has more essay questions, you may spread out these events and use them in several essays. This could also involve lengthening your description of the events. (The reverse process would be appropriate when changing from an application with many questions to one with only a few.)

- Similarly, the change in essay questions from one school to another may mean that you will no longer answer a question in which you had previously told your most important story. If so, you will probably want to find room for it in one of the essays you are going to submit to the new school.

- Another reason to change your essay is to shorten or lengthen it to conform to a second school's requirements.

  - To lengthen an essay, you may wish to include more examples, elaborate the examples you have already used, or even add additional main points.

  - To shorten an essay, keep your major points but reduce your elaboration of them.

- The hardest part of combining several essays into one is finding a theme that will unite them. If you can do that, it is a simple matter to link them with transitional sentences.

FURTHER READING

Stuart Berg Flexner, ed., *The Random House Dictionary of the English Language* (Random House).

William Zinsser, *On Writing Well* (HarperCollins).

William Strunk, Jr., and E. B. White, *The Elements of Style* (Macmillan).
The Economist Style Guide (The Economist).

APPENDIX
Personal Organizer

(Make extra copies of this form to have additional room for describing multiple schools, jobs, or other experiences, as necessary)

EDUCATION

School:

Degree: Date received:

Grade point average: Major/Concentration:

Minor: Relevant additional coursework:

Substantial papers written:

Activities:

Offices held/responsibilities/achievements (academic and extracurricular):

Honors and Awards:

Scholarships:

General questions about college (and any prior graduate school) experiences:

Why did you choose this school? In retrospect, was it a good decision? Why or why not? (Repeat for choice of major.)

WORK EXPERIENCE

Start with your most recent job and work backward in time. If you have had more than one job with the same employer, fill out separate data fields for each. Include all part-time as well as full-time jobs.

Employer: Division/Subsidiary:

Dates employed: From_____ To _____

Location:

Title/Position:

Beginning salary: Ending salary:

Bonuses/other compensation: Beginning: Ending:

Key responsibilities:

Who did you manage? To whom did you report?

Key accomplishments (quantify whenever possible):

Key skills that enabled you to accomplish these things:

Superiors' reviews (excerpts):

Reasons superior feels this way about you (think in terms of your achievements, skills, actions, etc.):

Reasons for taking the job:

Reasons for leaving the job:

Ways in which the job met your expectations:

Ways in which the job did not meet your expectations:

Important stories illustrating your leadership, analytical, managerial, creative, and other abilities:

What sources (including people) are there for developing further information about each story?

PROFESSIONAL ACCOMPLISHMENTS

Copyrights:
> Title:
> Date:
> Publisher/Publication:

Patents:

Title:

Date:

Number:

Professional certification:

Organization certifying:

Date certified:

Professional honors and awards:

Name:

Date awarded:

Organization awarding:

Reason for the award:

EXTRACURRICULAR ACTIVITIES (artistic, athletic, community, religious, political, etc.)

Activity: Dates of involvement:

Offices held/responsibilities/achievements:

Reasons for your involvement:

How does it relate to your other activities and interests?

PERSONAL QUESTIONS

Who are the four or five people who have most influenced you? (who and how?)

What are the four or five things you most admire in others? (in whom and why?)

What are your four or five most memorable experiences, whether great or small?

What was your greatest success, and what did you learn from it?

What was your greatest failure, and what did you learn from it?

What fear have you overcome? (how, why?)

What do your friends most like (and dislike) about you?

What are the four or five (or more) key words that would describe you? What on your list demonstrates this?

Do you have a personal motto or something that you frequently quote?

YOUR FUTURE CAREER

How has your interest in this career developed?

What are your career goals? What do you hope to accomplish in your life?

LEISURE TIME

What are your favorite books? Why? What have you read most recently? (Repeat for films, plays, music, etc.)

What do you like to do when given the time? Why? What do you most enjoy about it?

PULLING YOUR INFORMATION TOGETHER

At the conclusion of this exercise, list your major accomplishments in each category.

Business:

      1.

      2.

      3.

      4.

      5.

Education:

      1.

      2.

      3.

      4.

      5.

Personal:

      1.

      2.

      3.

      4.

      5.

Which events or activities represent turning points in your life (i.e., when you changed direction)?

Which events or activities reaffirmed your desire to continue your career in the same direction?

In what way are you different from a year ago? Why? (repeat for five years ago.) Think in terms of your personality, interests, personal and professional goals, and values.

How have your various experiences helped you to grow? What do they show about your abilities? What do they show about your interests?

Which of your experiences demonstrate the following characteristics? (This list is taken from the Chapter 4 analysis of what business schools are looking for in their applicants.)

CHARACTERISTIC   RELEVANT EXPERIENCE

Intellectual Ability

Analytical Ability

Imagination and Creativity

Motivation and Initiative

Maturity

Organizational/Administrative Skills

Ability to Work With Others

Leadership Potential

Self-Confidence

Ability in Oral Expression

Written Communication

Managerial/Career Potential

Sense of Humor

11

RECOMMENDATIONS

— EXECUTIVE SUMMARY —

■

Choosing recommenders correctly is critically important.

■

Approaching potential recommenders must be done carefully.
- Give them a chance to say no.
- Explain why you want an MBA, and why you have chosen these schools.
- Explain how important their recommendations will be.
- Brief them fully regarding what they should write.
- Emphasize telling relevant, rich stories.

■

Make their job as easy as possible.

WHY ARE RECOMMENDATIONS REQUIRED?

Applicants complain that recommendations are a waste of time because "all applicants can find someone to say something good about them." These applicants are right to believe that most people *can* find a supporter, but they are wrong about the importance of the recommendation process.

To understand how they can be both right and wrong at the same time, let us compare two applicants, George and Martha. Both George and Martha are 26 and have been working as sales representatives for a sporting goods manufacturer for three and a half years. They both went to a well-known school of Ivy League caliber.

George asks his former basketball coach and his favorite economics professor to write his recommendations. The coach says that George is a popular guy who really loved basketball and was a talented player. His economics professor notes that George loved economics and recollects George's oft-stated desire to make a lot of money.

*

Martha asks her thesis advisor and her current boss. Her thesis advisor considers her the best student he has had in the last fifteen years due to her dedication and analytical talents. He describes in some detail how she overcame two major hurdles in her thesis topic. He then explains that her writing was better than that of many of the junior faculty at the school. He also notes that he has formed his conclusion on the basis of teaching Martha in three different courses. Her senior thesis was the culmination of three years of working together. He concludes by saying that she is also one of the finest people he has ever met, citing her generosity in helping less talented students with their work. Martha's boss quantifies her standing as a sales representative. In her first year she was in the top 50 percent of reps; in her second year she was in the top 10 percent; in the last year and a half she has been one of the top 5

206

*

reps out of a total of 180. He explains that she was acutely conscious of having numerous shortcomings when she started, but was determined to study the best performers to figure out what she could learn. She also paid careful attention to what her boss said were her failings and what could be done to overcome them. He then illustrated her efforts by recounting how she overcame two specific problems. He concluded by stating that although approximately twenty-five people from the company had applied to top business schools in the last three years, she was unquestionably the best candidate of the lot.

Which one would *you* prefer as a study group partner? Martha is clearly the stronger candidate even though George got his recommenders to say good things about him. Martha, however, got a lot more mileage out of her recommendations. She chose the right people to recommend her. She also had them write about important attributes where business school and career success are concerned, and they did so in highly believable ways.

The rest of this chapter is devoted to analyzing how to get your best supporters to do the same.

WHAT DO ADMISSIONS COMMITTEES LEARN FROM YOUR RECOMMENDATIONS?

1. Your claims are true.

   Recommendations are examined first for the extent to which they confirm and support your claims and your positioning. If your essays state that you are a very successful deal maker for your firm, the admissions officers reading your file will look closely at what your boss has to say to see whether your claim is legitimate.

2. You have many qualifications.

   Recommendations play another important role. They are an opportunity to provide *more information about you*, preferably in the form of stories and illustrations of general points the recommenders wish to make.

> *One of the telltale signs that an applicant is not strong enough, \or has too little experi-ence,* is that the recommenders and the applicant himself all tell the same few stories. This suggests that the applicant has had only limited successes.

3. Your managerial skills are up to snuff.

   You must decide who should write on your behalf, determine what you want your recommenders to say, get them to say what you want said (in the most helpful manner), and get them to send in the recommendations on time. These are typically people over whom you have no authority, so you will have to use influence rather than clout. Thus the recommendation process is a test of your abilities as a persuader.

4. You can accurately evaluate others and their perceptions of you.

   If you end up choosing someone who writes a mediocre recommendation, your judgment will be questioned at the very least. It may even be assumed that you simply could not find two people who would say something good about you. A mediocre recommendation is death to an application. Bad recommendations are eternal damnation.

WHO SHOULD WRITE YOUR RECOMMENDATIONS?

Selecting appropriate recommenders involves sifting many factors. Here we will assume that you are to submit two recommendations. (In the next section we will consider what to do if you are asked to submit three.) In general, you will be expected to submit recommendations from people who know you and are well placed to address the key issues concerning your candidacy. As we have already discussed, you will want them to state that you have the appropriate managerial potential, intellectual ability, and personal character. There are two obvious types of choices for this:

- To address your managerial potential, a current or former boss
- To address your intellectual ability, a professor with whom you did a lot of work
- To address your character, either or both of these people

Your choice eases if there are not a lot of obvious candidates. For example, you may have reported to the same person at your company for the last three years, and he likes you and is willing to help you. By the same token, perhaps you did a great deal of work with one professor, and one professor only. If this is the case, you are more likely to be concerned about how best to approach and manage these two recommenders than about how to choose among many possibilities.

Most people, however, are not in this position. Some do not dare tell a current boss that they are considering leaving the company. Others figure that their boss is likely to sabotage any move they make to get ahead. Some of them did not work closely with any one professor, or it was too long ago for him to remember the experience. Perhaps he has since died; then what? Here is a starting point for choosing recommenders:

1. **The first rule**: Choose people who *know you well.* Do not choose people who are famous but will be able to say only that you seem like a nice person and apparently did a superlative job handing out fliers on a local street corner during the last senatorial campaign. Instead, choose people who can make the recommendation *credible* and *powerful* by illustrating the points they make with anecdotes that clearly show you at your best. Need we say it? The people who will be able to do this are those who know you well.

2. **The second rule**: Choose people who *genuinely like you.* Why? People who like you will take the time to write you a good recommendation. This is impressive in its own right. A recommendation that looks as though it took only five minutes to write suggests that that's exactly how much time the recommender felt you deserved. In contrast, a recommendation that looks carefully done and well thought out suggests that the recommender is committed to helping you. One other reason for choosing someone who likes you: she or he will try to put a positive spin on things, choosing examples that show you in a good light and describing them as positively as they can. Someone who does not much care may well write the first thing that comes to mind.

3. **The third rule**: Choose people who can address one or more of the key subjects: *your business skill, your brains,* and *your character.*

Business skill. The ideal person can address the following:

➤ Your maturity: ability to make well-thought-out decisions and retain your self-control under stressful conditions
➤ Your work habits
➤ Your self-confidence and poise
➤ Your creativity
➤ Your thoughtfulness
➤ Your ability to listen to valuable inputs
➤ Your ability to work with others
➤ Your ability to motivate others
➤ Your organizational and planning abilities
➤ Your other leadership qualities
➤ Your ability to analyze difficult problems (and to find a solution and "sell" it to others)
➤ Your overall managerial potential

Many of the above characteristics are quite personal in nature. For example, self-confidence is a personal quality, yet such characteristics are highly relevant to your business skill and managerial potential.

The person most likely to be able to assess your business ability is your current manager, preferably one who has seen you in operation over a period of time. You may not be able to use your current manager, however. If not, your next best choice might be a prior manager, someone to whom your boss reports (and who has seen your work on a number of occasions, even if at a greater distance than your manager), a client, or even a competitor or rival (such as one of your peers). If you do not choose your current boss, or someone else who is an obvious choice, it will be helpful to have your actual recommender explain why you have chosen not to have the obvious choice write on your behalf.

Brains. The ideal person can address the following:

➤ Analytical ability
➤ Quantitative skills
➤ Mental agility
➤ Healthy skepticism
➤ Imagination and creativity
➤ Communication skills (written and oral)
➤ Mastery of language
➤ Thoroughness
➤ Research methods
➤ Breadth of scholarly interests

The obvious choice to assess your brains will be a thesis advisor from your college or university. If you have not been in school for a long time, or your thesis advisor disliked you or has passed away, you may have to find a substitute. Anyone who has seen you work on difficult intellectual challenges is a possible recommender. This might be someone who taught several courses you have recently taken to improve your knowledge in a field related to your career, someone who has taught seminars to your department, or even a manager of yours who has had you do intellectually challenging work.

Character. The ideal person can address the following:

➤ Your sense of morality
➤ Your dependability
➤ Your motivation and sense of initiative
➤ Your sense of humor
➤ Your involvement with those close to you
➤ Your sense of civic responsibility
➤ How you deal with people below you in business or other organizations
➤ Your social skills

One or both of the people you have chosen to deal with the issues of business skill and brains should be able to address the character issue too. In other words, you do not need a spiritual or moral leader to address issues of character. The person you do select, however, must have seen you in a large number of different circumstances to be able to address these broad issues; his or her knowledge of you may have to be deeper than is required to address your intellectual abilities, for example.

These are the out-and-out rules for choosing recommenders, but the following criteria should also be considered:

1. *Choose someone able to support your positioning.* If you claim to be a marvelous accountant, at least one of your recommenders should be able to discuss just how good an accountant you really are. Failure to choose an accountant who has seen your work over a reasonable period of time would raise a major red flag.

   You should also try to take this one step further. Use your recommendations to address any potential weak spot in your application. If you are an accountant worried that the admissions committee will presume you to be humorless, as we discussed earlier in the book, this is your chance to prove what an engaging and funny fellow you really are. Similarly, if you are applying from a non-business background, try to find someone who can address your business skills, or at least the skills that would be most valuable in a business context.

2. *Beware the naysayers!* Certain personal characteristics of recommenders suggest that they will be effective in their support. Someone who is exuberant about life in general will be a good choice as she is likely to describe an average performer as marvelous, whereas a dour complainer might describe the performer as terrible. Similarly, an articulate person is likely to write a more impressive recommendation than a poorly spoken one.

3. *Seek out the voice of experience.* Be wary about choosing someone who is not obviously more senior, since it will look strange to have someone junior to you writing on your behalf. (This is potentially acceptable, but be sure to explain it.)

4. *Timeliness counts.* Choose someone who is reliable and therefore likely to complete your recommendation on time.

5. *Where did the recommenders go to school?* People who themselves graduated from your target school are ideal, since they clearly know what is required to succeed in the program. On the other hand, you are probably applying to numerous schools, so their advantage will not work across the board. By the same token, graduates of comparable quality schools can speak convincingly about your relative abilities.

HOW MANY RECOMMENDERS?

In general, schools ask for recommendations from two people, but some ask for three. As stated earlier, if only two recommendations are required, the general rule is to *get one from a former or current boss (or business colleague), who can address your managerial qualities,* and *one from a professor, who can address your intellectual abilities.*

If you are a younger or less experienced candidate, and you are asked for three recommendations, the third one may pose a problem. Given your relative lack of bosses or colleagues who could write effectively on your behalf, you might want to have another professor write the third recommendation. The problem here is that you will reinforce the impression of inexperience. So, at the margin, you should prefer a *slightly* weaker business colleague's recommendation to that of another professor in order to demonstrate the strength of your business experience.

Another issue arises when you have more potentially excellent recommenders than are called for. This is especially probable for more experienced applicants applying to schools that desire only two recommendations. Should you submit an extra recommendation or not? If the extra recommendation you are considering submitting reiterates points that have been made elsewhere, don't submit it. (Remember the admissions adage: "The thicker the kid, the thicker the folder.") On the other hand, if your recommender can add a truly different and important perspective on your candidacy, I would consider submitting it, but only if it is done in the right way. Approach your extra recommender and explain the circumstances. Then ask that he include with his recommendation a letter that you have written explaining what you are doing. This letter should state clearly that this is the extra recommendation, that the other recommendations are meant to be read first, and that this additional recommendation is to be considered only if the school would consider it appropriate. In other words, you offer this additional recommendation as helpful additional material to be consulted at the discretion of the admissions committee.

APPROACHING A POTENTIAL RECOMMENDER

The typical approach to a potential recommender involves a nervous phone call, in a pleading tone, asking for a big favor. The applicant is desperate to get a letter of reference, so she has to gather up her courage to make her phone call. Once she is on the phone, she hurries through the conversation, with little being done other than some meaningless pleasantries being exchanged and the all-important "Yes, I suppose I can write one for you" being received. This represents at best a completely wasted opportunity. In fact, it may prove to be worse than that.

Ideally, you should start the process about three months before the recommendation deadline. Begin your overture to a potential supporter by scheduling a 30 to 45-minute conference with her. (You will get a better response by having this meeting in person rather than by telephone.) Run it as a proper business meeting, with a typed agenda and outline of each matter that you want to share. Explain briefly where you wish to go in your career and what it will take to get there. Then note the skills and experience you currently lack, and how an MBA will provide many of those missing parts of the puzzle. Then tell her what is required in the application process, being careful to explain how important the applications are, including the recommendations. Tell her that you have been considering having one (or two) of several people write on your behalf.

Now comes one of the critical parts of the recommendation process. Make sure that each recommender is going to write a very favorable recommendation for you. The way to be sure of this is by giving the person a chance to beg off if she is unable to be highly laudatory. Ask if she believes that she would be the right person to write on your behalf. If she is uncomfortable about writing for you, because she knows that honesty would require her to be less than highly favorable, she will take this opportunity to suggest that someone else might be more appropriate. If she gives this kind of answer, do not press her. Thank her for her time and move on.

If, on the other hand, she is amenable to being a recommender, give her a further briefing. Tell her how much work will be involved, noting that you will make the process as easy as possible for her, thereby limiting her involvement to something under three hours. (If time is a major issue for her, suggest that you write a first draft which she can then quickly "adapt." See the discussions below in this regard.) Tell her which schools you are considering, and the reasons for each. Explain how you are trying to position yourself in general, and note any differences as to particular schools if necessary. Show her what questions she will need to answer about you, and how these relate to your desired positioning. Suggest "stories" she can tell about you, and how these will fit in with the questions. Provide her with enough detail to refresh her memory about these stories.

MAKING YOUR RECOMMENDER'S JOB EASY

Try to do as much of the work as you can, since your recommender is undoubtedly busy. Give her plenty of time to write the recommendation. Be sure to give her:

➤ The deadline for each application.

➤ Stamped, addressed envelopes.

➤ Several copies of each form, with the objective data already filled in (i.e., with your name, address, etc.).

➤ Copies of your own essays, and a description of your positioning strategy.

➤ If she is writing recommendations for all of your target schools, tell her which main points to discuss so as to satisfy the requirements for each school in one general letter (although she will still need to fill in the grid ratings for each school). Note that this requires you to know precisely which schools you are applying to.

➤ Samples of the work you did for her.

➤ A list of your recent (and past) activities, including why you undertook them, in light of your interest in and suitability for business school.

  – Provide "canned" descriptions of the stories you want to tell.

➤ An outline of what you wish her to discuss.

➤ Your résumé (c.v.)

Be sure that she understands what is important and how to write convincingly—i.e., with appropriate stories—for you.

If she wishes to write the recommendations herself, suggest that she write a general letter addressing each of the questions asked by the schools to which you are applying. Your outline material should provide her with the basis for writing such a letter, as you should point out to her. (Leave this material with her, of course.) The reason for writing such a general letter is that it will save a great deal of work. This letter can be made user-friendly by putting in bold print the topics being addressed in each paragraph, so that readers can quickly pick out the points that are of greatest interest to them. Your recommender may suggest that you do a first draft of the recommendations, which she will presumably alter to her taste later on—or she may ask that you write them, and she will simply sign them.

You might need to agree to write the recommendations, following our general guidelines about recommendations in doing so. Be careful, though. Many applicants make mistakes in this situation. (1) Some revert to the simplistic "he is extremely this, and extraordinarily that" instead of using appropriate stories to provide credibility. (2) They fail to make the recommendation sound as though this recommender actually wrote it. Putting yourself in her shoes will help you determine which matters she would emphasize, and how she would discuss them. (In fact, this is a step that you should take before you approach any possible recommender.) (3) Yet another mistake is to overlook the chance to tell stories that would otherwise not be told about you. Remember to bring new information to the table whenever you have the chance.

Whether your recommender writes your recommendations or has you do them, this well-thought-out approach to the matter will prove helpful in a number of ways. First of all, this approach minimizes the chance that you will end up with a lukewarm recommender. Second, your approach will have been highly organized and professional. If you had followed the nervous, pleading approach, why should she tell Harvard that you are a true professional destined for greatness? Third, you know in advance what stories she will tell. This means that you will retain control of the admissions process insofar as you have a number of stories you want told about yourself, without undue repetition. Fourth, following this process means that you will have a well-written recommendation. If your recommender writes it, she will almost certainly use your outline, just as she will treat the matter seriously since you have done so. If you write the actual recommendation, you can certainly manage to put together a good statement. Fifth, your professional approach means that your recommender is likely to improve her opinion of you, meaning that she will be a better resource for your future career than she otherwise would have been.

TIPS ON HANDLING DIFFICULT ISSUES

➤ If you find yourself in the position of writing all your own recommendations, formatting them differently and making them sound as if each recommender was the actual author will help camouflage their authorship. For example, you can format one as a letter and another in the question-and-answer format. Similarly, you can use different typefaces and font sizes.

➤ If you went to a second-rate or unknown university, or had mediocre grades even at a top school, you should have recommenders take every opportunity to discuss your analytical skills.

➤ If necessary, try to make a deal with recommenders, that they overlook your shortcomings and stay focused on your positive qualities.

➤ If you are unable to get a recommendation from someone the admissions committee would expect to write on your behalf, be sure to explain why either in the optional essay question or in a separate note.

➤ American schools are required to allow applicants to see the recommendations written on their behalf unless the applicants waive that right. You should waive that right because otherwise recommenders will not feel free to discuss your candidacy honestly. In fact, some will refuse to write a recommendation unless you waive your right to see it.

WHAT DO YOU WANT SAID ABOUT YOU? AND HOW CAN YOU INCREASE ITS VALUE?

A good recommendation should show that you are an outstanding individual, one who is an appropriate candidate for a top business school by virtue of having the appropriate management potential. It should also support your individual positioning strategy.

The following all add to the effectiveness of a recommendation:

■ It is well written. It is grammatically correct and reflects the thinking of a well-educated person.

■ It reflects substantial thought and effort. In other words, the person cares enough about you to spend the time to be as helpful as possible.

■ The person knows you well enough to provide several highly specific examples to illustrate her points. These should not be the same examples you use in your essays or that other recommenders note. As with your essays, the use of illustrative stories and examples will make the recommendation credible and memorable. This will also show that the recommender knows you well, thereby showing that you have not "shopped" for one.

■ She does not mention things best handled elsewhere in your application, such as your GMAT score.

- You are shown to be a distinctive candidate. The use of examples will aid this considerably.

- The person can discuss your growth and development over time. Your drive to improve yourself, in particular, is worth comment since your interest in learning and improving is part of what will make you a desirable student.

- Your recommender can explicitly compare you with others who have gone to this or another comparable school. Have her quantify her claims whenever possible. For example, instead of "intelligent," have her write "one of the three most intelligent people ever to work for me" (or, even better, "the third most intelligent of over one hundred top grads to work for me").

- The person shows how you meet the requirements, as she sees them, of a top manager or other leader.

The general impression should be that a person of very high caliber wrote a well thought out, enthusiastic recommendation for you.

HOW LONG SHOULD THE RECOMMENDATION LETTER BE?

The recommendation forms may provide limited space for a given response, but your recommender may want to write more. Should you or your recommender treat such space limitations as you do the limitations for essay writing? No. Recommenders are given much more latitude in choosing how best to write a recommendation. This is one reason why it is perfectly appropriate to use the one-size-fits-all recommendation, which does not even try to fit into the provided format.

THE ADMISSIONS DIRECTORS TALK ABOUT RECOMMENDATIONS

WHOM SHOULD YOU CHOOSE TO BE A RECOMMENDER?

➤ Choose the person who can speak to your strengths and weaknesses, who can give an accurate portrayal of you. We want good, solid information on candidates, so choose someone who can give it to us. *Brian Sorge, Kellogg*

➤ The biggest mistake is picking someone's title over intimacy of knowledge, choosing a senior V.P. who hardly knows who they are over a V.P. they work with daily. Having a Tuck alum write a recommendation would be very valuable IF the person knows you well. It's always apparent if it's just a casual acquaintance, and that's not useful. The second biggest mistake is choosing people who can't judge their professional or academic qualifications. A crew coach can talk only about character and personality. We'd rather have this as a third reference; it doesn't add as much value as a supervisor or professor could. *Henry Malin, Tuck*

➤ I think that writing your own recommendation letter is not a sound application strategy for several reasons. First of all, it shows that you haven't elicited the kind of regard from your manager that would cause him (or her) to expend the effort himself. Second, and more important, the applicant doesn't always know what things to emphasize and what things not. Letters from managers who have worked closely with people achieve a ring of authenticity by the range and vantage point of the remarks. It's the rare applicant who can duplicate that vantage point or who knows what might be significant commentary. The difference, of course, is a reflection of the years of experience. Typically, a manager is five to eight years out of school and that gives him a different perspective on things than someone two or three years out. *Fran Hill, Haas (Berkeley)*

➤ It's important that the recommender knows about MBA education or has worked with MBA candidates or MBA graduates. This helps them know how to evaluate candidates and to discuss the person in ways useful to our evaluation. *Connie Tai, Rotterdam*

MUST YOUR BOSS BE ONE OF YOUR RECOMMENDERS? (Maybe!)

➤ It's good to use your boss, but if you can't, use a former colleague who has since left the company, or a customer or supplier—someone you've worked with. *James Millar, Harvard*

➤ We advise people to use their current supervisor or, if that's impossible, a former supervisor. We would discourage them from applying without someone from their current job, someone who works with them every day, giving them a reference. *Henry Malin, Tuck*

➤ If your boss really knows your skills and accomplishments, it will be important to have him be one of your recommenders. We understand that it can be hard to have your boss write for you because it may compromise your work situation. If this is the case, mention it in the optional essay question. You can ask a co-worker, but this is not as satisfactory. The bottom line is that it is risky either way. If you ask your boss you increase the risk of trouble at work but increase the chances of being accepted. The opposite is true if you don't ask your boss. *Judith Goodman, Michigan*

➤ We require two work-related references, preferably from current supervisors. If you don't have two, maybe your supervisor's manager would be an appropriate choice. If you can't provide these two, you need to explain why. You want to avoid raising a red flag with the admissions committee regarding why you haven't submitted a letter from a current supervisor. You want to avoid giving the impression that it's performance related. *Fran Hill, Haas (Berkeley)*

➤ It is a good thing if your boss can write for you. We understand that it is not always possible to have your boss or even anybody in your organization. What we are looking for is somebody who clearly has worked closely with you and has observed you in a work situation, preferably over a long period of time. *I would argue that no matter where you work if you have built up credibility and you do have one or two people looking after you—interested in your career—they would always be prepared to give you a reference even if company rules say that they shouldn't. I think that people who are going to be successful will have one or two people watching over them.* *Carol Giraud, INSEAD (Paris region)*

How Should You Approach a Recommender?

➤ Sit down with the recommender, if at all possible, and discuss your career goals and aspirations. Discuss what you've learned from the company in your current position and your current manager, what you want to get from an MBA that the current position can't provide that you can procure more quickly in the context of a management program, and where you want to go with it. Frame your goals in such a way that a manager can then take his or her experience of you and his or her assessment of you and make comments that specifically address those issues. It's a very wise thing to do that. *Fran Hill, Haas (Berkeley)*

What Should a Recommender Say?

➤ You have to be brain dead not to pick someone who will say good things about you. The trick, though, is to have them distinguish you from the pack, to capture what your unique, valuable qualities are. *Jon Megibow, Darden*

➤ I would advise a recommendation writer to give specific examples, not be afraid to mention weaknesses, and, to the extent possible, show why the person is getting an MBA. It helps tremendously if the recommendation is well written, thoughtful, and polished. A "coffee break recommendation," one that involves a few scrawled comments and not filling in the grid, for example, is a real negative for someone; it's a missed opportunity. You should find out who writes recommendations well. *Henry Malin, Tuck*

➤ We are looking for people who have demonstrated that they can follow through on projects and accomplish things, not just get along with people. A great recommendation shows this. It has depth, examples which explain how and why this person is in the top 5 percent—it demonstrates what makes the person so outstanding. It should of course be well written. Responses do not need to be restricted to the tiny space on the form; it is perfectly acceptable if they are contained in a separate statement. At the opposite extreme, when we get a recommendation in which the person just checked the grid and signed it without responding to the questions, we wonder whether the applicant chose someone who didn't know him. Either way, it hurts his candidacy. *Judith Goodman, Michigan*

➤ A recommendation is most valuable when there's supporting information and when there are objective criteria used. If you're saying that this person is good interpersonally, tell us why and how he's good. Don't just say that he's the best assistant you've ever had, period. Support the point by showing us what has distinguished this person in your eyes. Explain what your frame of reference is. Give us a full description of this person's situation. *Brian Sorge, Kellogg*

➤ The recommender needs to identify this individual as someone special, being really a long way in front of his peers, and with very high potential. That is first and foremost. *Carol Giraud, INSEAD (Paris region)*

What Are the Worst Mistakes People Make?

➤ The biggest mistake: We are not impressed by a recommender's fancy title. Some make the mistake of thinking that the bigger the name or the reputation the more weight it will carry. This can actually work against someone—as brown-nosing. *Don Martin, Chicago*

➤ Too many come from very important people who simply don't know the applicant. Other recommenders just fill in the boxes and sign it. *Mary Clark, IESE*

➤ Relatively few recommenders take the time to provide substantial explanations, with accompanying stories and details, of what truly distinguishes an applicant. Most are content to say some nice things about him, but without being convincing. *Christy Moody, ENPC (Paris)*

➤ Sometimes recommenders brag to us about their companies instead of telling us about the applicant. *Connie Tai, Rotterdam*

OTHER

➤ You all too often see evidence of vindictiveness in recommendation letters. You wonder if it's the result of a stab in the back. If we ever have cause for concern, we call the recommender. *Fran Hill, Haas (Berkeley)*

➤ Virtually all of the recommendations rate the applicant as "above average" so we don't pay a lot of attention to them. Instead, we try to get a sense of the person by reading the answers to our questions. *Gabriella Aliatis, Bocconi (Milan)*

MAKING SURE THAT THE RECOMMENDATIONS ARE SUBMITTED ON TIME

The schools can keep you informed as to whether a given recommendation has arrived. If it has not arrived and time is getting short, contact your recommender and ask very politely how her effort is progressing and whether you can be helpful by giving her more information. This will tend to prod her into action without being annoying.

THE FOLLOW-UP

Be sure to send your recommender a thank-you note for her efforts and state that you will keep her informed as to your progress. This is simple good manners. If you need extra encouragement, remember that you may need her services again quite soon if schools turn you down this time.

If you manage your recommender well, the chances are that she will submit your recommendations well before they are due. What should you do, however, if you call your schools and learn that a recommendation is missing? You can certainly call your recommender to encourage her to submit it soon. On the other hand, you can take a subtler approach and send her a follow-up note explaining that you have completed the application process and are currently awaiting schools' decisions. If she has not yet submitted the recommendation, this should spur her into action. If this does not work, contact her again and see if you can help the process along in some way, such as by writing a draft of what she might say.

Keep her informed as to each school's decision. Also be sure to tell her what you have decided to do, such as attend school X and turn down school Y, and why. At this point it would be highly appropriate to send her a small thank-you gift such as a bottle of champagne or flowers. Very few people do this. It is not a terribly expensive gesture, but you can be sure that you will gain greatly in her estimation for having done it.

Do your best to stay in touch with her as you go through business school, even if this means nothing more than dropping a short postcard or E-mail message to her with a few comments about your progress.

In conclusion, remember that she is in a position to help your career for years to come and has already shown a distinct willingness to do so. You should do your best to reward her helpfulness. In fact, one sound reason for going to a top MBA program is to take advantage of the networking possibilities it offers. It would be ironic if you threw away a very good contact prior to arriving at business school by failing to treat your recommender appropriately.

SPECIAL NOTES FOR INTERNATIONAL STUDENTS

If you have a potential recommender who is not able to write well in English (or whatever language is acceptable to the school), you can help matters greatly by writing up some stories or even the full draft of a recommendation for her. To the extent that you write well in English, your recommender will be all the more likely to use what you have written rather than struggling with the language on her own.

EXAMPLES

These three recommendations were written for Canadian schools about a student then finishing his undergraduate business studies and hoping to get into an MBA program shortly thereafter.

FROM A CURRENT PROFESSOR:

Gordon Muller has been a student at the International Business School (Lippstadt) since October 1992; he will graduate in August 1995. I have known him since his first semester, when he took two EDP courses from me. His performance in those courses is indicated by his high marks. Even at that early stage in his career he was very much "on track," mastering materials which he knew would be important to his future career.

My next opportunity to work with Mr. Muller came this past summer when I critiqued his pre-diploma thesis. His thesis merited a 1.7 grade, which is quite rare here (1.0 is the highest possible grade and 5.0 the lowest). His thesis was a model effort. He undertook to examine the whole set of issues surrounding municipal waste collection in Germany. He analyzed everything from the legal requirements for waste collection, which are quite detailed, to the costing of such efforts.

The primary issues from a municipality's perspective concern how to estimate the costs which an outside firm will incur in collecting and disposing of waste and then negotiating with a firm a deal which will incent its behavior in the appropriate manner over the life of a long contract. Typical waste management contracts, prior to his consulting firm's involvement, generated 200–300% profit margins for the outside firms, making it clear that municipalities needed to get smarter and tougher in their bargaining behavior.

I found Mr. Muller's thesis very thorough in covering all of the relevant issues and in analyzing each one in depth. In fact, it was so well written that it is being published in the German waste management journal and also in the industry's management encyclopedia. He is clearly one of the industry's leading cost and negotiation specialists, which is quite an accomplishment for someone still completing his undergraduate studies.

Accomplishing what he has professionally has frequently necessitated being away from IBS but Mr. Muller has still maintained both a high level of classroom performance and an active involvement in our extracurricular activities. Despite his very busy schedule he seems always to be enjoying himself, retaining a great deal of enthusiasm for whatever he engages in. It is hard for me to think of someone who has contributed more to IBS. I undoubtedly speak for the whole faculty in recommending him wholeheartedly.

From a former boss, a consulting firm partner:

Mr. Muller began work for us as an intern. His was a most unusual internship insofar as we offered him a job once he had completed it. In fact, it was the first time that we had made a permanent offer to someone so young.

I have known him since he started work here. I recruited him for his internship and since then have been the manager for most of his projects. As a result I feel that I am well qualified to judge both his professional growth and his current abilities. When he first started work here he was tentative as most interns are. He soon became accustomed to the quality demanded of our people and his work, which in his first weeks was nothing special, rapidly developed so that by the end of his internship months it could be counted upon as worthy of the firm's name.

Municipal waste consulting work here involves a grasp of detail and of the big picture. Mr. Muller, for example, has to design a methodology for analyzing the 10,000 or so loads of waste collected under a typical agreement, which is especially important and difficult when hazardous waste is involved, then supervise collection and analysis of the data. He needs to gather other information, for example from interviews of everyone from truck drivers to CEOs and published materials, in order to understand the underlying costs of a particular municipality's waste business. Then he needs to understand the potential contractors, both the overall companies and their key employees, in order to set our negotiating strategy. Then he needs to project the future developments which might bear on waste collection for this municipality, such as local, state, and national government legislation which might be put into effect. The whole process is very complicated, but the result is highly worthwhile in terms of the sums which our municipal clients save.

Mr. Muller obviously bears a heavy responsibility in developing and analyzing the relevant information and writing our final report. He then is in charge of writing our presentation which will be given to government officials and other concerned parties.

This is an important piece of our consulting work. Mr. Muller is an excellent contributor to it. We expect him to continue to develop and to move up in our organization at a rapid pace. Getting an MBA at a first-class school such as yours will no doubt aid his development so we are happy to support his desire to do so. (Let me note that our reason for doing so is not because we feel that he is missing any particular skill which we consider essential. Rather, we think that he is already a very substantial contributor to our projects, both in terms of his own work and in helping others with theirs. He is an excellent analyst, very determined and thorough, and blessed with sound judgment. His skills and personality are very suited to the demanding work here.) I unhesitatingly recommend him—I think he is very talented and will contribute a great deal to your program.

FROM A FORMER BOSS, A LADIES' GARMENT MANUFACTURER:

Mr. Gordon Muller was our Regional Distributor slightly less than a year. That is, of course, a very short period of time, so I would ordinarily be reluctant to write a recommendation on the basis of such a relationship. The reasons for my writing on Mr. Muller's behalf, however, are substantial.

First, I had substantial personal exposure to his work. Due to my desire to get to know his capabilities I had him accompany me to Milan to examine the new fall collection. This was an important trip for my company. He showed me that he had a good "eye." More important, I saw that he could put himself in the position of our typical clients, understanding which items would most likely appeal to them and which would not. It is quite difficult to find someone who has a good personal sense of fashion but can also adopt the taste of others.

Second, I made several client visits with Mr. Muller. In each case I was going along with him to see how he would do and how the clients would react to him (and his youth). I figured that I would also be asked to contribute heavily to these meetings. In fact, the value for me was not from my persuading clients to buy, or covering up for Mr. Muller's mistakes. I was not the one doing the persuading, and he was not making mistakes which required correcting. He was extremely good at selling our lines. He connected very well both professionally and personally with the buyers.

Mr. Muller increased our sales markedly as our regional distributor. He also increased them outside his own region. While manning our booth at the Dusseldorf IGEDO (the world's largest ladies' apparel trade fair) he attracted customers from Spain and the UK for the first time. His languages probably helped him, but it was far more a matter of understanding these customers and their needs in a short time and responding effectively to them. He helped us open up two new markets which are now quite important for us.

He has a great future as a salesman. He brings all of the usual skills of a good salesman such as persuasiveness and charm, and also an intuitive understanding of the customer. He also brings an analytical mind, which is rare in my experience of salesmen. I wish that he were continuing to work for us. The best that I have managed to do is to have him continue to organize our semiannual fashion shows in Ludenscheid. This keeps him in contact with the industry, our company, and various customers who keep asking for him, which is the best way I know of trying to get him back.

Mr. Muller will be a success at whatever he does, including your business program. I recommend him absolutely without reservation.

HOW THESE RECOMMENDATIONS HELP HIS CANDIDACY:

1. Gordon Muller was just finishing his undergraduate degree at a private German business school when applying to MBA programs. In addition to wanting to have recommenders show that he was smart, determined, and so forth, he also needed to address the usual concerns about someone so young (22) applying for a graduate program. He tackled them in several ways. First, he selected two recommenders who could discuss his business experience. The normal impulse would probably have been to select professors, but using experienced business professionals highlights the fact that he has a surprising amount of business experience under his belt

despite his youth. Second, he made sure that both recommenders discussed his responsibilities and successes in such a way that it is clear he was acting as a mature, seasoned professional would be expected to act.

2. Each of these recommendations is written well, reflecting the time that the recommenders (or Gordon) put into them.

3. The professor's letter shows that Gordon was not just very successful as a student, it also shows the context for his success. It makes it clear that he handled a full academic schedule while also doing a lot of work at the same time. This again reinforces the message that this is a responsible, mature applicant.

4. The consultant's letter addresses Gordon's analytical capabilities. The professor's letter also did so, but having the consultant show that in the highly analytical field of consulting Gordon has been able to excel adds a useful, real-world perspective to his abilities.

5. The ladies' garment manufacturer shows that Gordon has valuable business skills, and personality, which are not necessarily expected in someone who is a strong student and analyst. Showing that he is a very good salesman who can handle older customers from around Europe, in various languages, suggests that he is a highly versatile.

6. Each recommendation letter makes it very clear that Gordon is a true standout. The professor talks about his exceptional academic performance, the fact that he is soon to be published in a leading journal, and his standing as an expert in his field. The consultant notes that Gordon is highly unusual in converting part-time employment into an offer for permanent employment. He goes on to show that Gordon performs a wide range of demanding tasks and excels both at the big picture and details in his projects. (His evaluation is particularly helpful because partners at major consulting firms generally have MBAs from leading schools and look to hire graduates from the same schools, so he is accustomed to evaluating top talent.) The garment manufacturer also shows that Gordon has been a top producer for him. The fact that his prior two bosses want Gordon to come back to work for them, with the garment manufacturer doing everything he can to lure him back, makes their evaluations of his performance all the more convincing.

RECOMMENDATION ORGANIZER

Name _____

Title _____

Organization

Mailing Address

Telephone   (office)   (home)

Fax   (office)   (home)

E-mail, etc.   (office)   (home)

Date to Make Contact

Date Contact Made

Schools He/She Is Writing For

Materials Given/Explained (and Date)

Further Materials to Be Supplied

Progress Checks to Be Made

     – Date/School

     – Date/School

Schools That Confirm Recommendation Receipt

Note: This form can be copied, or your own version computer generated, and used for each of your recommenders.

RECOMMENDATION BRIEFING OUTLINE

(The material below is meant to provide an outline to illustrate how you can structure briefing sessions with your recommenders to get them to provide you with the kind of recommendations you need.)

Reason I came to firm X:

My ultimate goals:

How an MBA would help me reach these goals:

Why I should get an MBA now:

Which MBA programs best suit me:

      Why/how:

My positioning/marketing for these schools:

How he/she can help me:

      Does she want to help me?

      Total time required: approximately 2–3 hours

Show application forms/explain that only "ticking the boxes" and writing a general letter is required.

      Show that the objective information has already been filled in, letters stamped, and so on.

Take recommender through outline of an appropriate letter.

      Include details of stories, copies of reports, and so forth.

Discuss style and form of the master letter.

Deadlines

12

INTERVIEWS

— EXECUTIVE SUMMARY —

■

Establish your objectives: conveying a good impression, imparting your strengths, demonstrating your knowledge, gaining information.

■

Prepare yourself by:
- Learning the most likely questions
- Knowing yourself and your qualifications vis-a-vis those of others
- Knowing the school
- Readying your own questions.

■

Practice via mock interviews, videotaping them if possible.

■

Familiarize yourself with the do's and don'ts of interviewing.

INTRODUCTION

More and more schools are interviewing most or all of the applicants they are seriously considering admitting. There are several reasons for this. One is that the greater emphasis upon "soft skills" in MBA programs means that an applicant's personality and social skills are more important than they were in the past. A second reason is that a person's interviewing ability is a very good indicator of how attractive he or she will be to employers at the end of the MBA course. An applicant with good "paper" credentials will be unattractive to a school to the extent that he or she is likely to be regarded as a loser by employers later on. A third reason for interviewing is that schools can market themselves better by meeting individually with applicants. This is particularly relevant for the elite schools, which tend to feel that they are all chasing the same few thousand absolutely outstanding candidates. These schools welcome the chance to get a jump on their rivals by better assessing candidates and by promoting themselves to their top choices.

Interviews offer schools the chance to learn much more about applicants. Some things are not readily determinable without a face-to-face meeting. These include your appearance, charm, persuasiveness, presence, and business mien. Interviews also provide an opportunity to probe areas insufficiently explained in the application.

Nevertheless, the interviewing policy of schools is not uniform. Kellogg and Michigan, for example, interview nearly all of their applicants, whereas Stanford and Texas interview none of theirs. Numerous other schools interview only those candidates who have passed their initial checks, whereas others interview only those who are borderline candidates—strong enough to warrant a close look, but not so strong that they will be admitted without an interview.

Some schools use only admissions officers to conduct their interviews, whereas others use alumni extensively, and still others use second-year students. The schools that rely on admissions officers alone are obviously unable to do in-person interviews with all applicants, due to the time and logistical constraints. For example, there is the problem of interviewing the candidate who is immersed in a round-the-clock project at a remote site on the north shore of Sumatra. Some get round this by doing telephone interviews; others simply evaluate the candidate on the basis of the file alone.

The need to do so many interviews results in (admissions office) concerns about the confidentiality of information revealed in the application. This is particularly true for those schools that use second-year students to conduct interviews. Many schools resolve these concerns by giving interviewers nothing more than an applicant's résumé (and thus none of the essays or recommendations) prior to an interview. Others have students and alums sign confidentiality agreements concerning the content of applications.

SHOULD YOU INTERVIEW IF YOU ARE GIVEN THE CHOICE?

Most people feel that they interview quite well, but the reality is vastly different. To become a good interviewee, you need to understand in advance what points you want to put across, what questions you are likely to be asked, and how to maximize your presentation to satisfy your needs and those of your interviewer. The keys to doing all this are to analyze what you will confront and then to practice performing under realistic conditions. Doing this will help you to avoid going blank, letting slip things you intended to avoid, forgetting to mention important points, or being unable to keep the interview flowing in a comfortable fashion.

If a school requests that you interview with them, it is ordinarily a mistake not to do so. Failing to interview may be taken as an indication of a lack of interest in the school or a tacit admission that you do poorly in one-on-one situations due to shyness or nervousness (or worse). There are often logistical considerations, of course, and schools are aware that it may not be realistic to expect you to travel 5,000 miles for a Wednesday morning interview, since it might necessitate your missing several days of work. The logistical barrier is not as great as it once was, however, now that schools have their representatives travel to most major cities and regions on a regular basis, or use alumni representatives to interview on their behalf.

Although it is generally appropriate to interview, if you are sure to make a poor impression, either improve your interviewing abilities or maneuver to avoid an interview. The people who should avoid an interview are those who are pathologically shy, whose language abilities will crack under the strain, or who are so contentious that they will inevitably get into a verbal battle with their interviewers. (Unfortunately, nearly everyone thinks that he or she interviews well. Very few people will eliminate themselves on the basis of poor interviewing abilities.)

INTERVIEW THEORY

Interview theory, seen from the school's perspective, can help you to understand how you will be evaluated and why. The underlying tenet of selection theory is that past behavior and success are the most trustworthy factors for predicting future behavior and success. Schools will attempt to determine how you acted in the past, and with what degree of success, in order to predict how you will act—and succeed—in the future.

BEFORE THE INTERVIEW

ESTABLISHING YOUR OBJECTIVES FOR THE INTERVIEW

The interview is important for all-too-obvious reasons. The fact that the school emphasizes the interview means that you have the opportunity to market yourself in a format in which most people do very little good for themselves. Some candidates are afraid of the interview and set themselves hopelessly limited objectives for it. They hope to get through it without embarrassing themselves. Or they hope that the interviewer likes them. You have the chance to make a very positive impression that will further your marketing efforts, so it is up to you to seize it. *Do not simply hope to survive the interview; be determined to achieve positive results.* Use it to reinforce all of your other positioning efforts.

You already have a marketing strategy in place, so go back to it when you are considering what you hope to accomplish in the interview. If you have positioned yourself as a true entrepreneur with great understanding of emerging technologies, for example, this positioning strategy will help you think through the interview and how to prepare for it.

Ask yourself the following questions at the start of your preparations:

1. How do you want the interviewer to think of you? What specific impressions, and information, do you want her to carry away from the interview?

2. How can you reinforce your strengths and address your key weakness(es)?

3. How can you show that you know a great deal about the school—that you are well prepared for the interview?

4. How can you learn whatever you need to know to decide which school to attend?

PREPARING FOR THE INTERVIEW

You should be mentally prepared to deal with four aspects of any interview. The first is understanding the format of a typical meeting as well as the special types of interviews that you may confront. You also must know what your objectives are, what the school offers, and what questions they are likely to ask.

1. TYPICAL FORMAT

No matter what type of interview is involved the format is likely to include:

- Welcome
- A few easy questions, perhaps about how you are, was it easy to find the location, and so forth
- Some comments about the school
- Detailed questions, perhaps tracking your educational and then work history, or your responses on the school's application form
- The chance to ask questions
- Conclusion

The first minutes of an interview may not involve substantive discussion, but they are likely to be important in forming the interviewer's impression of you. Therefore do your best to appear confident and pleasant even before you get to the heart of the interview.

The typical interview will last thirty to sixty minutes, although if it is with an alum it may be longer. In fact, alumni tend to differ from other interviewers insofar as they are generally chattier, more interested in selling the school, and less interested in "grilling" applicants than either admissions officers or students are. Admissions officers, in contrast, tend to run a smooth interview, and are likely to be extremely focused and to keep interviews very short (typically thirty minutes). Students are typically less smooth, ask very tough questions, and tend to assess applicants in terms of whether they would be an asset to the student's study group.

2. YOU AND YOUR OBJECTIVES

The University of Chicago uses the following interview evaluation form. It lays out very clearly the areas that are of interest to the school and thus the qualities you will want to show.

UNIVERSITY OF CHICAGO INTERVIEW EVALUATION FORM

Highly Descriptive	*Descriptive*	*Neutral*	*Descriptive*	*Highly Descriptive*

Comments:

Clear Communication Skills	vs.	**Weak Communication Skills**

Conveys thoughts and information in a clear organized way
Succinct; to the point
Good, active listener
Appropriate depth in answers
Persuasive; "sells" ideas well
Provides clear explanations
Appropriate expressiveness

Unclear; hard to follow
Goes off on tangents
Rambles, verbose
Too brief; information has to be drawn out
Overly factual; monotonous
Makes too many assumptions; not sensitive to needs of audience
Shows little or no emotion

Intellectually Curious

Asks probing questions
Exhibits an eagerness to learn
Open-minded
Seeks out new challenges and opportunities
Looks for unique ways to solve problems
Exhibits a broad interest pattern
Applies self fully; well disciplined
Curious about and understands key aspects of our program

Lacks Curiosity

Appears apathetic
Tends not to question or probe
Appears to be a "know it all"
Narrow in outlook
Intellectually lazy; may be bright but doesn't push self
Too often goes the "tried-and-true" way
Naive about our program or MBA programs in general

Strong Social Skills

Personable
Seems friendly and at ease with others
Appropriately assertive; states opinions tactfully
Outgoing; enjoys being with others
Cooperates within a team environment
Strives for leadership positions
Appropriate dominance in group environments
Good sense of humor
Appreciates humor of others
Shows enthusiasm and positive emotions

Poor Social Skills

Sarcastic, biting humor
Overly serious; formal
Loner; overly shy and quiet
Overbearing; domineering
Overly self-oriented
Distant; cold
Lacks tact; blunt
Avoids conflict
Overly critical or negative

Highly Descriptive	*Descriptive*	*Neutral*	*Descriptive*	*Highly Descriptive*

Comments:

Self-Confident

Projects a positive, professional image
and attitude
Speaks with conviction
Handles self well in interpersonal confrontation
Confident of intellectual skills
Looks forward to intellectual challenges
and new learning opportunities
Takes pride in accomplishments

Lacks Self-Confidence

Arrogant or cocky
Overly tentative; hesitant
Avoids eye contact
Easily threatened or intimidated
Overly concerned about academic
challenges
Overly critical or negative
Stays nervous; anxious throughout
interview

Committed to Building Relationships

Participates in groups
Seeks out relationships
Active in formal and informal organizations
Concerned about giving back to the organization
or group
Takes pride in past affiliations
Approaches new environments with
vigor and passion
Gets involved in community service and
extracurricular activities

Not Relationship-Oriented

Uninvolved with others
Not a social joiner
Just concerned about what he/she
takes out of groups
Waits for others to organize groups
and events
Lacks interest in outside activities
(high school, undergraduate,
work experience)

Hard-Working

Persistent; goes the extra step
Exhibits drive and determination
Willing to sacrifice
Takes initiative; doesn't wait for
others' direction
Enjoys and seeks out responsibility
High quality orientation
Views problems as challenges
High energy level
Goal-oriented
Ambitious

Lacks Persistence

Overly concerned with short-term
pleasures
Complacent; coasts along
Takes path of least resistance
Gets overly frustrated with obstacles
Low energy or overly hyper
Drifts; lacks ambition
Does not have well-defined career
goals or direction

Highly Descriptive	*Descriptive*	*Neutral*	*Descriptive*	*Highly Descriptive*

Comments:

Independent

Enjoys autonomy
Likes to be in control of situations
Self-sufficient
Comfortable working within
   ambiguous situations
Able to develop own goals and focuses well

Dependent

Looks too much to others for direction
   or guidance
Seeks out structure
Poorly focused; easily distracted

Flexible

Responsive to changing priorities
Able to juggle several tasks at once
Deals well with the ups and downs of
   academic and corporate life
Takes setbacks in stride

Inflexible or Overly Flexible

Overly concerned about things being
   a certain way
Flusters easily with obstacles
Rigid in beliefs
Wishy-washy

Summary Evaluation

Based on your comments and what you know about our school and its students and graduates, do you:

Feel that this person has well-thought-out reasons for getting an MBA?

Yes   No   Unsure

Agree that this individual is a good match with our program?

Yes   No   Unsure

Agree that this individual has a good understanding of our program?

Yes   No   Unsure

Feel that this individual would attend our program if admitted?

Yes   No   Unsure

Want this person in your class or organization?

Yes   No   Unsure

Vote to admit this person to the program?

Yes   No   Unsure

Overall Comments:

Please document the substance of your conversation with the applicant and your evaluation of the candidate. Please add any additional thoughts, positive or negative, which would assist us in making an informed admission decision.

This evaluation form may not capture everything that could be relevant in a candidate, but certainly captures enough to show you the way in which a school will assess you. Other schools, of course, have their own approaches, but these, without exception, are similar to the one shown above. The primary differences are that some schools use much briefer evaluation forms, whereas others highlight something particularly important to their own programs. Some of the programs that feature heavy quantitative demands probe applicants' experience using various quantitative techniques. One European school assesses candidates' internationalism. It focuses on language skills, understanding of other cultures, experience working in different cultures, and interest in the program's international dimensions.

3. KNOWING THE SCHOOL

Chapter 5, "How to Choose the Right School for *You*," examined many criteria relevant to that decision. It also detailed how to find the information necessary for making a well-informed decision. Let's assume that you have read that chapter and followed its advice prior to applying. Now that you are preparing for school interviews it would be a good idea to review the information you put together on each school you plan to interview with. In particular, you should be extremely familiar with the information that the school publishes about itself. If you tell the interviewer that you plan to major in international business, but the school offers no such major, you will look foolish.

If you are going to interview at the school itself, try to spend several hours in advance exploring the school and its environs. Talk with people in the cafeteria or lounge, paying attention to the attitudes they evince. Are they generally pleased with the school? Do they respect most of their professors? Do they think that the placement office is doing its job? Are there any particular problems concerning the facility itself, such as crime or lack of late-night restaurants that might matter to you? It always impresses an interviewer to see that you have taken the time and effort to examine the school up close rather than just reading some materials on it. Knowing what type of housing is available, or which professors students maneuver to take classes from, is the sort of thing that shows you to be both determined and resourceful. It also helps you to develop good questions to ask the interviewer without sounding artificial. Even if you are not interviewing on campus, take advantage of any opportunities to visit schools for precisely these reasons. (Interviewers invariably spot the applicants who have done their homework by visiting the school and learning what its program is really like.)

One last point: if you find out which specific person will be interviewing you, ask people you know who interviewed with the same school to see how the interview was conducted. How formal or informal was it? How rapid-fire? How long? How much was the interviewee expected to initiate, rather than just respond to, questions? How friendly was the interviewer? If you know how this person likes to conduct interviews you will be able to prepare more specifically.

The advantages of knowing the school thoroughly include:

- You will know that you are prepared, enabling you to relax somewhat during the interview.

- You will be able to ask intelligent questions about the school, thereby impressing the interviewer.

- You will show yourself as being highly motivated, concerned about your career, and in possession of the right work ethic, which will impress your interviewer.

4. ANTICIPATING THE QUESTIONS

The interviewer is likely to have two types of questions to ask you. One type is the set of questions she uses for everyone, such as, "Why do you want to attend school X?" The other type is a response to your résumé or file. If you have claimed to have had some marvelous successes, she may wish to probe to make sure that you have not exaggerated the results. Or she may wish to probe for gaps or weaknesses in your career to date. For example, one of the standard things to seek in a résumé is a period of unaccounted-for time. If such a time gap exists in your application, expect to be asked what you were doing then.

MOST LIKELY QUESTIONS

- ➤ Tell me about yourself.
- ➤ What are your career goals?
- ➤ Why do you want an MBA?
- ➤ Why do want to attend this school?
- ➤ Why should we accept you?
- ➤ What would you add to the program?
- ➤ What are your greatest achievements?
- ➤ What questions do you have?

The easiest question to prepare for is, "Do you have any questions?" Most interviewers will give you the opportunity to ask a few questions. You should be ready with three to five questions that reflect your concerns about the school. Keep these in your head rather than on paper, because having to look at your notes will slow the interview down and make it look as though you cannot remember even a few questions.

Another set of questions to expect is anything from the list of essay questions (which were analyzed exhaustively in a prior chapter). Prior to interviewing, review not only the questions you had to answer for this school—and, of course, your answers, since the interviewer may have read your essay answers shortly before interviewing you—but also those you answered for other schools and even those you did not have to answer for any program you applied to. Consider how you would have answered those too.

THE INTERVIEW QUESTIONS

The Chicago interview evaluation form reprinted above suggests some of the questions you can expect. In general, two types of approaches are common. In the first, you are asked more or less directly about the trait or competence the interviewer is interested in. For example, when trying to get a handle on your degree of independence, the direct interviewer might ask simply, "How much supervision and direction do you prefer?" The second approach tries to elicit information that will also allow the interviewer to determine whether, for example, you "strive for leadership positions," but it does so much less directly. In this case, the interviewer is likely to focus on various aspects of your past and current experience—in terms of your education, career, and personal life—to see how much supervision and direction you have had in various projects and whether that amount suited you. The questions that generate this information are likely to be more general, along the lines of, "Regarding that cost analysis project, what sort of relationship did you have with your boss? What did you like and dislike about this relationship?"

These more open-ended questions, where the focus is not made so obvious, are by now standard interviewing procedure. The more experienced the interviewer, and the more time she has available, the more likely she is to use the indirect approach.

You can prepare for both approaches by examining the following list, which covers the most common questions asked on each major topic—education, career, management orientation, goals, and personal life. Of course other questions are possible, but if you are prepared to respond coherently and consistently to each of the following, you will be ready for just about anything else you will encounter as well. Preparing for the following will force you to think through the main issues that are of interest to business schools.

UNIVERSITY EDUCATION (REPEAT FOR GRADUATE PROGRAMS AS APPROPRIATE)

Which school did you attend?

Why did you choose that one?

(Regarding a lesser quality school) Don't you worry that you will be overwhelmed by the quality of students attending our program?

Which factors most influenced your choice?

What was your major? Why?

In hindsight, are you glad you chose that school? What would you change now if you could? Why?

In hindsight, are you glad you chose that major? What would you choose instead if you could do it over again?

How many hours each week did you study?

Which courses did you do best in? Why?

Which courses did you do worst in? Why?

Do your grades reflect your abilities? If not, why did you not do better?

In what ways did your education prepare you, or fail to prepare you, for your career to date?

What did you most enjoy about college?

What did you least enjoy about college?

What extracurricular activities did you participate in? What was your role and contribution for each?

How did you pay for your education?

How would you describe yourself as a college student? Is this still true about you?

GENERAL TIPS REGARDING UNIVERSITY EDUCATION

1. Avoid portraying your university days as a social experience rather than an intellectual one if at all possible.

2. If your record is poor, show that you have since gotten serious.

3. Show that you were committed to learning, whether for its own sake or for the sake of your career.

4. If you have changed your goals or interests several times, show that you have been serious about at least one of them while pursuing it.

5. Portray both your academic interests and your extracurricular activities in terms of their contribution to your current (or then current) career interests.

6. Discuss your leadership experiences.

7. As to changes you might make if given the opportunity to do it all over again, a safe answer is one that would better prepare you for your eventual career, such as by providing further grounding in econometrics or multidimensional scaling if you are currently a marketing researcher.

8. If you are interviewing for admission to a part-time program, do not try to excuse a mediocre undergraduate performance by explaining that you were unable to focus well due to the need to work part-time as well as study. This combination of work and study will be your fate once again in the part-time program.

WORK EXPERIENCE (TO BE REPEATED AS APPROPRIATE FOR DIFFERENT COMPANIES AND JOBS HELD)

Why did you choose this profession?

Why did you choose this firm?

What is your job title? To whom do you report?

What are your key responsibilities?

What and whom do you manage directly?

Describe the financial aspects of your job: budget, revenues, costs, return on assets employed.

What are the key technical challenges of your job? Managerial challenges?

What do you do best/worst in your job? Why?

How could you improve your performance? What actions have you taken to make these improvements?

What have your major successes been? What financial or other impact have these had?

Did you achieve these on your own? Who else was involved? How?

What have you done that best shows your willingness to work hard/take initiative/innovate/exceed expectations?

How many hours per week do you work?

What do you like most/least about your position? Why?

What are the biggest challenges your unit faces? What are you doing to meet these challenges?

Where is your industry headed in the next five years?

Describe your relationship with your boss. What is good and bad about it? (Repeat for prior bosses)

How well are you rated by your boss? What does he or she most/least like about your performance?

Describe a failure on the job.

What are you doing to address your failings?

What would you change about your job?

How does your performance compare with that of others at similar levels in the company?

Describe your salary progression to date. How does this compare with that of others at similar levels in the company?

GENERAL TIPS REGARDING WORK EXPERIENCE

1. When discussing your boss, your description of what was good and bad about him will probably make it clear what you need, and also what you cannot tolerate, in a boss. This also says a lot about your own strengths and weaknesses.

2. Even when describing the characteristics you do not like in your boss, try to be reasonably sympathetic; otherwise you risk sounding like a malcontent.

3. Any job change should have been motivated by a desire for more challenges, more responsibility, the chance to grow, and so on. In other words, emphasize the positive, forward-looking reasons for making the change. Avoid the negative, backward-looking reasons for the change, such as being unappreciated, underpaid, or disliked by your boss.

4. If you were fired, confess to this fact if necessary, but be sure to note what you learned from the experience.

5. Working less than fifty hours per week may suggest that you are insufficiently motivated. A good answer will establish that you work as hard as necessary to achieve your objective.

6. Portray yourself as one who tries to meet or exceed the objective with as little time and effort as possible. You consider different approaches and look

to improve whatever systems are in place if such a change will make it possible to achieve such results with less effort in the future.

MANAGERIAL ORIENTATION

What is your management philosophy?

What is your managerial style? What aspects of it do you wish to change?

What have you done to develop those under you?

How much do you control those under you? How much freedom do you give them? How do you motivate them?

What do you do best/worst as a manager?

Are you a better leader or follower?

What would your subordinates say about you as a manager? Why?

GENERAL TIPS REGARDING MANAGERIAL ORIENTATION

1. Any response that chooses one managerial style over another is a mistake. Respond that this is situation-dependent.

2. When you are the person in a group who is most knowledgeable about a given situation, you take the lead, but you defer to others when appropriate.

3. You are very much output-oriented and not overly fussy about the role you play in a team, although you generally end up taking on a great deal of responsibility since you seem to welcome it and its challenges more than most do.

GOALS

What do you want to be doing in five years' time? Ten years? Twenty-five years?

What do you want to accomplish in life?

How have your goals changed in recent years?

Why do you want an MBA? What do you expect to get from it?

Which other schools are you applying to? Why? Why so many/few?

How did you choose these schools?

Which school is your first choice? Why?

What if you are not accepted at a top school?

GENERAL TIPS REGARDING GOALS

1. You want to show that you are committed to career success.

2. Showing that you have thought long and hard about your future career demonstrates your seriousness of purpose.

3. Regarding your long term goals, do not say that you want to lie on a beach somewhere. Saying this would show you to be overly stressed already, hardly an ideal attribute for someone trying to get into a challenging MBA program. Discuss instead how you arrived at your chosen goal in light of a consideration of your relative strengths and weakness, what you most enjoy, your background and desires, etc.

PERSONAL

Tell me about yourself.

What publications do you regularly read? Why?

What books have you read recently? What impressed you about that one?

What have you done to keep yourself current, or to develop your skills, in your field?

How do you feel about:
- China's advent upon the world stage?
- African internecine warfare?
- (Anything else on the front pages, especially if it relates to your home region or that of the school?)

How do you spend your time outside of work?

Is your current balance among career, family, friends, and interests the right one for you over the long term?

What activity do you enjoy the most? Why?

Who most influenced you when you were growing up? How?

Who are your heroes? Why?

What competitive sports have you participated in? Did you enjoy them? Are you competitive by nature?

GENERAL TIPS REGARDING PERSONAL QUESTIONS

1. When describing yourself, or what your long term goals are, be sure that a large part of your response focuses upon your career.

2. Take every opportunity to show that you are highly achievement oriented and do what you can to develop both personally and professionally.

3. At the same time, show yourself to be a sensible and well-balanced person with compelling outside interests, including but not limited to family and friends.

4. When talking about your interests, it does not much matter whether you read science fiction, monographs about the Napoleonic wars, or locked room mysteries, as long as you show that you are knowledgeable and enthusiastic regarding whatever you pursue.

5. These questions provide a natural opportunity to subtly strengthen your chosen positioning.

OTHER

Is there anything else you would like us to know about you?

GENERAL TIP REGARDING OTHER QUESTIONS

1. Remember your pre-interview objectives. If you intended to put across several major points, ask yourself whether you have succeeded in doing so. If you have, do not feel compelled to add anything. On the other hand, if you have not, mention briefly but persuasively the points you wished to make along with the supporting examples or illustrations you intended to use.

PREPARING TO DESCRIBE KEY EVENTS

You should be ready to discuss major and minor milestones in your personal, educational, and professional life. Some interviewers prefer to ask very general, open-ended questions to learn how well you can develop an organized, intelligent response. Questions of this nature often revolve around major events interviewers glean from your résumé or application. Prepare yourself by reviewing the relevant aspects of each event you expect to discuss. In the case of a successful business project, for example, you would want to recall:

The project's initial objective

Who originated it

Who was in charge

The resources available

The timetable

The activities undertaken

Your role
  - What you did well and poorly, and why
  - What skills you used
  - What you would do differently in retrospect

Other people's roles

The results

What went right and what did not, and why

Any conclusions this suggests about the department or company, whether of a strategic, operational, or organizational nature

It is a useful exercise to write down the half dozen (or dozen) most important incidents you expect to discuss on an index card, using this sort of approach for each. Carry these cards with you for reading when you are waiting or have a spare moment. Learn them well enough that you can produce a well-organized, apparently spontaneous summary of each of them at the drop of a hat, but do not memorize the stories by rote. Be prepared to be interrupted by the interviewer, and be ready to carry on with the story smoothly once you have answered his question.

WHAT DETERMINES THE LIKELIHOOD OF A GIVEN QUESTION BEING ASKED?

Questions are not generally asked without a reason. Some interviewers believe that certain questions should be asked of anyone, no matter what the person's circumstances. In interviewing for MBA programs, the most likely questions concern why you want to get an MBA, why at this school, what other schools you are considering, what you think you will contribute while at school X, and what you intend to do professionally in the near and long terms.

The other determinant of questions is, of course, you. Your background invites questions that may be quite different from those that would be asked of someone else. If you are in a nonbusiness field that seldom produces MBA candidates, you can expect questions concerning why you want an MBA. If you have a history of career success, but just got fired from your job, you can expect questions about what happened. If one of your credentials is relatively weak, you can expect questions about it. If you are an anglophone trying to get into a bilingual program, you can expect to have your second language probed.

A good interviewer, and often even a bad interviewer, will try to use the interview to learn as much relevant information as possible about you. Given that most interviewers will not have read your application, you can expect them to ask many of the same basic questions that appear on the various applications. One way to influence the course of an interview with someone who knows little about you is to take a résumé along. Most interviewers will use it as the basis for their questions, so they will ask about the items you choose to list on your résumé. They will also probe for internal inconsistencies ("Why were you paid so little if you were really in charge of the internal audit function?") as well as checking things that sound inherently unlikely ("How is it that you were in charge of conducting an audit of the internal controls in operation in the whole Swedish subsidiary when you had never done anything even vaguely related to such a field?").

The other items an interviewer will probe are things you and she have in common, or about which she is simply curious. ("What is the cheapest luxury trip down the Nile currently available?") The more that an interviewer takes this approach, the easier the interview is likely to be. Discussing interests you share is likely to provide an opportunity to share enthusiasms, which is generally easier to handle than responding to probing questions about why you left a good job after just fifteen months. Be sure, however, to keep to your own objectives. You can still make the impression you want by being articulate and well organized even when just discussing trips on the Nile.

PRACTICE

There are two ways that you can practice your interviewing skills and responses. The first is by doing mock interviews with others who are applying, or someone else who appreciates what is involved. This is a good first step to understanding what an interview will be like. The quality of the experience will depend in large part upon how prepared your interviewing partner is. If you can find someone who is willing to read your application carefully, and perhaps even read this chapter, then you are ready to get a good interview. The ideal person to team up with would be someone who is applying to the same schools, but has a very different background from yours, and who is willing to be tough when necessary in the interview. It can be difficult to find the right person, of course. (It is partly for this reason that Education U.S.A. regularly does mock interviews with clients, if necessary by phone, to give them a realistic view of what to expect.) It is not only fair, but also good for you, to switch roles with your partner. If you have to read her essays and data sheets with an eye to seeing what her strengths and weaknesses are, what she will contribute to the program, and the like, you will more readily understand how someone else will do this with you.

Your interview partner can tell you which responses were convincing and which were not (and why). Be persistent and force your interview partner to be specific in noting what worked and what did not. After all, the point is not what you say but *what your interviewer hears* that determines the success of your interview. In fact, simply saying things out loud will often cause *you* to hear what is not right. Speaking out loud often makes it clear that you are wandering instead of being focused, trying too hard to excuse some prior mistake, or pleading rather than convincing. Tape recording your practice sessions will make this apparent.

If you can videotape your practice interviews, by all means do so. Seeing yourself in action will help you to eliminate extreme gestures and repetitive phrasings. Particularly annoying is the idiotic-sounding, inappropriate use of "like" and "you know." Wear your interview outfit to make sure that it too passes muster.

The second means of practicing is to be sure that you interview first with the schools that matter least to you. If you are applying to three "likely" choices, make sure that your first two interviews are with schools in this category rather than the "possibles" or "stretches." This allows you to develop and refine your pitch and get rid of your first interview nerves without too much at stake.

It is a good idea to use both of these approaches if you can. Maximize the potential benefits by debriefing your partner, or yourself when you interviewed with a school, to be sure that you understand what worked and what needed more thought, and why.

PHYSICAL PREPARATIONS

PHYSICAL ENERGY

- Get plenty of sleep the two nights before the interview.
- Eat a solid breakfast or lunch on the day, so that you do not run out of energy.

APPEARANCE

- Arrive at the actual site slightly before the allotted time so that you do not need to rush and get nervous as a result. Find the restroom and check your appearance. Make sure that your hair is combed, tie straight and completely covered in back by the collar of your shirt.
- Make sure that your lipstick is not smudged, or on your teeth.

- Men should consider carrying an extra tie and perhaps a shirt, in case something is spilled at lunch. Women, similarly, can carry extra stockings, in case of a run.

LOCATION

- Be sure that you know where the interview will take place and how to get there (and where to park).

OTHER

- Take your business cards, several copies of your résumé, and a copy of your application.
- Take a copy of the university's brochure and other relevant information about the program to review if you get there early.
- Take the name and telephone number of your interviewer in case your car breaks down and you need to telephone her to notify her of your delay.
- Consider taking copies of the wonderful brochure you designed for your company, but do not take the two hundred pound, greasy widget that you manufacture.

STAYING RELAXED

A modest degree of nervousness is good because it gives you the energy to perform at your best. If you tend to be too nervous, try one of these techniques to keep yourself relaxed:

- ➤ Remind yourself that you have prepared thoroughly (assuming that this is the case) and that this preparation will see you through.
- ➤ Acting positive, by using the appropriate body language, will help you to feel the way you are acting. Positive body language involves keeping your head up, shoulders square, and eyes forward.
- ➤ A great friend of mine, before exams and cross country races, used to go off by himself and keep repeating, with concentration and intensity, "I am King Kong, I am King Kong."

DURING THE INTERVIEW

A considerable amount of the impact you have in an interview is achieved nonverbally; nonverbal messages may constitute over half of the message you deliver. As a result, it is highly appropriate to consider such factors as dress, physical comportment, and the like in order to maximize the chances of interview success.

DRESS

Business schools are inherently conservative places. The top graduates tend to go off into management consulting and investment banking, the professors consult to top multinational corporations, and the typical applicant is currently working in a corporate environment. This means that the style appropriate for a business school interview is a conservative one.

Rules for men:

- Wear clean, neatly pressed clothes and highly shined, black shoes. Socks should be black or navy blue and over the calf.
- Be sure that your clothes fit well. Be sure also that your clothes do not look as if you are wearing them for the first time, but they should not be so well worn that this is noticeable.
- Avoid wild colors or styles.
- Men will never go wrong wearing a conservative dark blue or gray suit with a white or blue shirt, or moderately striped shirt, and a conservative tie.
- Comb your hair and wear no cologne. It should go without saying that your shirt should be 100 percent cotton, long-sleeved, professionally cleaned and heavily starched. The tie should be pure silk and extend to the middle of your belt buckle.

Rules for women:

- Women should wear a suit or a dress, and no more than a modest amount of jewelry, makeup, and perfume.

- The length, color, and cut of your clothing are more fashion-dependent than is true for a man, but do not go wild.

- Try not to bring both a briefcase and purse because it is difficult to be graceful when carrying both.

- In the United States, wear pantyhose (no matter how hot the weather) and eschew bare arms.

    Rules for men and women:

- Do not wear such ostentatiously expensive clothes that you might offend your interviewer. For example, leave the Hermes tie in the closet.

- Your briefcase should be of good leather, preferably brown or burgundy.

- Be sure that you have invested appropriately in mouthwash, deodorant, and other hygienic necessities.

    You want to be remembered for what you said, not for what you wore (or failed to wear).

BEHAVIOR

PHYSICAL BEHAVIOR

Your goal is to be considered self-confident and relaxed. You can show this by remaining poised and thoughtful throughout the interview.

The rules:

- Greet the interviewer with a smile, an extended hand, and a firm handshake (matching the interviewer's pressure).

- Look the interviewer in the eye.

- Do not sit down until invited to do so.

- Do not put anything on the interviewer's desk.

- Do not smoke, drink, or eat anything even if invited to do so—not even if the interviewer herself does. This can distract either you or the interviewer, perhaps showing you to be clumsy or worse, without any chance of improving her opinion of you. If the interviewer offers you a cigarette, decline politely but not judgmentally by saying, "No thank you."

- Do not chew gum.

- Maintain a moderate amount of eye contact throughout the interview, perhaps 25 percent, but do not stare.

▪ Gesticulate moderately to make points, but do not go overboard.

▪ Remain physically stationary, without fidgeting. Interviewers often check your response to a tough question to see if you are exhibiting signs of nervousness (or lying).

▪ Maintain good rapport with the interviewer by being warm and smiling often. Do not, however, smile idiotically without stopping for the entire interview! Doing so will mark you as unbalanced or worse.

▪ Sit up straight, but not rigidly, and lean forward slightly. This will show that you are interested in what the interviewer has to say, and that you are businesslike.

▪ Listen carefully, and show that you are listening by nodding, grunting "uh-huh" occasionally, or saying, "I see" or "right."

▪ Avoid crossing your arms, or folding your arms behind your head.

▪ Keep your voice well modulated, but alive. Speak at a normal speed; do not rush.

ATTITUDES

The rules:

▪ *Be upbeat.* Be sure to emphasize your strengths. Do not discuss your weaknesses in any detail unless pushed to do so. And, never complain about anything that has befallen you. No complaint about a low GMAT score, or sickness during a math exam, or personality conflict with a boss or professor can improve an interviewer's opinion of you.

▪ *Flatter the interviewer, subtly.* Although a good interviewer will have you do 75 percent to 80 percent of the talking, that does not mean that you will be excused for failing to listen to her.

Adopt an attitude similar to the interviewer's. If your interviewer is deadly serious, avoid joking. If your interviewer is lighthearted and jocular, do not sit deadpan. In the first instance jocularity will make you seem frivolous, whereas in the latter instance seriousness will make you seem unintelligent.

Maintain more formality if your interviewer remains behind her desk throughout the interview, without even coming around to greet you initially.

▪ *Treat the interviewer respectfully, but not too respectfully.* Treat her as an equal, albeit one who temporarily is allowed to set the direction of the interview. Do not behave submissively.

Do not, however, use the interviewer's first name unless and until told to do so.

■ *Relax and enjoy yourself.* The relatively few people who enjoy interviews are those who view them as a chance to discuss important matters with an equal who happens to be interested in the same subjects. They view the interview as the time to learn more about the school as well as the chance to explain themselves.

A little nervousness is to be expected, but exhibiting substantial nervousness works against you insofar as a strong candidate is meant to believe himself well suited to interact at this level.

■ *Make sure that it is a conversation.* A good interview resembles nothing so much as a conversation.

If there is a pause in the conversation, consider whether:
- you have answered the question fully enough. If you suspect not, ask whether the interviewer would like you to add to the answer.
- you should follow up with a question of your own related to the same subject.
- you should simply sit quietly, without tension, with a pleasant smile.

Ask the interviewer questions to follow up on what she has said. This helps to build rapport and puts you on a more equal footing with her by getting you out of the role of interviewee answering questions. It is also the way normal conversations work, trading back and forth.

■ *Avoid sounding like a robot.* If you follow this book's suggestions and prepare thoroughly for your interviews, you run the risk of sounding preprogrammed rather than spontaneous. It is good to sound as though you have given thought to the relevant issues, but not as though you have memorized answers.

How can you avoid this problem? There are three keys. (1) Avoid a robotic monotone, or appearing to be reaching into your memory for what comes next in your rehearsed response. (2) Focus upon your interviewer. You should be able to remain relaxed, given that you know that you are well prepared, and this will allow you to stay focused upon how your interviewer is reacting to you. (3) Occasionally pause before you speak, seeming to get organized before starting.

■ *Look interested.* Avoid looking at your watch.
Do not appear bored, no matter how long the interviewer is speaking.

■ *Do not ramble on.* If your answer has gone on too long, cut your losses by briefly restating your main points.

HOW TO READ THE INTERVIEWER

The interviewer's demeanor will help to reveal her reactions to the interview. Smiles and nods clearly suggest that she agrees with what you are saying, in which case, think about what you are doing right so you can do more of it. Perhaps your interviewer likes the fact that you are backing up your abstractions with solid examples. Maybe you are keeping your cool when being asked very tough questions.

Looking away from you, frowning, or constantly fiddling with papers or pens may reveal disagreement or a lack of interest. If you sense that you are losing the interviewer, try to get back on track by asking the interviewer a relevant question or making comments that are sure to be winners, such as some self-deprecating humor or mention of the incidents that you feel show you in your best light.

It is important to keep in mind whatever the interviewer says in her opening remarks, because they may give you good clues as to what she values.

If you are talking too much, your interviewer is likely to start looking away, looking at her watch, or asking such questions as "could you just summarize this part?"

YOUR QUESTION TIME

A failure to ask questions if invited to do so risks leaving the impression that you either did not do your homework or do not particularly care whether the school admits you. Asking questions gives you the opportunity to show how knowledgeable you are about the process and the program as well as that you are taking a proactive approach to your career future.

If you are asked what questions you have, do not rush into asking them. If you have not yet had the opportunity to make one or two key points, ask if it would be acceptable to go back to the earlier question and then mention what you have just accomplished (or whatever). Even if these points are unrelated to any prior question, feel free to say, "I am glad to have the opportunity to ask you a couple of questions, but I hope you will forgive my wanting to mention two things that have come up since I applied. I think they might be relevant to the school's decision making, after which I will continue with my questions." Briefly mention the one or two points. Then go on to your questions.

Try to avoid questions that call for a yes or no response. To understand an area in depth, plan to ask several questions about it. One good way to do so is to ask your interviewer to compare, for example, her school and a major competitor (one that you are actively considering). She will probably mention several points, after which you can ask about one or more of them in greater detail, or ask her why she did not mention subject X.

If you think that the interviewer harbors major objections to you, try to get her to confess what it is she is concerned about, so that you can address her concerns, assuming that you have not yet had the opportunity to do so.

Some appropriate questions, in case you are stuck for something to ask, include:

- How do you expect the school to change in the near future?

- Has the character of the school changed in recent years? How? Why?

- Which top professors will be on sabbatical next year? Who will take their place?

If one reason for attending the school is that a certain professor teaches there, by all means ask whether the interviewer knows him or her, and if so, what he or she is like as a professor.

After asking several questions, if necessary you can fall back on the old standby: "I had a number of questions when the interview started, but you have covered them all."

Do not try to baffle the interviewer with questions you know she won't be able to answer. If she is an alum of the school, for example, she will not be privy to the school's rationale for its recent decision not to offer tenure to assistant professor X.

Being asked if you have any questions signals that the interview is coming to an end, so do not take too much time.

ENDING THE INTERVIEW

Be sure to smile at the interviewer, shake hands and thank her for seeing you, and leave with an energetic, confident demeanor.

Be careful not to be taken in by an old trick. Once you feel that the interview is over you may be asked a potentially revealing question as you are being shown out, on the assumption that you may have let down your guard at this point. Or the secretary may be instructed to ask a question such as, "How do you think you did?" in hopes of eliciting a telling comment. Assume that the interview is really over only once you have left the premises.

INTERVIEW WRECKERS

➤ Criticizing your boss or company

➤ Being too nervous to look the part of a successful, confident leader

➤ Appearing blasé about attending the school at hand

➤ Asking no questions

➤ Whining about past grades, low GMAT scores, and so on

➤ Blaming others for weakness in your profile

(Consult the interview evaluation form for more.)

GENERAL RULES FOR INTERVIEWS

The following advice is good no matter what type of interview or interviewer you encounter:

Do not criticize others. Do not criticize people you worked with or schools you attended. Otherwise you may be viewed as a chronic malcontent. Remain positive. You can still make it clear, for example, that a boss was limited in his ability to develop you, but without sounding critical. Simply state that he was expected to spend most of his time traveling to the regional offices, so he had no time left to worry about the development of his subordinates.

Assume that alumni interviewers do not have your file memorized. In fact, most interviewers will not even have seen your file. You can therefore expect to be able to make good use of the same incidents you discussed in your essays.

Be truthful. Do not lie in answering questions. Being honest, however, does not mean the same thing as being blunt, so do not volunteer negative information if it can be avoided.

Be yourself. Do not pretend to be someone other than yourself to impress your interviewer. Very few people are able to act well enough to carry it off successfully. Focus instead on presenting the best aspects of your own personality.

Never be less than highly courteous and friendly to the staff. The staff is generally in charge of all of the logistical elements of your candidacy, so do not alienate them. The admissions officers may also ask them to give their impression of you, so make sure that it is a positive one.

Do not try to take over the interview, but take advantage of opportunities to make your points. Interviewers want to feel that they are in charge of an interview, since they are likely to make decisions based upon the information they get about you. They need to feel confident that they will be able to get what they consider information relevant to their decision making, which may happen only if they are able to direct the interview. Taking over the interview may allow you to make the points you want to make, but the risk is far too great that your interviewer will react very negatively to this and resent your aggressiveness. Use of polite phrases in a confident tone of voice can keep your interviewer from fearing that you are trying to take over the interview: "Perhaps you wouldn't mind"; "I would find it very helpful if you could."

Do not ask the interviewer how you did in the interview. This will put him on the spot and will not do anything to improve your chances.

Stay relaxed. A good interviewer takes the following as possible indications that you are lying, being evasive, or hoping that he will not follow up a point:

- Fidgeting (such as twirling your hair, drumming your fingers, bouncing your leg up and down, or picking at a part of your body or clothing. Many people have a tic of which they are completely unaware. Use your mock interview partner or videotape to find yours, and then stop doing it.)

- Speaking much faster or more slowly.

- Pulling your collar away from your neck.

- Avoiding eye contact.

- Lengthy, convoluted response.

- Desperately looking for a drink of water.

- Coughing at length before starting a response.

Remain calm even in the face of provocation. An interviewer may be trying to annoy you to see how you respond. A senior manager, it should go without saying, is unlikely to be easily ruffled.

Answer questions concisely. Do not ramble. Do not take more than two or three minutes for any but the most involved, important question. In fact, two or three sentences is an appropriate length for the majority of answers. You can save time by quantifying whenever possible. ("I saved $275,000, which represented 13 percent of recurring costs.")

Structure your responses. Because you have prepared thoroughly (if you have taken this chapter to heart), you are in a position to respond with structured answers to most questions you will be asked. You do not need to start every response by saying "I did such and such for five reasons. Number one was . . .", but doing so from time to time will be impressive.

When you give a general statement, illustrate it with an appropriate example. ("I am comfortable in a very international setting. I have been able to work with people of all different backgrounds, such as when I managed a restaurant in New York that had Albanian cooks, Mexican busboys, Portuguese waitresses, a Greek owner, and a yuppie clientele—and I happen to be French, as you know.") Then go on to give an example in which nationality posed a substantial problem, and how you solved it.

Summarize any particularly lengthy answers you give.

Listen well. Be sure that you have understood what the interviewer is asking. If uncertain, ask for clarification of the question. Answering the question you thought was being asked, or the one you anticipated being asked, rather than the one she really did ask you, will annoy her and suggest that you are either dim or not paying attention. Listening well means more than paying attention to what is being said. It also requires that you encourage the interviewer by appearing interested. In addition, you should be able to sense the feelings behind the comments made.

Assume that anyone at the office may be an interviewer. Sometimes a junior employee will chat with you while you wait for the real interview to start, trying to get you to give your real reactions to the school or your own qualifications as though a junior person should be on your side rather than the school's. Expect any information you give away to be fed into your file immediately, maybe even given to your real interviewer prior to your upcoming interview.

SPECIAL TYPES OF INTERVIEWS

STRESS INTERVIEWS

Stress interviews are not much in evidence any more, but they still pop up often enough to merit comment. The idea underlying any form of stress interview is that applying enormous stress to an interviewee will cause him to reveal his *true* nature and likely performance under stress in the future. A failure to remain poised will reveal a person's supposed lack of confidence in himself.

What exactly is a stress interview? It can take many forms. You may be put in a position in which bright sunlight will be directly in your eyes, or your responses may be met by long silences. The tendency in this case is to try to fill up the awkward moments by adding to a response, thereby perhaps revealing information you would have been better advised to keep from view.

More likely you will be given too little time to answer questions. This sort of pressure is most readily employed when there are two or more interviewers, one preparing to ask you the next, perhaps follow-up, question while you answer the current one. As you start to answer a question, your response may be ignored or cut short and taken out of context, and the next question tossed at you as fast as possible. (Think of the movies you have seen in which detectives grill a suspect under a bright light.) The interviewer may dispute what you are saying and challenge you very aggressively. Your weaknesses can be pointed out at every turn. The interviewer can also be obviously hostile and rude. This will continue for some time, until you react, most probably by becoming angry or resentful that you are not being allowed to get your full answers out.

The key to this situation is to recognize it for what it is. If you know that it is a game, you can respond with suitable bits of gamesmanship. Once you know that you are deliberately being pressured, you have the opportunity to take control of the situation. (This is one of the few circumstances in which it is appropriate for you to take control.) If the sun is shining directly into your eyes, excuse yourself and move your chair to a more comfortable location. If you are being subjected to the silent treatment, respond by smiling at the interviewer and simply waiting for her to ask another question. If, on the other hand, you are being pressured verbally, start by leaning back, smiling, and not saying anything for a few seconds. Then restate the last question, "You have asked me whether this project was really successful." Go on to explain that there are, let's say, four parts to your response. Once you have done this it will be all but impossible for the interviewer to interrupt you until you have finished all four. Be sure to start each portion of your response by saying, "first," "second," and so on.

If you are interrupted again, lean back once more, smile again, and say that this approach seems a bit much and invite the interviewer to share information instead.

An international variation on the stress interview focuses on language. More than one applicant to INSEAD has spent the first half hour chatting in her native language about inconsequential, pleasant matters and then been required to respond to rapid-fire questions in French for the last half hour. The questions posed in French are invariably the tough ones, such as, "Why should we take you when we already have nine applicants from your company with higher GMAT scores than you have?"

GROUP EXERCISES

In a group exercise, you may be asked to work together with other applicants to solve a hypothetical problem or respond to a case. This is meant to test:

- whether you can think on your feet, and stay cool under pressure
- how creative or innovative you are
- your verbal communication ability
- whether you can work as part of a team
- whether you can lead others

These interviews are inevitably tricky because the other "team" members are all trying to get as much air time as possible, so that they are not easily led. In fact, the applicants often resemble nothing so much as the proverbial seals in a pond at the zoo, yapping for their trainer to throw them fish.

How do you determine your own strategy? Start by determining four things.

1. What type of exercise is planned
2. Your skill set and experiences as they relate to the exercise
3. The skill and experience levels of other applicants
4. Your risk profile: how much of a risk you are willing to take to impress the graders of the exercise, given how high you believe your standing is prior to the exercise

To stand out without looking like a publicity-crazed adolescent, consider prior to the exercise how best to position yourself. Do your homework regarding the exercise, too. Ask the admissions office what to expect in the exercise. Talk with people already at the school about their experiences with this or a similar exercise, or see if another exercise is planned for earlier in the same day, or the day before, and debrief participants as they exit.

For example, one applicant to London Business School was a Scandinavian who had just spent several years working in Asia. He decided that this gave him an ideal positioning opportunity. He knew that the LBS exercise would include a group of international students, some of whom might have weak English skills or be less aggressive than Americans tend to be in such settings. He figured that he could set himself up as the person who draws out the quiet team members. Asking their opinions, asking whether they agreed with what the last person said, would put him in charge of the group for a moment. (It is very difficult for one of the aggressive types who has just spoken to interrupt you because you are not ostensibly being selfish whereas his interruption will clearly be selfish. You can then go on to see whether their views can be reconciled with those already expressed and whether each side agrees with your synthesis. You show yourself to be active, to be concerned to involve everyone, and yet you are not acting selfishly.)

Another role you can play is to question those who have already stated their views. What facts or theories underlie their analysis? How do they feel that it fits with other views already presented (naming, perhaps, some possible area of conflict or agreement)? If you ask questions that are designed to help clarify the proceedings by getting people to amplify what they are thinking, you can contribute significantly to the quality of the discussion.

In general, your analytical approach should be to identify and evaluate alternative courses of action. Do not feel that you must be 100 percent certain that your view is correct before you will participate. If you do, you are unlikely ever to say much. Instead, take the approach that you will participate whenever there is a reasonable likelihood that you are correct. Then listen to others' views and defend your position if it still seems right, but be prepared to jettison it or compromise if it clearly is not. Do not fight to preserve a clearly incorrect view, since this is hardly a sign of maturity and good judgment.

At a minimum, make sure that your attitude is appropriate. Remain energetic and positive even if you are not able to put your views across. Do not give in to feelings of frustration or despair.

PANEL INTERVIEWS

Panel interviews are often conducted with harsh time constraints because they represent a large investment of resources (three or more people's time). This means that you should be particularly certain to arrive in advance. Explain that you understand that this format places time pressure on the proceedings, so you will strive to give very concise answers to questions, but you welcome requests for additional information.

Start each response by addressing the person who asked the question, then look at other panel members, and look back to the original questioner as you finish your response.

If you are asked questions by several people simultaneously, look at the most important (a chairperson for the panel) or someone who has not yet asked a question and ask her (with a smile) if she could please repeat the question.

FRIENDLY CHATS

One type of interviewer will come on as extremely friendly and casual. She will chat away about recent football results or the interviewee's favorite foods. When she shifts to business matters, she will be completely unthreatening and will agree with anything and everything you say. The danger is that she will lull you into totally dropping your guard so that you end up volunteering information that you would be better off keeping to yourself. You are inclined to consider a person who finds you agreeable, fascinating, and invariably correct to be on your side. Resist this temptation; your interviewer may just be using a technique to get you to open up about yourself.

SPECIAL INTERVIEW SETTINGS

RESTAURANTS

➤ Do not sit until the interviewer invites you to be seated.

➤ Consider the menu when the interviewer invites you to. Pick something midpriced, and do so without lengthy deliberations. Make sure that you choose something familiar and easy to eat. Avoid things that splatter or require eating with your fingers.

➤ If the interviewer orders a drink or first course, follow suit by ordering at least some mineral water so that you will have something to occupy yourself with while she is drinking or eating.

➤ Do not order too much, since this suggests a lack of discipline.

➤ Use your discretion regarding alcohol consumption. The safest rule to follow is that you should consume somewhat less alcohol than would be normal for a businessperson in the same circumstances. In Italy it might well be considered rude to refuse wine at dinner, whereas in America it would be considered a sign of incipient alcoholism to have a drink before lunch.

➤ In Europe, you should eat with both hands on the table. It is inappropriate both in America and Europe to place your elbows on the table.

➤ Do not criticize the decor or the food.

➤ Treat the waiters and busboys very politely.

➤ Wait for the interviewer to begin the business end of the discussion. She may prefer to wait until after the drink or first course has been consumed.

WHAT THE ADMISSIONS DIRECTORS SAY ABOUT INTERVIEWS

WHY ARE INTERVIEWS IMPORTANT?

➤ We have tried to correlate placement success and GMAT scores, undergraduate grades, years of experience, and everything else imaginable. The strongest correlation is with interview rankings. The personality strengths that are visible then are also what employers value later on. *Jon Megibow, Darden*

➤ We want to see if they are the right fit for the program, but applicants need to do the same and the interview is a good opportunity to do that. *Julia Tyler, London*

➤ We interview people to see how interested in the program they are. We want to know how enthusiastic they are. It's hard to know this sort of thing from the application alone. *Gea Tromp, Rotterdam*

➤ At the end of the day, you've got to go out and persuade somebody to give you a job and that happens in a face-to-face interview, so we want the interview to be an important part of our admissions process too. *Carol Giraud, INSEAD (Paris region)*

HOW IMPORTANT IS THE INTERVIEW?

➤ An interview is not required, but it is highly recommended, and we mean it. A person who lives in Boston and hasn't interviewed we assume is not interested in Tuck. We interview 85%–86% of our admittees. *Henry Malin, Tuck*

➤ For us, the essays may be slightly less important than they are for some other schools because you can always prepare your essays—rewrite them ten times. But you can't answer a question ten times in a face-to-face interview until you get it right. So for us that spontaneity is important in learning about a candidate.
Carol Giraud, INSEAD (Paris region)

WHAT DO YOU LOOK FOR IN THE INTERVIEW?

➤ I do the interview to get beyond the essays. I know *what* you've done; I need to know *why*. *Brian Sorge, Kellogg*

➤ The successful applicant will represent Tuck two years from now. We can polish somebody quite a bit in two years, but if they are a lump of coal rather than a diamond in the rough even we won't be successful with them. If they have serious problems in communicating in the interview, they are likely to have serious problems in the classroom. *Henry Malin, Tuck*

➤ We try to see if the candidate has more to offer than was apparent on paper. We connect a face/person with the application and hope that we can learn more about the individual in the face-to-face interview. *Linda Baldwin, UCLA*

➤ We look for team players. This quality is most apparent in interviews—we can tell how candidates feel about working with other people by the way they talk about it. *Mary Clark, IESE (Barcelona)*

➤ Interviews give us the chance to see who people are and to check a lot of the information in their applications. *Gabriella Aliatis, Bocconi (Milan)*

➤ We want to test their ability to engage in an argument and to withstand a challenge. We want to see if they can express their views clearly. We also look at the reasons someone wants to do an MBA, why more specifically at the London Business School. We'll look at his interpersonal skills. A lot of the work we do at London Business School is in a team environment, so we want to know whether someone will be able to cope with that. We want to be sure London Business School represents a good fit for him. And, at the end of the day, we want to know whether someone is going to contribute to the school and, having done an MBA, then go out and sell it for us. *Julia Tyler, London*

➤ Because INSEAD is different from other schools, we would expect an interviewee to know that, to know how it differs from other schools, and to be very clear about why he wants to come here. A very clear motivation for coming to INSEAD should be present. *Carol Giraud, INSEAD (Paris region)*

Who Does the Interviewing?

➤ We have our admissions officers, alumni (we have 850 volunteers), and second-year students do the interviewing. *Henry Malin, Tuck*

➤ We interview everybody. In contrast to U.S. schools, the admissions officers don't do the interviewing. Alumni and faculty do it. *Julia Tyler, London*

What Information Does the Interviewer Have About the Applicant?

➤ The interviewer conducts the interview "blind," on purpose. We want the interviewer to give an unbiased view of the applicant, which is impossible if the interviewer sees the folder in advance. *Don Martin, Chicago*

➤ Our interviewers generally work from the interviewee's résumé rather than a complete file. *Judith Goodman, Michigan*

➤ Unlike most schools, our interviewers have the applicant's folder. We don't interview everybody, and we don't use students to do the interviewing, so we can make sure that our interviewers have the data on interviewees. Schools that have students do interviews cannot share sensitive, confidential data with them, so they don't see applicants' folders. *James Millar, Harvard*

Advice

➤ A good interviewee will be succinct but persuasive about his accomplishments, show that he knows the direction he wants his career to take, make it clear why he wants an MBA and why he wants to get one at Michigan. This means that he knows the school and the curriculum and can explain why they are a good match for his needs. *Judith Goodman, Michigan*

➤ If you view interviews as information exchanges you will be more relaxed and sound more sophisticated than if you prepare yourself only for the purpose of responding to questions. *Linda Baldwin, UCLA*

➤ They should treat the interview like a job interview. They should be prepared about the school itself. They should talk with graduates and students of the program, not just read the brochures and guides. *Henry Malin, Tuck*

➤ People should be prepared (although too often they aren't). They need to know about the school and why they are there. The other problem is nerves. We try not to make it nerve-wracking, but people inherently feel that it is. They need to relax. They need to be themselves and be ready to discuss things and to have a good dialogue. *Brian Sorge, Kellogg*

➤ It's good to prepare, but not to be ready with orations you will deliver on topics you expect to be asked. You want this to remain a one-on-one exchange, not a series of canned speeches. *Fran Hill, Haas (Berkeley)*

➤ Know about the school and be prepared to state the reasons for your interest in it. You want the interviewer to feel that you've done your homework and are making some intelligent choices. *Fran Hill, Haas (Berkeley)*

➤ We are impressed when someone has done his homework and knows about our program— someone who obviously wants to come here. *Andrew Dyson, Manchester (England)*

UNUSUAL INTERVIEW FORMATS (notice that these exist only among European schools)

➤ If we question someone's academic ability, we'll use an interview to assess the person's intelligence as well as interpersonal skills. We may ask a business case question or have them do an impromptu presentation to test their business orientation and business skills. *Kal Denzel, IMD (Switzerland)*

➤ We give people a case to do. They're relatively brief. We give them an hour to write a response. *Professor Leo Murray, Cranfield (England)*

➤ We have an "observed group" situation as part of our interview day. We're not looking for someone to take over the group, to be aggressive and a leader; we're looking for someone to encourage other people, bring the best out in others, be a good team player. Five or six people would be asked to deal with a problem as a group. They'll be observed by an organizational specialist on the faculty (typically). It lasts for an hour. It's the process more than the result that interests us.
Helen Ward, Manchester (England)

BIGGEST MISTAKES

➤ Someone who doesn't know the program at all. It's not good enough to say that it's great or ranked number one. They need to know the style of the program and whether it will suit them. *Suzanne Cordatos, Wharton (Lauder Institute)*

➤ The biggest mistake people make seems to be arriving at the interview unprepared to ask specific questions about our program. If people are going to spend the time and money to come here, I would have thought that they'd have questions about our quite unique program. *Don Martin, Chicago*

➤ People tend to be either far too brief or too long-winded. *Judith Goodman, Michigan*

➤ One of the worst mistakes is to dominate proceedings, to wrest control from the interviewer. *Fran Hill, Haas (Berkeley)*

➤ It's unfortunate how many applicants have not thought out what they should expect us to ask. *Mary Clark, IESE (Barcelona)*

➤ Too few interviewees know much about our program before they interview and too few are ready enough that they have serious questions to ask about it.
Gabriella Aliatis, Bocconi (Milan)

➤ Too many people are too casual about the interviews. We expect them to treat interviews as they would a job interview in terms of their presentation (manner and appearance) and being prepared. But on the other hand, they shouldn't be so stressed out that they aren't open enough and friendly enough that there can be a good dialogue. *Carol Giraud, INSEAD (Paris region)*

HOW TO DEAL WITH THE INCOMPETENT INTERVIEWER

What marks an incompetent interviewer? Examples are: talking too much, going off on tangents, failing to maintain control of the interview, and dwelling on inconsequential matters. Here are some tips for dealing with the most common problems:

> *She talks too much.* The more an interviewer talks, the less information she can get about you. Build rapport with her by providing nonverbal encouragement. You do not want to offend her or be rude, but you still want to get some points across. Do so by appearing to agree with her, following up on one of her comments by immediately saying something like, "In fact, one of the things that first got me interested in school X was . . ." And, of course, take advantage of the break she gives you at the end of the interview when she asks if you have any questions. Phrase your questions as questions, but make sure that they are really short advertisements for yourself. For example: "I wonder whether my background—having a PhD in mechanical engineering and a lot of practical work experience in several industries—would be a good fit with the program at Acme University?"

> *She goes off on tangents.* If you want to get the discussion back on track, use such phrases as: "Let me be sure that I understand this correctly" (and then repeat the couple of key points briefly); "Could we go back to that first point, such and such"; "In our remaining time, I hope that we will have the chance to touch on the following points which are particularly important for me: X, Y, Z." Be very friendly and nonconfrontational, showing that you are not trying to take over the interview, but are instead trying to take advantage of an opportunity to learn more about the school or sell your own abilities.

> *She constantly interrupts.* Make a note of where you are in the conversation when the interruption occurred and recall this for the interviewer's sake when the interview recommences. She will be impressed that you have kept your focus while she was losing hers.

AFTER THE INTERVIEW

First, debrief yourself regarding what went well and what went poorly, and why. This will help you with later interviews for other schools; you will be able to anticipate what you might be asked concerning an apparent weakness.

INTERVIEW CHECKLIST

■ Clothing: My dress was/was not appropriate and comfortable.

■ My entrance, including handshake and greeting, was/was not positive.

■ My physical actions (smile, eye contact, body language, avoidance of fidgeting) were/were not appropriate.

■ Attitude: I did/did not appear confident, enthusiastic, and friendly.

■ Questions I handled well (list each, with what was good about your answer):

■ Questions I handled poorly (list each, with what was bad about your answer, and suggestions for improvement):

■ General comments:
  – I spoke too much/too little.
  – I did/did not establish rapport quickly and easily.
  – I stayed on a more or less equal footing with the interviewer.
  – I did/did not impress the interviewer without bragging.
  – I balanced sincerity and humor appropriately for this interviewer's style.

■ My ending questions were/were not appropriate (and sufficient).

■ My exit was/was not smooth and upbeat.

■ I was appropriately knowledgeable about the program (and the school).

■ Interviewer's impression of me:
  – Personal:
  – Professional:

Second, send a *brief thank-you note* to your interviewer. Note something that occurred during the interview to make it clear that this is not a form note. You can mention, for example, that you were glad to learn that it will be very easy to get moderately priced housing near the campus. The one absolute requirement of the note is that you get the interviewer's name and title correct, so be sure to get her business card during the interview.

SPECIAL CONCERNS FOR INTERNATIONAL STUDENTS

Interviewing in a language that is not your own is not easy, especially when you are under substantial performance pressure. This is precisely when your worst verbal tics are likely to show up, including mistakes that you have not made since early in your study of the language. Similarly, normal manners of speaking in your own language can be bothersome to others. Highly educated French speakers are accustomed to using a large number of "uh's" and, if anything, seem to gain respect for doing so. To English speakers, this same trait when expressed in English can be highly annoying. Check your performance under realistic conditions and go the extra step of asking a native speaker what verbal mannerisms are best eradicated.

Cultural differences manifest themselves at many points in an interview. For example, Americans at all social levels discuss a range of sports and expect others to follow them as well. A CEO would not find it odd to discuss baseball, football, or basketball as well as such sports as golf and tennis. In the UK, discussing soccer (i.e., football), darts, or other working class sports would be regarded as bizarre; CEOs would limit themselves to cricket, tennis (i.e., Wimbledon), or the like. Anyone doing business in America should expect sports to serve as a metaphor for business, with constant use of sports terms, whereas little sports terminology would find its way into a British business discussion.

The physical distance people maintain between themselves, amount of eye contact, and many of the behaviors discussed in this chapter are in fact culturally defined norms. Give some consideration, and some practice time, to incorporating these norms into your interview performance so that you will appear to fit into the school's cultural context.

The best way to prepare for a cross-cultural interview is, of course, to speak the appropriate language, and if possible spend time in the appropriate setting, for as long as possible immediately prior to the interview.

13

APPLICATION TIMETABLE

— EXECUTIVE SUMMARY —

■

Start the process as early as possible.
- Assess what you want from an MBA.
- Gather information about programs to determine where you should apply.

■

Apply as early as you can consistent with doing the best possible application.
- Applying early does not on average help your chances— unless you submit a truly unusual and complicated application—but it will give you some slack if factors beyond your control delay some aspect of your application.

■

Track your progress with the Master Application Organizer.

Schools basically use one of two types of admissions decision cycles. "Rolling admissions" involves considering applicants whenever they apply within the several-month admission cycle, and responding soon after receiving a completed application. "Rounds admissions" means that they look at the whole group of students applying by a certain date.

WHEN SHOULD YOU APPLY—EARLY OR LATE IN AN APPLICATION CYCLE?

The application cycle refers to the period of time during which a school accepts applications for a given class. In other words, a school might accept applications from December 1 through April 15 for the class beginning in September. This raises a question. Should you apply early (in December, for example) or late (in April) if you wish to maximize your chances of getting in?

WHAT ARE THE BENEFITS OF APPLYING EARLY IN THE APPLICATION CYCLE?

Assuming that the application is well written, an early application suggests that the applicant is well organized. If a school underestimates how popular it will be, the early applicants may be judged according to less stringent criteria than the later applicants. These are not major considerations, however, given the very slight impact of the first and the unlikely occurrence of the second (schools are quite good at knowing how to judge people throughout the cycle).

There is one major potential benefit to applying early, but it is significant for only one type of applicant. This is someone whose message is a complicated one and who therefore must give the admissions committee the time and mental energy to read his application carefully. This is unlikely to happen at or near the application deadline. Someone in this category should definitely apply early to ensure that his application is given appropriate consideration.

International students should seek to apply as early as possible since international credentials may add complexity to their application.

269

THE BENEFITS OF APPLYING EARLY

"Applying early does reflect a certain commitment to the school. Also, it would be disingenuous if I said that I read the 2000th application as carefully as I read the first. We all become a little fuzzy around the edges. The more complicated case would get a more attentive reading earlier in the process." *Jon Megibow, Darden*

WHAT ARE THE BENEFITS OF APPLYING LATE IN THE APPLICATION CYCLE?

Applying late in the cycle gives an applicant the opportunity to continue to build her credentials during the few months involved. This can be significant for someone with the potential to transform her application. For example, someone who expects a major promotion and salary increase might wish to apply after getting them rather than before.

The second potential benefit can occur if the school has misjudged its popularity and finds that fewer good applicants have applied than it expected earlier in the cycle, resulting in reduced admissions criteria for those applying late in the cycle. This is not likely to happen to any substantial degree.

CONCLUSION

A limited number of people will have such complicated applications that they should present themselves early in the cycle. A greater, but still limited, number of people will be able to improve their credentials substantially during the application cycle, and should apply late in the cycle. For most people, the most important timing criterion is to get the application done well as soon as is practicable; the earlier it is started the more opportunity there is to rewrite and reconsider—and even to have others help out by reading the finished product. Apply as soon as you can finish a truly professional application.

HOW LONG WILL IT TAKE YOU TO DO YOUR APPLICATIONS?

Most applicants underestimate the amount of time that a good application requires, thinking that they can do one in a long weekend or two. The reality is that many of the necessary steps have a long lag built into them. For example, approaching a recommender, briefing her on what you want done, giving her time to do a good recommendation for you, and ensuring that she submits it on time calls for months rather than days of advance notice. This is all the more true when you apply to six or eight schools rather than one; you have more application forms to get, more essays to write, and more recommendations to get submitted. Although work does not increase proportionally with the number of applications, the increased complexity as well as the number of additional things you need to do will inevitably increase your efforts.

The application process should start *at least one and a quarter years in advance* of when you would like to start business school. Thus if you wish to start a program in September, you should start work in June of the preceding year. This may sound excessive, but the timetable in this section makes it clear that this is an appropriate time to get serious about the process. One of the reasons this process takes so long is that schools generally require that applications be submitted three–six months in advance of the start of the program, meaning that you will have nine–twelve months to complete the process if you start at the suggested time.

Starting the application process late, or failing to work seriously at it until deadlines approach, leads to the typical last-minute rush and the inevitable poor marketing job. This book presents an enlightened approach devoted to the idea that applicants can dramatically improve their admission chances if they do a professional job of marketing themselves. This timetable is meant to reinforce the message that time is required for a successful marketing effort.

It is useful to establish your own timetable for applying. Ideally, you will be able to start about fifteen months before you begin your MBA program. Don't panic if you can't, since many people will, like you, need to condense their work efforts. It is still useful, however, to make sure that you use whatever time you have to your greatest advantage. Be sure that you note the dates that are fixed and immutable:

- GMAT (and TOEFL) registration deadlines and test dates
- Application deadlines themselves

The following is a typical schedule for someone applying to schools that begin in September, with application deadlines in March–April. It is intended not as an exact time line for you to follow, but rather as an illustration of the tasks and deadlines you will want to track.

APPLICATION TIMETABLE (Starting Dates for Activities) *

SPRING/SUMMER (i.e., fifteen months in advance of program start)

- Start considering specifically what you want from an MBA program, and whether an MBA is indeed appropriate.
- Develop a preliminary list of appropriate schools! Read several of the better guides, look at the most recent surveys printed in the leading business

and popular magazines, scrutinize the course catalogues and brochures of the schools themselves, and talk with people knowledgeable about the schools.*

■ Examine several schools' application forms, even if they are a year out of date, to see what the application process will involve.

■ Consider who should write recommendations for you (and be sure that you treat them particularly well from now on).

■ Start putting together a realistic financial plan to pay for school. Research financial aid sources and your likelihood of qualifying for aid. (Identify necessary forms to be completed and their deadline dates.)

■ Consider how you will prepare for the GMAT. Start by getting the *Official Guide for GMAT Review* and subjecting yourself to a sample exam under realistic conditions. If you are not a strong standardized text taker, are unfamiliar with the exam, or just want to save yourself the bother of preparing on your own, figure out which test preparation course you will take and when it will be available. International students will want to do the same regarding the TOEFL exam.

■ Start filling out the Personal Organizer in Chapter 10 to get a jump on the essay writing. Glance at the chapters covering what the schools want and how to write the essays (Chapters 4, 9, and 10) so you have some idea of what will be required in writing the essays.

SEPTEMBER

■ Send for the applications now! Many schools are inefficient about sending them out, especially to overseas applicants, so be prepared to have every third or fourth one fail to respond. If a school has not yet completed this year's application form, or is temporarily out of them, try to get last year's application form. The application tends to change very little from one year to the next, so even last year's form will give you a good idea of what to expect from the new application. (If possible, ask the admissions staff which essay questions have been dropped and which new ones added, if any.)

■ Register for the GMAT (and TOEFL) exam.

■ Read the chapters in this book regarding the essay questions, and the essay examples in the Appendix.

■ Develop a basic positioning statement; write a preliminary essay regarding where you are headed and why you want an MBA.

■ Take a GMAT prep course or begin an intensive GMAT self-study regimen (now or in upcoming months, depending upon specific course and exam dates).

■ Start visiting school campuses based upon a "short list" of preferred schools.

■ Request transcripts from the relevant schools, get military discharge papers, and so on.

■ Establish a file folder system for each school and note specific deadlines for each.

OCTOBER/NOVEMBER

■ Approach recommenders! (Assume the average one will take one month to submit the recommendations.)

■ Take the GMAT (and TOEFL) exam. The GMAT scores will take about four to six weeks to be reported to the schools. By taking the GMAT one administration earlier than necessary you give yourself the chance to retake it if you need to.

■ Attend Graduate Management Admissions Council (GMAC) or other MBA fairs.

NOVEMBER/DECEMBER

■ Do rough drafts of application essays.

■ Submit applications for financial aid from third party institutions (i.e., sources other than the schools themselves).

DECEMBER/JANUARY

■ Complete final drafts of application essays and forms; submit them.

■ Submit loan applications (for school loans) and any forms necessary for institutionally based scholarships or assistantships.

■ Contact recommenders who have not yet submitted recommendations.

■ Prepare for interviews by reading Chapter 12 in this book and by staging mock interviews with other applicants and friends.

FEBRUARY

■ Contact schools that have not yet acknowledged your complete file.

■ Finish remaining school interviews.

ONCE YOU HAVE BEEN ACCEPTED (or Rejected)

■ Notify your recommenders of what has happened, and tell them what your plans are. Thank them again for their assistance, perhaps by getting them a bottle of champagne or flowers.

■ Prepare to leave your job, and get ready for business school. (See Chapter 15, which discusses both of these points in detail.)

■ Notify the schools of your acceptance or rejection of their admissions offers, and send in your deposit to your school of choice.

■ If you have not gotten into your desired school, what should you do? Consider going to your next most favorite school, or perhaps reapplying in the future. (See the discussion in Chapter 14.)

SEPTEMBER

■ Enroll

* The materials and sources mentioned here are described in detail, along with how best to obtain them, in Chapter 5.

Notes: Each of the points made above is discussed in detail elsewhere in this book; refer to the in-depth discussions as appropriate. The timing set out in this schedule is of necessity approximate, since everyone's style of working and personal circumstances will vary. For example, if you are working in an Antarctic ice station, you will probably have to allow more time for most of the steps listed here. Using this schedule as a starting point, however, should give you a good idea of the sequence to follow, as well as the approximate timing. And it should go without saying that doing things in advance is always a good idea.

Special Notes for International Students: The application deadlines for the standardized exams (GMAT and TOEFL) are approximately two months in advance of the actual test date. Failure to observe deadlines will result in either an increased fee or the need to take the exam on a standby basis, with no guarantee that you can actually take the exam on that day. GMAT test preparation is not readily available outside the United States, so check carefully to determine where and when you can take a course. Because you must provide official translations of transcripts, recommendations, and the like you should allow extra time. The slowness and lack of reliability of international mail should also be factored into your timetable, both for tests and for the other elements of the application process.

Notify the school you have chosen to attend as early as possible so that you can begin the student visa application process. Depending upon your nationality and individual circumstances, this process may be either short and simple or lengthy and complicated.

WHERE ARE THINGS MOST LIKELY TO GO ASTRAY?

You should be aware of two different types of problems. *Problems that are partially outside your control (but not your influence):* (1) Some schools fail to send out a substantial percentage of applications upon a first request, or do so with a lengthy delay. The obvious solution to this is that you start requesting applications early and stay on top of the situation. (One of our German clients had a difficult time getting applications from two American schools. He kept requesting the forms by different media—telephone, letter, fax—and he enlisted his fiancée's help. She wrote and called for applications, too, and received an application form before he did, but it still took her a month.) (2) Your recommenders are another likely source of trouble. They are busy people who, despite their best intentions, are all too likely to need prodding to get the recommendations turned in on time, especially if they elected to write them themselves. As Chapter 11 suggests, you will want to make their job as easy as possible, and then stay on top of the situation.

Major problems that are within your control. The public mails are notoriously unreliable. This can be readily dealt with, however, simply by using Federal Express, UPS, DHL, or another private carrier whose reliability is greater. Urge your recommender to use this same approach if she is getting close to a deadline, and volunteer to pay for it, of course. Second, and critically important, your essay writing is all too likely to fall behind schedule, leading to last minute rushing and poor writing.

Start the whole essay writing process early and continue to give yourself time, on a regular basis, to work on them. You must be disciplined about this if you want to maximize your chances.

USING THE MASTER APPLICATION ORGANIZER

This organizer is meant to provide you with a framework for controlling the application process. You may well find that some steps take you a bit more or less time than this timetable allows for; adjust it to your own needs. The important thing is to have a firm schedule and keep to it. The sequence of activities will be approximately the same, no matter how long it takes you to complete them, so be sure that you do not skip a step.

MASTER APPLICATION ORGANIZER

SCHOOL	1	2	3	4	5	6	7	8

APPLICATIONS

Application Deadline

Target Completion Date

Date of School Visit

Interview Date

Target Mailing Date

Date Sent

_____

APPLICATION FORMS
   AND BROCHURES

Date Requested

Received Yet?

_____

GMAT SCORES

Date Taken

Date Requested

Has School Received Them?

_____

TOEFL SCORES

Date Taken

Date Requested

Has School Received Them?

_____

TRANSCRIPTS

Date Requested

Has School Received Them?

_____

ESSAYS

Target Rough Drafts Completion

SCHOOL	1	2	3	4	5	6	7	8

Essays *(cont'd)*

Outside Readings
   (by friends, etc.) Done

Final Drafts Complete

―――――――――

Recommendations

➤ Recommender 1

Date Requested

Date Briefing Completed

Date Finished

Date School Received

➤ Recommender 2

Date Requested

Date Briefing Completed

Date Finished

Date School Received

➤ Recommender 3

Date Requested

Date Briefing Completed

Date Finished

Date School Received

―――――――――

Financial Aid

Source (If Other Than School)

Date Information Requested

Date Information Received

Date Due

Target Mailing Date

Date Sent

APPLICATION ORGANIZER FOR EACH SCHOOL

SCHOOL

ADDRESS

TELEPHONE

FAX

E-MAIL

ADMISSIONS DIRECTOR

ADMISSIONS OFFICER DEALT WITH

      MET UNDER WHAT CIRCUMSTANCES

APPLICATION FEE

APPLICATION DEADLINE DATE

FINANCIAL AID/SCHOLARSHIP DEADLINE DATE

ACTIONS REQUIRED

      School's application, course catalog, and publicity materials requested

          Received by me

      Secondary research (reading standard publications on schools) completed

      Transcripts requested

          Received by school

      GMAT scores requested

          Received by school

      Recommenders approached

          All necessary material sent to them

          Recommenders' progress checked

          Recommendation 1 received by school

Recommendation 2 received by school

Recommendation 3 received by school

Application form details filled in

Application essays:	*rough draft completed*	*outsider reading completed*	*final draft completed*
Essay 1			
Essay 2			
Essay 3			
Essay 4			
Essay 5			
Essay 6			
Essay 7			
Essay 8			

Complete application photocopied

Application sent (by Federal Express or similar firm)/routing number _____

Interview status

    Required/requested

    Date (and any topics suggested)

School notified me of file completion

Financial Aid/Scholarship Form

    Requested

    Completed

    Mailed

Checked with financial aid office and financial aid file is complete

Note: Place this organizer in the folder you keep on each school, showing in detail what is only outlined in the Master Application Organizer.

Part *III*

ON THE ROAD
TO
BUSINESS SCHOOL

14

RESPONDING TO WAIT-LISTING, REJECTIONS, AND OTHER DISAPPOINTMENTS

— EXECUTIVE SUMMARY —

■

To optimize your chance of being accepted from a wait list, bring relevant new material to the attention of the admissions office.

■

When reapplying to a school, start by understanding the reasons for your initial rejection.

– Recognize that you will need to address these deficiencies to warrant reapplying.

*I*f you have followed our suggested approach you have applied to six–eight schools. Only one or two of them are likely to accept you and several others are very likely to turn you down. Prepare yourself for rejection by some of your choices. (In fact, if you get into every school, perhaps you haven't aimed high enough!)

Nonacceptance comes in many forms. You may be put on an administrative hold, wait-listed, told to apply again at a later date after you have remedied a specific deficiency, or just rejected outright. Your reaction should depend upon which of these categories applies and which school is saying "maybe," "later," or "no."

If one of your stretch schools says no, for example, you will probably react differently than if one of your likelies says no. Don't over-react to any single school's decision. The vagaries of the admissions process and the differences between schools mean that one school's decision does not have much predictive value in terms of what another school will do. (This is one of the reasons that we suggest applying to so many schools.)

RESPONDING TO AN ADMINISTRATIVE HOLD

An administrative hold means that the school was unable to make a decision on your candidacy within the normal time period, so your application will be held over until the next decision period. This suggests that your candidacy is strong, but the school will not know if you are quite strong enough until it has seen more of this year's applicants. (It also is possible that an administrative problem is causing the delay, but this is rare.)

Take the opportunity to send a short note reaffirming your interest in the program if the delay is scheduled to extend for more than about a month. If you have strong new information available—such as a promotion or greatly increased responsibilities—by all means, communicate it to the admissions office.

RESPONDING TO WAIT-LISTING

Being wait-listed means that you will be admitted to the program only if someone who has been accepted chooses not to come. In fact, schools know that a certain percentage of their admittees will choose other schools or decide to wait a year or two, so they routinely admit more students than they can actually take. The "excess" number admitted, however, is often not sufficient to make up for all those who declined admission. The wait list is used to manage this situation.

The trouble with being wait-listed is that you are not likely to get off the wait list and into the school until very late in the game. It is not uncommon for schools to call people on the wait list only days before the program's start or, indeed, some days after the start.

You should not wait in silence if you hope to improve your chances of admission. As you are likely to continue to augment your list of responsibilities and accomplishments during this lengthy waiting period, you should communicate them to the admissions office. The appropriate time to do so is whenever you have major news to impart—but not more than twice. By so doing you will also demonstrate your continuing interest in the program.

What information will be relevant to this process? And how should you communicate your new information? Any new information should show you to be even more the dynamic leader, thoughtful and mature decision maker, and so on, that the earlier chapters showed you how to portray. The one thing that makes your task easier at this point is that, having gone through all of the applications, you probably have a pretty good idea of where your applications were weakest and thus what sort of new information would be most helpful to your case. Knowing where your applications were initially weak means that you can be clever about bolstering these weak points in the months between the initial application and your follow-up communiqués. For example, if you know that one weak point is that your responsibilities have remained substantially unchanged for three or four years, there is no time like the present to expand them.

A sound strategy, whether or not you have dramatic new information available, is to send a short letter to the admissions committee that provides any useful additional information you have—and that also restates why you think you would be a valuable contributor to their program, and emphasizes that you still very much wish to attend it.

RESPONDING TO REJECTION

The first thing to do when confronting a rejection is to ask yourself how significant it really is. If you have already been accepted by a school you favor, the rejection is truly insignificant. If this is a school you very much wish to attend, however, a different reaction is appropriate.

The first step is to analyze why you were rejected. You may already know the reason, of course, if you were aware of one or two specific aspects of your application that were likely to keep you from being admitted. If you are not sure, you can always contact the school's admissions office to get their views on the matter. Some schools are willing to tell you why they rejected you. The schools most likely to do so are the smaller ones that have relatively fewer applications. Schools are most receptive to such inquiries during their slow periods, such as during the summer for programs with September starting dates. They will generally refuse to discuss the matter during their busy periods.

Beware, however, of what even these very helpful schools will say. They will address only substantive matters and will not comment on the actual application. They will not say, "Your essays were so sloppily written, and you revealed yourself to be so arrogant and insensitive, that we never want to deal with the persona you portrayed." For an understanding of the application itself, check it against the relevant chapters and examples of this book and ask an appropriate, objective person to do the same. (Or, call one of us at Education U.S.A.)

A school that is willing to discuss your rejection is doing you a real favor, so be ultra-polite in dealing with them. If you are defensive or hostile, which are natural reactions to being told that you are less than perfect, you will elicit less useful information from them than you might have if you had been appreciative and welcoming of their inputs.

SHOULD YOU EVER APPEAL A REJECTION?

If you have no truly dramatic new information to bring to the table, do not raise your blood pressure and that of the admissions committee by appealing a rejection. Admissions committees go to great lengths to give applicants a sympathetic reading of their files, by at least two and often three people, so you can count on the school's having considered your application material fairly.

Some schools, on relatively rare occasions, will be willing to reconsider an application based upon presentation of important new information. If you have such information and wish to appeal, contact the admissions office and explain the situation. See if they will entertain an appeal. If so, be sure to present convincing new information, reiterating that you do wish to attend this school and will contribute greatly if admitted. Recognize, however, that the odds against being admitted will be very long indeed.

SHOULD YOU REAPPLY IN THE FUTURE?

Some schools are good enough to tell you that they would be happy to have you reapply if you improve your GMAT score or get more work experience. This is generally a sincere comment on their part, so take it at face value.

The question of whether to reapply is of course a complicated one. If you got into one of your top choices, you might wish to attend it this year, instead of waiting, on the chance that you will get in next year to your first choice. The situation is more difficult if you got into your eighth choice, but none of your first seven choices. If you realistically think that you will be a stronger candidate in the near future, then it might be a good idea to wait and reapply with your improved credentials.

The important thing here is to analyze in what way you will, or could, be a stronger candidate. Cast a critical eye over your file. Look at it from the perspective of this book, analyzing each component. Was the component a relative strength or weakness for you at school X, given what the competition was probably like? If it was a glaring weakness, can you do something to improve it? Chapter 4 analyzed in detail what you could do to improve your credentials. If the fault in your application was not the application itself, but your credentials, consider what strategy you will employ to improve them. Ask yourself whether a successful effort will significantly change the nature of your candidacy. Also ask yourself whether you are being realistic in thinking that you can do what you are contemplating.

Then consider the application itself. Did you write polished, persuasive essays? Do you have reason to doubt that your recommenders wrote assertively and well on your behalf? Did you interview well? If the answer to any of these questions suggests that you have an opportunity to improve your application substantially, what will you do to make the improvements? Are you being realistic in thinking that you will put in the necessary time and effort?

Do not be lazy if you choose to reapply. Rewrite your essays to take advantage of your performance since your initial application, in light of what you have learned was wrong with that application. Consider using new recommenders, based upon their knowledge of your recent performance. If you use the same recommenders, have them rewrite their recommendations, incorporating new information about you to the extent possible.

WHAT THE ADMISSIONS DIRECTORS ADVISE REGARDING:

DEFERRED ADMISSION

➤ We offer deferred admission mainly to people still in college so that they can get some work experience under their belts. *Rob Garcia, MIT*

➤ We offer deferred admission to people who have the chance to do something particularly important in their careers. To keep people who have not thought through their futures from stringing us along, we require that they pay us their tuition now. They can go off for a year on their project, but if they do not attend London Business School next year, we'll simply keep their money. It's amazing how this clarifies people's thinking. *Julia Tyler, London*

WAIT LISTS

➤ Someone put on the wait list should tell us if they think we overlooked something. *Rob Garcia, MIT*

➤ One applicant successfully challenged her waiting list position by doing so in the nicest possible way—not saying, "I want to go up the waiting list," but, "London Business School is really important to me; let me explain again." So it was reasonable. She was aware of our constraints, but able to show that she was self-aware enough to know that she would benefit and contribute to us. She used the system politely. *Julia Tyler, London Business School*

REJECTIONS

➤ If I were turned down, I would call and make an appointment to discuss the reasons for my rejections. I would not insist on discussing it immediately, because the admissions person on the line will not necessarily have the file handy. *Rob Garcia, MIT*

➤ In the summer we give comments to those we rejected if they request them. We explain what was relatively weak in their applications. *Henry Malin, Tuck*

➤ We don't normally tell people why we rejected them, unless it's someone we want to encourage to re-apply. We would tell them verbally.
Andrew Dyson, Manchester (England)

REAPPLYING

➤ We don't penalize someone for having applied unsuccessfully before. Many people are successful the second time around. We want to see development in the areas that were weak. *James Millar, Harvard*

➤ This is a process, not life or death. If they don't get in they can continue to work and they can always re-apply. About ten percent of our class consists of people who were turned down in prior years. *Henry Malin, Tuck*

➤ If you intend to reapply, you should come have a chat with us to see what your chances are and what issues you need to address.
Andrew Dyson, Manchester (England)

OTHER OPTIONS

If a school that you wanted to attend has rejected you (for the moment) do not give up on getting an MBA. If you wanted an MBA for good reasons, there are probably a number of schools that can help you meet your needs. Most people who have investigated schools carefully, including those who produce the school guides and rankings discussed in Part I, sincerely believe that there are 100+ quality MBA programs in the world. So even if you applied to an unrealistic set of schools this time around, cast your net a bit more widely or reapply to schools you narrowly missed this time.

One last hint: Many schools have exchange programs that allow you to spend a semester or even two at another school. If you failed to get into London Business School directly, for example, you might still be able to attend it for at least one semester if you go to one of its many "partner" schools. This will give you much of the social and intellectual experience of attending it, as well as letting you tap into its network and list it on your résumé!

15

WHAT TO DO
ONCE YOU ARE ACCEPTED

— EXECUTIVE SUMMARY —

■

Take the necessary steps to reserve your place at your chosen school.

■

Upgrade your skills, as necessary, to be able to compete at business school right from the start. Do the necessary reading, or take the appropriate courses, to achieve reasonable skill levels in the following (if you have not already done so):

- Spreadsheet and Word-Processing software
- Accounting
- Economics
- Statistics
- Case Analysis
- Algebra (and Calculus)

■

If you have additional time, upgrade your knowledge in other areas as well.

ACCEPTING YOUR OFFER

If you are accepted by your top choice, be sure to send in your deposit to reserve your place in a timely manner. If you are accepted by one of your secondary choices before you have heard from your number one school, you may face a dilemma if you are required to send in a deposit immediately. Most schools have gotten so quick about responding to applications, however, that this quandary is no longer common. If you do encounter it, ask the school that has accepted you whether you can delay sending your deposit for a short time, and also ask your first choice school to speed up its decision making.

The one time when this is still likely to be a major problem is if you are accepted by a secondary choice and wait-listed by your first choice. You may not get off the wait list, or be definitively turned down, until the start of school. In this case, you may have to send in a deposit to your second choice, unless you are willing to risk being declined by your first choice school.

Another strategy is to ask your second choice school for a one-year deferment. This is a good idea *even if you are accepted by your first choice school.* There is always the infinitesimal chance of something going badly wrong at choice no. 1, so it does not hurt to have choice no. 2 available for the following year.

International students. As soon as you have chosen the school you will attend, begin the student visa process. In the United States, this means getting a Certificate of Eligibility (I-20) form from the school, which verifies that you have the appropriate credentials, language skills, and financial resources to attend the program. This form, along with accompanying financial documents, must be submitted to the local U.S. consular office to request the actual visa. This process is all too often delayed by either the school or the consular office, so it is important to begin it as soon as possible.

LEAVING YOUR JOB

Leaving your current job may fill you with joy, sadness, or a mixture of the two. No matter which, it is important to resign in a highly professional manner. Even one misstep can harm your future prospects.

Once you have decided to leave, step carefully. Do not pop into your boss's office and wax ecstatic over your new-found freedom. Instead, think about how much notice you should give. You will obviously give at least as much as is called for in your employment contract. Whether you should give more depends upon a balance of several factors:

- Are you likely to be regarded as a traitor or spy or bad influence?
  - If so, you may not be welcome in the office; you may be ordered to clean out your desk immediately.

- How hard and time-consuming will it be to transfer your knowledge and responsibilities to a replacement?
  - Must you be the one to train your replacement?

- How has the company treated others at your level who have resigned, especially those who are not going to work for competitors?

- What is your relationship with your boss?
  - If your boss is truly reliable, perhaps you can tell her in advance of an official announcement in order to give her time to make appropriate adjustments, without jeopardizing your paycheck.

- Does your company know that you have applied to schools? If so, you should tell them sooner rather than later.

- How much do you want to continue working? If you would just as soon have more time off before starting school, you do not need to worry about being dismissed too quickly.

RESIGNING

Schedule a meeting with your boss on a Friday afternoon, so that she will have the weekend to reconcile herself to your decision. Explain what you have gotten from your job and from her. Think in terms of what you have learned about your industry, analytical aspects of your job, people management skills, and how to present material (oral and written), and so forth. Then explain why you are going off for an MBA. (If your boss wrote a recommendation for you, all of this can be done briefly, of course.) Note that you are doing it as a smart career move rather than to get away from the work environment.

Give a short, simple letter of resignation. Then tell your closest colleagues of your decision. Once again, explain why you are leaving and how much you benefited from working with them. Not everyone will be happy about your news. Some will be sorry that you are leaving, whereas others will be envious. Just "grin and bear" any hostility you encounter.

To leave the best possible impression, be sure to:

- Complete any pending projects.
- Turn over all of your files, with detailed explanations regarding how you would suggest your replacement proceed.
- Train your replacement yourself, if possible.
- If you have people working under you, give them one last review.
- Ask for a concluding review of your own performance, assuming that your boss is not angry about your leaving.
- Consider mentioning what aspects of your position vis-a-vis the company could be improved, but only if you think your boss would be pleased to get this input.
- Consider scheduling a telephone call with your replacement one week after she starts work to help her out (and volunteer to call a second time at her discretion).
- Make every effort to stay on good terms with your former colleagues.

PREPARING FOR BUSINESS SCHOOL

RATIONALE FOR STARTING THE PROGRAM WELL PREPARED

If you are ambitious enough to seek a top MBA degree, you are probably also eager to do well in the program.

The easiest way to accomplish this is by starting the program well prepared. The student who is poorly prepared will find it difficult to succeed. The poorly prepared student is highly likely to struggle in the first term and barely get through the first set of courses. As a result, he will be perceived by his professors and fellow students as someone who has little to offer. He will be the case team member who contributes little except pitiful requests for assistance. It is very hard to overcome a bad first impression. The first impression of this student is likely to harden throughout the whole first term. The redemption process is not likely to start, if ever, until after the core courses have been completed. Only at that point will he be able to compete on somewhat equal ground with other students. At that point, it is likely to be too late to retrieve the situation entirely. After all, the students who performed well initially have been piling up points with professors and students, demonstrating over a lengthy period of time that they are capable analysts and managers. This will be reflected in the initial job offers to students, because most of them finalize their job situations long before they graduate. In fact, many students at two-year programs who take summer jobs at the leading consulting firms and investment banks will have accepted offers from their summer employers before the halfway point of the second year. This means that they will have capitalized on their first-year grades and reputations. The second year will be essentially irrelevant to the post-MBA starting job.

WHO KNOWS WHAT FROM THE OUTSET

How do the strong performers do it? Do they enter business school already knowing all that an MBA has to teach them, thereby negating the purpose of the program? There *will* be a few students who have already gained a bachelor's degree in business, then worked for a consulting firm for several years, and learned a great deal about business analysis and performance. These individuals are comparatively rare, however. Most students will have certain assets in terms of their prior course work and experience, but they will tend to have very limited knowledge of half of the core courses. Finally, some students will have no appreciable business experience or understanding.

There are thus three groups of entering students: know-it-alls, know-somethings, and know-nothings. The first group should do their best to maintain their enthusiasm for the whole of the program, since they tend to suffer from a very high rate of burnout. (This is understandable, given that they are often getting an MBA more to have the credential than to really learn something.) The second and third groups, however, can help themselves greatly by taking the time to prepare for the start of the MBA program.

THE ELEMENTS OF GOOD PREPARATION

Let's take a look at the core courses of a typical MBA program. Most programs require students to take a standard course (or two) in each of the following areas:

> Accounting
> Economics
> Finance
> Information Systems
> Marketing
> Operations Management
> Organizational Development/Human Resources
> Quantitative Methods

Several skills are not necessarily taught separately, but they tend to under-pin success in the core courses:

Computer skills, including spreadsheet analysis and word processing, in particular

Presentation skills, both oral and written

Calculus (in most programs)

Case analysis methods

Use of a financial calculator

Peter Robinson, in his excellent book, *Snapshots from Hell: The Making of an MBA* (Warner, 1994), shows what it is like to be underprepared for the start of business school. Robinson was a presidential speech writer who entered Stanford Business School without any perceptible quantitative skills or understanding. His resulting struggle makes painful, if often funny, reading. To avoid the nightmar-ish scenario of Robinson and other innumerates, take the following suggestions to heart.

SKILLS: THE BARE MINIMUM

Before you take another step, ensure yourself that your spreadsheet and word-processing skills are adequate. (Database skills are also useful, but not critical to success.) If you have not regularly used a computer for such tasks, plan to put in several dozen hours, making sure that you can do the following without dif-ficulty:

Word Processor: Enter and format text; add headers, footers and page numbers; change fonts and type size; copy, move, and save blocks of text; manage files; use standard tools such as find and replace, spellcheck, and center; work with tables; combine spreadsheet-generated tables and graphs with text; and, print a document.

Spreadsheet: Enter text and numbers; add titles and labels; enter formulas; use functions (such as sum, product, date, and dollar) in formulas; copy and move data; create charts; and print. You should be able to build a sim-ple income statement and balance sheet, using formulas to change data into usable information. You should also be able to link spreadsheets to provide summary data.

It is too late to start to learn such things once you are at business school.

Any introductory paperback that explains the basics of a standard program is suitable for this task. (Most schools, by the way, use PCs rather than Macs). If the school does not specify a given program, consider purchasing an integrated program that combines a spreadsheet, word processor, and database, such as Microsoft Office. A good introduction to this program in the Que series is Trudi Reisner, *Easy Microsoft Office* (Que, 1994), 294 pages, $24.99. (The publication dates listed herein are the latest ones available as this is being written. By all means, do purchase a later edition if one is available. And insofar as computer programs are also subject to relative obsolescence, ask the school for suggestions about which programs they currently recommend.)

Although this sort of introductory book covers word-processing in suitable detail, it is not really sufficient to provide the spreadsheet knowledge and experience required. It would be very helpful to get a second book for these purposes. If you take the Microsoft Office approach, a reasonable second book concerning Excel, the Microsoft spreadsheet package bundled into its Office suite of programs, is Joyce Cox and Joyce Cousineau, *A Quick Course in Excel 5 for Windows,* (Online Press, 1994), 163 pages, $12.95. This covers just about everything you need, from linking multiple worksheets to displaying data in charts and graphs, along with a reasonable number of practice exercises.

It is important to be able to use these tools quickly and easily. Thus you need to be able to put together a spreadsheet showing that you expect unit sales to increase at the rate of GDP increase plus 2 percent annually, energy consumption to remain proportional to volume, inventory to grow at the square root of the increase in unit volume, and so on, without being overwhelmed by the task. To do so, you must practice setting up a dozen or so spreadsheets. Many books provide appropriate examples. Simply get one that is keyed to your software package, entitled something like "Financial Analysis With Excel."

Where *presentation skills* are concerned, the best book available is Mary Munter, *Guide to Managerial Communication,* 3d ed., (Prentice Hall, 1991), 192 pages. This gives a good overview of how to approach both oral and written presentations. The advice is concise and very clear. You can expect to do a lot of presenting both at business school and in your future career. In fact, the more senior you are, the more presenting you are likely to do. This is one of the key skills to develop during your business school sojourn. Although you are not going to become an expert simply by reading Munter's book, it will help sensitize you to the issues involved in doing good presentations, thereby making the learning process at school that much faster and more effective.

Many programs require that incoming students be comfortable using *calculus* in various of their courses. Some of them have introductory math "boot camps" to get the innumerate up to speed. Anyone attending such a school should take as much calculus as possible before school starts, and not depend upon the boot camp alone. An appropriate course would give an overview of differential and integral calculus and, perhaps, introduce mathematical modeling.

If no courses are available, it should be a simple matter to hire a tutor to guide you through an appropriate text. The math used in business programs is definitely not as rigorous as that used in engineering programs, for example, and certain elements of calculus (and statistics, for that matter) are far more important than others. Texts for scientists or engineers will thus be more difficult than is necessary and will highlight techniques that will be of little use at business school. Ernest F. Haeussler and Richard S. Paul, *Introductory Mathematical Analysis for Business* (Prentice Hall, 1996) is a reasonable choice. Those wishing a more rigorous treatment can consult Deborah Hughes-Hallet, Andrew M. Gleason, et al., *Calculus* (John Wiley, 1994), 685 pages, $44.75 (Student Solutions Manual, $19.75), which covers the subject marvelously but is not for the fainthearted. It is well written and inclusive, but at a high level. Those seeking a more outline-like treatment are advised to try Edward T. Dowling, *Mathematical Methods for Business and Economics* (McGraw-Hill, 1993), 384 pages, $12.95, in the Schaum Outline Series. This covers equations and graphs, functions, systems of equations, linear algebra, linear programming, differential and integral calculus, and the calculus of multivariable functions. It is in outline format, though, and quite terse, so it is perhaps best used with the aid of a tutor. It does provide an immense number of examples and problems, however.

Those who have forgotten even math basics are advised to prepare with Peter H. Selby and Steve Slavin, *Quick Algebra Review: A Self-Teaching Guide,* 2d ed., (John Wiley & Sons, 1993), 232 pages, $14.95, which provides a thorough review and is quite suitable for self-study.

Even if you are attending a school that does not specialize in the *case method* of teaching, you are advised to prepare to handle business case analysis. All of the top programs utilize large numbers of cases in their classes. Becoming a good case analyst sooner rather than later will greatly ease your learning burden. One standard work on the subject is Robert Ronstadt, *The Art of Case Analysis: A Guide to the Diagnosis of Business Situations* (Lord Publishing, 1988), 189 pages, $14.00. This shows how to read and analyze a case efficiently, how to prepare it for classroom discussion, and then how to discuss it effectively in class. The approach is extremely practical, showing you how to do a complete analysis of a case—and also how to do useful analyses when you have little time available but still want to be ready to make a contribution to class discussion. The serious time constraints case method schools impose and the importance of class contributions upon grades (and reputations) mean that knowing how to make good contributions having done minimal analysis is a skill well worth developing. The book covers how to improve your classroom performance, develop effective study groups, and write good case reports. In addition, it discusses how to take case exams, another skill well worth developing. It also discusses some of the most important analytical techniques to be used in case analysis, including financial analysis and decision tree diagrams, and gives a brief overview of industry and market analysis. A not particularly satisfactory substitute for Ronstadt is Al Edge, *The Guide to Case Analysis and Reporting,* 4th ed., (System Logistics, 1991), 151 pages, $15.00.

The fluent use of a *financial calculator* is taken for granted by most students in business programs. The standard calculator for some years has been the Hewlett Packard 12C. (Hewlett Packard has added new, more powerful models, such as the 17BII and 19BII, to its line of financial calculators, but the 12C is still the business school calculator of choice as of this writing.) If you are not comfortable using a reasonably full-featured calculator, I strongly suggest that you learn how to use this one before getting to business school. The *Owner's Handbook and Problem-Solving Guide* provides a good guide to using the calculator. Do not feel compelled to read the whole thing, but do read the initial chapters, which show how to get started, and how to use the percentage and calendar functions, and the basic financial functions. Then read about "additional operating features." Glance at the chapters on statistics functions, real estate, investment analysis, leasing, and bonds. These features may not be meaningful at this time but they will prove immensely useful soon, so know what is available. Last, be sure to read the first half of the appendix concerning the automatic memory stack to learn how to make use of the calculator's memory capabilities. Another booklet, entitled *HP-12C Solutions Handbook,* is generally not included with the calculator, but it is well worth buying separately. It shows additional techniques you can use for investment analysis, forecasting, statistical analysis, and learning curve generation.

PREPARING FOR THE CORE COURSES

So much for the preliminaries; now let's look at the substantive courses. The key here is to avoid shouldering a full slate of courses for which you are not adequately prepared. If you have no idea of the basics of accounting or finance and you are going to take courses in both at the same time, along with several other courses in which you are comparatively weak, you will be in for a tough time. Limit yourself to only one quantitative or heavily conceptual course per term in which your background is a distinct liability. Notice that I emphasize the quantitative courses. Most students, whatever their backgrounds, feel that the non-quantitative courses, such as Marketing and Organizational Behavior, are the easiest to survive without any relevant background. The tough ones to survive are the quantitative courses and the heavily conceptual courses.

THE DIFFICULT COURSES

The quantitative (and thus difficult) courses are Accounting, Quantitative Methods, and to a lesser extent, Information Systems. Economics, Finance, and perhaps to a lesser extent, Operations Management, are a cross between quantitative and conceptual.

THE EIGHT CORE DISCIPLINES—GETTING A JUMP-START

ACCOUNTING. Taking the introductory accounting course at a top-flight business school is often a demanding proposition. The course is taught at a high level and unfolds very quickly. The inclination of the professor to speed is likely to be reinforced by the substantial number of accountants and financial analysts sure to be in the class. Do not try to get up to their level before class begins, but at a minimum you should familiarize yourself with double-entry bookkeeping, the accrual concept, and the basics of the balance sheet and income statement. Ideally, you should also have a nodding acquaintance with the concepts and principles underlying external financial statements—including the accounting cycle (from recording financial transactions to the preparation and analysis of financial statements)—as well as how managers use internal accounting information in their decision making.

A traditional means of preparing is the classic self-teaching text by Robert N. Anthony, *Essentials of Accounting* (Addison-Wesley, 1993), 211 pages, $29.95. This book takes you by the hand through a series of exercises that will teach you the basic vocabulary and methods of accounting. A good alternative is by Joseph Peter Simini, *Accounting Made Simple* (Doubleday, 1988), 162 pages, $12.00. If you are able, consider reading a book that shows some of the uses of accounting information. James Bandler, *How to Use Financial Statements: A Guide to Understanding the Numbers* (Irwin, 1994), 147 pages, $17.50, provides a good introduction to accounting data from the perspective of a user of the information. It is easy to read and makes a good companion to Anthony or Simini. Better yet, take an introductory accounting course at a local school. I suggest that you take the financial accounting course rather than the managerial one, or a class that combines the two fields.

The accounting knowledge you acquire will be of value in many of the other courses you take, so do not worry that you are overinvesting effort in learning accounting before business school.

ECONOMICS. Some schools teach just one economics course, perhaps calling it Managerial Economics. Others teach both microeconomics and macroeconomics. The important thing is to be used to the way in which economists think. Microeconomic concepts such as supply and demand analysis, price and income elasticity, complementary and substitute products, opportunity costs, game theory, and externalities should be part of your toolkit before you arrive at business school. Useful preparation would be taking a good microeconomics course at a local school. Many schools will offer an introductory course and an intermediate course. Take the intermediate one; the introductory course will generally be too lightweight to warrant the effort. Better yet, take a managerial economics course if one is offered. At the macroeconomic level, concepts concerning the problems of unemployment and inflation, monetary and fiscal policy, and the like should be familiar to you, although it is more important to be comfortable with micro- than macroeconomic thinking. If you are going to prepare in just one economics field, make it microeconomics rather than macroeconomics.

This is one field that will be very difficult to teach yourself. If you are unable to take an appropriate course, consider hiring a tutor to guide you through a suitable book. A very readable one, covering micro-, macro-, and a bit of international economics is Gary M. Walton and Frank C. Wykoff, *Understanding Economics Today,* 2d ed., (Irwin, 1989), 410 pages, $34.50. A good substitute is Stephen D. Casler, *Introduction to Economics* (HarperPerennial, 1992), 470 pages, $12.00. This covers both micro- and macroeconomics, and is also well-written. Another good substitute is John Duffy, *Cliff's Quick Review: Economics* (Cliff's, 1993), 156 pages, $7.95. This is a very good, but very brief, review of the relevant micro- and macro- issues. As such, it would be a good review for someone who had taken the relevant courses, but would probably be much too terse to be readable for an economics novice. No economics book is likely to be easy to read for anyone completely new to the topic, however, so using a tutor is likely to be an important factor in successful preparation.

If you feel up to the challenge of more difficult (and more expensive) material, consider *Fundamentals of Managerial Economics* (Dryden, 1993), 700 pages, $54.00, by Mark Hirschey and James L. Pappas. It covers only the microeconomic side, but it includes very good discussions of linear programming and finance topics such as capital budgeting.

FINANCE. The introductory financial management course will examine investment and financing decisions: sources and costs of capital, tax strategies, capital budgeting, optimal capital structure, valuation and portfolio analysis, and appropriate dividend policies. If you have the basics of related areas such as accounting and microeconomics under your belt, finance will not be a complete mystery. Nevertheless, several books offer good treatments of aspects of finance that will stand you in good stead. Burton G. Malkiel, *A Random Walk Down Wall Street* (W.W. Norton, 1990), 440 pages, $14.95, discusses modern financial theory and its relevance to personal investing. Although it focuses on investment decisions rather than financial management, its explanation of risk and return, basic concepts of valuation, the capital asset pricing model, and other foundation stones of modern financial theory makes it a good introduction to finance as well. It is highly readable despite being written at a high conceptual level. Robert C. Higgins, *Analysis for Financial Management*, 3d ed. (Irwin, 1992), 387 pages, $39.75, covers the usual financial management topics in a readable fashion. It is best read after preparing for accounting. A less readable book, which covers more topics but with little explanation, is Herbert T. Spiro, *Finance for the Nonfinancial Manager*, 3d ed., (John Wiley & Sons, 1988), 282 pages, $19.95.

INFORMATION SYSTEMS. The introductory information systems course typically focuses on the managerial issues presented by information systems development, deployment, and use. It is likely to cover strategic information systems, current and emerging technologies, and the system development life cycle. It is not devoted to teaching how to use software tools. (It is assumed that you are comfortable using such tools already.) A good overview of these issues is presented in James I. Cash et al., *Corporate Information Systems Management: Issues Facing Senior Executives*, 3d ed. (Irwin, 1992), $32.95. A good glossary, with extended discussions of key terms and concepts, is presented in Peter G. W. Keen, *Every Manager's Guide to Information Technology* (Harvard Business School Press, 1995), 290 pages, $18.95. *Pocket Information Technology* (*The Economist*, 1995), 218 pages, 10.99 pounds, presents a useful overview of the field. The same is true of *Pocket Telecommunications* (*The Economist*, 1995), 193 pages, 10.99 pounds, regarding the related field of telecommunications.

This field is uniquely subject to obsolescence, so the above publications should not be favored if something much more up-to-date is available.

MARKETING. The introductory marketing course looks at how to define markets, plan product lines, promote the products, establish and manage distribution channels, and establish prices. It will analyze buyer behavior, target market development, segmentation of buyers, etc. It is not necessary to have a lot of marketing background prior to getting to business school, partly because the concepts are more intuitively obvious than those in other areas. If you would like to increase your comfort margin, however, you could read the excellent *Introduction to Marketing* (HarperPerennial, 1993), 250 pages, $11.00, by Marjorie J. Cooper and Charles Madden. Like the other books in this series, it does a good job covering in a readable fashion the topics that are typically taught in intermediate-level undergraduate courses.

OPERATIONS MANAGEMENT. Operations management courses look at the planning and control of operations in manufacturing and service firms. Topics covered generally include forecasting, capacity planning, material requirements planning, just-in-time manufacturing, scheduling, facility layout, facility location, and quality management concepts. I do not suggest that you plow through a production and operations management textbook to prepare for this field. Instead, it would be helpful if you read one book to become familiar in a general way with the main issues. An interesting view of the Japanese operations management system, as contrasted with the traditional American one, is presented in *The Machine that Changed the World: The Story of Lean Manufacturing*, by James P. Womack, Daniel T. Jones, and Daniel Roos (HarperPerennial, 1990), 323 pages, $13.00. This provides a good overview of the two systems and along the way illustrates many important issues in manufacturing management in the context of the automobile industry. The book is quite good in discussing the relevant evidence in a readable fashion, and is of particular value in introducing new MBA students to methodological matters in a painless manner.

ORGANIZATIONAL DEVELOPMENT/HUMAN RESOURCES. This course can be taught from any of a number of different perspectives. A modern perspective is offered by looking at how organizations develop. A traditional way to teach is to focus on organizational behavior—how individuals and groups act within organizations, and how best to manage people in organizational settings. Another way is to focus on how to design the structure of organizations. Yet another is to look at human resource issues, such as how to recruit, select, train, develop, appraise, and reward employees. A combination of these views offers what may now be the most common means of teaching the course. The appropriate reading for this course will therefore depend upon the perspective the course adopts.

Some possible readings: A sensible view of organization development is offered in W. Warner Burke, *Organization Development*, 2d ed., (Addison-Wesley, 1994), 214 pages, $26.95. Many of the issues of organizational structure are laid out in Jay Galbraith, *Designing Complex Organizations* (Addison-Wesley, 1973) $26.95. The human resource issues are given a good overview treatment in Michael Beer et al., *Managing Human Assets* (Free Press, 1984), 288 pages, $27.95.

One major caution: do not do any of this reading until you are comfortable in the other areas discussed here. This subject is the one most people find easiest to pass and success in it is not generally rated as very impressive by other students. Thus reading to prepare for this field, if it displaced other preparation, would represent an overinvestment, and poor use, of time.

QUANTITATIVE METHODS. Quantitative methods for managers generally include decision trees, sensitivity analysis, scheduling and queuing theory, linear algebra and linear programming, and various statistical methods. The statistical techniques ordinarily covered include descriptive statistics, random variables, probability distributions, sampling techniques, statistical estimation, hypothesis testing, contingency tables, analysis of variance, regression (simple and multiple) and correlation analysis, and time series forecasting. (This course is almost sure to make extensive use of microcomputer statistical software, including spreadsheets.) It is not vital that you be up on all of these, but have a basic understanding of the standard statistical tools. An introductory statistics course is a valuable investment; otherwise, use a tutor to guide you through the basics. The book you use could be a standard statistical text for business, such as Edwin Mansfield, *Statistics for Business and Economics: Methods and Applications,* 5th ed. (W.W. Norton, 1994).

If you will be reviewing largely on your own, there are very few books that you can realistically expect to get through. The one that offers you the best chance is Terry Dickey, *Using Business Statistics: A Guide for Beginners* (Crisp Publications, 1994), 115 pages, $9.95. This is extremely readable, although it will take substantial work. It covers descriptive statistics, probability distributions, random samples, contingency tables, regression, confidence intervals, and measures of variability. Another possibility is Martin Sternstein, *Barron's EZ-101 Study Keys: Statistics* (Barron's, 1994), 199 pages, $5.95. This covers more material than Dickey, but it is covered in a slightly less intuitive way; it would make a very good companion to Dickey. Try reading Dickey first, then Sternstein. If you cannot find either of these, a possible substitute would be *The Little Black Book of Business Statistics,* by Michael Thomsett (American Management Association, 1990) 233 pages, $14.95. It gives a reasonably sophisticated view of the ideas underlying basic statistical techniques of importance for managers without drowning the reader in details or equations. It is concise and readable, although the math phobic might require help getting through it.

WHAT THE ADMISSIONS DIRECTORS ADVISE

HOW TO PREPARE

➤ We recommend that students take classes in calculus, microeconomics, a basic class in computers, and basic accounting (to get familiar with terminology and basic concepts). *Rob Garcia, MIT*

➤ Even for the undergraduate business major, depending upon how many years you've been out of school, a course in statistics or a quantitative methods refresher is always appropriate. You want to be up to speed from day one in the classroom. *Fran Hill, Haas (Berkeley)*

➤ For people who majored in the liberal arts or in certain of the social sciences (particularly international studies or political sciences), or, interestingly enough, architecture, the comfort level as well as the performance level improves dramatically to the extent that they take "remedial courses for business school." I think that it's absolutely critical for people with this background, and I think it's to be recommended for people with many other backgrounds, too. If you don't know algebra cold, for example, you'll be at a disadvantage on the first day of class. Sure, you'll get through it, but there's a question of how many hours you want to spend on your problem sets and how much anxiety you want to put yourself through. All of this can be remedied by enrolling in a local community college and taking a stats course, taking an econ course, etc., just so that you can familiarize yourself with the material.
Fran Hill, Haas (Berkeley)

➤ Computer literacy is a minimum-minimum. We run a pre-stats course, since so many people get stuck on that. We also suggest that people read the business strategy books to get the vocabulary. *Professor Leo Murray, Cranfield (England)*

FOR PEOPLE STILL IN COLLEGE

➤ People still in college who know that they may eventually do an MBA should take advantage of the opportunity to make sure that their basic skills are at a level they are comfortable with. For communications skills, that might mean taking a basic speech course or two and some additional writing courses. For people who are outside the technical/business realm it might mean homing in on quantitative courses. It would be sensible to take one or two accounting courses, some economics, and some math, at least through basic calculus and statistics. In the junior or senior year, plan to take the GMAT. Prior to doing so, do whatever is necessary to get a strong score. *Judith Goodman, Michigan*

FOR CAREER-SWITCHERS

➤ An arts graduate who wants to switch careers after getting an MBA needs to take full advantage of the opportunities in and out of class. She needs to get a start on her new career while she is at business school, some relevant experiences that will help her appeal to an employer in the field. If she were interested in consulting, for example, she could do some small business consulting on a part-time basis, whether she gets paid or not. This won't be possible, though, if she has to spend twenty hours of time preparing for her accounting or economics class. Many students who are economics majors don't waive the basic economics course, so competing with them when graded on a curve is tough if you have never seen economics before. *Linda Baldwin, UCLA*

FOR INTERNATIONAL STUDENTS

➤ For international students, we suggest a class in which they have to participate—in English—to get them used to that. This is a problem many of our international students face. *Rob Garcia, MIT*

OTHER READINGS

The texts suggested above were chosen on the basis of their readability and conciseness, and, in many cases, their low price. I have tried to find books designed to introduce readers to the key ideas and techniques that will facilitate further learning; I have not chosen books that will substitute for the actual readings in courses. In other words, following the preparation suggestions above will make it possible to follow a course at a top school without fear of being overwhelmed or of being unable to get the maximum out of the course.

These readings are not meant to be definitive. If you find a book that seems to cover the basic concepts in a readable fashion, by all means read it. If the books listed above are unavailable, not to your taste, or if you simply want to pursue the subject further, consider choosing one of the following:

The HarperPerennial series of business publications, as noted above, is a good set of books designed to appeal to those who need to grasp the material offered in an American undergraduate course at an intermediate level. As such, it is at an ideal level for someone who wishes to gain a substantial   understanding of a subject prior to entering an MBA program. These books retail in the United States for approximately $12.00.

A British series, published by Prentice Hall International (UK) Ltd., provides a good overview of a wide range of relevant topics. This series, entitled *The Essence of Management,* is not perfect for these purposes, however, insofar as it is written at a slightly too high level, and is perhaps overly concise. This is not to gainsay the fact that it is well written, but to suggest that it may be a bit difficult as an introduction to a subject. The following books are included in the series:

The Essence of Financial Accounting
The Essence of Management Accounting
The Essence of Economics for Managers
The Essence of Financial Management
The Essence of Information Systems
The Essence of Marketing
The Essence of Organizational Behavior
The Essence of Operations Management
The Essence of Statistics for Business

They retail in the United States for approximately $20.00 and in the UK for approximately 10.00–12.00 pounds.

Last, the Harcourt Brace Jovanovich Outline series offers possible substitutes in the following areas, but these are not truly reader-friendly, being in highly abbreviated outline form:

Principles of Accounting I & II

Calculus

Principles of Economics: Macroeconomics

Principles of Economics: Microeconomics

Financial Management

Principles of Marketing

Business Statistics

There are generally 250–300 pages and priced at about $13.00 in the United States.

Several books are available that aim to teach readers "the skills taught in top business schools," as Steven Silbiger's book *The 10-Day MBA* (William Morrow, 1993), claims. Silbiger, a Harvard MBA, does a better job than most in capturing some of the essence of MBA core courses in one volume; however, the aim of somehow duplicating the offerings of a serious program in 375 pages is, on its face, preposterous. The book virtually ignores information systems, does not do justice to microeconomics and the need for an understanding of supply and demand curves and the like, but it does do a fair-to-good job on marketing and, to a somewhat lesser extent, organizational behavior and finance. Its treatment of most subjects is simply too brief and limited to be of value to those who need a solid introduction to quantitative areas. If you are generally well prepared in quantitative areas and would like a very brief introduction to other areas, however, this is the class of the "one-volume MBAs."

HOW TO FIND THE BOOKS

Many of these books are readily available at academic or business bookstores throughout America. This does not mean, however, that you will be able to get all of those you might like, particularly if you live in a small town or in another country. Contacting the publishers directly is oftentimes far too time-consuming and effort-filled. We have generally ordered our books through Cody's (see Chapter 3).

SPECIAL NOTES FOR INTERNATIONAL STUDENTS

It is generally easier to order these books from a good bookstore in the United States rather than overseas, given that these U.S. bookstores are accustomed to dealing with the relevant publishers on a regular basis.

CONCLUSION

An entering student does not have to be at home in all of these areas, but the more he knows, the better. A reasonable minimum familiarity would include:

- Spreadsheet and word-processing computer software

- Robert N. Anthony, *Essentials of Accounting* and James Bandler, *How to Use Financial Statements: A Guide to Understanding the Numbers*

- Gary M. Walton and Frank C. Wykoff, *Understanding Economics Today*

- Terry Dickey, *Using Business Statistics: A Guide for Beginners* and Martin Sternstein, *Barron's EZ-101 Study Keys: Statistics*

- Robert Ronstadt, *The Art of Case Analysis: A Guide to the Diagnosis of Business Situations*

- Peter H. Selby and Steve Slavin, *Quick Algebra Review: A Self-Teaching Guide*

If you are going to attend a mathematically inclined program, read one of the more advanced math texts discussed earlier in this chapter.

Any level of knowledge below this basic familiarity is an open invitation to trouble!

A second tier of basic readings and other preparation would include:

- Burton G. Malkiel, *A Random Walk Down Wall Street*

- James P. Womack and Daniel T. Jones, *The Machine That Changed The World: The Story of Lean Manufacturing*

- Mary Munter, *Guide to Managerial Communication*

- Database and presentation computer software

- HP-12C Calculator use

One of the unfortunate aspects of trying to prepare for business school is that the courses that are most difficult to get through are the same quantitative/conceptual courses that are also the most difficult to prepare for on your own. Accounting, Quantitative Methods, and Economics are the principle stumbling blocks. It will be easier to tackle these prior to business school if you can take introductory courses in them at a local school. If not, do consider getting a tutor to help you because a good, or even adequate, tutor can take much of the fear and loathing out of your preparation. One of the great problems in trying to learn economics, for example, is running into one or two points that baffle you and prevent further progress, when having a tutor on call would allow you to get immediate help and thus to keep progressing.

The last point is the same as the first. If you reach business school without having prepared properly you will regret it. Anything that is difficult two months before the program starts will get much more so when you have to learn it along with all the other concepts and techniques that are being piled on you each day.

As with most programs nowadays, the University of Texas at Austin sends out a memorandum to incoming students about ten weeks before the program starts. It describes the estimated costs of the program, the hardware requirements for a student's PC, and suggestions regarding how to prepare for the core courses. I have excerpted some of the relevant portions to give you the flavor of their advice.

"If you have never had an accounting course or if you walk in fear of financial statements, don't worry. The MBA core course in financial accounting assumes that you have no background in accounting. But . . . with that in mind, we do move at a rapid pace. The advice is to obtain a copy of any Introduction to Financial Accounting text and review the first few chapters. . . . Also, obtain a copy of your company's annual report to shareholders. If your company is private, obtain a copy of a public company report. Read the report. Become familiar with the issues that are discussed. You may find that much of the language in the report is unfamiliar. You need to become familiar with the vocabulary of business. There is no time like the present to begin. Begin reading the popular press. *Business Week, The Economist, Forbes, Fortune,* and *The Wall Street Journal* are good places to start. Become familiar with the issues of the day and the names of the players."

The memorandum continues:

"For finance, economics, and statistics if you are comfortable with and can do the following, you are in good shape.

- Graph functions of one variable.

- Calculate the areas of triangles and rectangles.

- Solve two equations and two unknowns; (that is, find the point on a graph where two lines or curves intersect).

- Explain what a derivative is . . . and what the derivative represents.

- Calculate the first and second derivative of a function of one variable."

16

How to Get
the Most
Out of Business School

— EXECUTIVE SUMMARY —

■

Get your life organized before the first day of class.

■

Understand how best to manage your time.
- As Chapter 15 noted, adequate preprogram
  preparation is vital.
- Capitalize on the skills of others by structuring
  a strong study group.

■

Recognize that business school is about more than class work.

■

Keep stress under control.

■

Take advantage of the social (and networking) opportunities.

HIT THE GROUND RUNNING

To get the most out of business school, you must be ready to start working hard from the beginning of the first class. There are two keys to this. The first is to be organized and in control of your new life before classes start. Move into your new apartment and get it stocked and organized before classes begin. Don't be living out of a suitcase in a hotel and needing to look for an apartment and some furniture during the evenings when you should be doing your class assignments.

The second key, discussed at length in Chapter 15, is to be up to speed on the basics before you start classes. This means knowing how to use a spreadsheet and word-processing package as well as a financial calculator, being comfortable with some amount of calculus and statistics, being familiar with accounting and economics fundamentals, and of course being ready to participate fully in English (or the relevant language).

TIME MANAGEMENT IS YOUR BIGGEST RESPONSIBILITY

Business schools deliberately give you more work to do than any human could possibly manage to complete. They want to force you to do two things. First, they want to make you seek out help from other students, generally through study groups. This sort of team formation is exactly what businesses expect of their better employees, so it is appropriate for business schools to try to generate it as well. Second, you are expected to learn how to prioritize your assignments. Some readings are critical and you should do them thoroughly and well. Others are overly long and should just be skimmed for their main points. Still others are essentially for fanatics only and should (I hope) be ignored. Just as in any executive position, the potential work facing you greatly exceeds your time available to do it. You must learn what is most important for each course and focus on precisely that, doing additional work only as time allows.

Falling behind is the biggest trap you face. If you fail to keep up, you will face ever increasing problems. Falling behind results in a downward cycle: You have trouble following today's lecture because you hadn't prepared for it, so you must do extra work to make up for your lack of understanding of the lecture, meaning that you will never have time to get ready for tomorrow's lecture, underpreparation for which will mean that even more work is required to be able to make up for your lack of understanding of it, and so on.

Time management extends to your whole business school experience, not just your classes. This chapter recommends that you get involved in student clubs and sports, and get to know your fellow students and professors. You must learn how to do your classwork efficiently, as the following two sections discuss, and also decide in advance how you will spend your free time. Arrange your schedule to make time for the key activities you value most highly, and limit your involvement with other matters. You might have time to participate actively in two clubs, a sport, and a volunteer group, along with attending various career services workshops and special lectures that interest you, but you are unlikely to be able to participate in six or eight clubs and play as many sports, too.

CHOOSE YOUR STUDY GROUP WISELY

Study groups are an important part of business school for almost everyone. Some schools choose your study group members for you, but if you are allowed to choose your own study group, do so carefully; its makeup can be a major influence on your whole business school experience. You will rely on your study group in your first term. You will be able to use it as a sounding board before you present ideas in class, which will keep you from making some silly comments and encourage you to share genuine insights. You will also use it extensively to prepare assignments when you do not yet know how to reduce your work to manageable proportions by doing only the essential and skipping the rest. It will be very helpful in getting ready for your first sets of exams, helping you master concepts that are difficult for you but easy for someone else in the group.

Even after your first term or first year, a good study group will live on in importance. You may meet for major assignments and exam preparation in later semesters. If you picked the right group, you will have become close friends with some of its members. You will be able to help each other for years to come. In fact, this will be the core of your own contact network.

An ideal study group is invariably made up of individuals who are strong in very different aspects of business, yet who are personally compatible.

CUT TO THE CHASE

There are too many assignments in business school, and they are too long, to do all of them completely. You have two key ways to keep from being overwhelmed. One of them, described above, is to form an appropriate study group. The other, and arguably more important one, is to learn how to do the essential work first, and the inessential later (or not at all).

One group of students comes to business school trained in these techniques, so try to follow their example. Students who have worked in corporate strategy consulting firms like Bain & Co. and McKinsey have spent several years learning exactly this. What you will see them do is ignore extraneous detail and side issues and home in on one or two critical issues of a case. They will generate impressive analysis of those one or two issues rather than scatter their efforts and do unimpressive analysis of two dozen issues. They will be well prepared to discuss cases (or readings) on this basis, but they will not have had to expend prodigious amounts of work and late nights to do so. To work effectively, you must learn to see the forest rather than the trees, the big picture rather than only the details. You will do detailed analyses, but only as they relate to the critical issues.

DEVELOP SKILLS AND KNOWLEDGE THAT ARE VITAL TO YOUR CAREER (AND DIFFICULT TO DEVELOP OUTSIDE OF BUSINESS SCHOOL)

A number of skills beyond those taught in the core courses will be vital to your career progress. The softer skills include negotiation ability, oral and written communication prowess, and the ability to influence different types of people in a range of situations. Harder skills include the ability to price money, analyze currency risk, put together worldwide cashflow models for large corporations, or build econometric models of factors influencing demand for complementary products across various markets.

The time to build your intellectual toolkit is during the program. Take courses that will build strong skills rather than just give you the sort of knowledge you could readily acquire on your own. If a certain industrial marketing course involves learning little more than you could get by reading a standard text on the subject, take something like the marketing research course that develops advanced statistical modeling techniques instead. Select courses for the chance to develop the softer skills, too. Many graduates who have been out for five years or more say that the most valuable course they took, or the one they wish they had taken, was a negotiation course, because so much of what they do in every aspect of their jobs involves negotiating.

In addition, look for opportunities to build your skills in extracurricular settings. In particular, look for chances to give stand-up presentations whenever you can, because this sort of skill will be critical to your advancement throughout your career and it is something few people are ever truly good at.

**WHAT THE ADMISSIONS DIRECTORS SAY ABOUT GETTING
THE MOST OUT OF BUSINESS SCHOOL**

➤ Although academics are a substantial part of your MBA experiences, there is more to the experience. Learning how to structure teams, motivate people, manage differences with people, and lead are all parts of the MBA experience. The foundation for important relationships, both business and friendship, evolve not only during the two years of school but over one's lifetime. A portion of the time is spent in dialogues with professors and business executives that extend beyond the classroom presentation to meaningful exchanges, of ideas, opportunities and so on. This is a time in life to get the maximum out of your two-year investment. Learning a language, exploring areas of interest that have clamored for attention, and even traveling to new markets through exchange programs or DOJs (days on the job) are some of the benefits. Why make academics skill the only return on your investment? *Linda Baldwin, UCLA*

➤ People who don't know why they're getting an MBA miss a lot of opportunities; ten years later they realize what they could've gotten out of it and regret having just drifted through the program instead of paying attention to the opportunities that were all around them. *Brian Sorge, Kellogg*

➤ The type of person who goes grade-hunting, who even takes courses he's already familiar with in order to boost his grades, doesn't get as much as he could out of business school. *Andrew Dyson, Manchester (England)*

FOR CAREER-SWITCHERS

➤ Someone who intends to change careers should have either one definite career she is going to go into, or two or three possibilities for what she might do, things that she will explore over the next two years. She should have thought about it. She should try to get an internship in a relevant area. *Henry Malin, Tuck*

THINK OF YOUR FUTURE CAREER

Presumably, one of your primary reasons for being at business school is to propel your career forward. If you do nothing other than work hard for your classes, however, you will miss a large part of what business school offers in terms of career advancement. Several nonacademic parts of the business school experience are ideal for career enhancement, as are specific courses. Discuss with potential future employers and the career services office which skills you should master and experiences you should gain during the program. Some suggestions:

- Join student clubs that are relevant to your likely future career. For example, if you are interested in management consulting, join the management consulting club. You will have a chance to get to know the other members who are themselves interested in consulting. They will be valuable contacts in the future for information about the industry, job opportunities, and the like.

- Practice your skills in club settings and elsewhere. Businesses hire people who are leaders, communicators, skilled analysts—in other words, doers. You have a chance to demonstrate and refine these skills in various settings during business school, including by helping to run a student club, by working for a volunteer organization, or by working part-time for a business in a field related to the one you intend to work in upon graduation.

- Take advantage of the opportunity to get to know your classmates. You will learn a lot from their experiences and will profit from their friendships in the future, including in career terms. Staying in touch with them will provide you with important career advice and information.

- Get to know faculty members, especially in your chosen field. You will learn a lot more about a field if you spend time with the faculty members who are doing research in it. They will also be able to put you in touch with good industry sources to discuss the field and potential employers or specific job prospects. You *do* need to avoid the appearance of trying to cozy up to them simply to improve your grades or to benefit from their largesse without giving back as well. A sincere interest in learning about the field, on the other hand, will meet with a positive response.

- Take advantage of the professional services offered by the career services office. Take their résumé preparation and interviewing workshops, have them tape one of your presentations and a couple of mock interviews, and consult them about your career plans. These experts are a source of knowledge you would have to pay a great deal to consult outside of business school, so be sure that you do not waste an opportunity to get their input for nothing.

NETWORKING

One of the most valuable assets you will have upon graduation is your network of contacts from your MBA program. This network can help you to get jobs and even, through knowing whom to call for information and assistance, help you in your current job. The key to building an appropriate network is of course to make friends, avoid making enemies, and impress as many people as possible. The impression that you should make is of being clever, hardworking, a great team player, dependable, sensible, and comfortable working under pressure. In other words, your performance at business school will have a major bearing upon the network—as well as the skill base—you develop. Do not go to extremes in trying to network, however, because people trying to curry favor rather than develop relationships will always run the risk of annoying people.

KEEP STRESS UNDER CONTROL

The first months of business school are loaded with stress. You will probably be in an unfamiliar environment, surrounded by people you don't know, and be expected to produce more work faster than you ever have before. In addition, you may be competing with people of a higher quality than you have ever encountered before. This, combined with your high expectations for your own performance, can generate tremendous pressure.

Such pressure can be good or bad. Pressure can motivate you to work hard in a focused fashion. On the other hand, too much pressure can paralyze you and leave you unable to work or concentrate.

To avoid being overwhelmed by stress, *be aware of the signs.* If you feel panicked about not meeting your goals, or enraged about what is being asked of you, or you are feeling the physical symptoms of stress (such as a knot in your stomach, compulsive consumption of food, alcohol, or cigarettes, or tightness in your neck and shoulders), you may well be suffering from excessive stress.

Then *recognize what is causing* your stress. This is likely to be a combination of two things. First, you are demanding too much of yourself. You are expecting to complete every assignment down to the smallest detail, without using your study group for appropriate help. And you are probably expecting to get through the whole program without falling flat on your face a few times. Be realistic; disappointments and mistakes are a normal part of the learning experience. Second, you are failing to appreciate that business school programs deliberately give you more work than anyone can do in the time available.

This can be a rotten combination. You need to learn, as noted above, that you should expect only to complete the most important parts of your assignments, not all of them. You must carefully and firmly prioritize what you will do and what you will skip.

In addition, keep your everyday life under suitable control:

- Get regular exercise. Pick a sport you enjoy and devote half an hour or an hour to it at least five days each week. This will provide you with a suitable outlet for your anxiety, anger, and frustration.

- Eat properly. Too many late-night pizzas, or burgers wolfed down minutes before class, will eventually sap your energy and health.

- Get a reasonable amount of sleep, and make sure that once a week you get an extra couple of hours to help make up for your overly-demanding schedule.

- Last, do not let yourself be bothered by trivial annoyances. Learn to kid around with someone about the sillier aspects of your existence, including those that rile you despite their being not worth annoyance, let alone anger. For example, if you are cut off by a driver on the way to school, it is not worth screaming and yelling at him just because you are not suitably relaxed. The more such occurrences bother you, the greater the cumulative level of stress you will feel.

DON'T FORGET THE SOCIAL EXPERIENCE

Get involved in school life. Join several clubs, participate in a sport or two, and get to know your classmates and your professors. Involve your spouse in as many activities as possible, because it will enrich your experience to be able to share it with someone who truly understands what is involved, and he or she will enjoy the time rather than resenting your new and all-consuming lifestyle.

INTRODUCTION

This appendix contains 115 actual essays written, by 17 different applicants, for leading MBA programs. They address dozens of different essay topics. The applicants and their essays have been selected to give you the widest possible range of materials from which to profit.

The first four applicants all applied to the University of Chicago. They were chosen by Chicago's admissions director, Don Martin, according to my desire that they be from four very different people and of average quality for those admitted. In other words, these essays will show you exactly what you are competing against. They are of perfectly acceptable quality, but they should not discourage you. If you follow the lessons of this book you should be able to surpass each of these efforts.

The second set of three applicants—Melissa, Doreen, and Carol—is taken from Columbia University's files. Columbia's admissions director, Linda Meehan, was asked to supply several applications, again from people of widely differing backgrounds, but this time of superior quality. I think that this group's applications are of a somewhat higher average standard than the Chicago applications, true to my request, but I do not think that any of them should prove daunting to readers of this book.

The remaining applicants feature a high proportion of candidates whom Education U.S.A. helped apply. This is not true for all of them, but what *is* true is that all of their applications are of a high standard. They have been chosen because they offer good models for learning in addition to representing the widest possible range of backgrounds and future goals. Thus here you will find everything from an American commercial photographer to a Cameroonian electrical engineering consultant. The range of applicants, however, extends beyond questions of their job and university backgrounds. Approximately half of the applicants are women, the other half men. A slight majority of the applicants are American, but the others come from a range of countries. (My company operates in Europe as well as the United States and does not just pay lip service to the notion of globalization.) The schools they applied to include over a dozen leading American and half-dozen European schools.

You won't read page by page through this whole, lengthy section. The charts on the following pages are meant to facilitate your picking and choosing whatever is of greatest interest to you. For example, if you are coming from a traditional "feeder" firm or industry, such as management consulting or engineering, and want to see how others distinguished themselves, you can profit from the essays of more than half a dozen applicants. If you had a weak college record, examine the essays of Jon, Terry, and Doreen. If you want to see examples from minority applicants, look at Isabella (Hispanic), Melissa (African-American), or Albert (African). If you are from a public sector background, look at the applications of George, Debra, and Albert. If, on the other hand, you are from an artistic field, try Terry's. This does not exhaust the possibilities; whatever your circumstances, you are likely to find one or more applicants who were similarly situated.

To get the most out of this section, do three things:

- Read the best examples below—these of Roxane, Terry, Jon, Anne, and Joerg—to see how professionally someone can market him- or herself. These are textbook examples of good applications.

- Refer back to the discussion in Chapter 8 of overall marketing principles and the Chapter 9 analysis of specific essay topics you will need to address.

- Then look at the efforts of the people who most resemble you in terms of their backgrounds, critical issues they needed to address, and schools they were applying to.

Of course, you should not try to copy what these applicants have done. Instead, adopt the attitude of an admissions director and ask yourself just what worked and what failed for each applicant, and then ask what lessons there are for you.

(One last note: Some of the applicants wanted their full names used whereas others wanted only their first names used, or even wanted their identities lightly disguised by using a different first name or by eliminating the names of their bosses or companies. Thus there is no uniform policy followed here, except that of honoring the wishes of the applicants.)

OVERVIEW OF THE APPLICANTS AND THEIR ESSAYS

APPLICANT (Nationality— if not American)	JOB	EDUCATION	SCHOOLS (Applications Reprinted Here)	SPECIAL ISSUES
George (page 323)	Municipal government employee	BA, Social Sciences	Chicago	Switch from public to private sector
Isabella (page 326)	Insurance executive	BA, Hotel Management	Chicago	Analytical firepower
Robert (page 329)	Corporate banker	BA, Economics	Chicago	How to distinguish himself from applicant pool
Judy (page 332)	Consultant (technology)	BA, Mathematics	Chicago	How to distinguish herself from applicant pool
Melissa (page 336)	Strategy consultant	BA, Liberal Arts	Columbia	How to distinguish herself from applicant pool
Doreen (page 339)	Journalist	(Almost a BA)	Columbia	Quantitative abilities
Carol (page 344)	Account executive for garment manufacturer; formerly department store buyer	BA, Literature	Columbia	Quantitative abilities
Roxane (page 346)	Chemical engineer/ short-term planning analyst for oil company	BS, Chemical Engineering	Wharton, UCLA, Harvard, Stanford, Tuck, Darden	How to distinguish herself from applicant pool
Roger (German) (page 371)	Entrepreneur	BA, Economics	Wharton, Chicago, Michigan	—

APPLICANT (Nationality— if not American)	JOB	EDUCATION	SCHOOLS (Applications Reprinted Here)	SPECIAL ISSUES
Sylvie (French) (page 378)	Accountant	BBA, Accounting	Stanford, Babson	How to distinguish herself from applicant pool
Albert (Cameroonian) (page 384)	Electrical engineering consultant	BS, MS, PhD, Electrical Engineering	Columbia, Kellogg, Yale, MIT	Low GMAT score
Joerg (German) (page 392)	PhD internship; retailing consultant	BS, MS, PhD, Mechanical Engineering	Harvard, Kellogg (see Chapter 9)	Never worked full-time. Perpetual student? English abilities
Terry (page 399)	Commercial photographer	BA, German Literature BFA (Photography)	Rotterdam, INSEAD	Quantitative abilities Mediocre grades
Jon (Danish) (page 405)	Shipping executive	In-house company education	London, INSEAD	Lack of proper bachelor's degree
Philippe (French) (page 415)	Mergers & acquisitions analyst; formerly engineering project manager	BS & MS, Engineering MS, Technology & Policy	INSEAD	Too many degrees?
Debra (Dutch) (page 419)	College administration	BA, Education MA, Communications	IESE Nijenrode	Quantitative abilities Business orientation
Anne (French) (page 429)	Airport manager	BBA	INSEAD	—

THE ESSAY QUESTIONS, TOPIC BY TOPIC

Essay Topic	George Isabella Robert Judy	Melissa	Doreen	Carol	Roxane	Roger	Sylvie	Albert	Joerg	Terry	Jon	Philippe	Debra	Anne
Career plans/why an MBA, why this school, etc.	X	X	X	X	X	X	X	X	X	X	X	X	X	X
Work experience													X	X
Walk in another's shoes for a day	X													
What other career you'd consider	X													
Substantial accomplishments		X	X					X	X	X	X	X	X	X
Most valued accomplishments outside work									+					
Personal failure		X	X		X			X		X	X	X	X	X
Multi-experienced school body													X	
Contribute to school's diversity		X	X	X	X			X	+					
Challenged traditional thought of a group					X	X								
World's greatest problem					X	X		X						
Leisure/nonprofessional activities					X	X		+	+	X			X	

Essay Topic	George	Isabella	Robert	Judy	Melissa	Doreen	Carol	Roxane	Roger	Sylvie	Albert	Joerg	Terry	Jon	Philippe	Debra	Anne
Strengths and weaknesses								x					x		x	x	x
Leadership								x			x				x	x	x
Why an international program								x									
Show you'll succeed academically								x				x					
Challenging professional project								x				x					
Representative job								x				x					
Ethical dilemma								x				x				x	
How to teach ethics										x							
Contribution to your community								x				x					
People/events that influenced you								x		x						x	
Exceptional manager/person								x								x	
Biggest risk/obstacle									x								
Whom to invite for dinner/conversation										x				x			
Response to cross-cultural situation											x						
How to effect organizational change											x					x	x
Major trends in your industry														x			
Main factors accounting for your development															x		x
Alternative means to ensure your development															x		x
Why you studied what you did at university																x	
In 40 years, what will reviews of your autobiography say												+					
Optional essay															x		

The + sign for some of Joerg's work indicates that it is to be found in his Kellogg essays in Chapter 8.

— UNIVERSITY OF CHICAGO —
FOUR APPLICANTS' ESSAYS

GEORGE

Background Data:

Job:	Advisor to municipal government regarding urban economic development
Education:	Social science major, with multiple honors and awards, at a good university
Nationality:	American

Critical issues to address:

The biggest problems for someone trying to move out of the public sector are to show that he understands what the private sector is all about, has the skills and the mindset to make the switch, and will fit well in an MBA program.

---

1. **Why are you seeking an MBA from the University of Chicago Graduate School of Business, and what are your plans and goals after you receive your degree?**

My interest in pursuing a Masters in Business Administration began at the end of my public policy and administration studies, when I became intrigued by the role of government in promoting inner-city economic development. In addition to taking two courses at the Stern School of Business, I worked on a capstone project in which I analyzed economic development policies and programs in city X and conducted a case study of the MetroTech development in neighborhood Y.

After securing a position with agency Z, a key promoter of the MetroTech project, I began to work professionally on economic development projects designed to promote private investment and job creation in neighborhood Y. In this position, I learned the importance of business development to city X's diverse communities; businesses not only provided the jobs that allowed people to provide for themselves and their families, but also generated the wealth from which the city government draws taxes to support services and programs for the truly needy. In my position with neighborhood Y's Borough President, I had the opportunity to promote the borough's businesses by performing a detailed study of the garment industry and advising the Borough President on the city's commercial and industrial policy.

Although in this position I served as a facilitator of business growth and job creation, I wanted to be directly involved in managing companies and making investment decisions. I began to investigate business schools in the hope of identifying a program that provided in-depth exposure to the analytical tools and concepts needed to operate a successful business.

I became interested in the University of Chicago's Graduate School of Business (GSB) because of its reputation for providing a rigorous intellectual experience in which its students gain a solid foundation in business concepts and develop the analytical skills to apply them. Moreover, its focus on leadership, international education, curriculum flexibility, and job placement further convinced me of the compatibility of my skills, experience, and interests with the GSB program.

I am particularly impressed by the Leadership Exploration and Development Program, which highlights the GSB's serious concern for the development of leadership skills in its students. Through my experience in city X's politics, I learned the importance of strong and visionary leadership. Therefore, I look forward to the opportunity to participate in a LEAD program in which students not only discuss and analyze issues, but also practice leadership skills in seminars and workshops sponsored by corporate leaders. Because the GSB empowers its students by allowing them to plan, direct, and evaluate this required part of the curriculum, I also hope to develop team-building and leadership skills by serving as a LEAD facilitator.

I appreciate the GSB's respect for its students as further demonstrated by its flexible curriculum which would allow me to tailor the program to meet my needs and interests. With a limited number of required courses and the ability to take courses in other parts of the university, the GSB offers me more academic freedom than any other business school program I have considered. Moreover, the GSB would permit me to replace some of the required courses with higher level courses if I have mastered the material in other courses. Because of course work taken toward my Masters in Public Administration, including courses in statistics and finance at the Stern School of Business, the GSB's interest in having its students build upon their academic and professional background is especially important to me.

I am also impressed by the GSB's commitment to providing an international business education. With over 20 percent of the full-time students from outside the United States, I believe that the curriculum's focus on the globalization of business will be enhanced by the experiences and cultural backgrounds of my peers. In addition, the GSB's International Business Exchange Program (IBEP) will provide me with the opportunity to return to Vienna, Austria, where I lived and worked during my undergraduate abroad experience. Studying at the Wirtschaftsuniversität Wien will allow me to further my capacity with the German language and to build upon my prior professional work experience in Austria.

Since business school will require the commitment of substantial time and resources, the Office of Career Services' proven ability to generate professional opportunities for GSB's students is critical to me. By providing its students with access to the world's most prominent and successful companies, the GSB has assisted its students to achieve the third highest return on their educational investment of any business school. The success of GSB's students in making the transition from business school to challenging and lucrative positions is enhanced by an intense interviewing schedule that will expose me to a wide range of prospective employers.

After developing analytical, quantitative, and leadership skills, as well as an enhanced international business perspective, at the GSB, I intend to return to city X. With the strength of the GSB's reputation as the leading business school program in financial management, I believe I could obtain a position in the financial services industry. A position in municipal finance would be a natural career progression considering my background as an analyst of the borough Z budget, but I would also pursue opportunities with investment banks. I believe that a position with an investment bank would expose me to a large number of companies and industries, as well as allow me to apply an international investment perspective. Also, a large firm would provide the opportunity to learn about the structuring of sophisticated financial transactions and allow me to move into a managerial position as my skills and experience grew. This investment banking experience, coupled with the financial management skills developed at the GSB, would prepare me for a career as a venture capitalist.

2   If you could walk in someone else's shoes for a day, whose would you choose and why?

If I could walk in anyone's shoes for a day, I would choose those of Robert Kerrey, Senator of Nebraska, on the day that the Senate voted on President Clinton's 1993 federal budget proposal. Since the Senate was split largely along party lines, Senator Kerrey's vote would decide the fate of the most significant piece of legislation in President Clinton's first year in office.

I would like to walk in Senator Kerrey's shoes because I admire his determination to give thoughtful consideration to the budget's long-term effect on the nation's welfare at a time when he was under considerable pressure to make a politically expedient decision. Unlike most of his colleagues, Senator Kerrey had not based his support for the President's budget proposal solely on his party affiliation. Instead, he spent several days before the vote weighing political considerations against the strength of his belief that the President's budget did not reduce federal spending and the government's deficit fast enough.

Furthermore, I would choose to walk in Senator Kerrey's shoes on this particular day because I believe that people achieve self-awareness and growth through experiences that challenge their ethics and intellect. In this case, Senator Kerrey, a successful businessman and thoughtful politician, was forced to choose between the nation's future prosperity and the success of his own party's president.

3. If you could pursue any occupation regardless of education, training, special talent, or monetary barrier, what would it be and why?

If I could select any occupation without regard to limitations or barriers, I would choose to be a venture capitalist specializing in inner-city investments. I believe that in this occupation I could assist these communities to achieve self-sufficiency through economic development and generate a good return on my investments. I believe this economic development is most often achieved when private investors, motivated by profit, identify those potentially profitable companies with a comparative advantage derived from their inner-city location. Government could promote this private investment by reducing the capital gains tax on income derived from inner-city businesses. This tax benefit would overcome the real and imagined risks associated with inner-city investments.

In addition to giving inner-city companies access to a source of capital normally denied them, as venture capitalist I would provide consulting services to assist inner-city managers to most effectively capitalize on their competitive advantages of strategic location and proximity to markets. The City X garment industry, for example, has one important competitive advantage over producers in low-wage countries: their location allows them to respond to a production order from Manhattan designers or retailers in a number of days instead of months. Without the information processing technologies with which to implement "just-in-time" production, however, the managers of many City X garment firms fail to benefit from this competitive advantage.

By improving the performance of inner-city business through these financing and management services, I would increase the profitability of my investments. These returns would demonstrate to other venture capitalists that profits can be obtained through active investment and involvement in inner-city companies. Once the venture capital community recognized the potential profitability of inner-city investments, a new source of growth capital would become available to these companies.

These potentially profitable companies represent the inner-city's most promising opportunity to provide long-term employment at a reasonable wage for its residents. With the financial independence derived from this employment, inner-city residents could provide food, housing, and health care for themselves and their families.

ISABELLA

Background Data:

Job: Insurance executive (risk management) for four years

Education: Hotel management degree, with numerous scholarships and awards

Nationality: American (Hispanic)

Critical issue to address:

A hotel management degree leaves open the possibility that she lacks the analytical firepower for a program like Chicago's.

1. Why are you seeking an MBA from the University of Chicago Graduate School of Business, and what are your plans and goals after you receive your degree?

Upon graduation in 1990, I eagerly sought employment opportunities in the hotel industry. The weak economy, coupled with the lack of quality of career opportunities in the hospitality industry in 1990, encouraged me to reassess the direction of my future career. After completing a detailed job search, I was offered an opportunity at Corporation X as an account executive intern in the commercial insurance brokerage industry. Accordingly, I adapted quickly to the dynamic and competitive nature of the brokerage world by focusing on the service skills that I learned during my undergraduate studies.

During my first year of employment at Corporation X, I developed a unique, comprehensive foundation in the property and casualty insurance brokerage industry. I was involved in client presentations, risk-financing projects, account renewals, marketing exercises, proposal preparation, numerous seminars, and document translation from English to Spanish and vice versa. Overall, my technical knowledge of the industry was developed through both a classroom setting and general application. Upon completion of the account executive training program, I was offered a position as an account representative in 1991 and I was promoted to senior account representative in 1993.

During September 1994, Corporation Y invited me to interview with their senior management. At the time I was not seeking to change jobs. I had recently acquired a new property and casualty insurance account and was involved in several challenging risk management projects. Employment at Corporation Y, however, presented an invaluable opportunity for continued professional development. As a result, I joined their risk management department as an account executive during October 1994.

My contributions to Corporation Y were recognized by my colleagues during October 1995; with much pride, I received the prestigious *Q.U.E.S.T. for the Best* Award (Q. = Quality Work, U. = Unique Ideas, E. = Expertise, S = Service to Clients, T. = Teamwork). Only nine out of four hundred employees receive the award annually.

During my employment at Corporation Y, I have acquired substantive knowledge pertaining to the design and implementation of complex, sophisticated property and casualty insurance programs for Fortune 500 companies. As an account executive, I have more accountability compared to what I had in my previous position at Corporation X. In addition, due to my past experience in the management of hospitality industry accounts, I have been designated as a Hospitality Industry Specialist in order to concentrate on various segments of the hospitality industry, including hotels, casinos, athletic clubs, country clubs, restaurants, and racing facilities.

The insurance industry is competitive, challenging and fast-paced; as a result, upon completion of an MBA I plan to enter a different segment of the industry. I plan to synthesize my hotel administration degree and experience, along with my insurance background, by obtaining a position as a risk manager for an international hotel company. Within five years of serving as a risk manager, I will seek an appointment as Director of Risk Management and Insurance Services. An MBA from the University of Chicago will accelerate my professional development and facilitate the realization of my ambitions.

As a risk manager, I will have the responsibility of formulating cost-effective insurance programs including actuarial funding mechanisms such as self-insurance, paid loss retro programs, captives, and other cash flow techniques used to pay for losses including both damages to property and bodily injury to employees or third parties. These insurance or self funding programs cost millions of dollars a year. As a result, cost containment activities are a major priority. Therefore, I will also have the added challenge of motivating management to implement aggressive loss control systems that will decrease work-related injuries. Cooperation and team effort will determine the success of this endeavor. By developing a safer work environment, employees will be more productive and render higher quality service.

The hotel industry has recovered from a recession; consequently, occupancy rates and competition have increased substantially in the domestic and international hotel market. The insurance industry regularly shifts from a "soft market" that offers inexpensive property and casualty premiums to a "hard market" that, conversely, promotes expensive premiums. These two issues, coupled with the ongoing changes in the global economy, require a risk manager to develop a flexible, innovative, and proactive managerial style.

Participation in the University of Chicago's MBA curriculum will sharpen my leadership and managerial capabilities. Another factor, which I deem essential, consists of the University of Chicago's prominent global perspective. Participation in the International Business Exchange Program at the Instituto de Estudios Superiores de la Empresa (IESE), Barcelona, Spain, and collaboration with students from diverse countries will afford an unparalleled exposure to cultural diversity and develop substantive knowledge as to the globalization of business.

Ultimately, if provided with the opportunity, participation in the University of Chicago's MBA program will refine my technical know-how and managerial capabilities and afford an invaluable opportunity for personal and professional development.

2. **If you could walk in someone else's shoes for a day, whose would you choose and why?**

If I could walk in someone else's shoes for a day, I would choose to walk in my mother's shiny leather loafers. My mother has strolled and jumped through various challenges in her life. She has confronted obstacles with energetic optimism and contagious humor. Her vision, fortitude, and creativity have always guided her self-assured steps and ambition.

It takes an incredibly courageous individual to decide to pack up his or her belongings and immigrate to another country during her early thirties. My mother saw unparalleled professional and educational opportunities for her children in the United States. With sincere faith and confidence, she guided my father in the transition from life in Colombia, South America, to life in the United States.

It is through the application of creative endeavors that an individual develops and nurtures his or her willingness to see life from a different perspective. My mother has continually promoted cultural awareness and experimentation. Her accomplishments as an actress in Colombia and New York City reflect her creative convictions. By attending her rehearsals and performances I was consistently exposed to a myriad of personalities and I experienced innumerable episodes of humor, drama, and creativity.

Vigor, dedication, and resilience are pivotal components of my mother's character. For these reasons, I would welcome the opportunity to spend a day in her shoes.

3. **If you could pursue any occupation regardless of education, training, special talent, or monetary barrier, what would it be and why?**

Without doubt, I would savor a career as a fashion designer in the event that education, training, special talent, or monetary barriers were nonexistent. Apparel design has been a creative outlet that I have developed through the completion of several design courses and projects. After submitting a detailed proposal and portfolio, I was awarded a grant from the Cornell University council of the Creative and Performing Arts. During my fourth year of undergraduate study, I produced a fashion show promoting my collection entitled "The Latin Style." Vibrant colors, exceptional fabrics, and sensual shapes came together and celebrated the romantic evening. This enterprise proved to be a rewarding and valuable learning experience.

A fashion designer must be energetic, creative, self-confident, flexible, and resilient. Designers must cater to specific markets and satisfy the needs of those segments. The delivery of new lines of apparel is fast-paced, competitive, and invigorating. A designer must be in the forefront of the industry and deliver innovative creations that will entice buyers, journalists, and photographers. Ultimately, the customer, through his purchase decisions, determines the apparel designer's success. Nonetheless, I believe that true satisfaction is derived from the ability to help a client feel important, powerful, and elegant.

ROBERT

Background:

Job:	Five years of experience in corporate banking, with several promotions
Education:	Economics major at Duke University
Nationality:	American

Critical issue to address:

The only real problem is to distinguish himself from the large number of applicants from the same field, either by showing that he is truly a standout in this field or by showing that he is more well-rounded than others, or both.

1. **Why are you seeking an MBA from the University of Chicago Graduate School of Business, and what are your plans and goals after you receive your degree?**

Open the 1986 yearbook for Acme High School and under my senior picture you will see "future goals: doctor in radiology." At the time this made perfect sense. Ironically, a strong pre-med program was a major factor in my choosing Duke ahead of other undergraduate schools (which seemed to have stronger business programs). Yet, by my second year in college, I suspected that my true interests were not in the medical sciences. To confirm these suspicions, I applied for an internship program in a hospital. Here I discovered medicine was not for me.

During that sophomore summer, some mental regrouping led me to aspirations in the field of business. An initial fascination with the stock market, corporate news stories, economics, and my parents' businesses evolved into my current position as a derivatives trader/marketer. To continue to follow these interests, I believe now is the time to make a calculated move—attaining an MBA. An MBA at Chicago's Graduate School of Business will be instrumental in achieving my long term goals.

Following two years at the GSB I plan to join a capital markets unit with a dominant international presence. Employers with little understanding of global finance may wonder about my leaving my current career path in one capital markets group, only to join another later. But I believe that this is where I can most efficiently learn about expanding businesses into international markets. Ideally, immediately following graduate school I will be placed overseas, which should also open exciting avenues for my wife, who has a PhD in mechanical engineering. The combination of this added work experience and a GSB education will give me the practical knowledge for my long-term professional goal.

Long term, five to ten years after achieving an MBA, I intend to hop the banker/customer fence. Throughout my career I have admired the key managers responsible for their company's financial progress. As an advisor, I enjoy making financial suggestions that may influence a corporate manager's business strategy. My goal is to be in a position similar to these key managers.

As a manager, I hope to work within the finance group of a middle market manufacturer. While global trade becomes increasingly necessary for corporate prosperity, my skills would be desired by domestic corporations seeking expansion. My objective is to plan an essential role in assisting a company into foreign markets through acquisitions and strategic capital expenditures.

On a personal basis, long term goals include my wife, family, and community. I will remain actively involved in the community by continuing my association with Junior Achievement and Habitat for Humanity, coaching youth soccer, and perhaps working for the public service commission.

The Graduate School of Business is a critical component of this entire plan, both professionally and personally. Among the very best in business programs, the GSB is unique in that it concentrates on *all* the areas needed by a highly competitive financial manager on the international scene a decade from now. An MBA at Chicago will sharpen my finance and general management skills. While these skills have blossomed with six years of work, Duke University's liberal arts format did not provide the specific foundation I now desire. In addition, and perhaps more importantly, a Chicago MBA will teach me how to think like a manager and recognize what questions to ask.

As an undergraduate economics major, I admired that the overwhelming majority of my research was based on publications by University of Chicago faculty. Today, in addition to superior faculty, I am drawn to the GSB's team-oriented approach of LEAD, an international emphasis, and a diverse student body. The GSB's urban setting in one of the world's financial capitals is obviously a tremendous asset, not only from an academic perspective, but from a cultural perspective as well. I am anxious to choose from a large selection of electives in a curriculum that focuses on innovation. The combination of one of the broadest alumni networks and one of the strongest corporate recruiting programs worldwide is also vital to me.

In return, I believe that I can give fellow Chicago students a sampling of my experiences, possibly helping them to attain their goals as the GSB makes it possible for me to attain mine.

2. **If you could walk in someone else's shoes for a day, whose would you choose and why?**

"Houston, we have a problem. . . ." On board the Apollo 13, a crew of three scrambles to discern the cause, and effect, of a dramatic explosion. A gas is spewing from the side of the craft, and the oxygen gauge's needle begins to descend. It is April 12, 1970, and I am Jim Lovell, commander of the Apollo 13, about to face the ultimate test in crisis management.

I have chosen to wear Lovell's shoes for a day, partly for the excitement of flying in a spacecraft and for satisfying a childhood fascination—being an astronaut en route to the moon. However, my primary attraction to Lovell's position lies in understanding how he managed to overcome such an extraordinary set of circumstances. Clearly, Lovell was challenged by events for which he could never have trained. Coherent analysis and life-dependent decisions came from instinct and gut reaction.

Throughout that fateful period as Apollo 13 lost much of its vital oxygen and electrical reserves, the commander remained calm. Not only did he direct a frightened crew in close quarters while barreling into outer space, but he also managed a staff of hundreds on earth at mission control. Placed in the cockpit of the spacecraft, I wonder how I would respond while a series of mishaps occurred around me. Would I be able to innovate to effectively control others in a remote location and drive them toward a common goal? Would I be able to abandon a lifelong ambition of walking on the moon when it was just within arm's reach?

Lovell responded instantly to the changes dealt to him and put his own aspirations aside. I hope that, put in the same situation, I would react in a similar manner: recognize the big picture while paying attention to necessary details. A seasoned manager, Lovell quickly changed course and refocused. "Gentlemen, what are your intentions? I'd like to go home."

3. **If you could pursue any occupation regardless of education, training, special talent, or monetary barrier, what would it be and why?**

Anxiety swelled as two armed policemen escorted me through a metal detector into the city school. It was my first day as a teacher in the Junior Achievement program called Project Business. Introducing myself to the group of inquiring faces, I wondered whether these students would relate to me despite our cultural differences. Would they care? I did not realize at the time that the next two school years with JA would have such a profound influence on my life. If I were to pursue any occupation regardless of training, special talents, or other prohibitive factors, it would certainly be in a similar teaching capacity.

An evening news broadcast introduced me to Junior Achievement ("JA"). I volunteered to be placed at South Atlanta High School, where I would teach basic business principles to a ninth grade class. Initially, I volunteered because I had remembered the inspiration of coaching a youth soccer team in Winston-Salem, North Carolina; I thought JA would be similar. JA has given me new respect for those who can motivate, enforce self-discipline, and instill curiosity in others.

My passion for volunteer teaching in the community has carried over into the workplace. On a professional level, I relish the opportunity to speak before colleagues and customers. Explaining the complexities of derivative instruments has been a teaching challenge. In an effort to increase referrals, I have traveled throughout the corporate lending network of SunTrust Banks to conduct seminars on hedging. Likewise, as "derivatives" and "risk" have become synonymous to our client base, I have aggressively educated CFOs of concerned corporations (and their boards) in an attempt to combat a media-created frenzy.

Ultimately, my teaching efforts are rewarded, whether I am distributing JA diplomas to students or watching a customer finally understand a hedging product. Teaching others has taught me the importance of integrity and a good sense of humor.

JUDY

Background Data:

Job:	Two to three years of experience in consulting (use of technology)
Education:	Mathematics major at Yale
Nationality:	American

Critical issue to address:

As a consultant, she needs to distinguish herself from the large number of candidates with a similar background.

1. **Why are you seeking an MBA from the University of Chicago Graduate School of Business, and what are your plans and goals after you receive your degree?**

The managers of today and tomorrow need to understand the importance of keeping up with technology in order to remain competitive. Taking the recent popularity of large-scale mergers in the telecommunications industry as an example, we are seeing more and more companies striving toward more complete service offerings and massive geographic coverage. While bigger and better implies more efficient, it often means more complicated. It also means more work for the small competitor. Managers on all levels will need resources to provide information and tools for acquiring and using information. The technology that provides these resources is constantly being improved, but even the most advanced technology is useless unless it can be successfully applied. This is the greatest challenge that future managers will face. Successful management of technical change requires careful planning, to ensure a consensus among management, the developers, and the "front line" users of the new technology.

The process of technological change has always interested me. I have watched it, learned about it, and wondered about it throughout my employment. Even in high school, as the manager and statistician of a basketball team, I helped to computerize the analysis of player statistics. During college, I wrote batch files and manuals to help the business office of a magazine make better use of their computer resources. In my current position, I have participated in small-scale application development projects. I hope to continue in this direction and build a career in the management of technological change.

The implementation of change requires more than a background in technology. Those employees who stand to benefit the most from a new business process are likely to be unconvinced of the extent to which their work will improve. They may be afraid of computers, concerned about their job security, or unwilling to invest the resources for training. Managers trying to implement any type of change must motivate the people who are affected to support the change and guarantee its success. They must acknowledge the connection between the technology itself and the human resource that supports it. Change often requires a capital investment. Managers may not know how to determine the value of the investment and the expected impact on the bottom line. Yet even small companies will need to update the way to help them make that happen.

Such people must have a background in all management issues, including the management of human resources, marketing, and financial management.

I need to build such a foundation in management issues. I have always had ideas for change, but I have rarely had the authority, resources, or knowledge to implement change. I want to learn techniques for designing systems that address the user's needs, solve technological problems, and optimize the bottom line. I need to learn approaches to training and other human resource issues. I seek a deeper understanding of financial management and marketing. Over the next years, I will address these needs by earning an MBA and working in strategic consulting. I will improve my quantitative and technological skills, and I will develop an understanding of the nontechnical aspects of management. Ultimately I plan to have a leadership position in a consulting firm or to manage my own firm.

The Graduate School of Business at the University of Chicago is well equipped to prepare me for my future. The program provides a solid basis in general management, yet it allows for a concentration in a particular sphere. The course offerings in the areas of strategic management and information technology are relevant to the growth and survival of the modern company. The faculty includes some of the top minds in each field. The School attracts an intelligent and motivated student body, consisting of people who share my interests, such as technology management and small business consulting. The team-building focus, which starts as early as orientation, fosters the type of environment in which I will excel. I am certain that I will both gain a great deal from my fellow students and contribute to their experiences at the GSB.

In today's executive marketplace, there is no shortage of MBAs. In order to distinguish oneself and launch a successful career, one needs the appropriate credentials. I seek a degree in management from the Graduate School of Business because the GSB is uniquely qualified to provide the background that is required in order to manage technology.

2. **If you could walk in someone else's shoes for a day, whose would you choose and why?**

"There is a thing passing in the sky; some thick clouds surround it; the uninitiated sees nothing." (*Hani gve lewe ma negele ya nja gbili kaango kpowa ee to.*) Mende proverb, translated in Sylvia Ardy Boone, *Radiance from the Waters: Ideals of Feminine Beauty in Mende Art.* (New Haven: Yale University Press, 1986).

Sylvia Ardy Boone did not look like a typical Yale professor. Most people saw a quiet, heavyset woman who dressed in head-wraps and untailored clothes. To me, she was beautiful, successful, and admirable, clad in the graceful and flowing fabrics of the African people she studied. The above proverb, which she taught me, aptly describes her existence. Few members of the Yale community saw past the thick clouds surrounding this magnificent woman.

Boone's award-winning dissertation covered the expression of ideals of feminine beauty through art. Her subjects, the Mende of Sierra Leone, place a high value on secrecy and privacy. Researchers are not welcome among them. Yet Boone was dedicated enough to earn the trust of the Mende. She lived with them for extended periods of time, learning their language, culture, and art.

I met Professor Boone through an art history course. I knew very little about African cultures and the African-American experience, so I expected to be at a disadvantage. Happily, I was wrong. Professor Boone was one of the most caring and approachable professors I came across in college. She encouraged me to draw on my own experiences to understand the material and develop my own insights. I admired this introverted woman, who had the courage and commitment to live amidst a closed community.

Sylvia Boone died in her sleep about a year later. I learned from her obituary that she was the first African-American woman to be granted tenure at Yale. My respect for her increased, and I regretted the missed opportunity to learn more from her and about her. I would love to spend a day as this mysterious woman, this "thing" that passed in the sky.

3. **If you could pursue any occupation regardless of education, training, special talent, or monetary barrier, what would it be and why?**

If I could be anything, I would be a dancer.

Dance is a fundamental part of human existence. It exists in every culture, as ritual, as a rite of mating, as entertainment. Regardless of the reason for dance, it is always art.

Dance simultaneously interprets and is interpreted. Whether accompanied by song, instrument, or silence, dance is constructed of movements that are born out of sound, emotion, and spirituality. These movements, a sculpture in motion, in turn inspire the watcher, invoke thoughts and feelings, perhaps summon the rain.

Dancing is control and freedom, tradition and breaking from the past, taught yet ultimately found in the soul. When I dance, I am aware of every movement. I am conscious of moving the air around me as I float or cut through it. The floor beneath my bare feet, acting as my canvas, allows me to resist the forces of gravity and almost fly. Every stretch and contraction is calculated, yet each breath releases tension. While I study positions and techniques, I move beyond them to express that which defies words.

When I dance, I can see inside myself. I find my limits, and I exceed them. I find my burdens, and I set them aside. I attend to my joints, one by one, learning how they function. I seek strength, and it flows from deep within. And when I dance, I connect with others. We fuse together into an organism, a harmonious sharing and building of space. Each person may create a unique path through space, or all limbs may move with synchronous precision. The feeling of belonging cannot be broken.

If I could be anything, I would be a dancer.

COMMENTS

1. Remember that these essays represent a cross section of the essays that succeeded at a leading program. In other words, all of these essays were written by people who ultimately attended Chicago. Each applicant has done some things relatively well and other things relatively poorly. These essays have been included more to give you a realistic sense of the quality that typical (successful) applicants are turning out than to encourage you to mimic their efforts.

2. *George* has done a marvelous job, in his first essay, demonstrating that he understands Chicago's program very well. He is quite convincing in showing how it will be helpful to him. This is particularly useful for someone like him who needs to convince the school that he will not be a liability insofar as he has not been in the private sector. This first essay shows that he is very aware of what he can get from an MBA, thereby suggesting that he would fit comfortably in the program and making his desires for the future all the more credible. His second essay reinforces his political background, but may not do much more for him. On the other hand, his third essay allows him to show in concrete form what he envisions for his future. He does so in an unusual fashion because most people answer this essay in terms of their desire to be a deep sea diver, painter, or president, whereas he dreams of doing what he is going to business school for.

3. *Isabella* has written a good first essay: it shows her to have been very successful to date despite having had to take a job in a field rather distant from the one for which she had prepared at university. Her discussion of insurance reveals an analytical approach to the industry and to her career, thereby addressing the most serious potential concern likely to be voiced about her candidacy. Her second essay reveals her mother as an interesting and praiseworthy woman, and reinforces the fact that Isabella is a second-generation Hispanic. I am not sure that it does much more for Isabella, however, other than showing her to be a grateful daughter. Her third essay, similarly, does not advance her case dramatically, although it does sketch in some more about her interests and personality, thereby making one potential use of this question.

4. *Robert* has the problem of someone applying to MBA programs from a typical "feeder" field—how to distinguish himself from the many other applicants with similar backgrounds. He makes a good start in the first essay by engaging the reader's interest immediately. He shows how he ended up in business rather than medicine, which makes for good reading. In addition, he writes fluidly and well. His second essay, rather than humanizing him in a way that other applicants attempt for themselves, emphasizes his managerial interests. I am not convinced that a banker needs to persuade admissions officers that he is focused on business. He might have done better by taking more of a risk and showing more of himself. His last essay is on a good topic—teaching, especially of the underprivileged—and he does a good job of tying his alternative job to his actual one. On the other hand, he did not fully tie in how integrity and a sense of humor are integral parts of teaching. In other words, his conclusion seems to be tacked on as an afterthought.

5. *Judy,* with her educational background and work experience, has no particular issues she needs to address, other than the need to distinguish herself from the applicant pool. Her essays help her do this by showing her to be very well-rounded. Despite being a mathematics major, emphasizing her love of anthropology suggests that she is anything but a mere number-cruncher. The biggest drawback to her essays is that she discusses very little concerning her job and what she does well professionally. It is not clear from any of these essays what she actually does or what major successes she has had. She has thus missed an opportunity to impress the admissions committee with information about her career to date.

— COLUMBIA UNIVERSITY —
THREE APPLICANTS' ESSAYS

MELISSA PETERSON

Background:

Job:	Strategy consultant
Education:	Liberal arts degree from a leading school
Nationality:	American (African-American)

Critical issues to address:

As a consultant, she needs to distinguish herself from the large number of candidates with a similar background.

1. **What are your career goals? How will an MBA help you achieve these goals? Why are you applying to Columbia Business School?**

As a Business Analyst in the Strategic Services Practice of Andersen Consulting, I developed a passion for the variety, challenge, and intellectual stimulation that a career in management consulting affords. I enjoyed studying the management and operations of client companies, analyzing and formulating solutions to complex business questions, presenting findings, and managing client teams. In fact, everything about management consulting seemed perfect. However, something was missing. The constant travel and long workdays were forcing me to neglect my first love: community service.

I have always been conscious of the fact that my personal success was made possible through the efforts of those who came before me. Without the sacrifices of people like Thurgood Marshall and Susan Brownell Anthony, the opportunities that I have today would be far less numerous. As such, I feel a moral obligation to assist those less fortunate than I, and to ameliorate the world in some small way for coming generations. To date, I have fulfilled this obligation through noncommittal volunteer work. In the future, I will fulfill the obligation by embarking on a career that will allow me to utilize my consulting skills to serve the community.

My short-term career goal is to serve as a business consultant to a nongovernmental organization in a developing country or as a business consultant to a nonprofit agency in the United States. This will allow me to further hone my management skills while serving the community. Also, it will prepare me to realize my long-term goal of starting a business in an area of high unemployment. The most effective form of community service helps others to help themselves. By creating jobs, I would help people to become self-sufficient and to support their families.

A Columbia Business School MBA would provide me with an internationally focused management education, which would better prepare me to plan and act strategically and to predict and manage change as a consultant and as an entrepreneur. Studying entrepreneurial management and assisting minority entrepreneurs with their business issues would provide me with a theoretical and practical entrepreneurial education. In brief, a Columbia Business School MBA would help me to achieve my career goals by helping me to develop the skills that are necessary to succeed in today's global economy.

2. **In reviewing the last five years, describe the one or two accomplishments of which you are most proud.**

The two recent accomplishments of which I am most proud are related to my position as a Rotary Ambassador to Zimbabwe. The first started with a dream. For as long as I can remember, my fondest dream was of visiting Africa. Much as the adopted child who loves and cherishes her adoptive family, but still wonders who her biological parents are, I am a patriotic African-American who dreamt of sojourning in the land of my forefathers. So deep and strong was my desire to set foot on African shores that, in 1993, I dedicated myself to the fulfillment of the dream until I could visualize the sun rising above the veld, smell and taste the air after an ephemeral rain, and hear the wind thrusting through the leaves of the Baobab trees. I spent hours researching scholarships that would sponsor my trip to the continent and days completing scholarship applications and preparing for scholarship interviews. Hence, when I was awarded a 1994–1995 Rotary Ambassadorial Scholarship to Zimbabwe, a long-awaited dream born of diligence and desire had come true.

The second accomplishment of which I am quite proud was realized through my service as a Rotary Ambassador of Goodwill. Although I am not quite sure of when my fear of public speaking developed, my first efforts to combat the fear were made at the Bronx High School of Science when I enrolled in a forensics class and joined the debate team for a year. These steps were the beginning of a long and difficult battle to vanquish my fear of public speaking and to become an effective and persuasive orator. Throughout college I continued the struggle by actively taking on positions of leadership (such as the presidency of Onyx Senior Honor Society and the vice-presidency of the Bi-Cultural Inter-Greek Council), which required me to address large audiences, and by taking courses for which oral presentations were mandatory. As a result of these efforts, my oratory skills improved greatly. I learned to write persuasively and to communicate clearly and concisely. However, I still lacked the confidence that all good public speakers possess and this diminished the effectiveness of my orations. As a Business Analyst for Andersen Consulting, my skills continued to improve, but it wasn't until I began my service as a Rotary Ambassador that I noticed that my stiff, closed oratorical style had been replaced by a confident and open one. As a Rotary Ambassador, I give luncheon talks to Rotary Clubs upon request. Through these speaking engagements, I was able to triumph over my fears of public speaking by becoming a versatile and persuasive speaker. Both of these accomplishments stand as testaments to the value of hard work and perseverance.

3. **Discuss a nonacademic personal failure. In what way were you disappointed in yourself? What did you learn from the experience?**

Throughout my years at Our Saviour Lutheran School (grades K–8), I was lauded for my athletic and scholastic abilities. I was the captain and highest scorer of the women's basketball team and was graduated valedictorian of my junior high school class. As a result, I became very accustomed to being the big fish in a little pond. So, in 1988 as I prepared to begin my first year of study at the Bronx High School of Science (a highly competitive specialized school), feelings of self-doubt consumed me. I was plagued by the irrational idea that Bronx Science academics and athletics were fundamentally different and more difficult than the Our Saviour variety. This belief set the stage for my worst failure.

When I began classes at Bronx Science, I quickly realized that the material was no more difficult than that which I had tackled at Our Saviour. Having made this discovery, I began to excel in the classroom. However, I continued to doubt my aptitude for basketball. Was I really a good player or were my peers at Our Saviour and at the other Lutheran schools in that league substandard players? The opportunity soon arose for me to answer this question. Women's varsity basketball try-outs were held. When the 1988 team roster was posted, my name was not on the list. I had failed, but the competition had not beaten me. I had defeated myself. So sure was I that I would not make the team that I had not entered the trials. With this failure I lost my self-respect. In my eyes, I had done something unbelievably dishonorable; I had bowed to an irrational fear and called it master.

To restore my self-sovereignty, I tried out for the varsity team during my sophomore year. Although I hoped to make the team, doing so was not my primary concern. Through the act of competing, I was restoring my self-respect. When the 1989 roster was posted, my name was on the list. That year, I played more minutes than any other nonstarter. From 1990 to 1992, I was a starter and the highest point scorer on the team. I had succeeded on two levels.

From this experience, I learned the meaning of true failure. Failure only occurs when you do not try at all. If you make an effort, but do not succeed, there is honor and wisdom to be gained through the loss. Hence, you are better off than when you began. After all, success is not a destination—it is a journey.

4. **Columbia Business School is a diverse environment. How will your experiences contribute to this?**

Scientists have pondered the question of nature versus nurture for a long time. I believe that it is the combination of these two forces which molds an individual and shapes the contribution which she will make to society. As such, I hold that the contribution that my presence would make to the diversity at Columbia Business School is defined by my beliefs and values, which have been shaped by life experiences and heredity. That said, the adult experience that has had the most profound effect on my belief system and world vision has been my trip to and study of Africa.

Thus far, the most valuable lesson that I have learned on this trip is that everyone and everything in the universe is interdependent. This verity, which guided the lives of aboriginal men, was all but forgotten by many of those who advanced through the Iron Age. Men renounced their humanity by enslaving and subjugating fellow human beings and plundering the earth, thus disregarding the chains which link the fates of the planet and its people. However, our oneness cannot be ignored. The African continent abounds with testaments to our unity. In South Africa, time revealed that the fate of the Boers is inextricably linked with that of the Black South Africans whom the Boers once abhorred. In Angola and Mozambique, the lives of millions were permanently altered when a coup was staged five thousand miles away in Portugal. In other African countries, people starve as tribalism destroys their economies and dissolves their national unity. And nowhere on earth is man's dependence on his environment more apparent than in Africa, where water is such an important commodity that the strongest currency on the continent, the Pula, is named after it. All of this points to the conclusion that, for better or worse, humans must learn to coexist with the planet and with each other.

This belief, and the others which comprise my world vision, would allow me to contribute to the diversity of thought at Columbia.

COMMENTS

1. American schools, Columbia in particular, emphasize community service in a way that some European (and Asian) schools do not. Melissa's first essay therefore is ideally pitched for Columbia; it would be very good, but perhaps not perfect, for a school that focuses less on the question of what applicants will do for their communities' benefit.

2. One suggestion for improvement: to discuss something from her consulting work, because she includes virtually nothing from her professional life. Thus she gets relatively little mileage from her strong professional credentials, although she has other experiences that are interesting enough to talk about, so her presentation does not suffer greatly. This is due in part to her being quite different from what one would expect from a strategy consultant—more lyrical, less "data-driven."

DOREEN HEMLOCK

Background:

Job:	Journalist for fourteen years
Education:	Had not quite completed her bachelor's degree at Wesleyan
Nationality:	American

(Note: she was applying for a special program at Columbia. Journalists who specialize in business and economics are eligible for a one-year, nondegree program (the Knight-Bagehot Fellowship) that the Columbia Graduate School of Journalism offers, which includes classes at the Business School. Those who complete this program can apply for a second-year fellowship (the Wiegers Fellowship) through the Business School to complete their MBAs. Thus she was in her first year of study, applying to complete a second year and thereby finish her MBA.)

Critical issues to address:

None. (Her biggest issues, concerning why she would do further education in her mid-thirties and whether she could survive the quantitative aspects of the program, were essentially moot after she had gained a place in the first-year program. Nonetheless, her handling of these issues still comes through in the following essays.)

1. **What are your career goals? How will an MBA help you achieve these goals? Why are you applying to Columbia Business School?**

Journalism is not a career for me; it is a calling. There are deadline pressures. The low pay is frustrating. Politicians I cover are disrespectful. Yet I can think of no other work that is as challenging, stimulating and rewarding.

For the past 14 years, I have been based in Peru, Venezuela, and Puerto Rico, reporting and writing on business and politics for American, Latin American, and Caribbean media. Reporting has taken me far—to banks in Lima, electronics assembly plants in Haiti, coffee farms in Jamaica, corporate headquarters in Japan, and insurance offices in London, to name just a few places.

As a journalist, I have the chance to channel my curiosity, ask questions, learn, and give back to the community. I get to meet people, travel, research, and stay on top of current events. I get an opportunity to foster greater awareness and understanding. I get a chance to make a difference.

I became a journalist without even knowing it. The siren call sounded when I was transplanted from my native New York to the U.S. Virgin Islands. I wrote friends in New York about living without winter and with limited water supplies. I told them about high prices for food and low prices for liquor, about being a white minority and about life on a small Caribbean island. Even before entering college, I had my first job in media at the *V.I. Post* newspaper in St. Thomas.

To learn more about the region I call home, I pursued Latin American and Caribbean studies at Wesleyan University. There I embraced the idea that content should take precedence over form in journalism. I believe that editors and avid reading can improve one's writing style, but knowing a topic in depth gives added value to readers and distinguishes a journalist from the pack. I specialized in business and economic journalism in Latin America and the Caribbean.

Throughout the years, I have realized the need for continuing specialization. Today, I am focusing on finance through a Knight-Bagehot Fellowship in Business and Economic Journalism. My interest grew in the wake of the Latin American debt crisis and the North American Free Trade Agreement. I recognize that equity financing, short-term capital flows, and direct foreign investment have increasingly important roles to play in Caribbean and Latin American development. At Columbia, I've also learned that financial systems require solid information flows to efficiently allocate capital. Specialized financial reporting therefore proves essential in hemispheric development.

After Columbia, I plan to return to journalism to work in international business news, especially on Latin America and the Caribbean. There's a gap to fill, because business news on the hemisphere remains underreported in U.S. media. Washington rightly worries about immigration, drug trafficking and money laundering, and hemispheric free trade nowadays. Yet U.S. media still dedicate little space to the root causes of those problems in the economies of developing nations in the Americas.

Particularly disturbing for me is the scant attention given to the Caribbean Basin. The diverse, multilingual, and fragmented Caribbean runs the risk of marginalization in today's global economy, where even large nations feel compelled to form trading blocs to compete. The Caribbean's future has important implications for the United States and beyond. Clearly, international executives and policy makers could use more specialized economic coverage on Cuba, Haiti, Grenada, and Panama—to name just several nations that have surfaced as prime U.S. security concerns in recent years.

To continue bringing these issues to public attention, I plan to return initially to the *San Juan Star* newspaper in Puerto Rico, which has granted me a leave of absence during my Columbia studies. There, I plan to expand my freelance coverage, which already has included articles for *Bloomberg Business News*, the Caribbean News Agency, the *Denver Post*, and other media. Later, I hope to work at a large media outlet—likely in the United States. I believe that experience at a larger organization can provide greater access to editing and research resources, a more competitive environment to hone my skills, and a larger readership base for my work.

I also hope to use the knowledge gained through reporting at Columbia to help develop business and economic skills in other journalists in the Caribbean and Latin America. For starters, I am already planning several seminars at the *San Juan Star* on accounting and finance topics learned at Columbia Business School.

My ongoing year at Columbia has not changed my calling, but it has opened up new avenues to pursue my interests and expand my contribution through economic journalism.

2. In reviewing the last five years, describe the one or two accomplishments of which you are most proud.

In 1993, Puerto Rico's economic life was on the line. The Clinton administration wanted to slash tax breaks for U.S. manufacturers on the island—endangering 40 percent of the Puerto Rican economy and more than 150,000 jobs. But Puerto Rico's business community and its pro-statehood government could not agree on how to counter the attack.

At the *San Juan Star*, Puerto Rico's only English-language daily newspaper, I covered manufacturing and international trade. I knew that tax breaks were Puerto Rico's economic lifeblood. I jumped on the story. For seven months, I covered as many angles as I could find. I went to factories and interviewed everyone from hourly workers to CEOs. I interviewed top Puerto Rico executives, Washington officials, U.S. multinational lobbyists, Wall Street analysts, and Caribbean Basin leaders. Stories filled the business section front pages—and the hard work paid off.

The Star's in-depth coverage helped stimulate debate and action. It played a role in getting Puerto Rico business and government to adopt a more concerted approach to the issue. My articles were regularly faxed from San Juan offices to Washington and served as an important information source stateside, especially to U.S. government and business executives who could not read Puerto Rico's Spanish-language media.

After months of vigorous debate, Washington and Puerto Rico reached a compromise: The tax incentives were cut, but far less than initially proposed. I felt proud to have used my bilingual skills, business specialization, and networks to serve as a communications link of this vital issue. That year, the Puerto Rico Manufacturers Association named me Journalist of the Year, the island's top business reporting award. But more important, I felt I had contributed to the community at a critical time.

"Would you accept a Knight-Bagehot Fellowship?" the caller asked.

"Yes, Yes, Yes," I yelped. "I want it. I want it."

Years of work in the Caribbean and Latin America had brought me regional recognition, but the Bagehot was a sign that my efforts commanded respect outside the area as well. I was proud to have been chosen to study at Columbia and in New York.

Then came a roller coaster ride.

First was math camp. My confidence plummeted. I hadn't studied math since high school in 1973 and never studied even precalculus, let alone calculus. I cried over my problem sets—despite Prof. Peter Garrity's good humor. Then, I patiently started from scratch, reviewing addition, relearning algebra, seeking out help from teaching assistants and classmates, studying hard—and—I passed, barely.

Next came classes in accounting and finance, with a language that sounded strikingly similar to Chinese. I thought I would never understand. Yet, as the semester wore on, it started to make sense. I worked with colleagues and professors, hit the books and prayed for the best. By January, I was happily surprised when the call-in grading system electronically informed me of straight Hs at CBS.

I am very proud to have the opportunity to study at a university again and to have learned that hard work does pay off. I am energized by the challenge of grasping new concepts and hope to take on more. I enjoy the stimulation of tackling the new and meeting performance goals.

3. **Discuss a nonacademic failure. In what way were you disappointed in yourself? What did you learn from the experience?**

I should have completed my bachelor's degree years ago, but it has taken a return to academia at Columbia University to get me to do it. Not having the degree has been a personal failure. I have felt that I'd let my parents down, when they had worked so hard to put me through college. I also felt inhibited to seek full-time work in the U.S. media, fearing disqualification without a degree.

Still, for years I did not complete the senior essay needed to fulfill requirements for a Latin American studies degree from Wesleyan University. Working in small, understaffed newspapers in nations with huge development hurdles and with fascinating stories to cover, I had always been so absorbed by my work in journalism that I had never set aside the months to research and write the paper.

College had not been easy for me. I started at age 16, a time when I was moved more by hormones than homework. An impressionable teenager, I was confused by intellectually aggressive campus culture after years at a small high school in the Caribbean, where community meant more than competition. I took a semester off, but then missed the intellectual challenge, returning to Wesleyan only to seek exchange programs to try other environments for learning. I studied for separate semesters in Spain, at the University of Texas at Austin, and finally completed my required coursework for Wesleyan's Latin American studies program at Catholic University in Peru. Then, I decided to stay in Lima, lured by Peru's rich history, politics, and culture. I aimed to complete my senior essay there, hoping to write a case study on U.S. food aid in Lima's slums, an outgrowth of an urban anthropology course there. I never finished. In Lima in the early 1980s I could not find the documentation on U.S. policy that I needed, and, out of school, I lacked a professor to advise me on the project. I became engrossed in journalism and put the paper on hold—until now.

My current academic year at Columbia at age 36 has given me the time and tools to undertake the project, with the goal both to complete my Wesleyan requirements and to continue studies at Columbia to obtain an MBA. I am currently working with

Chazen Institute professor Ronald Schramm on an independent study on multinational business location decisions, focusing on tax incentive programs in Puerto Rico and Ireland. At Wesleyan, the Latin American Studies program director, Anne Wightman, also is working with me to ensure the paper fulfills requirements as a noncredit senior essay to allow Wesleyan to award me a bachelor's degree.

I am relieved to be redressing this failure and happy to re-embrace academia at Columbia. I have learned over the years to better appreciate the dynamism, debate, and stimulation a university environment offers. Columbia provides an especially rich environment by incorporating the resources available only in a global city like New York.

4. **Discuss your involvement in a community or extracurricular organization. Include an explanation of how you became involved in the organization, and how you helped the organization meet its goals.**

Fellow reporters active in the Puerto Rico Journalists Association had heard my pitch repeatedly: Why did we stand up for press freedoms in Puerto Rico and not speak out for press rights in neighboring countries? Why did we look at issues narrowly, in a local context, and not comparatively at how other places dealt with crime, privatization, and other issues?

My international perspective came from years reporting in South America and elsewhere in the Caribbean. Most Puerto Rico journalists had not reported off the island.

In late 1991, colleagues approached me to run for a position on the association's board of directors and, specifically, to focus on expanding international awareness among members. During my one-year term, I proposed and helped organize a conference on the press in Haiti.

The seminar came amid escalating repression and violence in that military-ruled country, including censorship and closure of radio stations and newspapers, as well as torture and even killings of Haitian reporters. About 75 people attended the event, mainly journalists. Speakers included, among others, two international news agency correspondents and a prominent Haitian-born University of Puerto Rico economics professor, who spoke on the role of radio news for Haiti's mostly illiterate population. I moderated and provided an overview of violations against the Haitian media, citing reports from Amnesty International and other human rights groups.

It was the association's first seminar on Haiti. The event helped meet the group's goals of defending press freedom and expanding international focus. A colleague also wrote an article for a U.S. media magazine, bringing the subject to the attention of U.S. colleagues as well.

5. **Columbia Business School is a diverse environment. How will your experiences contribute to this?**

As a business journalist specialized in Latin America and the Caribbean, I believe I help enrich Columbia's diverse environment in many ways.

First, as a reporter, I am unafraid to ask questions in public. In journalism, questions are a sign of inquisitiveness and strength. Colleagues in the entering MBA class have told me they're glad that I unabashedly ask professors to clarify concepts or explain complex graphs and equations in plain English. They say that my questions reflect their own concerns, but they are too shy to speak out. Many come from competitive corporate environments where questions tend to be seen as signs of weakness.

Second, my experience in the Caribbean and Latin America enlivens discussions on economic policy and globalization. In class, I ask questions about options for small, open economies and bring up examples from countries I've covered. Outside the classroom, I am working with a group of fellow students interested in the Caribbean and Latin America to organize events related to the region, including a panel on investment trends in Cuba and another on Caribbean stock exchanges.

COMMENTS

1. Doreen has an interesting tale to tell—returning to school in her mid-thirties to improve her knowledge of business and economics, not to get a job on Wall Street but to improve her coverage as a journalist. And, not surprisingly, given that she writes for a living, she tells her tale well. She makes it clear exactly why she wants to do an MBA. (Unlike most other applicants, she does not need to worry that she will sound like everyone else in the applicant pool.) She also does a good job of humanizing and individualizing herself with her discussion of her college experiences and how she failed to complete her bachelor's degree on schedule. Another strong point is her discussion of what she can contribute, based upon her experiences in first year MBA classes. She is in the unique position of having already taken her first year classes and is thus able to capitalize on what she already knows are her unique ways to contribute.

CAROL

Background:

Job: Formerly a buyer for a department store chain, now an account executive for a garment manufacturer

Education: Bachelor's degree in literature from a top quality liberal arts school

Nationality: American

Critical issue to address:

Showing herself able to handle the quantitative aspects of a top MBA program.

(I have excluded two of her four essays because they concerned matters too personal for general dissemination. The remaining two, however, are sufficiently interesting to merit inclusion on their own.)

1. **What are your career goals? How will an MBA help you achieve these goals? Why are you applying to Columbia Business School?**

I am pursuing a career in the apparel industry during a time when the industry is going through major changes. Many of my employment choices have been based on the changing nature of the business. Chapter 7 and Chapter 11 used to mean sections of a Charles Dickens novel. Now, Chapter 7 dissolutions and Chapter 11 reorganizations, mergers, and acquisitions are everyday vocabulary. Throughout my career in the apparel industry, I have recognized the inability of the industry to anticipate and promote the trends of the future. My work experience has taught me the pillars of merchandising, planning, and promotion, but my lack of experience and business fundamentals has made it difficult to initiate innovation. I believe that an MBA from Columbia Business School will enhance my managerial skills and give me the business knowledge I need to achieve my goals and be an innovator in the industry.

After graduating from college, I accepted a position in the executive training programs of a national department store. I set precedent by rising through the ranks in three years to become a buyer, responsible for my own business. As a buyer, I was responsible for analyzing, planning, developing, and distributing product to 49 stores. I developed and selected the merchandise for my department and reviewed selling history and pricing strategies to distribute the product profitably. I also managed and trained several assistant buyers and played an integral role in their development to buyer status. As the company became more integrated into the corporate structure of its parent company, the nature of my responsibilities changed. I became an accountant responsible for sales forecasting and budget reviews. What had been the essential focus of my job, the creative development and selection of product, was de-emphasized.

When a position became available with one of my suppliers in wholesale manufacturing, I saw it as an opportunity to be more involved in the development and marketing of product. I was soon offered a more challenging and stimulating job in a "start-up" division for a manufacturer of women's dresses and sportswear. As an account executive, I have brought to the table my in-depth knowledge of retailing. I have developed new accounts and have achieved high sales volume for the company. However, new and progressive methods of promotion and merchandising are not emphasized and the management of my company is not interested in diverting from established and archaic forms of marketing.

For retail chains and wholesale manufacturers to move successfully into the 21st century, it is essential that decision makers discard outdated methods of sales promotion and merchandising, replacing them with more effective and innovative forms of marketing. In an industry where women represent only a small percentage of senior management, I envision becoming a pioneer in this decision-making process. I believe that a Columbia MBA education will assist me in achieving my goals.

2. Columbia Business School is a diverse environment. How will your experiences contribute to this?

My in-depth knowledge of the apparel industry will contribute to the diversity of Columbia Business School's student body. My unique background in both retail and wholesale will offer insight into an industry that I do not believe is significantly represented in business school classes. My mature and experienced approach to teamwork will also be an asset to the Columbia Business School community.

In the past six years, the apparel industry has undergone tremendous changes. I have seen national retail chains merge, major retail chains merge, major retail stores go out of business, and established manufacturers file for bankruptcy. Through my work experience, I have insight into the impact of these changes on both the buyer and seller. As a buyer, I had to adapt to the variables in a changing industry. Now as a seller, I have had to be creative and find a niche for my product in a shrinking retail market.

My ability to forge strong relationships with my co-workers has been instrumental in my success in the industry. As a buyer, I worked closely with my manufacturers to turn around a down-trending and unprofitable department. This team effort was effective in improving the profitability of our business. Now, as a seller, I work with each buyer to develop our business based on the needs of the individual store. Using the same team approach, I have been able to successfully establish important business relationships and a strong customer base for my company.

My experience and knowledge in this turbulent industry can enhance the student body at Columbia Business School by contributing to the wealth of information that each student brings to an MBA education. My understanding of both sides of my industry has developed my appreciation for the ingredients required to create a successful business.

COMMENTS

1. Carol managed to address the question of her quantitative abilities elsewhere in her application.

2. Carol's background is unusual. As an English major working in the garment industry, she stands out from the applicant pool. She certainly recognized this and capitalized upon it in her essays. She does a very good job of demonstrating the extent to which she has (quite unexpectedly) found herself involved in business issues, thereby showing both why she wants an MBA and that she is prepared to enter an MBA program. She does this without ever losing the advantage of being from an unusual industry, which is part of her potential appeal for Columbia.

ROXANE

Background:

Job:	Engineer and, latterly, Short-Range Planning Analyst for a major oil company
Education:	Bachelor's degree in chemical engineering
Nationality:	American

Critical issue to address:

As an engineer, she needs to distinguish herself from the large number of candidates with a similar background.

WHARTON

1. **Please discuss your future career progression to date and your professional goals for the future. How will the MBA influence your ability to achieve your goals?**

I have been working for Chevron at the Richmond Refinery since graduating from college five years ago. I have held six different positions in the engineering and planning departments. As a result of this mobility, I have been exposed to several different areas of the refinery and have acquired a broad manufacturing background. The first three years of my career, I focused on developing my problem-solving and interpersonal skills. My engineering experience taught me to identify the root causes of problems and develop permanent solutions to them. Because many of the problems I was required to solve were too large for me to address alone, I learned to delegate and manage my time effectively. I also learned the importance of selling my ideas in order to get them implemented.

My fourth year at Chevron, I was assigned to the position of start-up engineer for a project to rebuild a processing unit that had been badly damaged by fire. The unit had been down for two years and was being rebuilt at a cost of $125 million. This unit was a major contributor to refinery profitability and I was instrumental in helping to bring it on-line safely and ahead of schedule. This experience was a major success for me and I began to advance quickly. I learned to see the problems I was solving in the context of the entire refinery rather than as isolated problems. I was able to identify business opportunities on my own and took the initiative to convince management to implement them. I was able to assimilate all the knowledge I had accumulated over the previous three years and my value to the organization increased rapidly.

Next, I was assigned to the position of process representative in charge of coordinating the process definition and process design of two major ($84 million and $20 million) retrofit projects. I worked with the engineering contractor to ensure project objectives were met at the lowest possible cost. After the process designs for these two projects were approved, I was assigned to my present position as Short-Range Planning Analyst. In this assignment, I develop the short-range refinery operating plan focusing on maximization of refinery profit in a dynamic market-driven environment. I also work with Supply and Distribution to develop these plans and coordinate the efforts of the refinery operating divisions as needed to ensure smooth implementation of new processing schedules. This position has increased my involvement in the financial aspects of our business.

I am applying to the Wharton MBA program at this time because I have come to a crossroads in my career. As I have gained experience and received increased exposure to the business side of the oil industry, I have become aware that my engineering training has not prepared me adequately to deal with the broad strategic questions faced by senior level managers. I am seeking an MBA to supplement my work experience and gain high intensity exposure to the other business functions which are important to running a successful business. In addition, I am applying to the Lauder Institute to further develop my French language skills and improve my cultural understanding of France and the rest of Western Europe. I am interested in the joint degree program because it will allow me to shift from an engineering to a management career and will allow me to incorporate my interests in language and culture into my work.

My future career goal is to advance to a senior-level management position dealing with international management strategy for a multinational corporation. I am interested in strategy because I feel my strongest skills are in identifying the root causes of problems and developing and implementing lasting solutions to them. Because I am able to see problems in the context of the big picture, I am able to identify opportunities which will not only result in profits today, but will also increase flexibility and adaptability which will result in increased profitability tomorrow. I am especially interested in international corporate strategy, because of my strong interest in working overseas.

In addition to my personal interest in working in a language and culture other than my own, I have been influenced by the international aspect of my current position. During my tenure at the Richmond Refinery, products sold into the export market have become increasingly important to our refinery's profitability. Chevron's planners and oil traders typically come from the engineering ranks and often lack the business skills necessary to analyze the refinery's competition in these markets. As a result, the export market is viewed not as a viable market worthy of cultivation, but as a dumping ground for products, which allows the refinery to operate at capacity.

Wharton's emphasis on international business and its joint degree program with the Lauder Institute fit well with my future career goals. I am not pursuing an MBA degree with an emphasis in operations expressly because my experience is in this area. I am interested in gaining a well-rounded understanding of each functional area of business with an emphasis in multinational management so I will be able to deal with broad strategic issues in an international environment.

2. **Describe a situation in your life when you actively challenged the traditional thought of a group. What level of impact did you have on the group?**

One situation where I actively challenged the traditional thought of refinery operations management took place last year when I was the process engineer assigned to two heavy oil processing units. One of these units provided feed pretreatment for the other. I was approached by Operations Coordination and was asked if Widuri resid, a low value fuel oil stream, could be fed to the upstream of the two units. This would allow a portion of the resid stream to be upgraded to gasoil, a high value intermediate product. I agreed to address the technical aspects of the problem and asked Operations Coordination to deal with the logistics.

When we reconvened to finalize the plan, it became apparent that the logistical constraints would render the project uneconomical. Having gathered the physical property data, I realized that the Widuri resid could be fed directly to the downstream unit. I suggested we bypass the feed pretreatment step entirely. This would allow us to upgrade the entire stream rather than only a small portion of it as the original plan would have required. In addition, it would avoid some of the operating costs.

Operations Coordination was enthusiastic, but I knew it would be difficult to sell the idea to Operations. A resid stream had never been fed directly to the downstream unit and I knew Operations would be concerned about damaging the catalyst in that unit. This was a major operational change, but I was confident it would work. I gathered the necessary data and developed a plan which included a good monitoring program and contingency plan. This would allow us to identify and respond to any unexpected problems if necessary. Two weeks later I organized a meeting for all the interested parties and presented my plan which anticipated and addressed management's concerns. The following day the resid was being fed to the downstream unit. This project resulted in profits to the refinery of $8 million over a five-month period.

This project marked a change in my career in terms of maturity and initiative. Prior to this, my efforts were focused primarily on my own sphere of operation. The success of this project gave me the self-confidence to assert my leadership skills. I began to approach problems from a refinerywide perspective. In addition, I began to challenge traditional approaches and offer more innovative solutions.

3. **In your opinion, what is the world's greatest problem? Why?**

I believe the world's greatest problem is the disparity of wealth between the developed and underdeveloped nations of the world. While the plight of the poor in Third World countries is relatively unchanged from ancient times, the standard of living in the Western World has increased dramatically since the Industrial Revolution. This disparity of wealth is a problem because in modern times the world has become increasingly interdependent. The spread of Western ideas throughout the rest of the world began with the discovery of the New World and accelerated as a result of European political supremacy in the eighteenth and nineteenth centuries and improvements in communication in the twentieth. As a result, more people than ever before share Western ideals and strive for Western success.

While this is in many respects a positive aspect of European colonialism, it also has a negative side. Third World nations often try to industrialize their countries overnight. This often leads to disastrous political and social policies which attempt to duplicate Western success without taking into account the cultural and environmental constraints of the country in question. While the Western experience can serve as a model for Third World countries, it is by no means a blueprint. The West owes much of its success to the virtues of capitalism, but the West did not get rich by the sweat of its own people alone. Exploitation of natural and human resources in colonial possessions was also a major contributor to Western success. As the West increased its wealth, it learned to value the environment and was able to afford to enact strict environmental laws. In addition, as life expectancy increased and cultural attitudes toward women in the workplace changed, population growth in the West stabilized. These changes took nearly a century in the West. In underdeveloped countries today, rapid industrialization causes extreme cultural and environmental pressures. These special circumstances must be considered when helping Third World countries to develop.

Population pressure is a major aggravation in the attempts of underdeveloped countries to industrialize quickly. While a large population should equate to significant global power, it seldom does in Third World countries. The most obvious influence preventing many highly populated countries from becoming very powerful is poverty. While in some cases this is due to a genuine lack of resources, in others it is caused by rapid increases in population which quickly overcome successes in improved technology and planned investment. In other cases, the pressure to feed a growing population results in shortsighted policies which often lead to environmental degradation. For example, in Brazil, the Amazon Forest is being cleared at an alarming rate to provide land for grazing cattle. Unfortunately, the top soil in this area of the world is only inches deep and quickly erodes away. As a result, additional forest must be cleared. Clearly this is not a sustainable policy and could eventually lead to widespread famine. Experience in developed nations has shown that population growth slows considerably with an increase in standard of living. When parents are confident that their children will live to be adults, they tend to have fewer children. Helping the Third World to increase its wealth through industrialization should help to slow the exponential population growth in these countries.

As appalling as many of us find large-scale environmental destruction, it is not enough for the West to simply require that the Third World stop these practices. After all, in many respects these countries are only doing what the West did during its colonial era. If the West wishes to protect the environment in the Third World, it must provide technological assistance. This is not only our responsibility, but will also benefit us in the long run. The rain forest is just one example of the biodiversity which exists on our planet. Many of the species which inhabit the rain forests may be of use to us in the future as technological advances are made. In addition, maintaining biodiversity is important to life on Earth. It is advantageous to have a wide variety of plant and animal species in order to survive climatic changes. (I am referring to the inevitable climatic change which occurs naturally as a result of continental shift. I am still not convinced that the Greenhouse Effect exists.) Standardization of plant and animal life to those species which are superior today could be disastrous as these species may not be able to adapt to and survive in the climate of tomorrow.

Finally, the West must show a sincere commitment to helping underdeveloped nations industrialize while preserving their environments. This applies not only to our governments, but to individuals as well. I have moral and ethical difficulty with our approach to solving environmental problems here at home. For example, as a people we Americans lobby to prevent oil drilling off the coast of California and in the Alaskan National Wildlife Refuge. However, we do not make any substantial effort to reduce our consumption of petroleum products. Instead, we drill for oil in Third World countries where we can exploit cheap labor and avoid many of the costly environmental regulations imposed on industry in the United States. Is it right to prevent drilling in our own country which has the strictest environmental controls in the world only to turn around and develop oil fields in Third World countries? Is this what we call preserving the environment? Are the rain forests in Papua New Guinea any less beautiful than the coast of California? Who are we trying to fool?

Clearly the West must move to help underdeveloped nations industrialize. This should help to stabilize their populations and slow environmental degradation. It will allow the people of these countries to live the healthy and comfortable lives that those in the West enjoy. An additional benefit is that it may help to stabilize the governments in Third World countries, which could reduce the number of people killed needlessly in revolutions and civil wars. However, it is imperative that we consider cultural differences in the countries we try to help before attempting to prescribe a solution. Only then do we have a chance of elevating the rest of the world to our standard of living while preserving the environment for future generations.

4. **What nonprofessional activities do you find inspirational? At what level do you participate in these activities?**

Traveling is my principal interest outside of work. I spend all of my vacation time visiting foreign countries because I enjoy experiencing different cultures. Traveling has forced me to remove my small town blinders and open my mind to other ways of doing things. Traveling has shown me that the American way of doing things is not the only way and that flexibility and sensitivity are absolutely necessary to get along with others. I have found that this applies not only to people of different nationalities but also to fellow Americans whose views may be different from my own. These experiences have benefited me both in my personal life and on the job and I believe they will be an asset for me at Wharton.

I also study French in my free time. I studied French in high school but was unable to do so in college due to the large number of courses required in the engineering curriculum. I recently resumed my studies because I was planning a trip to France. While in France, I became even more enthusiastic about studying French because of the satisfaction I received from communicating with the French in their own language. I have even found it to be useful here in the United States. While I was doing volunteer work for the Mill Valley Film Festival, I met many interesting people of various nationalities. All of these people spoke French in addition to their native language and I was excited to be able to participate in their conversations. I found that my ability to speak a language other than English increased the respect these people had for me. I believe it went a long way to dispel their beliefs that Americans are culturally insensitive and egocentric.

Literature, especially nineteenth century European literature, is another of my primary interests. My final semester, I took a literature course which was the most enjoyable class I had while in college. I have found reading to be an easy and inexpensive way to increase my exposure to the world. Because an author portrays the world through his or her eyes, reading has exposed me to many different philosophies of life and has helped me to better define my own. Reading books from many time periods with many different types of characters has taught me that people are people and the pursuit of happiness is a universal goal. While this seems to be an obvious point, I believe this realization has made me more sensitive to other people's needs and concerns.

I should note that not all of my leisure activities are cerebral in nature. I love to scuba dive for the sheer pleasure of it. Diving makes the mysteries of the undersea world accessible. The ocean is a whole new world full of strange and exciting plants and animals and is the only place where you can feel as if you are floating in space. Nowhere on land can you find the magnificent colors and variety that make up the underwater landscape.

UCLA

1. **Please give a brief, candid evaluation of yourself. Include some discussion of the abilities and other attributes you believe are your strengths and some discussion of areas that you would like to develop more fully. How do you think others perceive you? What do you consider most unique or distinctive about you?**

My strongest attribute is my conviction to follow through with what I believe in. I show a tremendous amount of proprietorship in the projects to which I am assigned. During my tenure at Chevron, I have developed a reputation for getting the job done and I am often sought out by management to implement new or controversial ideas. I am always looking for better ways of doing things and focus my efforts on long term improvement. Because I do a good job at recognizing my customer needs, I am continually being recruited by those I have previously worked for.

My good written and oral communication skills ensure that I am effective in dealing with people at all levels of the organization, from peers to executives. This has enabled me to sell my ideas and motivate groups into action. The emphasis I place on getting input from others contributes to the overall quality of the solutions I recommend.

Finally, my excellent planning and organizing skills enable me to complete my projects on time or ahead of schedule. I am consistently told that I get more work accomplished than my peers. This is because I carefully prioritize my work and leverage my time by getting others involved as appropriate. By developing good working relationships with others, I am able to spend more of my time identifying and proposing solutions and less of it working out the minor details.

My greatest development opportunity is to learn to control my frustration with people who are resistant to change. I have very little patience with people who are willing to accept the status quo when better solutions are within easy grasp. Because I am always looking for better ways of doing things and am willing to take risks, I find it difficult to identify with those who do not. I set very high standards for myself and others and I always strive for high quality output. However, I believe that I will be even more effective if I learn to be more tolerant of those less competent than myself.

I believe my operations background will distinguish me from many of my classmates. This is especially true because women continue to be relatively scarce in heavy industrial environments. My ability not to just survive, but to succeed in this environment has contributed to my personal growth and has increased my self confidence over the years. In addition, I believe that my experience in manufacturing will enhance the learning experience of my fellow classmates as it will provide a much needed perspective on how things are really accomplished in the field. For those students who are not familiar with the tremendous inertia working against change inherent in a large manufacturing facility, my experience will provide insight and, at times, a reality check.

2. **Discuss two or three situations in the past three years where you have taken a leadership role. How do these events demonstrate your management potential?**

A recent situation where I have taken a leadership role took place last year when I was the process engineer assigned to two heavy oil processing units. One of these units provided feed pretreatment for the other. I was approached by Operations Coordination and was asked if Widuri resid, a low value fuel oil stream, could be fed to the upstream of the two units. This would allow a portion of the resid stream to be upgraded to gasoil, a high value intermediate product. While at first glance this appeared to be a good idea, it quickly became apparent that the logistical constraints would render the project uneconomical. However, I realized that the Widuri resid could be fed directly to the downstream unit. I suggested we bypass the feed pretreatment step entirely. This would allow us to upgrade the entire stream rather than only a small portion of it as the original plan would have required. In addition, it would avoid some of the operating costs.

Operations Coordination was enthusiastic, but I knew it would be difficult to sell the idea to Operations. A resid stream had never been fed directly to the downstream plant and I knew Operations would be concerned about damaging the catalyst in that unit.

This was a major operational change, but I was confident it would work. I gathered the necessary data and developed a plan which included a good monitoring program and contingency plan. This would allow us to identify and respond to any unexpected problems if necessary. Two weeks later I organized a meeting for all the interested parties and presented my plan which anticipated and addressed management's concerns. The following day the resid was being fed to the downstream unit. This project resulted in profits to the refinery of $8 million over a five-month period.

Another situation where I was able to demonstrate and develop my leadership skills took place approximately eight months after I began working at Chevron. My supervisor suggested that I begin planning for a major plant turnaround which would take place the following year. He wanted me to begin the work, but he made it clear that I might be replaced by a more experienced engineer as the shutdown approached. No one with my level of experience had ever been in charge of a $7 million turnaround at Chevron.

I did not want to do all the groundwork only to turn it over to someone else later on, so I decided to make myself indispensable. I began the work a year in advance compared with the usual six months. I worked closely with maintenance and the other engineering groups to define the scope of the work early. I set up a method of tabulating the work list which eliminated the need for long, drawn out meetings. The shutdown planning proceeded very smoothly.

Early in the planning phase of the project, I was asked if it would be possible to move the shutdown date up six months. Because I had begun the work early, this was possible. The shutdown was a major success and was completed ahead of schedule due to careful planning and cultivation of good working relationships.

These projects demonstrate my willingness to "grab my projects by the horns" and see them through to completion. I am willing to take risks but am careful to identify possible problem areas and develop contingency plans to address them. This has led to my success in selling ideas in a very conservative organization. I am able to develop good working relationships with others because I recognize the unique contribution of each person working with me on a project. This allows me to leverage my own time by utilizing all of the resources available to me. My excellent planning and organizing skills not only increase my own productivity, but also make it easier for management to decide on a course of action when I make a proposal. By clearly identifying the problem and outlining possible solutions, the best answer is generally clear.

3. **Why have you decided to enter an MBA program? Why have you decided to apply to the UCLA MBA program in particular? What other options for next year, aside from remaining in your current position, have you seriously considered?**

I am applying to the UCLA MBA program at this time because I have come to a crossroads in my career. As I have gained experience and received increased exposure to the business side of the oil industry, I have become aware that my engineering training has not prepared me adequately to deal with the broad strategic questions faced by senior level managers. I am seeking an MBA to supplement my work experience and gain high intensity exposure to the other functions which are important to running a successful business. In addition, I am applying to the International Fellows

Program to further develop my French language skills and improve my cultural understanding of France and the rest of Western Europe. I am interested in this program because it will allow me to shift from an engineering to a management career track and will allow me to incorporate my interests in language and culture into my work.

My future career goal is to advance to a senior level management position dealing with international management strategy for a multinational corporation. I am interested in strategy for a multinational corporation. I am interested in strategy because I feel my strongest skills are in identifying the root causes of problems and developing and implementing lasting solutions to them. Because I am able to see problems in the context of the big picture, I am able to identify opportunities which will not only result in profits today, but will also increase flexibility and adaptability which will result in increased profitability tomorrow. I am especially interested in international corporate strategy, because of my strong interest in working overseas.

In addition to my personal interest in working in a foreign language and culture, I have been influenced by the international aspects of my current position. During my tenure at the Richmond Refinery, products sold into the export market have become increasingly important to our refinery's profitability. Chevron's planners and oil traders typically come from the engineering ranks and often lack the business skills necessary to analyze the refinery's competitive position in new markets. At times it is even difficult to identify the refinery's competition in these markets. As a result, the export market is viewed not as a viable market worthy of cultivation, but as a dumping ground for products, which allows the refinery to operate at capacity.

UCLA's strength in international business, in conjunction with the International Fellows Program, fits well with my future career goals. I am not pursuing an MBA degree with an emphasis in operations expressly because my experience is in this area. I am interested in gaining a well-rounded understanding of each function of business, with an emphasis on multinational management so that I will be able to deal with broad strategic issues in an international environment.

Prior to deciding to pursue an MBA degree, I researched overseas career opportunities. I quickly realized that an MBA degree with linguistic training would greatly increase my chances of finding employment in Europe. In addition, it would give me the necessary skills to move into a management position. While it is possible for me to move into management while working for Chevron, it is unlikely that I would be given an overseas assignment for many years. An MBA will allow me to function as a manager outside the oil and chemical process industries and the International Fellow Program will be an asset to me in making contacts abroad.

4. **What leisure and/or community activities do you particularly enjoy? Please discuss their importance in your life.**

(See Roxane's essentially identical answer to Wharton essay 4.)

5. **For applicants to concurrent degree programs, the Arts Management Program, or the International Fellows Program only: Why specifically are you applying to the program you have selected? How does an MBA fit in with your professional interests?**

I became interested in international business as a result of the traveling I did after graduating from college. Traveling stimulated my interest in foreign cultures and each time I planned a new trip, I put an increasing amount of effort into researching the history of the area I intended to visit. This effort resulted in far more rewarding travel experiences than I otherwise would have had. This trend culminated in a trip to France that I made just prior to deciding to return to business school. After returning from this trip, I knew that I needed to incorporate an international focus and the use of my second language into my career.

At the same time, I began to consider returning to school for an MBA. My involvement in the development of an export program while employed at Chevron made me aware of some of the special considerations of working in international markets. I decided that an MBA would give me the business skills I lacked and it could open the doors to an international career.

It was not until I began researching graduate management schools that I learned about the International Fellows Program. I was thrilled to find that such a program existed because it was so perfectly suited to my interests. Prior to discovering this program, I had expected to have to continue my French studies in my own time. This program will not only allow me to become more proficient in French, but will also enable me to get valuable experience and make important contacts overseas.

In summary, I am applying to the MBA/International Fellows Program because I have a strong interest in international business and believe that language skills are necessary to work successfully overseas. If I am not admitted to the International Fellows Program, I intend to continue my French language studies in my spare time.

HARVARD

1. **What evidence can you present to demonstrate your capacity to perform well academically in the Harvard MBA program?**

    I believe my grades are a good indication of my academic ability when additional consideration is given to the time I devoted to outside activities. I graduated with Distinction in Chemical Engineering while working 25 to 36 hours per week to put myself through school. In addition, I devoted a significant quantity of time to my dancing (jazz, tap, and ballet). Because I believed I would benefit in the long run by leading a balanced life, I did not devote my time exclusively to my studies. Instead, I set priorities and managed my time which allowed me to lead a well-rounded lifestyle. As part of the prioritization process, I set a personal goal to maintain a grade point average of 3.5. I achieved this goal, which enabled me to graduate as the top chemical engineer in my class.

    In addition to my past academic performance, I believe I would function extremely well in an environment where the case study method of teaching is utilized. My success at Chevron has been directly related to my willingness to voice my opinions and my ability to develop creative solutions to problems. In addition, I work well with others and am able to take others' ideas and incorporate them into workable solutions. I believe these strengths will allow me to perform well at Harvard and contribute to other students' experiences as well.

2. **Discuss a professional project which challenged your analytical skills.**

While engineering is by nature an analytically challenging profession, I am able to single out one project that was particularly challenging. Three years ago, I was asked to determine why we were unable to meet a product specification unique to export jet fuel. It was assumed this question could be answered easily by "finding out what others do." Unfortunately, "others" were not in the export jet fuel market; this time, we in the Richmond Refinery were the pioneers.

After consulting my counterparts at other Chevron refineries, our technical experts in the home office, several jet fuel experts in the home office, and several jet fuel experts throughout the petroleum industry, I realized I would have to solve the problem on my own. This problem was especially difficult to solve because the specification was sensitive to the synergistic effects of different sulfur species in the jet fuel components. Because we use several components to blend jet fuel, I set out to identify a blend of jet components which would not result in synergistic effects. This recipe would be used for export jet fuel.

I had many different combinations of jet fuel components hand-blended together and tested for this specification. Using this method I was unable to produce even one off-test result. I then attempted to duplicate the recipes of actual off-test blends to produce an off-test result. If I could not produce an off-test blend, the results of the on-test hand blends would be suspect. I was again unable to produce an off-test result.

A careful review of the data revealed that the material used in the hand blends had been sampled from the piping leading to the jet tanks while the off-test results for the actual blends were sampled at the tanks. I began to suspect a problem with the tanks themselves. After additional testing, I confirmed that this was in fact the problem. I recommended a solution which was quickly implemented. This project has resulted in profits of tens of millions of dollars for the refinery over the last several years.

3. **While recognizing that no day is typical, we ask that you describe a representative work day.**

I begin my day as a short-range planner in the refinery by reviewing the previous day's operation. Next I attend a meeting with Operations Coordination to discuss operating problems and items of interest for the day ahead. After the meeting, I present the plan and associated economics for an upcoming test run to the operating superintendents. The test run objective is to establish the viability of substituting a new lower cost feed stock for the feed stock currently fed to a critical operating unit. This is a very controversial issue because it involves a fundamental change in the operation of the unit, so I am careful to back up my assertions with the data.

I then return to my office to finalize the operating plan for the winter season. I use a linear optimizer to determine the most economic refinery operation. I review the output and identify any work which must be completed by the various operating divisions prior to its implementation. After receiving approval for this plan from the refinery manager, I set up a meeting with the operating assistants and engineers to discuss the plan and their role in its implementation.

In the afternoon I have a meeting with my inventory reduction team. I am the leader of the "Breakthrough" effort identified by executive management as one of the five key areas on which our corporation should focus its efforts to reduce operating costs. We discuss our efforts to date and identify lack of communication along the supply chain as a major obstacle to reducing inventories further. After the meeting I return to my office to call another member of a related inventory team to discuss the communication problem.

This related team is a cross-functional decision support systems (DSS) team assembled to provide information to the individual inventory reduction teams throughout Chevron. As a "user representative" I discuss my team's concern about the communication problem and the lack of reliable supply and demand data for making inventory decisions. We decide that an enterprisewide logistics planning tool would make dramatic improvements in inventory and cash flow management. We agree to present our idea to the rest of the DSS team at the next monthly meeting.

4. Describe an ethical dilemma you have experienced firsthand. How did you manage and resolve the situation?

My junior year in college, I was offered a summer internship working in a metallurgical laboratory for Gold Fields of South Africa Limited. The opportunity to work overseas while gaining valuable work experience prior to graduation was very appealing. I accepted the job and immediately completed the paperwork required to obtain a South African work visa. In addition, I began planning the details of a trip I would make to Europe on my return. I wanted this experience so badly that I turned down an excellent opportunity to work at the Argonne National Laboratory outside of Chicago that same summer.

I was offered this position in the Fall of 1985. Early in 1986, the political situation in South Africa began to deteriorate rapidly and a State of Emergency was declared by the South African government. Several friends working for Gold Fields assured me that I would not be in danger if I were to go to South Africa. However, my conscience began to get the better of me. I attempted to justify accepting the job offer on the basis that I should see the situation firsthand in order to judge it. In addition, I was well aware of the importance of South Africa to our nation's supply of strategic minerals. I believed that American involvement in South Africa was necessary to ensure change in that country's racial policy while assuring that America's strategic interests were tended to.

As the situation worsened, however, I found my decision to go to South Africa increasingly difficult to justify. I could no longer ignore the pleas of the African National Congress to remove outside support of a racist government. I knew that I was offered the serious position because South Africa was experiencing a serious "brain drain." By agreeing to work in South Africa, I personally was supporting the racist policies of the Afrikaaner government. As much as I hated to do it, I had to cancel my plans.

In retrospect, it is still a difficult problem. It is impossible to judge a problem as complex as apartheid from the thirty-second news briefs provided by the media. Had I gone to South Africa, I would have gained valuable insight into this problem that I could never hope to get from the outside. This experience would have given me a different perspective about racial tensions in our own country. However, I still cannot justify the personal growth I would have realized when there was much more at stake for the people of that country.

5. **Describe your three most substantial accomplishments and why view them as such.**

Financing my college education

Financing my college education is easily my most substantial accomplishment. My parents were divorced and my mother was working was a secretary so she could not afford to pay for my education. While my father could afford to give me some assistance, he would not because he felt I would appreciate my education more if I financed it myself.

My father was right! I financed my education through a combination of scholarships, grants, loans, and work. When I graduated with Distinction and landed a great job with a major corporation, I had no one to thank for my success but myself. This sense of accomplishment proved to me that I can achieve anything I put my mind to regardless of the odds.

TKC start-up

I recently held the position of Start-Up Engineer for a project to rebuild a processing unit that had been badly damaged by fire. The unit had been down for two years and was being rebuilt at a cost of $125 million. Because this unit was a major contributor to refinery profitability, it was critical that it come back on line quickly and safely. I was very excited to be presented with such a challenge.

I worked with Operations to develop operating procedures for the new unit and helped to train the operators. I expedited catalyst delivery which allowed catalyst to be loaded into the reactors three months earlier than planned. This prevented catalyst loading from becoming a choke point for the project and was instrumental in starting up the unit a month ahead of schedule. I also implemented a long term monitoring program which allowed information required to maximize the unit's profitability to be learned quickly.

The start-up proceeded very smoothly as a result of careful planning and excellent procedures. Because of my success with this project, I have been moved into positions of increased responsibility and visibility twice in the past year. My greatest satisfaction, however, comes from the respect I gained with the operators and operating management because of my hands-on approach to this project.

A-Train shutdown

After working at Chevron for approximately eight months, my supervisor suggested that I begin planning for a major plant turnaround which would take place the following year. He wanted me to begin the work, but he made it clear that I might be replaced by a more experienced engineer as the shutdown approached. No one with my level of experience had ever been in charge of a $7 million turnaround at Chevron.

I did not want to do all the groundwork myself only to turn it over to someone else later on, so I decided to make myself indispensable. I began the work a year in advance compared with the usual six months. I worked closely with maintenance and the other engineering groups to define the scope of the work early on. I set up a method of tabulating the work list which eliminated the need for long, drawn out meetings. The shutdown planning proceeded very smoothly.

Early in the planning phase of the project I was asked if it would be possible to move up the shutdown date six months. Because I had started planning early, this was possible. The shutdown was a major success and was completed ahead of schedule due to careful planning and cultivation of good working relationships.

6. Discuss a contribution you have made in your community.

The most satisfying contribution I have made to my community was participating in the Tutor Richmond Youth program. In this program Chevron employees contribute their lunch hour once per week to tutor youth from the community surrounding the refinery. This is a very poor community that is high in drug use and violent crime.

The student I tutored was a bright young lady in the eighth grade whose ambition was to become a nurse. I was aware that she looked up to me and considered me a role model. While this was flattering, I was not aware of the responsibility that goes along with being a role model until she asked me to read a letter from her boyfriend.

The letter was very sexually explicit. At first I was not sure what to do, but I decided she would not have brought the matter up had she not wanted to talk about it. Difficult as it was, I felt I needed to discuss the letter frankly with her. We talked about her future as a nurse and how an untimely pregnancy could ruin her plans. We discussed the pressures of being an adolescent and the option of waiting until she was ready to have sex. Finally, we talked about birth control and safe sex.

I do not know what has happened to her since that year. I only know that she, as well as all the other kids in her community, face incredible obstacles to success growing up in the neighborhood they do. Just how difficult it can be to break out of the trap of poverty became vividly clear to me that day. I can only hope that the year I spent as her friend, and the discussion we had that day, had a positive influence on her life.

7. Discuss a situation in which you influenced a group.

(See Roxane's essentially identical answer to Wharton essay 2.)

8. What are your post-MBA career plans?

My future career goal is to advance to a senior-level management position dealing with strategy and international management for a multinational corporation. After five years of engineering and planning experience at an operating company, I have come to a crossroads in my career. As I have gained experience and received increased exposure to the business side of the oil industry, I have become aware that my engineering training has not prepared me adequately to deal with broad strategic questions. I am seeking an MBA to supplement my work experience and gain high intensity exposure to the business functions which are important to running a successful business.

I am interested in strategy because I feel my strongest skills are in identifying the root causes of problems and developing and implementing lasting solutions to them. I am especially interested in international corporate strategy, because during my tenure at the Richmond Refinery, products sold into the export market have become increasingly important to our refinery's profitability. Chevron's planners and oil traders typically come from the engineering ranks and therefore lack the business skills necessary to analyze the refinery's competitive position in new markets. At times it is even difficult to identify the refinery's competition in these markets. As a result, the export market is viewed not as a viable market worthy of cultivation, but as a dumping ground for products, which allows the refinery to operate at capacity. I am seeking a general management education so that I will be equipped to deal with these types of problems as a senior level manager.

STANFORD

1. **Each of us has been influenced by the people, events, and situations of our lives. How have these influences shaped who you are today?**

Growing up in a single parent family has shaped who I am more than any other factor. My parents separated when I was ten years old. My mother, who had never worked outside the home, suddenly had to support my sister and me. Shortly after starting her first job as a secretary, she injured her back and had to have surgery. This kept her out of work for six months. During this time, she received only seventy-five percent of her already meager salary. To make things worse, my parents' divorce was not yet final so my father was not paying child support.

These were especially difficult times for our family. We nearly lost our home and could not afford to heat it. My mother applied for food stamps but did not qualify because she owned a car and was unwilling to give it up. She could not give up the car because she would have no way to get to work when she had recovered from her injury (there was no public transportation in Reno at the time). Somehow we managed to survive these difficult times through sacrifice and help from friends and family.

I learned many important lessons about life during this period of my childhood. This experience brought our family closer together and showed us that with sacrifice and hard work, we would always be able to get through the hard times. It has also given me a greater appreciation for the things that I now have. While I am happy to have a well paying job and look forward to even more success in the future, I am very aware of how fortunate I am. Because I began working when I was fourteen years old, I was able to learn the value of hard work at an early age. I developed a strong sense of determination and the belief that I could have all the money and success I wanted as long as I was willing to work for it. The difficult times I endured during my childhood are largely responsible for the work ethic that has resulted in my success to date.

When I was sixteen, my mother remarried and we moved to a small town east of Reno. This experience also had a major impact on my life. Life in a small town was very difficult for me. While my sister and I acquired instant popularity after moving there, it was still difficult to truly break into such a close-knit society. Having come from a larger city, I found many of the people in this town to be rather close-minded. I often found myself as the sole defender of outsiders, minorities, and others who did not fit the small town mold. I also spoke up and challenged conventional ways of doing things if they did not make sense. This outspokenness often caused me problems and kept me out of organizations such as Honor Society. However, I believed that it was more important to stand up for what I believed in than to yield to peer pressure. This conviction has remained with me through the years. I continue to fight for what I believe in rather than conform to the status quo in order to keep from making waves. While this is often the more difficult route, I believe it is the right one.

I left home a week after graduating from high school and moved back to Reno. I found a job and enrolled at the University that summer. I was able to finance my entire education through scholarships and work. While it required a tremendous amount of effort and focus to work part time and graduate at the top of my chemical engineering class, I was still able to devote much of my spare time to dance. I had always wanted to become a dancer when I was growing up but we could never afford the lessons. However, when I entered college I was able to obtain a dance scholarship at an off-campus dance company. To attain success with so many demands on my time required me to learn to manage my time effectively. This period of my life was a lot of work but was also the most rewarding. When I finally graduated and was offered a job at Chevron I had no one to thank but myself. To this day, when I am feeling down or running low on self-confidence, I think back to this accomplishment.

In recent years, traveling has been the major influence in my life. Now that I am working full time, I am able to travel every year. Traveling outside the country has allowed me to meet people with many different viewpoints and priorities in life. This has forced me to examine my own beliefs and challenge my assumptions of the kind of life I want to lead. While I will always want a successful career, I now know that there is more to life than just work. I spend my spare time reading literature and history and studying French because I believe that it is important to have a well rounded education to get along with people of all types.

All of these events have shaped who I am today. I have a very high work ethic and am determined to achieve the goals I set for myself. I work hard and expect to be compensated for my efforts, but because of my modest beginnings I am always aware and appreciative of how far I have come. I believe this makes me more sensitive to the positions of those less fortunate than I am. Finally, my travels have forced me to remove my own small town blinders and have opened my eyes to all that our diverse world has to offer.

2. **How do you see your career developing? How will an MBA further that development? Why are you applying to Stanford?**

I am applying to the Stanford MBA program at this time because after five years of engineering and planning experience at an operating company, I have come to a crossroads in my career. As I have gained experience and received increased exposure to the business side of the oil industry, I have become aware that my engineering training has not prepared me adequately to deal with the broad strategic questions faced by senior level managers. I am seeking an MBA to supplement my work experience and gain high intensity exposure to the other business functions which are important to running a successful business. In addition, a general management education will increase my career flexibility. Without a formal business education, it would be very difficult for me to change business functions or move into a senior level management position outside the chemical process industries.

My future career goal is to advance to a senior level management position dealing with strategy and international management for a multinational corporation. I am interested in strategy because I feel my strongest skills are in identifying the root causes of problems and developing and implementing lasting solutions to them. I am especially interested in international corporate strategy, because during my tenure at the Richmond Refinery, products sold into the export market have become increasingly important to our refinery's profitability. Chevron's planners and oil traders typically come from the engineering ranks and therefore lack the business skills necessary to analyze the refinery's competitive position in new markets. At times it is even difficult to identify the refinery's competition in these markets. As a result, the export market is viewed not as a viable market worthy of cultivation, but as a dumping ground for products, which allows the refinery to operate at capacity.

Stanford's emphasis on a general management education fits well with my future career goals. I am not pursuing an MBA degree with an emphasis on operations expressly because my experience is in this area. I am more interested in gaining a broad understanding of each of the functional areas of business so I will be able to deal effectively with issues which impact the entire organization. In my current position as a Planning Analyst, I recommend changes in operation designed to increase refinery profitability. Historically, Planning Analysts at Chevron only considered refinery operation when making these recommendations. However, as the business becomes more complex and competitive, additional aspects such as payment terms and inventory carrying costs should also be incorporated to ensure profit maximization. Because I have had very little exposure to the other functional areas, it has been very difficult to incorporate these operating costs into my economic analyses.

Finally, an MBA will give me the skills necessary to be an effective change agent. While "fighting fires" often leads to a successful career at Chevron, this is not an effective form of management. Many of these problems occur as a result of poor planning. I believe that problems should be anticipated and avoided. By adopting a broader perspective and a strategic viewpoint, change can be managed and the road into the future can be made smoother. While I have incorporated these ideas into my career to date, I believe a general business education will allow me to apply these strengths more effectively and at a much higher level in the organization.

3. **The issue of diversity increasingly is recognized as a critical element of successful workplaces. What specific changes would you implement in your current company to address inequities and/or enhance diversity?**

As the workforce becomes smaller and more poorly educated, it is becoming increasingly important for companies to not only accept but nurture diversity in their organizations. To be competitive, companies must hire the most qualified candidates available. They can no longer discriminate on the basis of gender or ethnic background if they expect to hire the most productive workforce available. Economic necessity will ultimately break down the barriers that women and minorities currently encounter in the workplace.

I personally have seen this phenomenon at my own company. Oil refineries typically do not have particularly good track records in terms of diversity. As a result, my company is currently facing a crisis with respect to encouraging diversity in the workplace. Because we do not have women and minorities in highly visible positions, we are finding it increasingly difficult to attract young women and minorities to our company. As a result, we have not been able to hire the most qualified college graduates.

A top-down approach is required to facilitate cultural change in a large organization. If diversity is to be valued at the bottom levels of an organization, it must be very clear that it is valued at the top. First, management must be educated as to what constitutes diversity and how discrimination occurs. While blatant discrimination still exists, subtle unconscious discrimination is far more common. Unless people are aware of what constitutes discrimination, they will continue to discriminate unknowingly.

As part of the educational process, the benefits of diversity should be stressed. Diversity is becoming increasingly valuable in the workplace because it introduces concepts from a wide range of viewpoints and ultimately results in more innovative solutions. While the workforce in the refinery is becoming technically more diverse, those people who conform to traditional role models continue to be the most successful. As a result, the organization suffers. I have seen countless cases where the most qualified person was passed over for a promotion because he or she did not "fit the mold." This is particularly devastating because the "mold" does not exclude people only on the basis of gender or race, but also on the basis of educational background, age, and personality. By employing narrow definitions, the organization ultimately suffers.

To break down these paradigms, management must focus on work products and results rather than work processes when making promotional decisions. For example, our management has been reluctant to place women in line management positions because it was feared that women would not be tough enough to handle the job. However, many women are more effective than men in dealing with the blue collar workers because they are able to develop good working relationships with them. What is important is not how tough women are, but whether or not they will get the job done. Because management is focusing on work processes rather than results, women are being placed in "nice" staff jobs rather than the highly visible line supervisor positions.

A final topic is minority outreach programs. While these can be effective, they can also create animosity among other workers who fear reverse discrimination. However, the dismal record of our company for hiring minorities requires that we implement special programs to develop minorities for our future workforce. If these programs are to be successful, they absolutely must be based on performance. Hiring minorities to meet quotas only encourages labeling and ultimately hurts those people it is designed to help. By developing and hiring only candidates who can perform at the same level as their peers, we will break down the stereotypes which currently pervade our workplace.

4. Describe a day in your life you would like to relive.

The day I would most like to relive is not just a day but an entire era of my life. That era begins the day I entered college. While my college career continues to be one of my most substantial accomplishments, with the experience I now have, I would have done some things differently. For example, I would have worked hard at my engineering studies but I would have taken more liberal arts courses. My last semester I took a literature course which ended up being the most enjoyable class I had in college. While I continue to read widely in my spare time, I miss the classroom environment where I could discuss my impressions with others. Since leaving college, I have not found anyone who is interested in discussing literature. This class made me realize that there are many things I am interested in besides engineering and business and I would have liked to have had more exposure to them while I was still in the university environment.

I would also have taken the opportunity to live abroad. I never seriously considered doing a semester overseas because I was worried about the expense and I was afraid it would force me to add an additional year to my studies. While both of these concerns were legitimate, I now know the benefits would have far outweighed the costs. Having had the opportunity to travel since graduating from college, I realize how much my life is enriched every time I leave the country. This aspect of my life has become one of the most important to me and I intend to work overseas at some time during my career. I want to experience a foreign country from the perspective of a resident rather than just a tourist. I am especially fond of France and have recently resumed my French studies.

I also would have spent more time deciding where I wanted to attend college. I did not apply to any schools other than the University of Nevada-Reno because of the expense. I now know that I would have been able to finance my education one way or another and that cost should not have been the only factor. In addition to thinking about where I wanted to go, I would have challenged my ideas of what I wanted to do. I decided to be an engineer my junior year in high school. After that time, I spent all my effort on achieving that goal. Since women are still rare in engineering, I had many people tell me that I would not succeed in accomplishing this goal. This provided me with even more drive and focus to get the job done. However, once I finished college, I found myself asking if this was the right career move. Ultimately I decided that it was, but I found it disturbing that I might have spent the previous four years working toward a goal I really did not want. I vowed never to jump so blindly again.

Fortunately for me, this is an era that I can "relive." Now that I have examined my professional goals and decided that graduate business school is the next career step I really want to take, I am once again faced with the chance to do the things I did not do the first time around. Now that I am more mature and have a better idea of what is really important to me, I will be sure to take full advantage of all that this opportunity has to offer. I will take an active role in organizing study tours to foreign countries, take a wide range of elective courses, and join student organizations that will allow me to meet people with similar interests.

TUCK

1. **Discuss your career progression to date. What factors have influenced your decision to seek a general management education? Based on what you know about yourself, how do you envision your career progressing after receiving the MBA degree? Please state your professional goals and describe your plans to achieve them.**

I have been working for Chevron at the Richmond Refinery since graduating from college five years ago. I have held six different positions in the engineering and planning departments. As a result of this mobility, I have been exposed to several different areas of the refinery and have acquired a broad manufacturing background. The first three years of my career, I focused on developing my problem-solving and interpersonal skills. My engineering experience taught me to identify the root causes of problems and develop permanent solutions to them. Because many of the problems I was required to solve were too large for me to address alone, I learned to delegate and manage my time effectively. I also learned the importance of selling my ideas in order to get them implemented.

My fourth year at Chevron, I was assigned to the position of start-up engineer for a project to rebuild a processing unit that had been badly damaged by fire. The unit had been down for two years and was being rebuilt at a cost of $125 million. This unit was a major contributor to refinery profitability and I was instrumental in helping to bring it on-line safely and ahead of schedule. This experience was a major success for me and I began to advance quickly. I learned to see the problems I was solving in the context of the entire refinery rather than as isolated problems. I was able to identify business opportunities on my own and took the initiative to convince management to implement them. I was able to assimilate all the knowledge I had accumulated over the previous three years and my value to the organization increased rapidly.

Next, I was assigned to the position of process representative in charge of coordinating the process definition and process design of two major ($84 million and $20 million) retrofit projects. I worked with the engineering contractor to ensure project objectives were met at the lowest possible cost. After the process designs for these two projects were approved, I was assigned to my present position as Short-Range Planning Analyst. In this assignment, I develop the short range refinery operating plan, focusing on maximization of refinery profit in a dynamic market-driven environment. I also work with Supply and Distribution to develop these plans and coordinate the efforts of the refinery operating divisions as needed to ensure smooth implementation of new processing schedules. This position has increased my involvement in the financial aspects of our business.

I am applying to the Tuck MBA program at this time because, after five years of engineering and planning experience at an operating company, I have come to a crossroads in my career. As I have gained experience and received increased exposure to the business side of the oil industry, I have become aware that my engineering training has not prepared me adequately to deal with the broad strategic questions faced by senior level managers. I am seeking an MBA to supplement my work experience and gain high intensity exposure to the other business functions which are important to running a successful business. In addition, a general management education will increase my career flexibility. Without a formal business education, it would be very difficult for me to change business functions or move into a senior level management position outside the chemical process industries.

My future career goal is to advance to a senior-level management position dealing with strategy and international management for a multinational corporation. I am interested in strategy because I feel my strongest skills are in identifying the root causes of problems and developing and implementing lasting solutions to them. I am especially interested in international corporate strategy, because during my tenure at the Richmond Refinery, products sold into the export market have become increasingly important to our refinery's profitability. Chevron's planners and oil traders typically come from the engineering ranks and therefore lack the business skills necessary to analyze the refinery's competitive position in new markets. At times it is even difficult to identify the refinery's competition in these markets. As a result, the export market is viewed not as a viable market worthy of cultivation, but as a dumping ground for products, which allows the refinery to operate at capacity.

Tuck's emphasis on a general management education fits well with my future career goals. I am not pursuing an MBA degree with an emphasis on operations expressly because my experience is in this area. I am more interested in gaining a broad understanding of each of the functional areas of business so I will be able to deal effectively with issues which impact the entire organization. In my current position as a

Planning Analyst, I recommend changes in operation designed to increase refinery profitability. Historically, Planning Analysts at Chevron only considered refinery operation when making these recommendations. However, as the business becomes more complex and competitive, additional aspects such as payment terms and inventory carrying costs should also be incorporated to ensure profit maximization. Because I have had very little exposure to the other functional areas, it has been very difficult to incorporate these operating costs into my economic analyses.

Finally, an MBA will give me the skills necessary to be an effective change agent. While "fighting fires" often leads to a successful career at Chevron, this is not an effective form of management. Many of these problems occur as a result of poor planning. I believe that problems should be anticipated and avoided. By adopting a broader perspective and a strategic viewpoint, change can be managed and the road into the future can be made smoother. While I have incorporated these ideas into my career to date, I believe a general business education will allow me to apply these strengths more effectively and at a much higher level in the organization.

2. Evaluate a recent experience that required the use of your leadership skills. What impact has the experience had on your personal and professional development?

My biggest leadership success took place last year when I was the process engineer assigned to two heavy oil processing units. One of these units provided feed pretreatment for the other. I was approached by Operations Coordination and was asked if Widuri resid, a low value fuel oil stream, could be fed to the upstream of the two units. This would allow a portion of the resid stream to be upgraded to gasoil, a high value intermediate product. I agreed to address the technical aspects of the problem and asked Operations Coordination to deal with the logistics.

When we reconvened to finalize the plan, it became apparent that the logistical constraints would render the project uneconomical. Having gathered the physical property data, I realized that the Widuri resid could be fed directly to the downstream unit. I suggested we bypass the feed pretreatment step entirely. This would allow us to upgrade the entire stream rather than only a small portion of it as the original plan would have required. In addition, it would avoid some of the operating costs.

Operations Coordination was enthusiastic, but I knew it would be difficult to sell the idea to Operations. A resid stream had never been fed directly to the downstream unit and I knew Operations would be concerned about damaging the catalyst in that unit. This was a major operational change, but I was confident it would work. I gathered the necessary data and developed a plan which included a good monitoring program and contingency plan. This would allow us to identify and respond to any unexpected problems if necessary. Two weeks later I organized a meeting for all the interested parties and presented my plan which anticipated and addressed management's concerns. The following day the resid was being fed to the downstream unit. This project resulted in profits to the refinery of $8 million over a five-month period.

This project marked a change in my career in terms of maturity and initiative. Prior to this, my efforts were focused primarily on my own sphere of operation. The success of this project gave me the self-confidence to assert my leadership skills. I began to approach problems from a refinerywide perspective. In addition, I began to challenge traditional approaches and offer more innovative solutions.

3. **Describe the characteristics of an exceptional manager using an example of someone whom you have observed or with whom you have worked. Illustrate how his or her management style has influenced you.**

I have been fortunate to have had the opportunity to work closely with our Refinery General Manager since being assigned to the position of Short Range Planning Analyst. Mike Hannan has made dramatic improvements in our refinery's profitability since becoming Refinery Manager two years ago. Historically, the refinery was operated for the sake of engineering rather than making money. This is because Chevron's managers come from the engineering ranks and generally prefer solving engineering problems to solving business problems. To make matters worse, the corporate research and engineering staff is located next door to the refinery. Because of its close proximity to our refinery, the research department was continually using our refinery as a giant pilot plant. As a result, our refinery provided more than half the research company's revenues even though Chevron has a total of eight refineries and several chemical plants. Thus, research projects occupied an excessive amount of the refinery employees' time and diverted their attention from making the refinery a profitable business unit. In fact, the refinery's financial performance was so poor that it was in danger of being shut down.

Mr. Hannan immediately focused on solving this problem. He was able to focus the efforts of all refinery employees by clearly stating his objectives in a mission statement. This made it very clear that it was important to reduce operating costs and increase light product yield. Because the employees were now able to understand their role in the larger context of the refinery, teamwork improved and people began to find innovative solutions to problems that were previously viewed as handicaps inherent to an older manufacturing facility. In less than a year, our refinery became a top performer in the Chevron system.

Mr. Hannan also required that capital projects be funded from the refinery's revenues and the refinery return money to the corporation. This requirement forced close scrutiny of all capital projects and only those projects which were consistent with the refinery's mission statement were funded. This dramatically cut the number of frivolous projects and helped to keep the research company from using the refinery for test programs that were inconsistent with our business objectives.

Mr. Hannan focused on not only the primary business functions, but the support functions as well. For example, our public affairs policy has always been developed independently of the business plan and was executed in a rather random fashion. The budgeted sum of money was distributed to anyone who asked for it on a first come, first served basis. Mr. Hannan required that the public affairs budget be consistent with our business plan. Money would be given preferentially to the community surrounding the refinery to improve our relationship with our neighbors. Because the ability to get environmental permits is critical to completing our capital projects, a good relationship with the community is absolutely necessary. By focusing our public efforts in this area, we are improving the likelihood that the community will view us as good neighbors and support us in our efforts to obtain permits.

Mr. Hannan also improved the work environment in the refinery. He empowered people by putting decision making authority at the proper levels. Previously, decisions were made at very high levels in the organization by those who were furthest from where the actual work was completed. This resulted in inefficient use of the employees' talents and often resulted in less effective solutions to problems. In addition, Mr. Hannan has fostered an environment where risk taking and creativity are rewarded. Employees are beginning to step out of the old conservative ways of doing business and are making dramatic improvements in their work processes. Now even the employees at the lowest level of the organizational hierarchy feel they can contribute.

Because Mr. Hannan has focused all aspects of the refinery on the same goals, all employees are able to see how they fit into the organization and how their efforts contribute to the bottom line. I have seen the morale at this refinery increase dramatically since these changes were implemented. This has resulted in a more profitable refinery and a more pleasant work environment. Mr. Hannan has had a tremendous influence on me because I have been able to see first-hand how an effective manager works. By providing clear focus and objectives, he was able to mobilize all the employees and accomplish many of the goals he outlined in his mission statement.

I am lucky to have an office two doors away from Mr. Hannan. He enjoys developing bright young people and often comes into my office to share his philosophies of business with me. I have a tremendous amount of respect for him and take his advice to heart. Now when I begin work on a new project, I clearly define how the project will contribute to the refinery's bottom line. I have begun to think more strategically and look not only for the answers that best suit our needs today, but will also serve us in the future. I continually challenge the status quo and take calculated risks knowing that I will have some failures. Because the problems I solve in my current position cross operating divisional boundaries, I am dependent on the assistance of people from all over the refinery to solve them. I have learned how to identify who is best suited to solve particular problems and how to get them involved in the planning process. This has resulted in improved planning and more profitable refinery operation. I believe that working with Mr. Hannan has helped me to take the first step toward becoming a manager rather than just an engineer.

4. What are your principal interests outside of your job or school?

(See Roxane's essentially identical answer to Wharton essay 4.)

DARDEN

1. Specifically address your post-MBA short- long-term professional goals. How will Darden assist you in attaining these goals?

(See her essentially identical answer to Stanford essay 2.

2. The Darden School seeks a diverse and unique entering class of future managers. How will your distinctiveness enrich our learning environment and enhance your prospects for success as a manager?

My broad manufacturing experience will enable me to bring a unique perspective to the learning environment at Darden. During my employment at a large oil refinery, I have worked in various aspects of manufacturing including the design and operation of the equipment used to produce a wide variety of petroleum products. In my current position, I plan the operation of the refinery as a whole to maximize profit in a dynamic, market-driven environment. I believe that my experience in manufacturing will provide a much needed perspective on how things are really accomplished in the field. For those students who are not familiar with the tremendous inertia working against change inherent in a large manufacturing facility, my experience will provide insight and, at times, a reality check.

My experience will provide yet another unique insight into the diversity issue. I have spent my career working in an environment in which traditionally very few women have worked. I have had to learn to deal with people who doubted my abilities based on my gender alone. I have been able to build a very good professional reputation in an environment where women are often labeled as weak and unable to survive in the difficult refinery atmosphere. The perspective I bring with respect to the diversity issue is unique and will enhance any discussions which take place on this subject.

I am willing to speak my mind, which is critical in a classroom in which the case study method is utilized. In addition, I work well with people of varied backgrounds and am able to utilize the specific strengths of others to develop workable solutions to problems. In a team environment, one is required both to give and take. I have had the chance to develop these skills in my present position. Because teamwork is essential to the success of the case study method, these skills will be invaluable to me at Darden.

Finally, I spend all of my vacation time traveling and devote much of my free time to reading and studying French. Traveling has forced me to remove my small town blinders and open my mind to other ways of doing things. Traveling has increased my awareness of the fact that the American way of doing things is not the only way and that flexibility and sensitivity are absolutely necessary to get along with others. I have found that this applies not only to people of different nationalities but also to fellow Americans whose views may be different from my own.

These experiences have benefited me both in my personal life and on the job, and I believe that they will be an asset for me at Darden.

3. **Describe a significant leadership experience, decision-making challenge, or managerial accomplishment. How did this affect your professional/personal development?**

(See her essentially identical answer to Tuck essay 2.)

4. **What is the most difficult ethical dilemma you have faced in your professional life? Upon present reflection, would you have resolved this dilemma in a different manner?**

(See her essentially identical answer to Harvard essay 4.)

COMMENTS

1. There is a lot to like in Roxane's essays. She does a very good job of distinguishing herself in several ways. First, she successfully positions herself as a woman who has had to work hard for the success she has enjoyed. She is from a relatively poor family from a very small town, so her career success owes a great deal to

her determination and cleverness rather than her family's situation. Second, she shows that she is a very talented engineer by emphasizing her highly profitable successes. This is all the more impressive for the fact that there are very few women to be found in her sort of industry. Third, she demonstrates that her talents are not limited to engineering. Her essays are very well written, suggesting that her communication skills are much better than might be anticipated. In addition, her 730 GMAT score had her in the top 2 percent in both verbal and quantitative ability, again demonstrating her intellectual balance. Fourth, she shows that she has already had substantial managerial success and yet would still benefit substantially from an MBA. One of the factors in her managerial success is the fact that she understands how to work with and through other people. Her political savvy appears well developed. Her teamwork and political skills are valuable items at a time when business schools emphasize these "softer" skills. Last, she makes it clear that she will bring a lot to her classmates in terms of her relatively unusual skills, experiences, and attitudes.

The net result is that she appears to be an engineer who is very skilled at her job, but brings much more to a school than just engineering knowledge. Given the great number of engineers applying to leading business schools it is useful for her to be able to position herself both as a top quality engineer and as more than just an engineer. (The "have your cake and eat it too" approach.)

2. I have included several different versions of her "why I want an MBA" essay because she has recast it to suit each school to which she applies. In applying to the joint MBA-International Studies MA program at Wharton, for example, she emphasized her interest in international strategy and in the development of a strong second language. For Stanford, on the other hand, she emphasized her interest in general management. She was not dissembling in mentioning these different areas, merely highlighting whichever of several actual interests was most pertinent to the given situation. Note that she is able to support each of these positioning efforts. The Tuck essay features a combination of the Wharton and Stanford essays, giving a good demonstration of how to recycle essays. Tuck essay 2 (on leadership) is another good example of recycling, this time of Wharton essay 2 (on challenging the thought of a group).

3. Her weakest essay is probably Wharton's "what is the world's greatest problem." This is a hard one to write because it asks the respondent to pontificate on a subject that is seldom a matter of true expertise. Although that is probably the case here, she at least manages to avoid embarrassing herself with a truly naive essay, while still gaining credit for being reasonably knowledgeable and concerned about more than her own engineering field.

4. In Tuck essay 3, note the masterful exposition in the opening paragraph. She informs us of the context in which her manager was operating, thereby giving us the opportunity to understand the rationale and significance of his actions.

ROGER

Background:

Job: Entrepreneur

Education: Bachelor's in economics from a German university

Nationality: German

Critical issue to address:

None.

WHARTON

1. **Please discuss your future career progression to date and your professional goals for the future. How will the MBA influence your ability to achieve your goals?**

My career path has been rather unorthodox. While I was still a student I started my own firm. For the first four years this consisted of embroidering terry-cloth textiles for department store chains. I began the business for two reasons. I had spotted this niche market which offered what I thought was a chance to make a fair amount of money. Of course, the reason that I was even thinking in those terms was that I had a strong desire to work for myself, because I very much enjoy having the opportunity to "create" something.

Getting this business established required that I put in long hours making sure that the machinery worked, that our deliveries would be made in spite of a truck breakdown, etc. I had to learn most things from scratch, since I had essentially no experience related to anything I was now doing. My biggest obstacle may have been the first one I faced, selling non-existent product to department store chains (which order only on a chain-wide basis) before I even had a company. I solved this as I solved other problems, by learning all that I could about the problem by doing library-type research and talking to everyone I could find who had experience of the issues involved, and then pushing and pushing until something worked out.

I eventually had a bit of money put aside, so I was able to take the next step in building my business. I rented a store of my own in which to sell our textiles. I expanded our output by adding four machines, which allowed me also to expand the range of our output. This expansion allowed us to serve the hotel trade as well.

The business certainly expanded from a sales perspective as well. Turnover for the first year was 120,000 marks. By the sixth year we enjoyed revenues of 2,400,000 marks. This was in spite of the fact that our underinsured store burnt to the ground early in this sixth year (1989). Oddly enough, this cloud had a silver lining to it. We received a great deal of press coverage and our ensuing special sales led to the development of a greatly expanded clientele. We designed a new store which was truly state-of-the-art and much larger than our old one.

We then expanded our product line and added several more stores. Last year's results showed turnover of 10.8 million marks and strong profitability, despite Germany's poor business climate.

I very much hope to be able to continue "running my own show" in the future. But I hope to run a much bigger, more complex one. To do so will require a much greater understanding of things which I have grasped at only the most practical of levels, such as marketing and finance. I therefore view an MBA as an essential step to taking this large step forward. I am in the fortunate position of having developed strong enough managers under me that I can be away from day-to-day supervision of the business, so now is a perfect time to make this investment in my managerial future. My choice of Wharton is due both to its reputation for overall excellence and to its strong entre-preneurial program.

2. **Describe a situation in your life when you actively challenged the traditional thought of a group. What level of impact did you have on the group?**

This question does not really apply to my situation. For the past decade I have been running my own business. As the boss of a small company which I started myself, I have not been answerable to anyone. Also, my principal community and social activities have not involved challenging a group's traditional thought.

Consequently, in order to respond to this question, I will have to go back to a not terribly important event of some years ago. When I was first trying to get into business I wanted to embroider terry-cloth textiles for large department store chains. Such chains buy only on a chain-wide basis, so I had to be prepared to manufacture on a scale suitable to a chain's potential requirements. To do so required buying some machinery at a price of 40,000 marks for each of several machines. I had very little money, so I needed to get my financing elsewhere.

I approached my local banks for a loan. The bankers I had to deal with were in their fifties and sixties. They were quite conservative in their views of life as well as lending; one might describe them as stodgy rather than simply conservative. They were uniformly hostile at first to an inexperienced, very young fellow who wished to run a business for the first time. Winning them over to my point of view required several things. The most important thing I did was that I kept at it. I did not give up even in the face of their discouraging attitude and remarks. I also went to great lengths to show them that I understood what the business was about, and that I was prepared to work extraordinarily hard to be successful.

The combination of persistence and knowledge eventually convinced them to take a chance on me, which was good for them as well as for me.

3. **In your opinion, what is the world's greatest problem? Why?**

The world seems to be presenting too great a choice of major problems. I am by no means certain that there is a single "greatest" problem, but I shall respond in the spirit of the question. Lack of tolerance for peoples who are different from one's own group is not merely extremely widespread but also has had, and will continue to have, catastrophic consequences.

The lack of tolerance I am talking about can be in terms of others' political, religious, racial, or ethnic backgrounds or beliefs. The particulars of a given situation may differ from those of other situations, but the key element is an unwillingness to allow other people to pursue their own lives in the fashion they choose.

My concern about this problem may owe a great deal to my being German. The "particulars" of our own history are all too well known in this regard. Lately various new problems, or rather similar sorts of problems which have bedeviled our history, have surfaced. The elements of this latest series of episodes are perhaps unique to Germany—the number of refugees; the laws prohibiting them from working, which makes them appear lazy to those who remain ignorant of the law (or its consequences), while at the same time granting them benefits at least as good as those granted to the unemployed; the impact of a recession; and, of course, the cessation of the parental role played by the East German state. The net result has been uncertainty and fear, two emotions which have had such terrible consequences in German history.

Other examples are similarly all too easy to find. The Northern Ireland battle over economics and religion. The religious (and historical) battle between Arabs and Jews. The remarkable upheavals in the former Soviet empire. The efforts of the Malays to keep ethnic Chinese subordinate. The list starts to feel endless, even though I have just begun.

The fact that innumerable such conflicts exist is clear. The sad thing is that modern weaponry offers the chance for killing beyond the proportions considered possible even in nightmarish novels a century ago. While human beings are unlikely to exist without substantial conflict, the sad thing is that progress on other fronts has been matched neither by the diminution of "tribal" hostilities nor by the improvement of peace-making mechanisms. I fear that the next decades may have such terrible tolls in human lives, due to conflicts arising from tribal intolerance, that we may yet view the Cold War as a "golden age."

4. **What nonprofessional activities do you find inspirational? At what level do you participate in these activities?**

My principal interests outside my job have been sports, especially volleyball, and a community project which aims to bring together people of different ages.

I have been playing volleyball ever since early in high school. What I liked about it right from the start was the uncomplicated way in which you can make friends and the different types of groups you can get to participate. I have played with my classmates, colleagues from my job, youngsters at the local sports club, and people I just met at the beach while on holiday. The only equipment needed is two poles, a rope, and a ball, and then off you go.

What fascinates me about volleyball is the amazing transition one makes from being an individual to being part of a team. The team changes character as the players rotate to new positions, and as the requirements change from needing a spike to needing a dig, etc., just as the teams themselves change after each game ends. Who has winners? Who can stay for just one more game? The game is extremely swift, with each change in requirement for success rewarding different attributes, so the team that acts most like a real unit and marshals its skills, without individual egos or simple confusion getting in the way, is most likely to win. The challenge of taking a group of strangers, or rivals in some other aspect of life, and making a *team* of them is a constant challenge which I love.

My interest in community work is somewhat similar. Several years ago several friends of mine and I decided to try to do our part in ameliorating some of the difficulties faced in living in our suburb. This suburb of Frankfurt was built in a rush in the seventies. It consists largely of high rise apartment complexes. Although the facilities are good, there is no sense of community to the environment.

We asked the local Protestant church for space in which people could meet. They agreed to provide this and to advertise forthcoming events in their newsletter. We also advertise the existence of this group and its activities at bulletin boards in the area.

Our focus is getting people to contribute whatever it is that they most value about themselves or most want from these interactions. One elderly woman with time on her hands baby-sits and cooks for several of the single mothers in the area. One pensioner who is a skilled tinkerer enjoys showing others how to take care of their apartments and appliances. Various young people are happy to do the shopping for elderly invalids. And so on. We also organize regular bus trips to local spots of interest, like a winery, dripstone cave, or picnic grounds.

Many dozens of people now feel that they know their neighbors and are part of a real community.

CHICAGO (Selected)

1. Why are you seeking an MBA from the University of Chicago?

As a German entrepreneur who would like to expand his current business, I believe an MBA is necessary for me at this time.

My career path has been rather unorthodox thus far. While still a student, I started my own firm. For the first four years, this consisted of embroidering terry-cloth textiles for department store chains. I began the business for two reasons. I had spotted this niche market which offered what I thought was a chance to make a fair amount of money. Also, I had a strong desire to work for myself, to "create" something, and was delighted to take the opportunity available to me.

Getting this business established required that I put in long hours making sure the machinery worked, that our deliveries would be made in spite of truck breakdowns, etc. I had to learn most things from scratch, since I had essentially no experience related to running a business. I learned as much as possible through doing library-type research and talking to everyone I could find who had experience with the issues involved. Then I pushed and pushed until something worked out.

I eventually had a bit of money put aside, so I was able to take the next step in building my business. I rented a store of my own in which to sell our textiles. I expanded our output by adding four machines, which allowed me also to expand the range of our output. This expansion allowed us to serve the hotel trade as well.

The business certainly expanded from a sales perspective as well. Turnover for the first year was 120,000 marks. By the sixth year, we enjoyed revenues of 2,400,000 marks. That year we designed a new store which was truly state-of-the-art and much larger than our old one. We then expanded our product line and added several more stores. Last year's results showed a turnover of 10.8 million marks, despite Germany's poor business climate.

I very much hope to continue "running my own show" in the future. However, I would like to run a much bigger, more complex one. To do so will require a much greater understanding of things which I have grasped at only the most practical of levels. In particular, there are two areas I must address if I intend to be successful in this expansion: control systems and finance.

Thus far, my business has been run through personal management, literally being on the spot to address any problems that arise. I would like to move toward a more "professional" management style, putting a management structure in place that would provide a built-in control mechanism. I have benefited from the fact that my business is a community-type enterprise, where I know my clients and employees personally. This has cultivated a certain loyalty to me, but in the long run, reliance on this overly personal view of things could be detrimental to the expansion of the business.

My desire to understand more about finance relates to my desire to expand my business. Right now I think that I understand too little about how to analyze my financing needs, and will consequently be unable to raise substantial sums of either debt or equity.

My interest in a rigorous, theoretical approach to such subjects—to balance my purely experiential understanding—drives my desire to attend the University of Chicago. Since I already have much practical experience, I am not interested in a case method program which simulates the "real world." I am looking for a serious quantitative approach to finance, as well as hard-edged marketing skills to supplement the intuitive grasp I already have. I am in the fortunate position of having developed strong enough managers under me so that I can be away from the day-to-day supervision of the business, so this is an ideal time to pursue the MBA.

I think I would be able to contribute to the school in terms of being a German entrepreneur who has been running a business for ten years. I understand firsthand retailing in Germany, including the legal framework, customer attitudes, and the general business environment of post-reunification Germany. And I am an extremely outgoing person who gets along easily with others.

I believe the MBA would supplement my developed interpersonal and practical skills, and give me the necessary "hard skills" to see my business expand into the next decade.

MICHIGAN (Selected)

1. **What was the biggest risk that you have taken or most substantial obstacles you have overcome?**

The biggest risk I have undertaken is opening my own business. There were a number of major obstacles I overcame at every point in the expansion of the business.

The first major obstacle was my own youth and inexperience. I started the textile embroidery business when I was 21. The first thing I had to do was to sell nonexistent products to department store chains (which order only on a chainwide basis). At first, many managers were reluctant to even hear my pitch; they saw me only as an untested "kid." After analyzing my first failures, I saw that there was no way I could get around my inexperience. Instead of trying to act smooth and experienced (which came off phony), I decided to turn my youth to my advantage, by conveying enthusiasm and energy. Soon, I had these same managers chatting and laughing (and signing orders). I learned a lot those first few years about communicating with, and influencing, people.

Another challenge came when I requested my first bank loan. After two years, I had established a fairly large clientele of department store chains and needed to invest in four new machines at a price of 40,000 marks each. The bankers I had to deal with were in their fifties and sixties and were quite conservative in their views of life as well as lending. They were uniformly hostile at first to an inexperienced, very young fellow who wanted to run a business for the first time. Winning them over to my point of view required that I really keep at it. I went to great lengths to show them that I understood what the business was about, and that I was prepared to work extraordinarily hard to be successful.

As the business took off, and I matured both in personal and professional life, other challenges arose. I arrived at a point where there was a ceiling of profit in the textile embroidery business, and I needed to diversify into other products. After many hours of research, visits to the chamber of commerce, and personally handing out surveys at the local mall, I decided to focus on the group of women consumers between 25 and 50 with a large disposable income. I diversified into upmarket hardware, tableware, and electrical appliances, and firmly entrenched myself to do battle with the other fellow at the mall who was selling similar products. By pointed advertising campaigns, and a clear view of my clientele, I established my own niche in this market, and saw, despite competition, a dramatic increase in profits.

These challenges (and many others) contributed to my personal and professional development. I saw that hard work and exploiting one's strengths (while working seriously on one's weaknesses) was the way to make a gamble pay off. I have matured along with my business, and am eager to seek even greater challenges as my skills and ambitions increase.

2. **Imagine that through the marvels of technology, you have the ability to relive one day of your life. What day would you choose? Why?**

The day in my life I would like to relive was a day of tremendous relief, after what started as a potential disaster. After six years in business, my underinsured store burned down (on the one-year anniversary of the new store). Just two days before the fire, I had called the insurance agent to request more coverage (we were about 30 percent underinsured). After the fire, the insurance agent said there was nothing he could do, based only on a spoken telephone agreement. However, several people in the agent's office had heard our conversation (he was using a speaker phone), and they went to the Board of Directors with this knowledge. The Board took up the matter and we were told we would have to wait several weeks for a decision on whether the agreement constituted a viable contract.

Meanwhile, two weeks later, we set up a hallway stand in the mall to sell our products. We were used to doing about 15,000 marks per day, and figured we would be lucky to make 5,000, just enough to tide us over. A seeming miracle happened, however. Not only did we make the usual amount of money, but in fact on that day, we grossed 100,000 marks! We could barely keep up with demand, fostered by the press coverage about the fire in the local newspaper. (In fact, these elevated profits continued for weeks on end.)

On the same day, I got a call from the insurance agent, who said the Board had decided to consider our telephone conversation a contractual agreement, and was willing to put up the money required to pay for the damages. I can't say that this day ranks among the most enjoyable in terms of fun; however, after two weeks of constant worry, I slept ten long hours, and felt an immense sense of relief.

In fact, this cloud turned out to have a silver lining. Not only were we able to stay in business, but the press coverage brought us an expanded clientele, and the profits we made in a relatively short period allowed us to invest in a second store.

COMMENTS

1. In the first Wharton essay Roger recognizes his unusual position as an entrepreneur and looks to capitalize on it by immediately bringing it to the reader's attention with his opening phrase. This frames the essay and has one ready to see what makes him unusual. (Note, however, that he does a more effective job of showing why a given school is appropriate for him in his Chicago essay, which he anchors more firmly to what is unique about Chicago.)

2. Later in this first essay he shows that he bootstrapped his way into the business, starting with very little indeed and needing to work very hard at unglamorous tasks. Later in the essay he shows the remarkable progress he made from this humble start. This includes showing that he has become a real manager insofar as he has developed strong managers under him. Saying that they could handle the business while he goes off for two years of education makes his managerial skills clear.

3. His record marks him as a serious businessperson. He is therefore wise to show the other side of his character by talking about a nonbusiness issue in essay 3; the world's greatest problem thus is intolerance rather than some business or economics issue. In the following essay, discussing his sporting and community interests performs the same function. (Were he from a nonbusiness background, I would have preferred to see him take every opportunity to discuss business issues to show that he is going to fit into the school.)

4. Discussing sports, as he does in Wharton essay 4, is not generally particularly interesting insofar as most of the candidates for business schools have participated in them. Here it is useful, though, because it shows that he is not a loner and, for that matter, fits the profile of a typical applicant in some ways at least, and will thus fit in well to the school's social life. Similarly, discussing his community work shows that he has a heart.

5. His Michigan "day to relive" story is a marvelous tale. It is interesting and shows that he has accumulated a substantial amount of community goodwill.

SYLVIE

Background:

Job: Consultant (formerly an accountant)

Education: Accounting degree from a good French business school

Nationality   French

Critical issue to address:

As an accountant, she needs to distinguish herself from the large number of candidates with a similar background.

STANFORD

1. **Each of us has been influenced by the people, events, and situations of our lives. How have these influences shaped who you are today?**

I was raised on a small family farm located in the southwest of France, about twelve kilometers from Albi. For many years I regarded my childhood as a disadvantage, but I have come to realize that in fact the determination and teamwork I learned as a child continue to serve me today.

I lived with my parents, my brother, my grandfather, and the two youngest brothers of my father. Because my father lost his mother when he was young, he raised his brothers along with his children.

My father was a great influence in my life. He had a calm strength and determination, as well as a deep affinity with nature. Even though he had health problems and financial difficulties he refused to abandon the farm. He believed that independence and self-determination were necessary for survival. I remember the day in the garden shed when I was seven years old, helping my father extract honey from the bee hives. He said, "bees spend their lives working together to produce honey for people. It is the same for our family." Because the links in our family were strong, we were able to work together toward a common goal. It is this spirit of productivity and collaboration which inspires me.

I worked on the farm with my family for eighteen years: harvesting grapes and corn, milking cows, cleaning animal stalls, feeding hens, pigs, and rabbits, and tending the vegetable garden. During the school year I had to ride my bicycle four kilometers to school every morning, and back again in the evening. At night I was responsible for feeding the animals, after which I did my schoolwork and went to sleep, exhausted. I did not have much of a social life because all my time was divided between school and work on the farm.

I attended secondary school at Lycee Bellevue in Albi, the nearest city. In 1981 I passed the Secondary Education Baccalaureat in Mathematics with High Honors, thereby proving to my father that I had inherited his determination. Because of my parents' financial difficulties my studies were financed by my own earnings, partial scholarships, and bank loans. When I first arrived at Ecole des Cadres in Paris, I felt an outsider because most of my classmates were the children of business executives.

There are still quite pronounced class distinctions in France, and I was sometimes looked down upon by other students as a result of my modest origins. I started to hide my family's occupation even when, during school holidays, I went back to work on the farm. We all came back to school well tanned, but I may have been unique inso-far as I did not get my tan from being on a beach.

My shame resulted from the usual combination of peer pressure and the desire to fit in. I came to view the value of my background quite differently once I graduated first in my class at Ecole des Cadres. I realized at last that my upbringing had been a great advantage. I still view it as by far the most important influence upon who I am today. A few examples will probably make that clear.

I have never had anything "given" to me. I had to struggle to break away from the typical future that awaited most of my classmates in the countryside. I had to strug-gle both financially and psychologically to succeed as a student in Paris, and then again as a businesswoman. I consequently recognize an opportunity when I see one and do my best not to waste it.

When I had a chance, through scholarships, to go to a prestigious university, I seized it. I took fullest advantage of the opportunity too, not just in terms of getting top grades or producing my prize-winning thesis. I spent extra hours in the library researching issues that were only touched upon in class, such as special planning techniques and cost control methods. During research for my thesis I spent twenty hours each week at FR3, a public television station, in order to learn from the inside how it functioned. I was also elected class representative, despite my provincial upbringing, and managed to work part time as a cashier to help finance my studies.

As a certified public accountant I saw the opportunity to learn the workings of various industries. Each project represented for me a chance to learn about something new, whether it be the transportation, real estate, communication, or nuclear industries.

Even in my personal life I have tried to seize every opportunity available to me. For example, when the real estate market was favorable, I bought an apartment which I then spent two years refurbishing. As my finances were limited, I did this construction piecemeal, living in the midst of planks and pipes, until I saw my dream realized.

2. **How do you see your career developing? How will an MBA further that devel-opment? Why are you applying to Stanford?**

The MBA is an important step on the way to creating my own business. It would build on the strong quantitative and leadership skills I already have, and provide me with three important skills necessary for my undertaking: a broader perspective on business and management; experience working collaboratively in groups; and a creative approach to entrepreneurship. I have chosen Stanford for its excellence in each of these three areas.

My long-term professional goal is to create my own business: a financial advisory firm for small to medium-sized companies. The focus of this enterprise would be on non-routine financing and investment decisions which smaller firms lack the in-house expertise to handle without assistance.

After seven years of professional experience I have acquired some of the skills neces-sary for my undertaking. My experience, however, has been limited in scope. While my education and work at Deloitte-Touche prepared me to deal expertly with accounting and auditing, I lack a more general view and understanding of business. My desire to learn more about business, and to do so in a more free-flowing environment, prompted my move to D.G. Conseil. While this experience has been valuable, I have not yet gained a sufficient understanding of numerous functional aspects of business or, indeed, a general management perspective. My lack of these things is one reason for wanting an MBA at this time. Another is that I have had very little professional experience in working in collaborative groups, which I view as important to my own managerial development, particularly in light of my desire to start my own business. A third reason for my interest in an MBA is that I would like as much exposure as possible to entrepreneurial theory and practice.

These three desires, when matched with the strengths of Stanford's program, made clear to me that the GSB would be an ideal fit for me. Its general management emphasis, emphasis upon teamwork, and, of course, its remarkable tradition of producing successful entrepreneurs, make its program most desirable for me.

I would be remiss if I did not admit that its sterling reputation (in France and elsewhere) also plays a role in my thinking.

3. **Create your ideal small group with whom to have a conversation. You may choose anyone and any topic. Explain your choices and why they are important to you.**

I would like to gather together four very different people in order to discuss the notion of success. The reason that "success" is a topic of interest to me is that I have worked very hard throughout my life, and enjoy doing so, but I know that I have never really asked myself why I work as I do, or why I enjoy it the way that I do. I suppose that now is as good a time as any to open the inquiry.

My first conversation partner would be Epicurus, the founder of a school of thought which emphasized a nearly hedonistic approach to life. His notion of "carpe diem" suggested that life is to be lived to the fullest, albeit with an underlying suggestion that pleasure in its simpler forms is the likely, perhaps even appropriate, outlet.

My second conversation partner would be a far more spiritual individual. The specific representative of this approach to life is not particularly important to me, but I will choose Gandhi as a conventional choice to speak for this very different set of values. His view that one's life is to be valued to the extent that one helps others while leading an extremely modest existence oneself represents a view opposite to the sensation-centered Epicurus.

My third partner would be Shakespeare, or at least the Shakespeare represented by the idea that "nothing is but thinking makes it so." (I hope that this translation from French back into English is accurate.) The idea that one's objective circumstances are unimportant relative to the way one understands or views them provides a perfect counterpoint to the Epicurean and spiritualist views.

My fourth partner would be my father, insofar as his views are much more pragmatic and earthy than any of the other participants. (Of course to the extent that I am my father's daughter I suppose that he would not be strictly necessary to this discussion, but I am reluctant to deny him a chance to participate in this company.) He considers that a successful life is based on your attitude to life, regardless of what you achieve in a practical sense. In other words, you are successful to the extent that you make it clear to your family and friends how much you care about them, and by trying your hardest, with enthusiasm and courage, to promote the interests of those closest to you.

I would enjoy very much the discussion which I would try to foster concerning how one might view the successful life. The group I have chosen should provide a very good balance of competing perspectives, which would no doubt be well presented. (I hope that my father and I would come close to holding our own.)

4. How would you teach ethics? Can ethics be taught?

I suspect that it is most appropriate to respond to these questions in reverse order. I think that ethics can indeed be taught, but I think that there are very clear limits to the impact it will generally have upon people who are already in their mid to late twenties. I think that the Jesuits were (are?) probably right in their view that the critical learning period regarding large moral issues is up to the age of seven. Therefore, I think that the largest influence upon a child is inevitably going to be its environment in the early years of its life, most especially its family. The impact of learning later in life is likely to be modest in comparison.

This does not mean that I am altogether pessimistic about the possibility of influencing people by the time they reach adulthood, but I think that one must inevitably have somewhat limited objectives. The objectives should probably be to influence "some of the people some of the time." An appropriate course in a business school should probably aim to give a reasonable overview of the different notions of ethics which have been developed through history. These notions should then be applied to the business environment in which students will again soon be working.

The application of these ideas should be quite realistic, given the tendency of many to shrug off this sort of subject as so much hot air. This suggests that a case study approach is probably necessary. The application also needs to look very carefully not just at the different options open to the participants, and the ethical implications of each option according to the various theories, but also the likely outcomes of each option. By outcomes I mean the impact upon the companies involved, their customers (suppliers, employees, etc.), and the individuals involved—in terms of their careers at their respective companies, and also in terms of the psychological impact of each possible course of action.

In other words, I think that such a course when presented to people of this level of maturity and sophistication cannot be "preachy" or simple-minded. Rather, it must be "real world" in nature as well as on a par with the level of difficulty of other courses in the curriculum. Otherwise I fear that it would invite being taken less than seriously.

BABSON (Selected)

1. How do you feel the Babson MBA can help you attain your specific career and personal goals for the five years after you graduate?

The Babson MBA is an important step on the way to creating my own business. It would build on the technical skills I already have through my work as a CPA and marketing manager, and provide me with entrepreneurial skills, as well as a broader, global view of business.

I have chosen the Babson School first because it accents entrepreneurship. My long-term professional goal is to create a financial advisory firm for small to medium-sized companies. The focus of this enterprise would be on nonroutine financing and investment decisions, since many small firms lack the expertise to handle this. In order to pursue this goal, I would like exposure to American-style companies as well as courses in general entrepreneurial theory. My experience as CPA for Deloitte-Touche prepared me to deal quite expertly with accounting and auditing methods, but the firm had a rigid, hierarchy type of structure, which did not allow me to define my own functions or gain entrepreneurial experience. I would take advantage of internships offered through Babson in order to see firsthand the structure of an American business. I think this would provide a model to consider in my own undertaking, as well as introduction to American-style management.

I also believe a Babson MBA will help broaden my business perspective. After becoming frustrated with the rigid structure in Deloitte-Touche, I moved to a consulting firm, DG Conseil, a much smaller company which allowed me to create my own position as marketing manager. This job did give me more management responsibility, but I in no way feel ready to risk opening a business at this stage. I simply was not exposed to enough situations that one likely encounters as entrepreneur. Because Babson stresses real management case studies, this education would give me tools in a short time to rise to different occasions presented by the real world. Also, I am not satisfied with just knowing a little about French companies. I would like to make my perspective broader, as more and more firms do business across borders. I would also like a chance to use English in my career and I think it is best to study business issues in this language, which is even in Europe considered the "language of business."

Naturally I would not be ready immediately upon graduating to open a business. I would like to work for two to three years in a consulting company, with greater responsibility than I had at DG Conseil. Because my background is so technical, many firms are reluctant to hire me, even if I can most surely do the job. The Babson name and qualification would make me more marketable to businesses, which ensures that I get good position, responsibility, and experience soon. I would especially like to work in the States, and hope even maybe to establish contacts for future work while at Babson. Its closeness to Boston would make this an easier search, or at least give me ideas about what sort of company to pursue before coming back to France.

Because Babson promises an entrepreneurial foundation, plus a broad business perspective, as well as its location in a place in America I have always wanted to live, I am quite committed to this school as my first choice for the MBA.

COMMENTS

1. Sylvie's determination is brought out in terms of being just a "farm girl" who has never had things given easily to her. By writing an optional essay that conveys in concrete, evocative words her origins, she was able to show how much she has pushed to get where she is in life (a successful Parisian businesswoman). Showing herself to be from a farming background separates her from the majority of candidates who have a predominantly middle-class background.

2. She shows that whatever she has undertaken, she has accomplished in an exemplary way, always going beyond what is required of her:

    A. She not only went to college (a considerable feat in her circumstance), but graduated first in her class.

    B. In materials not included here, she mentioned that she completed her CPA requirements in two years, instead of the usual five or six, which necessitated her working evenings and weekends and sacrificing her vacations.

3. Her provincial background, strong undergraduate academic performance, and years of successful work experience are all worth emphasizing, both for their own sake and to counteract the impact of a low GMAT score. The first of these factors suggests a reason for not performing so well on the GMAT, whereas the latter factors suggest her underlying analytical skills.

4. The same is true of her small-group essay. She shows that her provincial background and undergraduate accounting study do not prevent her from discussing obscure historical figures. Discussing how the group should work as a group suggests that she has given some thought to the question, because implicit is the question of why you have selected them together, not just individually. In addition, showing her gratitude to her hard-working father strikes a very nice note. It would have been nearly impossible for this to work as well if she had not demonstrated her independence and maturity via her schooling away from home and two successful jobs. Had she been applying right out of college, her invocation of her father would have suggested immaturity rather than gratitude.

5. Her ethics essay is very well reasoned and well stated. The depth and sophistication to most of her answers rebuts the provincialism and weak GMAT indictments.

6. Her essays reveal her to be very hard working. Her key themes, which she establishes very successfully, are clearly persistence and hard work.

7. Her Stanford application is superficial, however, in showing how Stanford could help her. Her Babson essay, in contrast, does a very good job of demonstrating that she understands the nature of the Babson program and knows precisely how it will be useful to her.

8. She writes nearly lyrical essays, especially for an accountant. This is uncommon and very useful, especially for a non-native English speaker.

ALBERT

Background:

Job: Electrical engineer/consultant

Education: Doctorate in electrical engineering

Nationality: Cameroonian

Critical issue to address:

Low GMAT score

COLUMBIA

1. Discuss your career plans, and what has influenced these plans.

I would like to attain a high-level management position in a large international firm. I have come to realize that my current career path will not easily permit me to reach my goal, which is why I am considering an MBA at this time. Several factors have led me to this realization.

While I began my career as an assistant instructor of computer science in Cameroon, it might be more appropriate to view my three and three-quarter years with Electricité de France (EDF) as the starting point.

This project (described in Essay 2) was decisive in determining my career path. I was satisfied with this project from an analytical point of view, but not in other ways. My position as researcher and the bureaucratic nature of this public enterprise gave me little opportunity to implement the changes my research clearly called for. The introduction to management (I was entirely responsible for the project), along with the frustration at my lack of influence, made me determined to seek a more influential position in which I could push abstract achievement into practical value. This realization made me turn away from the idea of becoming a scholar, and made me resolve to seek a career in the business world.

This sense of frustration at my lack of influence led me to take a job as project engineer for Cap Gemini Sogeti. I manage small groups of three to four engineers, working in close collaboration with clients. This work has given me the opportunity to examine firsthand several types of industries, including communications, aeronautics, transportation, and heavy industry. I have been pleased by many aspects of my job: I enjoy being a group leader; I enjoy being in a position to influence our clients to take positive action; and I have enjoyed working in a variety of industries and countries.

I am now at a point when I would like to take another large step in my career. I am proficient at, and well regarded for, what I currently do. However, I wish very much to move into high-level general management. I do not want to forsake the skills I have, but rather, through greater management skills, to bring them to bear with greater impact. Evolution to managerial positions for technical experts is a slow process, and at least in France, there seems to be a ceiling for those who are considered foremost as engineers. This prompts my desire to seek the MBA at this time.

After completion of MBA studies, I hope to join a firm like Cap Gemini, but in a different position. I hope also to be able to work in my native country, Cameroon. This latter desire may have to wait for a time, but eventually I intend to return to Cameroon. If opportunities to benefit my country are unavailable to me once I have the necessary set of skills, I will start my own firm. I believe that an MBA will provide me with the necessary management skills to take a leadership position in these future endeavors.

2. Describe the two accomplishments of which you are most proud.

My most substantial accomplishment was the completion of my PhD doctoral dissertation at Electricité de France in 1989.

My project was to model the dynamic behavior of power system loads. Loads are the consumption of electricity in a power system. I was required to analyze the production-consumption balance, which is critically important because electricity cannot be "stocked." Whereas production was known because it was determined by EDF, consumption was unknown since it depended mainly on users.

I consider this my most important accomplishment for three reasons. First, it was the most highly analytical project I had encountered. Numerous variables had to be defined and means of measuring them determined in order to create a software package that would encapsulate this knowledge. From this point of view, the project was quite successful. I created an elegant software package, which is still in use at EDF, and I was invited to publish and present a paper at the IFAC conference in Austria.

Second, I was introduced to the rigors of management. I had to manage input from experts, organize campaigns of on-site experimentation, and present clear progress reports both to my PhD committee and to EDF managers, whose interests were not always compatible. I had full responsibility for the project and completed it on schedule in four years. Finally, as I mentioned in the first essay, this project largely determined my career path.

Another achievement which I am proud of was a professional project at Cap Gemini Sogeti for FANSTIC, a European program which studied air traffic control. I was pleased to be chosen as a representative for the French contingent of a pan-European program. I was able to meet engineers from Greece, the Netherlands, Belgium, and many other countries. In addition, the program was a cutting-edge study of new technologies at a research center established expressly for this purpose. Being able to hold my own in, and also to add value to, a group composed of some top European engineers greatly increased my personal and professional confidence, and gave me a clear, positive perspective on my own abilities.

From a career perspective, I realized that technical experts all over Europe share the same plight. It is very difficult for them to gain access to broad management. Their access to management positions proceeds through "natural evolution" which often takes ten to fifteen years, and still often remains limited in scope. This realization prompted me to begin considering the MBA as a means of achieving my goals.

3. Discuss your involvement in a community or extracurricular organization. Include an explanation of how you attained your position in the organization and how you help the organization meet its goals.

Young Cameroonians in France intent upon a business career lack the "networks" that can be helpful in giving career advice and support. Several friends and I decided to change this by forming the National Association of Cameroonian Executives, a group which provides a support system to Cameroonian business people in France. We meet regularly to discuss how to obtain a work permit, formulate a goal-oriented career plan, manage conflicts at work, etc.

While the organization originally started as a local group in Paris, interest in the group has caused us to expand to the national level. We now have over 250 members. Our increased size has allowed us to formulate more ambitious goals. For example, later this year we will host a conference which will bring together international companies with operations in Cameroon and young Cameroonian professionals working in France.

I am very proud of the success of our group, and am inspired by the feeling of community and commitment it brings. It means a great deal to me to be able to help my fellow Cameroonians reach their professional goals. Personal advancement without benefiting one's community is ultimately not rewarding.

4. **Discuss a personal failure.**

In 1988, ten friends of mine and I established a computer engineering consultancy. I did this "on the side" while still working for EDF. Part of our activity was devoted to transferring computer technologies to Africa.

At the beginning we met with some success, winning contracts both in Cameroon and in France. Two factors, however, eventually led to the dissolution of the business. Our group of partners had differing views on how to pursue the market, which the geographic dispersion of the company, and the fact that this was a part-time activity for many of us, made it difficult to resolve. Also, our undercapitalization limited the time we had in which to build agreement among the management team. Within two years, time had run out for our company.

I was naturally quite disappointed at having missed what seemed to be a great opportunity. Our group offered a wide range of talents and abilities, plus we had good market prospects and strong support from decision makers in Cameroon. It also seemed that we shared a rare blend of enthusiasm and commitment, fostered by the fact that we were all close friends engaged in a collaborative effort.

My objective had been, naturally, to establish a successful business. However, I eventually learned that enthusiasm and hard work are not enough in this regard. To achieve success in such a venture, a well-thought-out management structure is required from the beginning. In addition, even though the venture was unsuccessful, it gave me a taste for the freedom and excitement of setting up my own company, a possible option for the future. From this experience, I know that I must augment my management skills, including organizational ones, in order to succeed in such a project in the future.

5. **Describe a cross-cultural situation in which you were challenged and how you responded.**

This question is not simple to answer, because my entire life, as an African pursuing a business career in Europe, is a cross-cultural challenge! I am constantly reminded of my position as an outsider, and have had to cultivate much judgment and flexibility in navigating my professional life.

One aspect of this situation that particularly challenges me is the individualistic nature of French society. Life in Cameroon is much more community-oriented, and it is considered selfish to pursue solely personal aims. While I appreciate the relative freedom of this individual pursuit, I am sometimes distressed by the egotism and jealousy caused by this individualistic notion of success. I am especially disappointed by the lack of group spirit.

I adjust to this situation by devoting considerable time to the Association of Cameroonese Executives, which allows me to help others in my community. Also I try to bring a sense of group commitment to professional projects in my current job, which I think others appreciate and seem to respond to in the same spirit.

6. What has motivated you to apply to the Columbia Business School?

My reasons for wishing to attend Columbia are quite simple. My criteria for a business school are a perfect description of Columbia. I would like a program which is American but very international, located in a large east-coast city, and offers a well-balanced academic program.

I have wide exposure to European business, so I would prefer to learn more about American methods. In addition, I look forward to having the chance to pursue subjects in depth via a two-year program rather than a one-year one. These factors point me toward America, and especially toward Columbia.

KELLOGG

1. Briefly describe your career progression to date.

I began my career as an assistant instructor of computer science in Cameroon. This was just a means of paying for my studies at that time, however, so it might be more appropriate to view my three and three-quarter years with Electricité de France (EDF) as the starting point.

I was charged with modeling the dynamic behavior of power system loads, a project which also served to meet my PhD requirements. Loads are the consumption of electricity in a power system. I was required to analyze the production-consumption balance, which is critically important because electricity cannot be "stocked." Whereas production was known because it was determined by EDF, consumption was unknown since it depended mainly on users. I had to gather valid technical information, manage input from experts, organize campaigns of on-site experimentation, and present clear progress reports both to my PhD committee and EDF managers. The project was extremely analytical in nature, as it required numerous variables to be adequately defined and means of measuring them determined, in order to then create a software package which would encapsulate this knowledge.

I was satisfied with this project from an analytical point of view—insofar as I completed an elegant software package and had my thesis published and presented at the IFAC conference in Austria—but not in other ways. My position as a researcher, and the stratified bureaucratic nature of this public enterprise, gave me little opportunity to influence the implementation of needed changes.

My consequent dissatisfaction led me to take a job as project engineer for Cap Gemini Sogeti. I manage small groups of three to four engineers, working in close collaboration with clients. My work has extended across a variety of industries, including communications, aeronautics, transportation, and heavy industry. I have been pleased by many aspects of my job: I enjoy being a group leader; I enjoy being in a position to influence our clients to take positive action; and I have enjoyed working in a variety of industries and countries.

I am now at the point where I wish to take another large step in developing my career. I am highly proficient at, and well regarded for, what I currently do. I wish very much to move into general management, however, and the natural career progression for an engineer into general management is very slow. That is why I am hoping to pursue an MBA at this time.

2. **Your background, experiences, and values will enhance the diversity of Kellogg's student body. How?**

I believe that there are two things which separate me from the majority of applicants, and which would thereby enhance Kellogg's diversity.

The first is that because of my experience as a technical consultant I have had the opportunity to work in a variety of industries. My clients have included SNCF (the French national railroad system), RATP (Paris public transport), FANSTIC (a European community program which brought together engineers from across Europe to study air traffic control), Deutsche Aerospace, Volvo, IKEA, and many others. In group discussions I would be able to offer valuable information not only on technology and information systems, but also on the implementation of these in several types of industries. I have firsthand knowledge of both public- and private-sector enterprises and would be able to compare them in terms of management, culture, and business environment. For my classmates who were considering working abroad, I would be a source of information about business culture in France and Europe generally.

My African origin is another aspect which would bring diversity to Kellogg. I grew up in Cameroon and received my undergraduate education there. I have maintained a commitment to my community, while at the same time integrating myself into European professional life. (Because I am an outsider I have never taken European culture and business organization for granted; the pressures to adapt have given me a degree of sensitivity that many others lack.) It has been my experience that many are ignorant of the political and economic situations of Africa, and I would be able to offer valuable information and advice to those who were interested in doing business in Africa. I hope to be able to establish contacts while at school, both as a service to those who wish to go to Africa and also with the goal of developing my native country, to which I am most committed.

I hope that I would also add to the diversity of the social life at Kellogg. I am eager to share my own customs with others, whether it be discussing politics and traditional life, or sharing meals, soccer games, and stories. Americans are famous for their openness to new cultures, and I am eager to be a part of this cultural exchange.

3. For fun I . . .

The activity I appreciate most during my leisure time is to play soccer with friends. We meet regularly on Saturday afternoons at one of the Paris stadiums, organize in two teams, and have a match.

This is so enjoyable because it is completely informal and spontaneous. (We are not even registered as a permanent club at the police station.) The teams change every time, so that we have a chance to play with and against each of our fellows. These meetings also give us a chance to chat, to laugh, and to relax from the difficult work week. From time to time, we even organize weekend excursions to other cities (Orleans, Rennes, Rouen, Strasbourg) to meet our comrades there. The usual program consists of sightseeing in the morning, soccer throughout the afternoon, and dancing in the evening until our strength gives out.

4. I wish the Admissions Committee had asked me *what my conception of leadership is*.

Since the moment I opened my eyes, I saw the French and English in power in Cameroon, dominating our society with their superior strength and technology. Their "leadership" of our society failed because they had only very selfish goals. The native governments which replaced them also failed, due to lack of skill rather than lack of community orientation. I see many examples at work of such leadership through force, rather than knowledge, and without community orientation. I view them as leading to imminent danger as a result.

A traditional Cameroonian views himself as part of a larger community. Consequently, a leader should work as part of the community, influencing people through his knowledge rather than his hierarchical authority, being successful because of his knowledge and because he is seeking what is best for his group, not mere personal glory. I try always to bring this spirit to my work.

YALE (Selected)

1. Please describe your learning goals in the MPPM training as applied to your career plans.

I hope to move from engineering to general management. Part of the reason for this is a simple need to keep growing personally and professionally. Another reason is that I have a great desire to be able to manage not just something technical, but rather a whole operation. Underlying these desires is my devotion to Cameroon: I think that I can make the most positive impact upon the country by being more than an engineer. By being a general manager with a strong technical background I hope to be able to work for, or establish myself, a company which will have a positive, modernizing impact upon the country.

Yale's program is of particular interest to me because my background is in both public- and private-sector organizations. I am unable to say whether I will work in one rather than the other sort in the future. In all likelihood, I will end up working in both.

Whether I am in the public sector or the private one, I feel that I do not yet understand enough about the nontechnical, managerial dimensions of issues. I hope to learn much more than I currently know about marketing, finance, organizational development, and, indeed, about general management. (One of my reasons for applying to a two-year program, by the way, is because I think that it will be beneficial to have more instruction than is available in one of the ten-month European MBA programs.) I hope to learn enough from the MPPM program so that, with a little further seasoning in terms of experience, I can lead a large, integrated team of professionals. In other words, I hope to be able to be in charge of the type of effort my friends and I once undertook (as I described in essay 1), but with the appropriate degree of understanding of "the big picture."

MIT-SLOAN SCHOOL OF MANAGEMENT (Selected)

1. **Describe a situation you encountered in your employment or educational experience that required organizational change. Tell how you would effect that change as the manager in charge and what skills you expect to learn at MIT to help you accomplish this.**

My work for Electricité de France (EDF) involved some very large experiments which had to be conducted on site without shutting down the rail network. The engineering difficulties involved in doing this were often immense. On the other hand, the managerial difficulties were, if anything, even greater.

My first step, after designing my desired "campaign," was to discuss the experiment with the local technicians who would have to help me carry it out. I needed to make sure that they understood what would be involved, just as I needed to learn from them of any local complications—often political—which would necessitate changing target dates (or even sites).

My next step was to convince the head of my department that this was both necessary and doable. Then my department head had to contact the head of the department of the local site to get his approval, without which no work could possibly proceed.

This background work was just a prelude to the formal approval process. Formal description of the experiment, along with all possible requirements and work schedule implications, had to be provided to the local site's department head. He would ordinarily respond to this about two months later. He would often deny the request because he received no direct benefit from the activity, whereas his department might be inconvenienced by the work. His was not the only department which had to agree to the work. Various finance departments, for example, needed to approve.

The basic problem was that EDF was highly departmentalized, despite being in a business requiring a system-wide view of many activities. This tendency was exacerbated by the fact that almost no one understood, let alone sympathized, with the activities of another department. Very few people, for example, have ever worked in more than one department. Neither are there in place liaison offices or standing committees to coordinate information and activities between the departments with the greatest need to work together. This is despite the fact that many activities naturally cross many of the company's departmental boundaries.

My suggested solution to the problem of excessive departmentalization of the company is, first, to acknowledge the existence of the problem, and, second, to institute the job rotation and other programs noted above as lacking.

I think that EDF suffers from not looking at the overall picture of the business it is in. I am applying to MIT because I think that it offers me an opportunity to learn about technology management as one aspect of general management. In other words, I expect to understand this overall picture by learning about the functional disciplines I know too little about now, and by combining functional knowledge with organizational understanding. (It has not escaped my attention that MIT's faculty includes famous organizational specialists like Dr. Schein.)

COMMENTS

1. Albert was easily able to overcome his weak GMAT score by emphasizing his strong educational background and the heavy analytical component of much of his work.

2. It was important to make it clear that he was truly African rather than largely Europeanized, to retain the uniqueness value of his being African, a rarity among applicants at top business schools. Thus he emphasized his commitment to his community by talking about his intention to return to Cameroon, his founding of the Cameroon Executive Association, his Cameroonian soccer pals, etc.

3. By the same token, he needed to show that he could succeed at a top business school, so he discussed his success at French universities and with a top consulting engineering firm.

4. To help make up for the low GMAT score, he also discussed his highly analytical dissertation topic on power system loads.

5. Columbia essay 2 gives a good explanation of a technical problem. It is clear why it mattered to him, and he shows that despite being a doctoral dissertation it had a real-world dimension as well.

6. He consistently elevates himself by elevating the group that he is dealing with. By praising his company, he also encourages a school to believe that he would also be a good advocate for it later on.

7. In Columbia essay 4 he shows that he understands why his effort failed and does a good job of tying it to his need for an MBA. In addition, as an engineer it is useful to emphasize his business experience to show that his interest in an MBA is eminently sensible.

8. His discussion of why he wants to attend Columbia, however, is very thin. Simply noting that it is international and in a large East Coast city does not do justice to the program.

9. Note how good he is at telling stories. He sets things up by describing the story's background, establishes the conflict, and then describes the resolution.

JOERG (See also his Kellogg application in Chapter 8, "Marketing Yourself.")

Background:

Job: Working as an intern to finish engineering doctoral
                  degree project

Education: Finishing doctoral degree in mechanical engineering at a
                  leading German university

Nationality: German

Critical issues to address:

Lack of full-time work experience.

Having already pursued master's and doctorate degrees, is he a perpetual
student?

A German doctoral student in engineering inevitably runs the risk of being
regarded as a humorless nerd.

Is his English close enough to perfectly fluent to allow him to succeed in a
case method program?

HARVARD BUSINESS SCHOOL

1. **What evidence can you present to demonstrate your capacity to perform well
    in the Harvard MBA program?**

    I am assuming that there are several requirements for superior academic performance
    at Harvard. First, that one must be able to sort, assimilate, and master a large amount
    of data. Second, that one must be bold enough to contribute in the competitive atmos-
    phere of case-based classes. And third, that one should be of a cooperative enough
    nature to benefit his or her study group. I am thus assuming that intellectual ability
    (of a certain nature), competitiveness or aggressiveness, and a cooperative spirit are
    the desired components of a potential MBA student. (The last two may be taken to be
    in conflict, but I view them as situationally based in this regard.)

    My intellectual capabilities, and especially my ability to process information extreme-
    ly quickly, are evident from my success in my undergraduate, master's, and doctoral
    engineering work. I have taken far less time to complete my studies than the average
    student does—about 2.5 years less, worked far more on the outside to support myself,
    and still stayed in the top one-tenth of my class throughout my studies at what may
    be Germany's finest engineering program. On top of this, I fully expect to have a sub-
    stantial patent result from work I have directed, as discussed in another essay.

    My competitive spirit is probably already suggested by the above. My determination,
    my desire to seize opportunities, on the other hand, may not be quite so obvious at this
    point. In fact, I think that I have almost routinely made much more of situations I have
    been in than would have seemed possible for most people. In order to pay for my mas-
    ter's studies, for example, I did some computer consulting work for a marketing con-
    sultancy. I was able to demonstrate quite quickly to the owner (Mr. R. Wehmeyer), that

I was willing and able to acquire new skills, so he ended up hiring me to perform various types of marketing work as well! I did analyses of upmarket male and female customer purchase criteria regarding different types of clothing, boutique site selection criteria, etc.

My verbal abilities should not be an issue in regard to competing for air-time in classes. I have held my own in this regard, in English, in wide-ranging scientific discussions with senior colleagues in the United States at the University of Wisconsin, Madison, in Japan, and in Germany.

My cooperative spirit is perhaps best demonstrated by my leading a team of researchers and technicians on my hair and fiber "shape stability" research project, discussed in other essays. This "team" is a team in name only. Its members are parts of different organizations, working in different places, and have been lent to me only on a "dotted line" basis. I can get results from them only to the extent that I can motivate them. This involves everything from convincing a technician to stay late to get additional data for me up to convincing a department head to allocate more money for me to buy experimental equipment. As my referees probably make clear, I have been highly successful in leading this team.

In sum, I think that I am well equipped to pursue an MBA at Harvard.

2. **Discuss a professional project which challenged your analytical skills.**

While working for the Wehmeyer consultancy in spring 1991 I was asked to analyze Mauritius' potential as a source of textiles. Several textile firms were located there. They offered what appeared to be decent quality textiles for a low price, making them possible alternatives to Hong Kong and Singapore suppliers.

The problem was that the real quality of cloths the manufacturers produced could not be determined simply from a test sample. Because this would be the first such contract for one of the local firms it was necessary to analyze its capabilities carefully.

Besides doing various analyses of the country concerning its infrastructure, etc., I had to analyze the quality of the cloth regularly woven there (as opposed to what might have been done specially for a sample). I used an expert system I developed to reveal the reason for specific failures in textile materials. I designed a system in the form of a "failure tree," using specific graphs and text shells connected by number codes. This system enables one to analyze woven material by tracing back faults to their specific mechanical, operator, or raw material problems.

I examined regular cloth—not samples—from each of these firms. I determined that one firm in particular would be a highly acceptable supplier, but that the others were inevitably going to encounter quality problems given the difficulties they were revealing via their current output. Our client decided to engage this firm as a supplier.

3. **While recognizing that no day is typical, we ask that you describe a representative work day.**

8:00 A.M.   I hand my last night's written work and letters to my secretary, check for time changes in today's meetings and notify colleagues of new developments affecting their work.

8:45 A.M.   I discuss yesterday's experimental results with a technician and plot today's experiments,taking account of what happened yesterday. Then I have Purchasing buy appropriate materials for future experiments.

9:30 A.M.   Update session with department managers at which budgeting and marketing changes are discussed, as are new developments from the labs— especially those with budgeting or scheduling implications.

10:30 A.M. Appointment with sales manager from Rodenstock company to discuss their instrumental equipment and performance and ask him for cost estimate.

11:30 A.M. Ask colleague in chemistry department for help concerning some experimental difficulties.

12:00 P.M. Meet my academic research advisor and people from various departments (marketing, other research group) for lunch.

12:45 P.M. Drive to patent lawyer's office to discuss new technical drawings and other ideas to see whether we might be infringing upon any existing patents.

2:15 P.M.   Call our sister research department in Hamburg to discuss the problems with their last batch of hair samples and then to order a new batch. Afterwards I visit a technician I hope to convince to do some experiments for me.

2:30 P.M.   Prepare presentation of recent results, about the impact of silicon-based shampoos on hair, for tomorrow's presentation to marketing. I compare our products to our competitors' in this regard.

4:00 P.M.   I lead a discussion concerning future experiments which will involve the use of our scanning electron microscope to determine the porosity of chemically treated hair.

5:00 P.M.   I go to the library to make copies of articles, patents, and specifications concerning my experiments and design work.

5:30 P.M.   End of the day tasks: I check today's letters and faxes and tomorrow's timetable, evaluate data from today's experiments, and dictate letters to chemical companies (in order to get a specific polymer for some new tests).

6:00 P.M.   My last hour is spent working on drawings for my robot hand.

7:00 P.M.   I leave the company, taking with me the articles I copied in order to do some background reading about recent developments in related fields.

4. Describe an ethical dilemma you have experienced firsthand. How did you manage to resolve the situation?

I designed a device to measure the shape stability ("body") of hair and fiber. This device, however, can only work in a climate-controlled room. Such a room eliminates the temperature and humidity changes which upset the ability of the device to monitor changes in shapes.

I needed to purchase such a climate-controlled room for my work. The cost to my company would equal approximately 40 percent of my total project budget, so it was very important that I minimize this expenditure.

The companies which offer this sort of room are, with one exception, "West" German. The exception is an "East" German company. Given the reunification of Germany, I had a strong personal desire to buy from the "East" German company in order to benefit the poorer section of our country. The problem was that their product was markedly inferior to the other companies' products.

I discussed the dilemma with the "East" German company, which did all it could to help me (and thereby help itself). Together we searched for ways to improve their product. They had remarkably motivated employees who were willing to work extremely hard, but that was insufficient to overcome all of the design defects involved. We searched for ways to cope with these design defects, such as buying in some parts from "western" firms, but we could not find a way to achieve the narrow tolerances my project required.

I reluctantly bought a room from one of the "western" companies.

5. **Describe your three most substantial accomplishments and explain why you view them as such.**

1. My finest accomplishment is nearing completion at the moment. I have been in charge of a complex research project at Hans Schwarzkopf GmbH, which should result in a patent in which I will hold a one-fourth share. The project itself, as I describe elsewhere on another essay, involves the building of a device to measure the shape stability ("body") of human hair in order to measure objectively and reliably the effectiveness of permanent wave products.

I was chosen to manage this project because of my expertise in fiber analysis, gained during my master's degree study. (A moderate competence in chemistry, such as I possess, was also required.) The actual task, however, has required as much managerial as technical skill.

My job has involved pulling together various strands of analysis in a rich mix of fields, including robotics, organic (peptide) chemistry, and image analysis employing a variety of mathematical techniques. I need to do some parts of this work myself, delegate and supervise the rest, and provide the necessary machinery and materials for the whole team. Thus the need for me to be both scientist and manager.

The project is on schedule for a planned patent application in early 1993. A likely patent is one measure of success, but I also value this project for another reason. I have had to manage a far-flung, disparate group of people in a variety of organizations, who did not necessarily owe me any loyalty or favor, in the complex process of developing a new machine, and I have succeeded in doing so.

2. My second most important accomplishment will be the completion (in spring 1993) of my BA, MA, and PhD in Mechanical Engineering in approximately two and a half years less time than the average student requires, without sacrificing the breadth or depth of my studies. In addition, this will have been done at Germany's finest engineering school.

I very much wanted to have a "practical" engineering capability, not just academic/laboratory skills, so I sought out a wide range of traineeships in German and Japanese companies. These ranged from production engineering in a Japanese "just in time" factory, through foundry engineering in one of the biggest steel manufacturers in Germany, to computer-aided design engineering in a German nuclear power station company. I also managed to hone my academic abilities by taking, for example, an assistantship at the University of Wisconsin, Madison, which allowed me to work on advanced mathematical theories relevant to computer aided engineering for polymer processing work.

I had to support myself through my studies, since my parents are disabled. As a result, I worked part time for two business consulting firms throughout large parts of my education.* Despite my efforts to gain a great deal of hands-on engineering experience and my need for income, I was still able to progress extremely rapidly through these degree programs while maintaining a top 10 percent class rank.

3. My third accomplishment relates to my work for a marketing consultancy, Rudolf Wehmeyer Marketing Beratung. This work provided me with an opportunity to gain valuable business experience while also allowing me to realize that I have some talents useful in the business arena.

I began my relationship with the firm as a computer consultant, employed by Consultax. Wehmeyer appreciated the work I performed for it sufficiently to lure me away from Consultax. Wehmeyer's business focused on consulting to clothing firms, so it thought I could be of value with my background in both computers and textile engineering. Despite my lack of marketing experience, I was chosen for projects which required an understanding of both marketing and information systems.

Wehmeyer chose me for this work, in fact, because I had succeeded in a complex project of exactly this type for Wehmeyer itself. Wehmeyer had a chain of clothing stores which was using an antiquated order entry and inventory management system. It wanted to be able to perform these tasks in a simple manner, but it also wanted to gain marketing advantages as well, by tracking marketing sales trends by region, store location, type of customer, garment, color, size, etc. My work required that I understand their marketing efforts as a prelude to designing an appropriate information system.

Wehmeyer saw that I could understand quickly the connection between marketing desires and information system requirements, so it recruited me. Although I began as a system "expert," I ended up doing a lot of pure marketing work. I am proud of having been able to switch fields so successfully. (Besides feeling a degree of pride, I was also motivated to seek out a variety of business courses to audit in preparation for an eventual business career.)

*I had sought this work because I could not subsist on the poorly paid apprenticeship offered to German engineering students. This consultancy work, although not closely related to my studies, nevertheless offered the opportunity to make the money I needed. It was my good fortune that it changed my career orientation as it did.

6. **Discuss a contribution you have made in your community.**

I have long been involved in the International Club in Jülich, which is dedicated to helping the foreign scientists, and their families, who came to work at the Forschungszentrum

Jülich (Jülich Research Center). It was due to my membership in this club that I came to get a student out of the People's Republic of China.

I met Fanzhia Ling* after she had broken her arm in a bicycle accident. I helped her to get worker's compensation, then helped her get back the pension payments she had previously made to the government (based on the fact that she will not retire in Germany). I now manage this money for her, which is the only independent source of funds she has. All of her official earnings were split fifty-fifty with the PRC government (which we have kept ignorant of this other sum).

Fanxhia Ling went back to China, at which time she told me that she wanted her money kept as a secret reserve account for her son, Li Ling,* who hoped to come to Germany to study in the future.

I eventually arranged for Li Ling to come to Germany, but only after countless interventions for him. Li Ling began German lessons in Xiang. After six months of study he applied for a passport, while I simultaneously arranged for him to be admitted to the University of Cologne. My family served as his financial guarantors as well. The University's acceptance was conditional upon his passing a German exam and arriving at the University before March 1989.

The Chinese government refused him a passport. I arranged for the University of Cologne to postpone his enrollment, giving him time to reapply for a passport. He was given oral approval for a passport, but this was withdrawn after the Tiananmen Square events (in which he was tangentially involved, in Xiang). I got the University to renew its offer of a place once again. I also telephoned Li Ling's father to request that he speak with the Chinese ministry about his son. He was unable to do this initially, because the ministry was sealed off in the aftermath of the Tiananmen Square events. He eventually did reach the appropriate official and miraculously convinced him to issue a passport.

The last phase of this effort concerned the refusal of the German embassy in Beijing to issue Li Ling a visa, based on its view that Li Ling did not speak German well enough to qualify for a student visa. I spoke with the embassy. The embassy relented and agreed to issue a visa. Then, however, the official in charge of this left on vacation, necessitating a second round of convincing yet another official, in order to secure Li Ling's visa just days before the University year began.

Li Ling is now an excellent student at Cologne and he does indeed speak German fluently.

*This is a pseudonym; her/his real name, as well as the actual university attended and other relevant details, should remain disguised.

7. Discuss a situation in which you influenced a group.

My research project at Hans Schwarzkopf GmbH, discussed elsewhere in my application, requires that I motivate people who have been temporarily "borrowed" for my project. These researchers and technicians come from three different independent groups in the research department, all with large responsibilities and tight deadlines facing them.

The challenge of getting output from resources I do not own could be tackled in several ways. I decided to act opposite to the manner in which other research department project managers typically act. They try to pressure people and to control their actions directly. This attempt at direct, tight control does not seem to work very well. The people being controlled resent the heavy-handed approach and rebel.

I decided to emphasize friendliness and involvement instead of direct control. For those interested in the intellectual elements of the project, I explain at great length the goals of the whole team and how interesting their work will be. I keep them informed about the interesting developments across the project. For those interested in a more personal work relationship, especially with a leader of one of their projects, I find time to discuss their personal and work-related problems. In general I try to make the team's members feel part of a group, one which is engaged in important and interesting work, and one that can succeed only if their own efforts measure up.

The results seem to me to be an endorsement of this approach to motivation, at least in my current environment. Our project is on schedule and on budget. And, I have not done anything like setting fictitious deadlines or publicly belittling someone—which would prevent my working with these same people again. In fact, our collaborative effort will make a second project that much easier to manage than the first has been.

8. What are your post-MBA career plans?

I have pursued my education in mechanical engineering to the doctoral level because of my interest in technical manufacturing matters. My interest in getting an MBA stems from my desire to work in manufacturing industries in ways which require both engineering and business experience.

(I know that this route to a business career—via an engineering doctorate—may seem odd to Americans, but to Germans it is perhaps the most respected route to such a career.)

My short-term plans are to work in marketing for a reinforced composite material company, such as Mitsubishi, Du Pont, or ICI. My in-depth knowledge of the technical side of this industry, combined with my continuing interest in the field, suggest that this is an area I should focus on. Eventually I would hope to be involved in establishing new markets in the Far East, combining my own interest in that region with the opportunities provided by rapidly industrializing markets.

My long-term plans are to own and run a business in a related field which focuses on a niche market (which I hope to spot while working for the above-mentioned reinforced composite material company). By the time I set out to develop or purchase such a specialized and focused company, I expect to have the marketing and general management skills that, combined with my technical capabilities, will allow me to do a first-rate job leading such a firm.

COMMENTS

1. Overall, this is a very well written, complete, unified application. Joerg shows that he has had plenty of real-world experience despite having been a student throughout the last seven–eight years. In addition, he provides the German context to his education, which shows that his pursuit of so many degrees is actually appropriate for someone seeking to get to the top of German industry. He also shows that he is quite well-rounded and has a deep humanitarian streak, thereby eliminating the

"humorless nerd" problem. (His listing, in the résumé part of the application, of his travels, sporting activities, and other hobbies also helped in this regard.) His very good command of English is demonstrated throughout the essays, helping to eliminate fears that his English would not be sufficiently good to survive an American MBA program, even a case method program.

2. Joerg's first essay makes it very clear that he understands what an MBA is all about, and in particular, what Harvard's case method system of education involves. He is then able to demonstrate that he possesses the requisite capabilities.

3. His third essay shows the great variety of his tasks and also avoids lapsing into professional jargon. In addition, he constantly talks about working with people, which is a useful counterbalance to his working as a laboratory engineer. The message is that he is able to communicate and work with nonengineers.

4. He succeeds in showing a surprising amount of business analysis and other experience for someone without lengthy full-time work experience. In fact, he makes it sound as though he has been working all of his life. This is meant to address the issue of whether he has sufficient work experience to be ready for an MBA program.

5. In essay 5 he handles a technical discussion with great clarity. This is always a plus, but especially when applying to a case method school (like Harvard) that emphasizes clarity of expression more than most.

6. In essay 5 he also discusses dealing with customers, again emphasizing that he is not just a laboratory nerd.

7. His discussion of his efforts to help get someone out of China is impressive both because of the results and because it is clearly not just a résumé blurb like signing up to help at a community soup kitchen two weeks before applying to business school.

TERRY

Background Data:

Job:	Commercial photographer
Education:	Bachelor's degrees (2) in German literature and fine arts
Nationality:	American
Other:	Based in Germany

Critical issues to address:

Is he quantitatively able enough to survive the program?

Is he analytical enough, given his mediocre college grades and work in an industry not noted for analytical skills?

Does he know enough about business and MBA programs to be sure that this is the right step for him, and are his goals for the future realistic enough that he will be employable when he finishes an MBA?

ROTTERDAM SCHOOL OF MANAGEMENT

1. **What are your career objectives? In what specific ways would attendance at the RSM help you to fulfill these intentions? (Explain how your study plan fits in with your previous training and your career objectives.)**

I trained as a photographer and have, since graduating six years ago from the Art Center (Pasadena), run my own commercial photography business in Munich. In this time I have learned a great deal about the advertising industry specifically and about business more generally. But I feel that I have reached the limit of what can be done here. I have surpassed my initial goals and, in fact, outgrown them. Having run a small business, I now want to learn how to manage a larger business, either my own or someone else's. This is why I want to earn an MBA; it is the most efficient way to learn all the components of how to run a business on a larger scale.

I understand a great deal about certain aspects of marketing and marketing imagery. I have gained much experience in analyzing customers and in intuitively understanding their needs and wishes. I have also dramatically improved my knowledge of selling in the past six years. Yet I want to study all the other principal aspects of running a business in much greater depth as well. And whereas I may know about these things for a small company in my particular industry, I would like to explore them on a larger scale and independent of my own particular business sector (advertising).

After completing an MBA I see myself working in marketing, either in a corporate structure or as a marketing consultant. Business-to-business marketing would be my area of choice, as opposed to consumer marketing, but I believe it would be a mistake to limit my future possibilities too soon. That would go against the reason why I want an MBA, which is to broaden my knowledge of business and my horizons, not to narrow them.

Although marketing is my natural field, I want to be able to perform well in other areas of business, too. Even if I do in the end spend the bulk of my career in marketing, I believe a solid knowledge of all aspects of business is indispensable for success at the highest levels in marketing. Just as a modern manager must be able to communicate with people of diverse cultural backgrounds, in order to effectively operate in the worldwide market, in the same sense he must also be able to communicate effectively with the various members of other departments of the company. For example, I suspect that a major hindrance to managing change effectively is the inability of many people within a company to see problems and changes from the other person's (and department's) point of view.

I want to get a high-quality MBA, with a marketing emphasis, from a very international school, preferably one located in Europe. RSM, with its strong core curriculum and attractive marketing electives, not to mention its outstanding reputation, fits my needs perfectly. I believe that RSM would provide an excellent "bridge" between my previous work experience running my own business and my future career marketing goals.

2. **Please give an account of your personality (your strengths and the traits that you would like to improve).**

I would describe myself as Creative, Inquisitive, Resourceful, Self-Confident, and Organized. *Creativity* is the one trait without which I could not imagine myself. Whatever I am doing, be it private or business, active or passive, I think about how I could do it differently, in a way perhaps no one has before. My *inquisitiveness* as a child was so well known that my friends often called my by the nickname "Questions." Fortunately this natural curiosity of a child has never left me. I was drawn to commercial photography through this curiosity, along with my desire to use my creativity and *resourcefulness* professionally. I was also attracted by the opportunity to work with so many different types of people and businesses, as is possible in advertising.

Self-confidence can be both a strength and a weakness. It has helped me a great deal in many aspects of my life, for example in starting up my own business in a foreign country. But it can have a negative side, for example when I become overconfident and neglect to analyze a given situation carefully enough.

One of the first things clients tell me they notice about me is my passion for *organization*. A large part of my clients being German, a nation notorious for its organizational zeal, makes this praise all the more remarkable. This strength also leads to my greatest weakness: my habit of getting too involved in the details, even on occasions when it would be better to concentrate on the general picture. Being aware of this tendency helps me in my effort to improve it.

3. Discuss your interests outside of your job.

At the risk of it sounding like a cliché, I must admit that my greatest interest in life is my family. As the father of a four-year-old daughter and two-year-old son, I am daily confronted with such endless curiosity, energy, enthusiasm, and other sources of joy and fascination that I would hardly require any other interests. Nevertheless I do have many other areas of interest, which I pursue whenever possible. The first one began early in my life—*internationalism.* My parents raised me in a very international atmosphere. From my fifth year on we spent every other summer traveling outside the United States, principally in Europe, but also through many other parts of the world. The alternate summers we traveled throughout America. These travels imbued me with an insatiable interest in the world, in all of its many cultures and nations, not just in their present state, but throughout history. They also were critical in forming my own view of myself. I do not see myself as an American living and working in Europe. I see myself as an international person with a European cultural base. This strong international aspect of my childhood's family life has, not so coincidentally, also been carried over into my adult family life: my wife is half Italian and half German. Our children are consequently citizens of three different countries. At home we speak English, German, and Italian.

I am also very interested in history and *literature.* I was torn between the two when it came time to choose my major for my first undergraduate degree. I wanted a major which would allow me to pursue a strong liberal arts education, and both were well suited. In the end I chose German Literature over history because of its added benefit of giving me the opportunity to learn a second language at the same time. Nevertheless, history remains one of my greatest interests, particularly ancient history. When I can find the time, I especially enjoy reading original texts from ancient authors.

Another strong interest of mine is *astronomy.* Although I was able to take only one general course on astronomy while at university, it is a subject which never ceases to fascinate me. The infinite vastness of the subject, and the endless possibilities involved in theorizing about the nature—past, present, and future—of our universe, is indescribable. One aspect of astronomy which I find especially interesting is its nature as a science where one can spend an eternity studying it purely from the perspective of physical laws and mathematical equations, or equally well studying it strictly from a philosophical point of view as the ultimate subject of metaphysics.

I also enthusiastically enjoy *sports.* Tennis is my favorite sport, and the one I have participated in on a competitive basis as well as recreationally. Aside from tennis, I also enjoy skiing, squash, and golf.

4. Describe a situation when your objectives were not met and what you learnt from it.

Aside from working for companies through their advertising agencies, I also work with many companies directly, usually with their marketing departments. In one such case I was given the job of producing an image for the cover of the annual report of a large German bank. This single image was of immense importance to the bank. They wanted it to incorporate many different symbols of their diverse business activities. I set myself the objective of producing an image which would satisfy all of their needs.

This developed into an extremely complicated production. Logistically it was necessary to plan, organize, and then construct a complex set in the studio. Creatively it was a challenge to develop an image which could communicate so much without departing from the bank's established corporate imagery. I was successful in designing and building the studio set and in developing what I regarded as an appropriate image. This "success" was for naught, however, because I failed to maneuver successfully the complex hierarchy of decision makers inside the bank's marketing department. At the first level of authority, the person I dealt with initially had no real authority to make decisions on her own. Hence she could give me information as to the client's wishes, but she could not make commitments as to how these should be visually realized. At the second level, her boss, who could, was only sporadically available for consultation, even though the project was being done under great time pressure. At the third level, the person ultimately responsible for the annual report was essentially unavailable. This structure of building walls between each level of authority made it impossible for me, within the given time constraints, to determine what the client really wanted to communicate and how.

I had failed to establish at the outset of the project exactly what they wanted from me, and to make clear the degree of communication I would require of them in order to complete the project on schedule. Because of this failure they did not use my photographs. This experience showed me the great importance of determining the goals and structures of cooperation—how two partners intend to work together—at the outset of a collaboration.

COMMENTS

1. Terry is very successful in addressing each possible issue raised by his candidacy. His quantitative abilities are addressed in part by his GMAT score and his noting in his interview that he had already enrolled in a Managerial Economics class and had begun receiving individual tutoring in calculus. He addresses the issue of his analytical abilities indirectly by presenting his essays in a very persuasive way and by discussing hobbies that have an intellectual component (such as astronomy). He addresses the business interest and knowledge issue by demonstrating that he has long been in business insofar as his photography operation is first and foremost a business.

2. Note how he gets right into a discussion of his business background and success at the beginning of the first essay. He knows that one of the concerns he needs to address is the extent to which he has a business background, appropriate goals for an MBA program, knowledge of what an MBA program entails, etc. He goes a long way to answering these concerns in the first half of this essay. Similarly, his comments about his goals for future employment sound sensible. He shows that industrial marketing would not be too much of a stretch from what he has already done. Last, his discussion of managing change and communicating within companies sound like a young corporate executive's views rather than those of a photographer, further emphasizing his solid business background. The message: He is a businessman who happens to be in the commercial photography business, rather than an artistic spirit unaware of business.

3. Terry's discussion of his outside interests in essay 3 suggests that he has strong intellectual interests, in history and astronomy, to lend depth to his self-portrait. In terms of the critical issues he faced, this helps deal with possible concerns about his analytical capability. His discussion of his sporting interests is meant to show that he will fit in with the young executive crowd at business school, rather than to impress anyone with his great skill or unusual interests. (As a photographer, the questions for him concern whether he can fit in with the business school environment, not whether he can stand out in terms of bringing something unusual.) The essay's initial focus on fatherhood marks him as mature. The rest of the essay shows him to be thoughtful and interested in the world. He would probably be an interesting and engaging conversational partner.

4. His last essay shows him as a photographer, which is nearly absent from the other essays and is thus important here. It also shows that he has had extensive involvement with corporate organizations and issues, which is relevant to the concern about his business background and understanding.

5. Terry had his recommenders address his analytical capabilities (in addition to all their other comments), which was a sensible move, given his mediocre undergraduate results. (It should be mentioned, however, that he did extremely well in his second bachelor's degree.)

INSEAD (Selected)

1. Describe what you believe to be your most substantial accomplishment to date, explaining why you view it as such.

Coming from America to Europe to establish my own commercial photography business is an accomplishment of which I am quite proud. Setting up one's own business for the first time is probably always difficult; doing this far away from home is a further challenge. After managing to overcome the hurdles of German legal codes and permits, I had to learn how to market myself and my services. My lack of local contacts required that I make endless phone calls, introductions, and presentations. The result of this lengthy marketing blitz was that my presentational and marketing skills, in English but even more so in German, improved dramatically.

To be successful I also have had to manage ad hoc teams on a routine basis. One has to be able to work together with an incredibly diverse group of people in commercial photography. To maximize the team's performance requires learning what is important to whom, and what is not, and how to get the best out of each person—to discover their strengths and put them to use. Given the extreme time constraints common in this industry, it is impossible to work alone. Teamwork is crucial both within my own studio, and with all the external parties involved: client, ad agency, production services, etc.

A prerequisite for my work is being able to lead a team. I am ultimately responsible, but all members of the team bring in fresh input and ideas. The atmosphere is one of great openness for new insights, possibilities, and differing opinions. Thus the potential exists for this creativity to turn to chaos. It is up to me to be a veritable circus leader, integrating the different inputs, troubleshooting the ongoing project to be sure that each person is contributing what is needed at the right moment, and controlling the flow of events through to the postproduction conclusion. In an environment where people come together for one project rather than on a long-term basis, this integration and control function is of crucial importance.

I view the experience of setting up my own business as my most substantial accomplishment to date because of the great challenge it represented to me—and as a result of all that it has given me the opportunity to learn. Part of that learning is to have faith in my ability to meet difficult challenges.

2. What would be your main contribution during your time at INSEAD?

My main contribution at INSEAD would be the unique set of skills and experiences that I have acquired in the course of my professional and private life. On the professional side, I feel I would fit very well into INSEAD's mixture of different business backgrounds. Also, I am used to working very hard, an absolute necessity when running one's own company. At the same time, I feel I can offer other students some unique qualities to balance their particular professional backgrounds: I would come into the program from the entrepreneurial side and also from the artistic side. As an entrepreneur I have learned a great deal about: how different cultures require different approaches for making business connections or selling; how important it is to recognize priorities specific to a given business; how to recognize the "unwritten" guidelines that clients often ultimately use when deciding with whom they will work; how to invest energy, time, and capital wisely and effectively, taking chances where the potential is worthwhile and yet recognizing when it is time to "write off" a bad investment; and taking responsibility not just for one's own actions, but also for the entire business. As a photographer, I have learned to see things from a more creative perspective than most "normal" business people. I would also contribute to the diversity of the school's intellectual base through my strong visual and design sense. I can bring these viewpoints to discussions and team projects as a contrast to the likely views of students from a more traditional corporate background.

On the private side, I feel I would contribute to INSEAD's very international atmosphere. As I mentioned earlier, as an American who has spent a large part of his life traveling and working outside of America, I am used to dealing with people from many different cultures. In fact, my wife is half Italian, half German. Our children are consequently citizens of three different countries. At home we speak English, German, and Italian. Last, but not least, I would contribute my legendary (!?!) sense of humor and natural talent for making friends.

COMMENTS (regarding the two INSEAD essays)

1. In the first essay, Terry makes a good case for being a good team player and leader in an interesting business setting. He goes into some detail regarding how his projects function because it is unlikely that the admissions committee knows much about the commercial photography business and yet it is important that they see how he functions in his own milieu.

2. He starts the second essay by noting that he is from a business, not just an artistic, background. He is implicitly showing both that he would fit into the school, but is different enough from the usual applicant that he will also add value through his artistic and creative abilities. This is a critical point: A creative type can be a useful addition to a program because he is different, but if he is too different, and too unfamiliar with the business and academic environment he will face, he poses a large risk to the school.

3. Although his discussion (in essay 2) of the entrepreneurial skills he will bring to the program is not particularly impressive, the important point is that he does have this entrepreneurial side, which adds immeasurably to his value as a creative "type." After all, few creative, artistic candidates will also bring this entrepreneurial business perspective as well.

JON

Background Data:

Job at time of application:	Shipping executive
Educational background:	In-house "degree" from his shipping company, plus part-time business school coursework
Nationality:	Danish
Other:	Mother tongue Danish and Faroese, ultrafluent English, Thai

Critical issue to address:

His lack of a "proper" bachelor's degree could suggest a lack of analytical firepower in addition to lack of a credential.

LONDON

1. **Our students participate in the MBA programme for many valid reasons, for example: to change from a specialist to a broader career; to move upward within an organization; to change organizations or industries; to change job function or to work in a different country. Please explain why you wish to earn an MBA qualification. There is no "right" answer, so please be as frank as you can.**

I wish to earn an MBA qualification as it will significantly assist me in achieving my career goals.

Since I was 19 years old I have known the type of career I wanted. Working for seven years in a highly international environment, with a two year stay in the Far East, has only confirmed my decision.

I want a management position working for a multinational concern in a foreign country. Experience has shown me that I possess the personal qualifications needed to become a successful manager, and I feel that I can reach the very summit of a multinational concern significantly faster if equipped with the management tools taught at London Business School.

All of my experience has been in shipping, with just one company. As valuable and enjoyable as it has been, I recognize that I would be best served by exposure to new concepts and experiences. I want to get to the top of a large multinational, but to do so (even in shipping) will require that I develop knowledge and skills beyond those I now have. For example, as I note in the next essay, I want to gain a more profound understanding of finance and corporate strategy.

I also want to understand the nature and operations of other industries, since it is clear that no one industry such as shipping contains the best example of how to approach the full range of problems that I will encounter in my career. This exposure both to intellectual concepts and practical knowledge is most easily found, I suspect, at a highly reputed business school. I suppose that I could learn some part of what I seek by working for another firm in a different industry, but I certainly doubt that I will learn as much in a short time. After all, an MBA is meant to be a highly organized intensive learning experience.

An MBA will allow me to work without boundaries. It will assist me in becoming a truly "global executive," a career path which is the logical consequence of my upbringing and education, as I have always considered it one of the largest intellectual challenges in life to work and function in a culture different from my own.

My conclusion is that the education I am looking for is best achieved by earning an MBA qualification from London Business School. Its international environment will train me for future work in foreign cultures with foreign languages and, last but not least, significantly different ways of doing business.

I already have substantial management experience and I want further management education, but not the one-size-fits-all type of education. I want to be able to pursue certain key areas in real depth. As I mentioned above, I intend to focus on finance and corporate strategy. These are the factors which have led me to London Business School.

2. **Please explain what your experience at work tells you about your likely strengths and weaknesses as a manager and how you hope to see your career progress over the five years following the MBA programme. Please include an assessment of the effect of not obtaining a place on the MBA programme.**

The key word to describe my career progress and personal development over the next five years following the MBA programme will be: international. I determined many years ago that I want to pursue an international education and career and that focus remains unchanged. I am ready to work in any country in the world, as long as the job is challenging and rewarding.

In five years I anticipate working in a management position for a multinational company in a foreign country. I know one of my responsibilities will be to explore new business opportunities, both outside and within the borders of the country in which I am working. This responsibility will preferably lead to extensive deal-making and possible joint ventures, during which I will make full use of the finance and corporate strategy skills I have obtained at London Business School. All through my career I have been involved in new business projects of that kind and I have found it to be extremely challenging and stimulating.

No matter where in the world I work, I will continue expanding my knowledge of foreign cultures and languages. My interest in these issues has always been substantial and I expect my education in that field to continue for the rest of my life.

The internationalization of business has created a pool of expatriates who are working for foreign companies in foreign countries. These global executives speak several languages and know an industry or a foreign country very well. This group of people will inevitably grow over the next five years following the growing globalization of the business world, and I want to continue being a part of it.

If I do not obtain a place at the MBA programme I will still continue to pursue my career plans. I will, however, be forced to seek the necessary managerial tools elsewhere. This solution will obviously be more time consuming.

As described earlier, I am presently pursuing the second half of the Danish management education, H.D. This is not, however, on the same level as London Business School. I will continue with the H.D. if I am not accepted at London Business School, but I would be sorry to lose the opportunities which London Business School offers.

3. **Please describe what you believe to be the major trends in your industry.**

I believe that there are three major trends in the fuel oil industry:

- decreasing availability of fuel oil
- deteriorating quality of fuel oil
- implementation of drastic measures to prevent oil spills

Decreasing availability of fuel oil

Fuel oil is a by-product of the refining process when refining crude oil. It is primarily used for utilities and as fuel for larger vessels (when used in the maritime industry fuel oil is referred to as "bunkers").

Up until now, fuel oil has been readily available. In older refineries the fuel oil output amounts to 30%–40% of the crude oil volume processed. However, by means of advanced technology, this share is being significantly reduced. Newer refineries install so-called cat-crackers and hydro-crackers to break the molecular compounds in the crude oil. These refineries yield a larger amount of distillates, leaving only 10%–15% of fuel oil.

Refineries can also choose to install so-called cokers (at a cost of approximately US$ 1 billion per refinery unit). These refineries are so efficient in the refinery process that they leave no fuel oil at all.

Deteriorating fuel oil quality

Not only does the improved technology in the refining industry lead to lower fuel oil output but the quality of the fuel oil is also deteriorating. When refiners become better at extracting the best products such as gasoline and gas oil from the crude oil, the by-product, the fuel oil, is of a lower quality.

The increasingly poor quality is forcing the major shipping lines to take measures to protect themselves against fuel oil that is not within the international ISO specifications.

A.P. Moller has, as a direct consequence of the deteriorating fuel oil quality, introduced the concept of "predelivery testing" when bunkering around the world. The introduction of such a concept is necessary to protect the shipping companies against fuel oil which does not live up to the ISO specifications. A predelivery test is carried out by an independent surveyor 24 hours prior to the bunker delivery. The fuel is analyzed and compared to the ISO standards.

This way of avoiding expensive and time consuming off-loadings of nonstandard fuel from the vessels is slowly spreading in the market. The major shipping lines are beginning to copy the principle of never accepting a bunker delivery without a predelivery test. In the case of A.P. Moller, the concept has dramatically decreased the number of debunkerings.

Oil spills and OPA-90

As a consequence of the "Exxon Valdez" disaster in Alaska in 1990 the United States implemented the "Oil Pollution Act of 1990" (called OPA-90). The law makes it impossible for carriers of crude oil to limit their financial liabilities in case of an oil spill. As an example of the amounts involved, the U.S Coast Guard is requiring that all vessels taking bunkers in U.S. territory must present a bank account with a minimum deposit of US$50 million to cover the first part of the cleaning job after a possible oil spill. Possible environmental damage is notoriously difficult to quantify, which leaves open the possibility that a company could be held responsible for highly speculative damages.

The introduction of such drastic measures has been a hard blow to my industry. It is presently very difficult to buy fuel oil in U.S. ports. The majority of well-established oil companies have totally withdrawn from the U.S. bunker market—companies such as Texaco, Shell, and Mobil. The oil majors have withdrawn from the U.S. bunker market as they cannot afford to pay the insurance needed to meet a claim from the government in case of an oil spill.

The bunker industry in five years

I could easily foresee that in five years' time no vessels would take bunkers in U.S. ports since the consequences of an oil spill in U.S. waters are fatal for almost any company with the present U.S. legislation. Several U.S. suppliers have already seriously considered supplying bunkers in international waters.

Due to tighter and tighter availability and a deteriorating fuel oil quality, the marine industry could very well be forced to change from fuel oil to gas oil. Gas oil is a better product which is extracted at an early stage of the refining process. The availability is more or less unlimited and the quality superb.

However, due to the heavy investments required to take full loads of gas oil, the change from fuel oil to gas oil might not happen within the next five years, but rather within the next ten. The possible change from fuel oil to gas oil would significantly change the competitive situation in my industry. Japanese shipping lines are already using gas oil on board some of their vessels and the engines on board these vessels are built for that purpose.

That means that if the change occurs, the Japanese will have a major competitive edge by being one or two years ahead of their competitors with regard to investments in new engines, etc.

4. **Please describe a situation, either work or personal, where you faced particular frustration or difficulty. What was the outcome and what did you learn from the experience?**

I have chosen to describe the situation when I was repatriated to Denmark after having stayed in the Far East for only a little over two years. I had expected to be there for perhaps a decade or more. I found my unexpected repatriation frustrating and difficult to handle.

My contract in Thailand was open-ended. When I had stayed in the Far East for only a few months I was approached by the Far East Manager himself. He told me that I, and a few others in similar situations in countries in the Far East, should consider ourselves "life-time expatriates." He now believed he had gathered the strongest team possible in the Far East and had thus decided that all future job rotations should be among ourselves. He saw no reason to waste valuable experience by sending people to other parts of the world.

From that day on, I started planning my life accordingly. I traveled intensively in the Far East, not only in my capacity as Quality Coordinator but also during weekends and holidays. I made an effort to understand the various cultures in the Far East, to get to know the distinctions between the countries, and to familiarize myself with the A.P. Moller offices throughout the region.

After having stayed for two years in Thailand, I was approached by the Personnel Department in Denmark and told, much to my surprise, that I was to take up a position in the Oil Purchasing Department in Copenhagen. I was to become the right hand man for the manager of the department. My specific responsibilities were to be Far Eastern purchases, with a total budget of US$ 90 million. One of the A.P. Moller vice presidents, whom I had worked for before I was sent to Thailand, had made a strong case to get me for the position. The manager of the department had for some time needed someone with the ability to analyze potential cost savings and evaluate the existing working procedures.

The frustrating thing was, however, that I felt that this transfer was definitely not the best use of the company's resources. It had taken me two years to build a good network of national and foreign business people operating in Thailand. I spoke the language better than any Maersk expatriate before me and was in the unusual position of having the locals behind me in every project I initiated.

I would have liked to see the results of the projects which I had worked hard for: the establishment of a well-functioning marketing section, the foundation of the Danish Chamber of Commerce, my recommendation for our company to enter into business in Laos, the implementation of a Total Quality Management system, and last, the strong relationship to our multinational customers that I had built during my stay.

Also, on the personal level I felt frustrated. For two years I had done everything to assimilate myself to the life in a foreign country—the life that I had always wanted—and now I was going home. It was difficult not to feel that this was a step backward.

The ironic thing was that when I came home, I got the most interesting job I have ever had, and being responsible for the Far East, I could utilize a lot of the experience I had gained by living there. I still traveled in that part of the world, mostly in Singapore and Hong Kong, and in the Copenhagen office I soon obtained a position as a bit of a Far Eastern expert.

It was, however, in my position as a right-hand man for the manager that I realized the true potential of my new assignment. Working in Copenhagen, I was much closer to the actual decision makers on the strategic level than I could ever be working for an agency such as Maersk Thailand.

I soon obtained a position as deputy for the manager of the department and by January 1, 1995, I was officially made Assistant Manager. I have for two years now been involved in a number of projects, some which were initiated by Mr. Maersk McKinney Moller himself, and have had the rare opportunity to present my recommendations directly to the top management of the company. I would never have had the opportunity to participate in meetings with Mr Moller, at the age of 26, had I stayed in the Far East.

My initial frustration at not being able to see the long-term results of my efforts in Thailand proved to be without reason.

5. **If we asked three of your closest associates to describe you, what would they say? Which adjectives would they use and why? What would they say are your strengths and weaknesses?**

Very early in my career in the Oil Purchasing Department, I was exposed to the higher levels of the A.P. Moller hierarchy. The Vice President of the Group showed me the confidence allowing me to participate in meetings concerning the long-term strategy for the Group's oil purchasing activities because I was perceived to be responsible.

I have a **strong sense of focus** and managed to pass my exams without losing focus at work (please refer to "Higher Education"). The same year as I passed the exams I was promoted to Assistant Manager (deputy) of the Oil Purchasing Department. (An equivalent managerial level has as of today only been obtained by four people from the class that graduated in 1990. This places me among the top 10% of my year.)

People who work for me would say that I possess **strong leadership abilities** and that I am a motivator. The daily price negotiations within my department follow a certain routine and it takes approximately two months to become familiar with a new area like, for example, the Arabian Gulf. Therefore I have introduced a rota system that makes sure that every employee becomes familiar with all areas of the world and that everyone is facing new challenges every day instead of routine work.

My immediate superior in Thailand would mention the word **empathy**; the ability to understand signals and interpret the feelings of other people. He would also mean the ability to adjust, to create confidence, and to get a decision through without the use of force.

My sense of empathy was put to a test when I first arrived in Thailand. My superiors had very high expectations for some of the projects that I was responsible for and I was determined to make these projects a success. At the same time, I had to realize that I was a very young manager, only 22 years old, working in a culture in which age automatically means respect and authority and in which you under no circumstances can make anyone "lose face," especially not people older than yourself.

I have a **restless nature**. Fortunately, with my present job, I never have to look far to find new challenges as the interests of my company cover the whole world. Once a procedure has proven cost efficient in one part of the world, I take the experiences gained and implement them in ports similar in character around the world in order for A.P. Moller to stay one step ahead of competition.

I can be **intolerant** at times—that is, if I feel that some of the players on my team are not totally committed. To achieve goals and stay ahead of competition, commitment is essential and when met with a lack of same, I find it very difficult not to voice my dissatisfaction. I am also rather **impatient**. If it has been decided what course of action to take, I find it very hard to wait. I prefer action over waiting any day.

I hope my closest associates would describe me as **a good friend**. I try to help the people I care about and it is extremely important to me to have a good relationship with my family and friends.

6. **If you could choose any three people who have ever lived to join you for dinner, whom would you invite and why?**

If able to choose freely among people who have ever lived, I would invite the Norwegian writer and member of the resistance movement **Nordahl Grieg**, the Danish philosopher **Soeren Kierkegaard**, and the Danish businessman and shipowner **Maersk McKinney Moller**. These three people have all in their own way contributed to the way I think and the way I want my future to be.

The topic of the dinner should be: **"Commitment to your own life and commitment to changing things for the better."**

Nordahl Grieg was a Norwegian poet and writer who died in 1943, shot down over German territory while serving as a pilot in the Royal Air Force.

When the Nazis invaded Norway in 1940, he was entrusted with the Norwegian gold reserves by the king. He flew the gold reserves to England and joined the RAF. There he started working as a news speaker in the broadcasts to the Norwegian resistance movement and until the day his plane was shot down he gave the Norwegian people the same faith in victory as Winston Churchill was able to give the rest of the free world.

What makes Nordahl Grieg outstanding in my eyes was his determination to fight for what he believed in. Even though he was a poet and a writer he still had the vision to see that ideas alone are not enough. Idealists will always be defeated by aggressors if they are not able to be equally disciplined. He had the will and determination to do what had to be done.

Soeren Kierkegaard was a philosopher who in the nineteenth century was able to make his small country known around the world. His works concentrated on the subjects which have interested people throughout time: how should life be lived, and, what is the meaning of life.

Kierkegaard was for a short while engaged, but soon had to realize that he was totally unable to commit himself to marriage or any other close contact with his fellow human beings.

What fascinates me about him is that even though he was unable to live a so-called normal life, he was still able to write brilliant books about subjects such as "the meaning of life."

In his book *Either-Or* Kierkegaard describes the relationship between aesthetics and ethics. Being a philosopher, he is trying to establish whether life should be lived in an aesthetic or in an ethical way. His conclusion was that the correct road to travel was somewhere in between, and without ethical values and commitment life is not worth living.

My third guest for dinner would agree with that statement. Maersk McKinney Moller is the owner of the A.P. Moller Group. His father, the late A.P. Moller, founded the company, and under Maersk McKinney Moller the company has grown to be the largest shipping company in the world. Moller has earned respect all over the world. He is the only non-American who has ever been on the Board of Directors of IBM and he has received more distinctions than any Danish businessman before him.

It is, however, not the distinctions but rather his business ethics which have made him respected all over the world. He has a motto that Nordahl Grieg would also agree with: "He who has the ability also has the duty," and he has lived by it all his life. He, and his employees with him, has had the ability to build a large concern without losing focus on the ethical values necessary to survive in the business world in the long run.

Another of Moller's mottoes sounds like a cliché, but has proven highly workable as a company motto. Through this motto one gets a good understanding of his perception of how life should be lived: "Everything that is worth doing is worth doing well."

Working for Maersk McKinney Moller has taught me that he is a man with a strong determination to do the best he can. He has managed to imbue the whole A.P. Moller group with that same way of thinking and has through his own life shown how far one can get with determination and personal commitment.

I believe that the participants in my dinner party, including myself, would agree that the will to do your best is a very important qualification if you want to succeed in the business world. Success will then follow, like an unintentional side effect of your personal commitment to a cause larger than yourself.

COMMENTS

1. Jon had an interesting combination of a weak educational background and an extremely successful career to date. He needed, therefore, to emphasize the latter and either camouflage the former or show that it did not matter because his inherent abilities were sufficient that a lack of formal education should not be of concern. In fact, he did all of these things. He made sure that he capitalized on his successful, varied career by telling a wide range of stories from his business life. He camouflaged his lack of traditional education by referring to classes he was taking, by discussing everything in a very logical and well-thought-out fashion, and by explaining work he had done that had a very analytical component. These approaches, taken together, made it clear that he has plenty of intellectual horsepower.

2. In the first essay, Jon shows that he knows two strengths of the London Business School program and is a very appropriate candidate for it insofar as a strong grounding in finance and corporate strategy are exactly what he wants. He also states a clear rationale for getting an MBA.

3. In essay 3, he demonstrated a strong overall strategic understanding of his industry, showing that he has not just remained in a cubicle, but has instead considered the context in which he is operating. Indeed, his analytical discussions, plus good prose, belie his lack of formal education.

4. Note his emphasis in essay 6 upon a writer and a philosopher, part of the effort to overcome his modest academic credentials. He also chose to emphasize his "Danishness" by choosing two Danes and one Norwegian, only one of whom is known to the outside world. This is a useful counterbalance to his internationalism, which is evident throughout his discussion of his Asian experiences and his desire to operate internationally. The Danishness suggests that he is not stateless and will indeed bring a Scandinavian as well as global perspective to bear during the program.

5. Note how positive he is throughout these essays about his career to date and his prospects. Similarly, he is very positive about his company. He notes that it is a top company, suggesting that he must be a top-quality manager to be working for it. His very positive approach, which includes being a veritable booster for his company, suggests that he will probably be a booster for the business school he eventually attends, something that cannot fail to have value for a school.

INSEAD (Selected)

1. Describe what you believe to be your most substantial accomplishment to date, explaining why you view it as such.

During my first year in the Oil Purchasing Department of A.P. Moller, I managed to totally eliminate volume cheating involving Maersk vessels in Singapore.

The large amounts of money involved in the oil business in Singapore have attracted criminal elements to the trade, resulting in the regular theft of 5%–10% of the fuel oil that ships purchase.

The problem lies with the barge operators who are acting as subcontractors to the major oil companies. Due to the difficulty of obtaining solid evidence of the cheating, these problems have been more or less accepted by the trade and the Singapore authorities for years.

By joining forces with the suppliers, however, I managed to eliminate these problems for all Maersk vessels. In short, the "cure" was:

1. I made it clear to our suppliers that I wanted to get to the bottom of this problem and that I expected their assistance. I used our Vice President to open the doors.

2. In cooperation with selected suppliers I developed a performance questionnaire that enabled our vessels to report on the performance of the bunker barge and crew directly to the supplier and to my department.

3. Through intensive joint lobbying we persuaded the Singapore authorities to implement a licensing scheme for bunker barges to decrease the number of dishonest barge operators.

4. In cooperation with the Port Authorities of Singapore I managed to make the rules for barge operations inside the port limits far more flexible, thus eliminating the barge operators' main excuse for bad performance.

5. I made it a rule that every captain should visit my department when in Copenhagen, in order for me to have firsthand knowledge of developments in Singapore.

I regard this as my most substantial accomplishment as I managed to save approximately 4 million dollars (U.S.) of recurrent annual costs.

2. **Briefly describe a situation taken from school, business, civil, or military life, where you did not meet your personal objectives, and discuss what you learnt from this experience.**

One of my functions while working in Thailand was that of Quality Coordinator. I had been educated in the concept of Total Quality Management (TQM) in Denmark, and it was my responsibility to implement this concept in the various work processes of the Thai staff. Before leaving for Thailand, I made the objectives of the corporate office my personal objectives and promised to fully implement TQM within the first year of my stay in Thailand.

When I arrived in Thailand, I was shocked to see how low the educational and professional level of our Thai staff actually was. It was obvious that the corporate office knew nothing of the actual situation in Thailand when the decision to implement TQM was made. It would take at least another five years before the staff could be made ready to get any substantial benefits from the concept. Until then, trying to implement it would create more problems than it would solve.

I soon had to realize that I was not going to meet my personal objectives. When I had realized that, much to my surprise, I felt a sense of relief. I felt that my hands were free and that I was able to act again, and instead of implementing the TQM concept I implemented proper job descriptions for all local staff. This way I paved the way for a future implementation of TQM and at the same time eliminated a substantial amount of double work and routines that were not adding to the goals of the company.

The experience taught me to trust my own judgment and the importance of understanding the needs of the parties involved before working out strategy and goals. Had I forced the TQM concept through, the result would have been disastrous. By understanding the actual needs of the local staff I managed to turn a major failure into a win/win situation.

COMMENTS

1. I have included these two essays because they provide interesting examples of two of the most common essay topics. In each case, Jon does a good job of explaining the situation and how (and why) he succeeded or failed.

PHILIPPE

Background:

Job:	Project manager of air force command and control system. Later, mergers and acquisitions associate for a high tech group.
Education:	Bachelor of science degree from Ecole Polytechnique, MS from ENSTA, and MS from MIT
Nationality:	French

Critical issue to address:

Does he need a fourth degree?

INSEAD

1. Give a candid description of yourself, stressing the personal characteristics you feel to be your assets and liabilities.

What I perceive as a major asset resides in the fact that I am extremely rigorous. I am strongly committed to well-done things and I wouldn't do or produce anything that looks approximate or amateurish. Consequently, I am considered a very reliable person. Also, I have always been perceived as trustworthy. Whether this relates to natural openness and honesty, or to a good capacity to listen to and to care for others, the fact is that people trust me, not only on a professional basis, but also as a confidant or an adviser. Third, I have a good ability to communicate: I am always very clear in my explanations and presentations, and I know how to make a meeting lively and productive. Besides the fact that I am a hardworker full of energy (which I believe every applicant to INSEAD is), I also have a communicative enthusiasm when undertaking something, combined with a good sense of humor.

On the liabilities side, I lack confidence when it comes to subjects that are not in my area of competence. This type of situation makes me feel uneasy since I am not in a strong position to argue. This is one of the reasons why I am applying to INSEAD: I need to acquire skills in finance and management related topics. Also, I have to pay sustained attention so as to curb a tendency to disperse myself in various activities of interest to me. I can say that I succeed in focusing on priorities, but this requires a steady effort from me.

2. **Describe what you believe to be your most substantial accomplishment to date, explaining why you view it as such.**

During my three first years of professional experience, I was in charge of the conception, development, and implementation of a large scale command and control system for the French Air Force. When I started the project, there were five major companies involved in specific parts of it (Dassault for the aircraft, Aerospatiale for the missiles, Sagem for guidance systems, plus two other software companies). There also were two distinct chiefs of staff on the Air Force side, each with his own operational requirements. Last, I had to understand the deterrence concepts in order to conceive a global computer-based system. That was indeed a big challenge, since I had to integrate all the points of view of the different interlocutors, as well as the technical characteristics of the different subsystems. I also had to get all these people around the same table so that they would work in the same direction, using the same language. This required a good deal of diplomacy. The responsibility of the global coordination and of the good achievement of the project was entirely mine.

When the system was finally accepted and used by the Air Force, I knew I had accomplished something. Not only did I develop aptitudes in communicating with multiple persons, in negotiating contracts within a given budget, and in making things happen, but I also keep from that experience the pleasant feeling of paternity of this system, now fully operational at the Strategic Air Command, that a part of myself is embedded in it.

3. **Briefly describe a situation taken from school, business, civil, or military life, where you did not meet your personal objectives, and discuss what you learnt from this experience.**

When I was finishing my master's studies at MIT, that were sponsored by the French Ministry of Defense, I was so interested in the research work I was conducting (i.e., information system modeling) that I wanted to pursue this research through a PhD. Therefore I applied to the doctoral program in MIS (management information systems) at the MIT Sloan School of Management. The admission cycle was such that I received my admission to the program more than six months after I started working for the French MOD in Paris. There was then a conflict of interests between my personal objectives (going back to MIT) and the priorities of the Defense Department (the completion of the system I was in charge of). Finally, although I strongly insisted, my hierarchy did not allow me to go back to the United States.

From this experience I learnt several important points:

- ▪ We are not living in a world of absolute independence, and in that sense such a situation, where personal objectives were confronted by superior priorities, enhanced my own maturity.

- ▪ Indeed it turned out that it is a greater accomplishment to honor one's commitments than to satisfy one's personal objectives regardless of these commitments.

- ▪ In most dissatisfactions there is something positive; in that case I learnt that to run a technical project can be as enriching and stimulating as conducting research.

4. **Comment on the main factors which you believe account for your academic and professional development to date. Explain your career aspirations and why you choose to apply to INSEAD now.**

At the end of Polytechnique, I thought that even if I wanted to work in private industry I should take the opportunity to get acquainted with government affairs since such an opportunity is only given once and not to many people. And indeed I do not regret this choice; I've been given large responsibilities in my first job as a project engineer. My second appointment was a great challenge since I moved from the very technical side of defense activities to the policy side: I dealt with vast subjects like the relations between France and NATO on nuclear policy issues; this was not only challenging but also highly exciting.

But after these four years I realized that if I wanted to pursue my initial idea to work in industry I should move to the private sector rapidly. The times when civil servants joined companies after fifteen years or so of governmental service are now over: with the European build-up, the influence of national administrations will decrease, and most of the action will take place within industry (the current restructuring of the defense electronics and armament business is a good example). Therefore I decided to join the MATRA group by the end of 1988, for at least two reasons: its private status and the European composition of its capital.

My career aspirations, which of course coincide with Matra plans, are to become within a few years the operational manager of a European-based entity within the group, with full responsibility for profits and losses. The other idea of the corporate vice-president for strategy is to have me working with him as a member of the corporate staff for several months, so that I get used to the corporate strategic issues and that I bear them in mind when I assume operational responsibilities. To achieve these objectives I need to develop skills and knowledge that I am now lacking, i.e., in finance, accounting, and general management. These are the reasons why I am applying to INSEAD, which is moreover attractive to me because of its European orientation.

5. **What means of ensuring your personal and professional development are you seriously considering as an alternative to INSEAD?**

First, Matra has set up an internal management program that is designed to give to its participants a basic knowledge in managerial topics. Besides this, since it lacks the international dimension, Matra and I are also considering intensive programs (15 weeks or so) for management development in leading business schools.

6. **What do you feel you would contribute during your time at INSEAD?**

I can bring and share with other INSEAD people what I learnt from my professional experience:

- a very good knowledge of government-business relations, of government policy-making and decision-making process;

- the practice of negotiation, either in contracting or in international policy issues;

- how to appreciate the changes in East-West relations and the political build-up of Europe, topics that are today subject to major attention;

■ how the industrial strategy of a high tech group like Matra is handled, bringing in actual examples.

On top of that, I think that I can also bring a positive contribution in class sessions as well as in team work, through personal qualities such as enthusiasm, intellectual curiosity, a good sense of humor, and a permanent good mood.

7. If you wish to discuss any matter, other than the items of information already requested, please develop it here.

1. I am enclosing three letters of recommendation instead of two, because I think that INSEAD should have an appreciation of the three aspects of my past experience: academy, government, and industry.

2. I would like to make a short comment about the fact that I am applying to do a fourth degree. I want to stress that there is nothing special about this since I got the three first degrees within four years (between age 20 and 24); Polytechnique is meaningless without an "École d'application," which lasts two years, and I spent that second year at MIT instead of ENSTA through an equivalence agreement. This explains how I will have 60 months' full-time work experience by the fall of 1989 and that I am not diploma-addicted.

COMMENTS

1. Philippe was and remains one of France's high-fliers. When applying to INSEAD, he had everything going for him: a stellar academic background and outstanding experience both at the defense ministry and at one of France's leading companies. His only potential liability was his "excessive" number of degrees.

2. His first essay shows that he may have weaknesses, but he is on top of his tendency not to prioritize sufficiently and he can therefore control it. He claims in the first essay that he can explain matters well, something that later essays demonstrate in spades as he treats technical topics with ease (despite writing in his second language).

3. In the fifth essay he makes it clear that his company thinks the world of him insofar as they are looking around for how best to develop his talents.

4. The sixth essay focuses on his intellectual capital, the knowledge he has that he will bring to INSEAD. He is, for example, very clear about his technical and business-government relations strengths. This is particularly helpful to evaluations of his talents. He goes a helpful step further by showing that he is the type to share that knowledge and contribute positively.

5. His extra contribution (the "optional essay," number 7) is ideal. He addresses the very specific issues that warrant attention and does so very efficiently.

DEBRA

Background:

Job:	Marketing and admissions director for an American college in Europe
Education:	Bachelor's degree in teaching, master's degree in communications
Nationality:	Dutch
Other:	Strong languages

Critical issues to address:

Her quantitative abilities are likely to be called into question, given her very nonquantitative schooling and job history.

Her human resources orientation raises questions about her toughness. (This is probably even more the case for a woman.) And is she sufficiently business-oriented in general?

IESE (Barcelona)

I. DESCRIBE YOUR WORK EXPERIENCE

As Associate Director of Admission and Marketing I report directly to the Dean of Admission of College X in City Y, USA. On a day-to-day basis I report to the Dean of College X in Europe. The Dean, the Business Manager, and I form the management team of the Institute.

Working for College X in Europe has been much like an entrepreneurial experience. I was one of the first employees of this degree-granting branch of an American college in Europe, founded in the early 1990s. Preliminary marketing research for this venture had been limited, and none of my American colleagues had experience in recruiting students for a European-based degree program. Without much guidance, I developed and implemented marketing strategies, reaching out to prospective students, their parents, and the guidance community. In addition, I developed and implemented admission procedures to support the marketing activities. In the first year of the program we enrolled 35 students, and this number grew to 50 in the second. By 1993, our third year, we realized a more than 100 percent increase in enrollments with a total of 115 students.

From the beginning I have been involved in nearly all aspects of the College's operation, including: resolving personnel hiring and contract issues, implementing an academic advising and registration system, contributing to curriculum development decisions, designing the billing procedure, and finding housing for both students and faculty, among others. The variety of my responsibilities has enabled me to acquire a broad insight into the workings of an organization, and to apply my analytical and managerial skills. Over the course of my employment at College X, other professional positions have been filled, allowing me to hand over a number of responsibilities and to develop marketing and admission strategies to a more sophisticated level.

II. PROFESSIONAL AND OTHER QUALIFICATIONS

A. In addition to the academic and professional activities already mentioned, describe other activities that you have participated or presently participate in. This includes college, university, community, athletic, political, or cultural organizations. Also include articles published, awards won, professional titles obtained, etc.

I am a member of the regional Public Relations Association of City Z (in Europe), through which I keep up with current developments in my profession, meet colleagues in the field, and learn more about the industries in the area. Since November of 1993 I have been enrolled in an economics class at a local college, out of general interest and to prepare for entrance into an MBA program.

I have an active interest in the arts, in particular fiber arts and sculpture. Whenever possible I try to find the time to put my interest in the arts into practice. Since completing my undergraduate program, I have taken a course in silk-screen printing, and currently I assist in teaching a desktop publishing workshop.

I am always involved in at least one sport, to keep my body in shape, to relax, and to socialize. In secondary school, I played badminton; during my undergraduate studies, I was an active volleyball player; while living in the United States I sailed and worked out in the gym, which I continue to do now in City Z (in Europe). I have also participated in several group vacations, learning sailing and canoeing.

Upon graduation from my undergraduate program I went abroad to improve my foreign language skills. I took intensive French and German language classes, in which I increased my foreign language skills, as well as my knowledge of Swiss, French, and German cultures.

As a secondary school student I assisted in organizing summer camp activities for children. Indeed, I have always been an active participant of the groups of which I am a member, whether during work, study or spare time. I make the effort to organize social gatherings and group excursions to bring colleagues or peers away from the formal environment and to thus strengthen group ties.

B. Describe any position of leadership you have held. Please indicate whether you were elected or appointed to the positions held and show the dates of involvement and scope of your responsibilities.

Although I have not held any officially appointed or elected leadership positions, I would characterize my role in a number of groups and organizations in which I have participated as the informal leader and the person who creates group cohesiveness.

In my current professional position, for example, I have received the trust of both my superiors and colleagues. On a regular basis, the Dean as well as my co-workers turn to me for advice, and to discuss troublesome work issues. My ability to listen, coupled with my analytical reasoning and problem-solving skills, helps others to identify the source of the problem and to find creative solutions. Due to my involvement at all levels, I am often able to act as the mediator between parties.

Because organizations constantly require adaptation to the new needs and demands of a changing environment, I believe that it is important for employees at all levels to identify areas which need modification, and to propose ideas for improvement. I therefore actively stimulate and challenge colleagues to take responsibility for bettering their work practice and environment wherever possible. Doing so has contributed to cultivating an enthusiastic and dedicated staff, in which the individual members feel responsible for, and instrumental contributors to, the success of the organization.

From secondary school on, and in particular during the years I spent abroad, I have been engaged in numerous formal and informal group settings. During my undergraduate studies I served as an orientation leader during the new student introduction and I was the founder of a student volleyball team. On many occasions I have organized social gatherings and group excursions, such as a study trip to a major fibre art exhibit in Switzerland and several long weekend trips. These activities have had a positive influence on the groups I participated in, in that they have unified group members, and have often made me the informal leader, the person members turn to for facilitating group decisions.

C. State what the reasons were for choosing your university studies.

When I completed secondary school I was quite young, just about to turn 17, and not quite ready to make a career choice. Because the Dutch education system does not offer a broad liberal arts education, I chose a profession I was familiar with, teaching, and a field which would allow me to apply my creative skills, fine arts. However, during the final years of my bachelor's degree program, I came to the conclusion that neither secondary school teaching nor the creative arts gave me satisfactory intellectual fulfillment. Upon evaluation of my personal strengths and career aspirations, I decided to enter the field of public relations.

I spent two years abroad, improving my foreign language skills, and acquiring work experience in public relations. Through this experience I realized that, in order to find the professional challenge I was looking for, I needed to further my education in the field. This prompted my decision to enter a master's degree program in Business Communication and Public Relations at College X in the United States where I acquired both theoretical knowledge as well as practical experience in business communication.

D. Indicate the reasons why you wish to follow an MBA Program and how the Bilingual MBA Program will fit in with your career plans.

My overall aim is to apply my strengths and experiences in those environments which offer me a challenge, that is, an opportunity to continue to expand by personal boundaries.

My current position as Associate Director of Admission and Marketing for the international branch of an established American college, has allowed me to apply my knowledge and skills, and to experience and contribute to the development and growth of a new organization. In this position, I apply public relations primarily as a marketing tool, with activities which are predominantly forms of one-way communication. However, I find that my particular interest now has become focused on the function of public relations and business communication, which is much broader than serving as a marketing tool alone. The task of the business communication manager is to act as a liaison between an organization and all of its publics, including its employees, stockholders, the community, the media, and the public at large, among others. In this role he/she is responsible not only for communicating management issues to the public, but also for monitoring public opinion and analyzing its possible impact on the organization. The findings of the communication manager thus contribute to the strategic planning process of the organization.

My immediate goal is to acquire a position in the communication department of a medium to large international organization. In the longer term, I aim at managing such a department, and eventually I wish to apply my knowledge and strengths as a consultant. In order to achieve these goals, I find it imperative to supplement my business communication education and to reinforce my marketing management experience, by pursuing an MBA education.

As communication member or consultant, I will be a member of, or consultant to, the general management of the organization. Because I will be dealing with all publics and all facets of the organization, this will require an understanding of the organization in its broadest possible scope. The MBA program will strengthen my general business knowledge, and my knowledge of economics, corporate finance, business policies, strategic management, organizational behavior, and political trends affecting business in particular. The emphasis on the interrelation of these individual business areas through the case methodology used at IESE is of particular interest to me because it will provide me with the knowledge and experience necessary to identify and analyze those complex public issues which impact an organization.

I also chose IESE to pursue my MBA degree because it offers a truly global program. I have been engaged internationally, through work and study, for the past six and a half years, and have enjoyed and learned much from the intercultural interaction. I wish to continue to be engaged internationally in the future, both personally and professionally. In addition, I believe that current business practitioners can no longer afford to ignore their competitors over the border. Mergers and takeovers change many industries into multinational conglomerates with new communication demands, and more and more companies employ immigrants coming from a variety of cultural backgrounds. These intercultural settings require internationally educated managers— managers who have proven to be able to operate successfully in multicultural settings. The bilingual MBA program offered by IESE provides the education and experience in just such an environment, through its international curriculum, faculty, and student body. In addition, becoming fluent in Spanish will greatly enhance my effectiveness for working in international settings.

E. Given your experience with employers or educational institutions and given the opportunity to effect one change, what would that be? Describe how you would implement the change and what difficulties you would expect to encounter.

The organization I currently work for, College X, is not at all consistent in communicating with external publics via its printed materials. Each individual department—undergraduate admission, graduate admission, continuing and external education, alumni relations, and the European campus—develops its own printed materials. This creates a variety of communication pieces ranging from prize-winning quality to desktop experiments. I would like to bring all of these efforts in line with one another, and to do so I would propose the following.

A publication manager should be appointed who will be responsible for all publications emanating from the college. This individual, who will possess excellent writing skills and knowledge of graphics and design, will write most of the materials him/herself. He/she will be assisted by a graphic designer and will be able to call upon external copy writers and/or designers whenever necessary.

There will be four primary benefits from this approach:

a. A single publication manager will ensure consistency in the use of language, logos, and images.

b. Consistency in promotional materials will increase recognition among target audiences and will thus increase recognition of the college as a whole.

c. Through multiple use of graphics and pictures, and by negotiating large contracts with printers, the college will save in production costs. This will allow even those departments who work with small printing budgets to produce representative and effective promotional materials.

d. Individual departments will no longer have to spend time on production of publications, which will account for significant time savings in offices with few employees such as my own.

The major problem I expect to encounter is resistance to change. Most offices on campus have been in charge of their own publications for as long as they can remember, and each individual office believes it is doing a fine job on its own. Even though not directly competing, there is a sense of rivalry among the offices and they do not have much faith in each others' marketing capabilities. It will therefore be important to allow each office to contribute to the appointment of the publication manager and to allow for their direct input when it concerns a publication produced for their use.

---

1. **Give a candid evaluation of your personality, just as you see yourself.**

I am successful in my current position at College X, primarily because of my analytical reasoning skills, combined with my ability to think creatively. Due to these strengths, the Dean of the College involves me in many organizational decisions beyond my marketing responsibilities, including budget planning, curriculum development, and student life concerns. My resourceful nature has caused one of my colleagues to describe me as a level-headed problem solver, and many of my co-workers often seek me out to discuss troublesome work issues. Due to my involvement at all levels, I sometimes act as mediator in the case of a conflict or communication problem. I enjoy applying my versatility and flexibility to tackling these diverse matters, and doing so has allowed me to gain insight into the various aspects of a managerial function.

Another one of my prime assets is my ability to communicate. During my three and a half years abroad, in which I lived in four different countries, I was able to adapt with ease to new environments, situations and people, which was largely due to strong interpersonal communication skills. In my current position, in which I inform prospective students, their parents, and college counselors about the educational opportunities offered at College X, my success relies heavily on excellent interpersonal communication and oral presentation skills.

I perform at my highest level under pressure. My current position requires me to constantly maneuver a variety of tasks which have the tendency to become urgent all at the same time. It is under these pressing circumstances that I am most energetic and productive.

I have a natural drive to organize and to create structure, which has been essential for my professional accomplishments. As public relations assistant at Essilor International in Paris, I was completely in charge of the logistics and execution of foreign group visits to the parent company in France. Careful planning, excellent timing, an eye for detail, and regular communication with my colleagues in the international subsidiaries and the local plants were imperative to meeting the expectations of the participants and ensuring smooth and enjoyable visits. In my current position, I have successfully developed and implemented operational structures for the admissions office, as well as for the organization as a whole.

A liability that I face is my tendency to be somewhat of a compulsive perfectionist. I often find myself adding criteria onto the task at hand right up until the deadline. Improving my time management skills and forcing myself to realistically assess quality versus time invested will help me to improve my work efficiency.

Perhaps typical for a Dutchman, I have a direct approach and am a results-oriented person. When bureaucracy, internal politics, and rooted procedures stand in the way of getting the job done, I sometimes tend to lose my temper. I am learning that the most direct approach is not necessarily always the most effective, and that it is sometimes necessary to first build a good working relationship before starting to work on the task at hand.

My professional career is very important to me, and I therefore devote a lot of time and energy to my job. To find satisfaction in my work, it is important that I believe in the organization I work for, the product or service it delivers, and its management style. Because I frequently go beyond the call of duty, I continually need to monitor maintaining a healthy balance between my professional and personal life.

2. **Describe two substantial accomplishments and one failure in a professional, academic, private, or family endeavor and explain why you view them as such. Mention also what you learned from them.**

   1. One of my most substantial professional accomplishments to date is marketing the new branch of an American university in Europe. Its success is demonstrated through its growth from 35 students in its initial year, 1991–1992, to 50 in its second, and a more than 100 percent increase to 115 students in its third year. This effort, combined with my involvement in the general management of the organization, has contributed significantly to its overall success.

I see this as a substantial accomplishment, due to a number of obstacles I had to face to achieve this.

▪ For the first year and a half, until I started reporting to the Dean of Admission on the U.S. campus, I found myself with hardly any professional guidance. Relying on limited preliminary research, I was responsible for defining targets and developing marketing strategies. At first this created some anxiety for me, but I soon started to appreciate and exercise the independence it offered. In addition, I had to learn to maneuver among the varying and sometimes conflicting demands of the interim director, the incoming dean, and the vice president for external programs located in the United States.

▪ From a marketing point of view, the biggest obstacle was, and continues to be our tuition. College X has a long tradition of educating communication professionals and, through its educational balance of theory and practice, offers a viable alternative to the existing communication education programs in Europe. However, attracting students to College X has been a challenge because of its costs. As a private, not-for-profit university, College X is entirely tuition driven. Fees are therefore ten to fifteen times higher than those of most public universities in Europe, and this means that (1) only a small percentage of the general population can afford our education, and (2) we are operating in a market where people are not accustomed to paying for their education.

▪ Finally, from day one I have been involved in nearly all aspects of the College's operation. Through this broad range of responsibilities, described earlier in this application, I have gained significant insight into the workings of an organization and, among other things, have learned how to manage people and deal with working under pressure. However, at the same time this wide variety of responsibilities has seriously diverted my time and energy from my primary responsibilities, marketing and admission.

2. Another major accomplishment is my successful career change from education to business. I entered my master's program at College X with business experience obtained solely through my position as public relations assistant at Essilor International in Paris. In a relatively short period of time I mastered the theories of the field of business communication and was able to apply my newly acquired knowledge to case studies, research projects, class discussions, and an internship. In my current position I have shown that I have been successful not only in marketing the organization, but also in quickly moving into general management duties through which I have contributed significantly to the overall development of the organization.

3. A situation in which I did not reach my objectives occurred toward the end of my undergraduate studies. For the final project, a fellow student and I decided to design and produce a visual theater performance in which objects, instead of actors would play the leading roles. In addition to the design and construction of the objects, we were also responsible for the choreography, sound, and lighting of the performance. Although both of us had worked on a similar project before and could thus anticipate the work involved, our plans went beyond what could be considered realistic. After three months of brainstorming, planning, and designing, we had to come to the conclusion that a project this ambitious could not be carried out by a team of just two people. Notwithstanding our excellent cooperation, we decided to break up as a team, and I started a new project on my own. A year later I graduated with a successful sculpture exhibit.

The most important thing I learned from this experience is the necessity, at the initiation of any project, to establish goals carefully, outline the means to reach these goals, and test the feasibility of reaching them in the time available. Had we conducted this exercise during the planning stage of our project, we would have been able either to downsize the magnitude of the final production, or to get additional people involved to assist us with the sound and lighting, for example.

This particular experience was important to me, because the year of primarily solitary work in a studio taught me a lot about myself. Even though solitary work allows one to fully concentrate on acquiring new knowledge, I felt a lack of stimulation which comes from cooperation with other people. It became clear to me that, whatever career I pursue, interaction with others is crucial to finding satisfaction in my work.

3. **Describe an ethical dilemma you have experienced. Discuss how you managed the situation.**

To get a quick start recruiting College X's first European class, the U.S. campus employed four persons for the admission office including an admission coordinator (myself), and two recruiters. Contracts ran from January through June, at the end of which the positions would be evaluated based on performance and program staffing needs.

Both full-timers wanted to, and assumed that they could, continue their employment with us. At the time they were hired, the U.S. campus gave them the impression that they would have a fair chance of continuing beyond their first contract period. However, toward the end of May, the U.S. campus decided that the admission staff was to continue as a two-person office; that is, my position and that of one assistant. After careful evaluation, the Dean and I concluded that neither one of the current recruiters was the optimal candidate to fill the position. Both were College X graduates, and possessed a great deal of enthusiasm to get prospective students excited about the College X programs. However, both lacked a certain maturity and professionalism, which we felt was particularly important in their contacts with guidance counselors and parents. In addition, now that the admission office was being reduced to two professional staff members only, I felt that it was important to get an assistant who would contribute to developing and implementing operational structures for the admission office. Neither one fit that profile.

The U.S. campus's decision about the new configuration of the admission staff did not come until the end of May. It then took the Dean and me another couple of weeks to define which qualifications were needed for the newly defined admission assistant position. This brought us to mid-June, close to the end of the recruiter's contract period. Because all this evolved very late, we had not communicated the new scenario to the two people involved. The fact that their contracts might not be renewed came therefore as a surprise to both of them.

College X had no legal obligation to offer to renew their contracts. Both expired in June, and no commitments had been made for continuation of employment thereafter. However, the combination of late decision making and poor communication created false expectations and caused an ethical dilemma for the Dean and me.

In addition, even though it was clear to me that we needed a stronger candidate to fill the position, I found it difficult not to renew the contracts of these two employees, who had both worked hard and been loyal to the organization. In the Netherlands, employment provides a fair amount of security. Even though this is changing under the influence of economic recession and values adopted from other cultures, I grew up with the idea that an employee is fired only when he/she is guilty of serious misconduct, or when the company is forced, because of financial constraints, to reduce the total workforce. I therefore also felt a social obligation toward these employees.

The moral dilemma created was whether we should base our decision solely on what would be economically most beneficial for the organization, or whether we should take into account the College's social responsibility to these employees. In addition, the situation had become more complex than necessary because of late decision making, and consequently a lack of timely communication with the employees involved.

After careful consideration, our final decision was to hire one of the recruiters in a services position, not to extend the contract of the other, and to advertise the position of admission assistant. This enabled us to hire an admission assistant who was better suited for the newly defined admission position, thus strengthening the competence of the admission office. The recruiter who was offered a new contract obtained a position for which he was much better qualified. The person whose contract was not renewed did not find alternative employment in the area, and eventually returned to the United States.

4. **Give the name of an individual who has positively influenced your professional, academic, private, or family life. Describe what that person did and how it affected you personally.**

A person who has very positively influenced my professional career has been my father.

First of all, he has been for me an inspiring example of a successful businessman. As a farmer's son, he combined his personal interests with a career in business, working the major part of his life in the agricultural industry. He worked for an organization in which he was able to utilize his entrepreneurial talent; as director of Cebeco International Projects he initiated many successful agricultural projects in developing nations as well as in the former Soviet Union. His professional endeavors have contributed to the agricultural development of these countries as well as to the success of the organization for which he worked.

Second, my father has always acted as my advisor and mentor on important educational decisions, without at any moment forcing his advice on me. When I decided to make a career change, he was instrumental in helping me to map out my future career path. He has stimulated me to go abroad to improve my language skills and eventually to enter a master's program, which has had a very positive influence on my personal and professional development.

Finally, he continues to act as an objective external consultant regarding some of the personal and professional dilemmas I encounter. His pragmatic, down-to-earth approach helps me to see complex issues from a new perspective.

NIJENRODE (NETHERLANDS) (Selected)

1. **During your study at the Nijenrode International MBA Program, you will be part of a diverse multi-cultural, multi-experienced community. What rewards and challenges do you anticipate in this environment, and how do you expect this experience to prepare you for your future personal and professional endeavors?**

Living and working with people from various cultural backgrounds has broadened my views of other values, opinions, and beliefs, and has made me look with more criticism at my own. Working in a multicultural environment has also exposed me to new challenges. It is one thing to go out for a drink with a non-Dutch national; even though you have to settle on the choice of a bar, you can each choose your favorite drink. It is something else to work out a business proposal or to solve an organizational conflict with someone who did not grow up with the same set of values and beliefs as you did. It is these types of situations I expect to also engage in at Nijenrode.

I believe that it is important to continue to develop intercultural knowledge and communication skills, because tomorrow's business world will be even more global than it already is today. Most traditionally national industries can no longer ignore their competitors on the other side of the border; mergers and takeovers change many industries into multicultural conglomerates with new communication demands; and more and more companies employ immigrants coming from a variety of cultural backgrounds. These intercultural settings require internationally educated managers; managers who have proven to be able to operate successfully in a multicultural setting. Nijenrode provides the education and experience in such a setting.

The multi-experienced community brought together in a Nijenrode class allows its participants to benefit and learn from each other's professional expertise. Also, in a relatively short period of time, the group members acquire insight in a broad variety of industries and organizations. This multi-experienced community offers a challenge in that it forces one to cooperate with people who come to the field of management from different disciplines, and with various business perspectives. The Nijenrode class thus mirrors an organizational setting, in which one is also required to closely cooperate with colleagues who come from a variety of professional backgrounds.

Finally, upon graduation, this multicultural and multi-experienced group of people is expected to branch out in a variety of disciplines, all over the globe. This will create a strong international network of personal and professional contacts.

COMMENTS

1. Debra managed to show that she had the "people person" qualities to be expected of someone in education and also emphasized the business aspects of her education work, thereby showing that she was not a high risk candidate. She showed herself to be knowledgeable about business and clear (and realistic) regarding where she was headed and how an MBA could help her get there. She also gets full credit for being a very interesting candidate who is not at all like the usual accountant/engineer/banker/consultant applicant.

2. She failed to get the most from her application in one way. She showed herself to be a leader, but did too little to draw attention to this. In essay B she is too modest; she ran this office and should have claimed the credit for her actions. Similarly,

her discussion in essay 3 of whether to fire two workers concerns a down-to-earth problem constantly faced by managers. Unfortunately, she does not drive home the point that she took the lead and swayed the decision.

3. In essay C, she notes how young she was when she chose the field she would enter, a subtle way of excusing her failure to choose something appropriate for her and also of indicating her surprising determination to get on with things. Completing high school at 16 indicates that she has more firepower and determination than might be expected of an almost–high school teacher.

4. In essay D, she shows that she knows what business is all about by discussing her interest in consulting. This is also her chance to show that she understands what an MBA is all about, and that she recognizes exactly how it can help her. By the same token, she knows what IESE has to offer—its case method of teaching and bilingual program in particular.

5. In essay E, she is persuasive in discussing what she would wish to change in her job, but she could have been more so had she provided specific numbers regarding the impact her suggestion would have, particularly the likely cost savings.

6. Her description of herself in essay 1 as a results-oriented Dutch person is a good counterbalance to the presumption created by someone being in education (and thus being viewed potentially as a waffly bureaucrat).

ANNE

Background:

Job: Airport manager

Education: Bachelor's degree in business and master's degree in law

Nationality: French

Critical issues to address:

None. She is a strong candidate who merely needs to communicate her numerous strengths. She graduated in the top 10 percent of a good undergrad program, did well on the GMAT, and has had very strong operating experience in a very international industry (airlines). The only concern is that she be able to present herself in a manner reflecting her abilities.

INSEAD

Work Experience/Job Description

I started working for AirInter in 1987, just after completing my original studies. I worked for six months as an attaché direction (assistant) for the Strasbourg-based regional manager. When I returned to the company after doing my degrees at the Faculté de Droit, Aix en Provence, I was the assistant manager to the Lyon station (i.e., airport) manager. I very much liked being at the point of contact with the customers, ground staff, and flight crews.

I therefore applied to be a station manager myself, eventually getting the job in Mulhouse which I have held up until my recent pregnancy leave. One could divide the job into four components.

The first is the management of 150 people, with an operating budget of 45–50 million francs and a capital budget of approximately 10 million francs. The management responsibility is nearly total. The station manager decides how many people to hire, whom to hire, and how to train them; the manager also manages the facilities and finance functions, deciding, for example, when and how much to invest in replacing equipment, in addition to running the ongoing operations of the facility.

The second component involves seeking out "handling agent" business for other airlines. This means that one performs all the ground functions to enable KLM, for example, to make daily stops at the airport. In other parts of the AirInter system this is a simpler task because the company generally has a monopoly at each airport. Because this is not true at Mulhouse, the marketing and bidding processes are trickier. This part of the business, by the way, currently generates revenues of approximately 15 million francs, a substantial increase over the last several years.

Third, the manager must be "on call" at all times. The airport runs nearly twenty-four hours a day, and it is on an international border, so there are constantly major decisions to be made. For example, the recent Airbus 320 crash at Mont St. Odile took place near Mulhouse, necessitating that I head to Strasbourg, the airport nearest the crash, to help the overwhelmed manager there.

Fourth, I represent the company's interests in front of the airport authorities. This is particularly important in Mulhouse for two reasons. The first is that we do not have our customary monopoly position there, having to share the airport with Swissair. The second is that we are the world's only binational airport, with both Swiss and French authorities having power. In commercial, immigration, and security matters, things are much more complex in Mulhouse than elsewhere because of the multiplicity of interested parties, making good representation of the company all the more important.

Further descriptions of the challenges involved and my relative success in handling them are to be found in the essays.

1. **Give a candid description of yourself, stressing the personal characteristics you feel to be your assets and liabilities.**

My assets can be divided into three general categories. The first is that I have **strong interpersonal skills**. I work well with a wide range of people, whether young or old, French or German, graduate or laborer. For example, I was regarded as a strong team player when I worked on the AirInter corporate staff with other young graduates. Later I managed a group of 150 ground employees and commercial staff—essentially none of whom had a university background—as station manager at Mulhouse airport, and developed such a good working relationship that we were virtually unique in having no work stoppages during my tenure. [The personal characteristics underlying this probably include the fact that I am very much bien dans ma peau (comfortable with who I am) and not overly emotional on the job. This calm under fire is particularly valuable as a station manager in the airline business, being respected by all, and making it very comfortable for people to work with me.]

The second is that I am a **good analyst**. While station manager at Mulhouse, for example, I was unable to learn from our controle de gestion (accounting) people whether we made money as handling agents for other airlines. So, before bidding on such work, I did an analysis of this business which revealed its underlying costs, thereby enabling me to know how and when to bid for it. The costs of this work are highly complex because of the large number of different groups involved in performing it, without keeping proper activity-based cost data, and, because the complexity added to the system due to the need to handle additional types of aircraft, is inherently difficult to quantify.

The third is that I am very **hard working and determined**, something I may have acquired from my immigrant parents.

My weaknesses are also quite clear. I am not a really creative person, being more of a practical nature. I dislike personal confrontations and go too far out of my way to avoid them. For example, I sometimes prefer to redo something a subordinate has done poorly rather than confront him with his mistakes. By the same token, I may be too demanding of my subordinates and colleagues and be inappropriately disappointed when they appear not to be as committed to the business as I am.

2. **Describe what you believe to be your most substantial achievement to date, explaining why you view it as such.**

My most substantial accomplishment was making a real success of my first operational job, that of station manager of Mulhouse Airport. I faced several barriers that made my ultimate success all the more pleasing. I was the only person ever to be given such a post without many years (typically twenty-plus) of experience in a station. In fact, I had only eighteen months' experience, and none managing people, at the time. In addition, the airport I was given is one of the most complicated in the AirInter system. (Mulhouse is the world's only binational airport, being operated jointly with Switzerland.) Perhaps of significance as well is the fact that I was the first woman to be made station manager.

My success in this position can be measured on several dimensions. The first is that we turned this airport into the model for the whole AirInter system in terms of early adoption of new techniques. If, for example, other station managers want to learn about computerized check-in of international passengers, formerly done manually, they are told to see how Mulhouse does it. Second, we managed to operate throughout this period without any strikes or work slowdowns, even in the face of a mechanics' walkout throughout much of the rest of the system. This was due to our willingness to listen carefully to what each of our work groups felt, and to what they knew about how best to run the business. We also managed to integrate the Air France and AirInter operations when the two firms merged without serious disruptions. I personally felt pleased that I was able to manage supervisors who had an average of twenty-five more years of experience and three fewer degrees than I did.

3. **Describe a situation taken from school, business, civil, or military life, where you did not meet your personal objectives, and discuss what you learned from this experience.**

I was made assistant manager in Lyon approximately four years ago. I started with high expectations but left after just one year with none of these expectations realized.

Despite getting on well personally with my manager, I never found a way to work well with him. He gave me virtually nothing to do and thwarted my efforts at carving out areas in which I could work. The basic problem was that he was new at his job and was unwilling to delegate because he did not yet understand what his own job entailed.

This was a bad situation which I initially hoped would improve of its own accord. Nothing happened, however, until I pushed to get another assignment.

What I learned was quite simple. The inability to work in a positive manner was devastating to me. I was not able to report to work and just read memos all day or stare out the window. I also learned that personal compatibility is not sufficient to guarantee professional compatibility as well. In addition, I reaffirmed my basic notion that the world is not waiting to give me the job; I have to manage my own career just like I have to manage any other task I care about.

4. **Comment on the main factors which you believe account for your academic and professional development to date. Explain your career aspirations and why you chose to apply to INSEAD now.**

The characteristics I mentioned in Essay One—having good interpersonal skills, being a good analyst, and being very determined—have contributed significantly to both my academic and my professional development. The additional factors to note are two. My academic progress resulted in part from my great curiosity about my studies; I greatly enjoyed being a student. (And thus, perhaps, my graduating from the Faculty of Law with high honors.) My professional development undoubtedly owes a great deal to my enthusiasm about the airline industry.

I hope to remain in the airline industry, preferably on the operational side, albeit in higher positions. I very much enjoy the general management nature of dealing with customers on the one hand, and all of the airline's staff (such as flight crews, commercial agents, ground crews, and the corporate staff) on the other.

My reasons for wanting an MBA are set forth in Essay Six. My reasons for wanting to attend INSEAD are also described there. The reasons that I wish to attend INSEAD now are quite simple. With the birth of my baby I have reached a natural break point. Also, I have now gained enough practical experience to benefit from additional education.

5. **If you were given the opportunity to effect one change in your work environment, what would that be? How would you implement this change?**

I would change the compensation and promotion system. Right now AirInter operates just like a government bureaucracy. Promotion and pay are determined by a combination of seniority and exam results. As a station manager, I cannot reward more that three or four of my 150 employees, and that only with a 3000 franc bonus. Not only am I basically unable to reward good performance, I am unable to penalize poor behavior. This is clearly inappropriate in a company which should be attuned to the coming global competition in the airline industry, a competition which will require far better performance than we now manage.

Changing the system will be a major task. At my level in the company, I currently try to work around the problem by seeking to allow one employee to take a promotion exam a few months ahead of schedule, or whatever. The real task, however, is system wide. To convince the more conservative, not to say lower performing, part of management that this is necessary will not be easy but it will be simple compared to changing union attitudes.

I am not able currently to commission a consultant to compare our performance levels with those of leading American carriers, or to lay out a disaster scenario of how fast we will go bankrupt in the event of unfettered competition in the future. In any event I am not sure that such major change can be made absent a crisis, although the British Airways change is certainly worth studying. As a personal matter, I intend to pay close attention to questions of organizational change at business school, particularly as they can be applied to this sort of service industry. If possible, I hope to study exactly this case so as to help to push AirInter's management and unions at least a bit in the right direction.

6. **What means of ensuring your personal and professional development are you seriously considering as an alternative to INSEAD?**

I have concluded that an MBA is the right step in my professional development at this time. I want to get more of a senior management perspective than I saw as a veritable kid at Ecole Des Affaires de Paris (EAP) years ago. Now that I know how a company functions, and what is particularly relevant to the industry that I have chosen, I am anxious to get started on a top program.

The two programs that I have looked at seriously are those of INSEAD and IMD. I want top programs devoted to development of senior, general managers. I also want a one-year program because I think that two years represents a greater time commitment than is appropriate given my current level of knowledge and operating experience. Last, I want a very international perspective given the increasingly global nature of the airline business, making these two schools the natural choices in Europe.

If I am not admitted I shall consider other career options. It will be difficult to gain the perspective I am seeking at AirInter because several of its attitudes run directly counter to those appropriate for the future. It is, for example, run by engineers with little marketing and no customer orientation. Consequently, if unable to pursue an appropriate MBA, I shall try to get a job with a non-French company with a real devotion to marketing and customer service. This will probably mean an American carrier.

7. **What do you feel you would contribute during your time at INSEAD?**

My background in the airline industry gives me several things to share with my classmates. I have learned a great deal about the airline industry for one. Also, I have had several years of running a 150-person operation, working not just for a French company but with several large international carriers as clients as well (in our handling agent capacity), all within the unique binational structure of Mulhouse Airport, which requires constant cooperation and negotiation with my Swiss counterparts. In addition I have managed groups of people very different from myself, insofar as they are true "blue-collar," unionized employees.

These experiences have contrasted with the work I initially did as a corporate staff employee at corporate headquarters, so I know that this perspective will be a bit different from what the typical management consultant or banker will bring. Because I enjoy working on teams with very different sorts of people, due to what I can learn as well as my own opportunity to contribute to their learning, I look forward to participating in such groups at INSEAD.

COMMENTS

1. Overall, this is an exceptionally successful effort that highlights Anne's numerous strengths and takes full advantage of being a relatively senior person, with an unusual job, when compared with other applicants. Note too that this is a very lean application; there is no excess to her essays.

2. In her job description, she does an admirable job of quantifying her responsibilities as well as explaining what they are. The latter is important for a job which is not likely to be well known to admissions officers.

3. Her first essay is very effective. She presents a convincing case for her several strengths, focusing on a limited number of them rather than simply listing a large number. She handles her weaknesses in the right way by listing several that are believable, but not disabling, without dwelling upon them.

4. In the last line of her second essay she shows that she may be "overeducated," but is still very practical at heart, thereby addressing one potential issue.

5. One small flaw: in essay 3 it is not clear that she has extracted all potential learning from her failure. She makes it sound as if it was all her boss's fault, but is that necessarily true? On the other hand, she has gleaned important personal career management information from this experience, recognizing that rather than indulge in recriminations she should simply move on.

6. In essay 4 she does something few applicants do; she relates her successes to her personal and professional strengths. In other words, she ties together essays 1 and 4. By showing how her strengths have contributed to various professional successes and her professional development, she makes those strengths clearer and more believable than they otherwise would be.

7. In essay 5 she shows two positive things about her: she bears heavy responsibilities (150 people work under her) and she is aware of the international aspects of her business (which she makes clear by discussing American and British operations).

8. In essay 6 she makes clear why she needs a second business degree: her first one was done when she was still a youngster and she needs the sort of senior management perspective that is not part of a BBA education and would, in any event, be nearly irrelevant to nineteen-year-olds.

9. Throughout the application she shows how international she is. Whether she is discussing the organizational change efforts at British Airways or discussing what is involved in running a binational airport, she makes it clear that a truly international program like INSEAD's is her natural home.

INDEX